the cinema of WES ANDERSON

DIRECTORS' CUTS

Other selected titles in the Directors' Cuts series:

the cinema of TOM DICILLO: *include me out*
WAYNE BYRNE

the cinema of ROBERT ALTMAN: *hollywood maverick*
ROBERT NIEMI

the cinema of HAL HARTLEY: *flirting with formalism*
STEVEN RYBIN (ed.)

the cinema of SEAN PENN: *in and out of place*
DEANE WILLIAMS

the cinema of CHRISTOPHER NOLAN: *imagining the impossible*
JACQUELINE FURBY & STUART JOY (eds)

the cinema of THE COEN BROTHERS: *hardboiled entertainments*
JEFFREY ADAMS

the cinema of CLINT EASTWOOD: *chronicles of america*
DAVID STERRITT

the cinema of ISTVÁN SZABÓ: *visions of europe*
JOHN CUNNINGHAM

the cinema of AGNÈS VARDA: *resistance and eclecticism*
DELPHINE BÉNÉZET

the cinema of ALEXANDER SOKUROV: *figures of paradox*
JEREMI SZANIAWSKI

the cinema of MICHAEL WINTERBOTTOM: *borders, intimacy, terror*
BRUCE BENNETT

the cinema of RAÚL RUIZ: *impossible cartographies*
MICHAEL GODDARD

the cinema of AKI KAURISMÄKI: *authorship, bohemia, nostalgia, nation*
ANDREW NESTINGEN

the cinema of RICHARD LINKLATER: *walk, don't run*
ROB STONE

the cinema of BÉLA TARR: *the circle closes*
ANDRÁS BÁLINT KOVÁCS

the cinema of STEVEN SODERBERGH: *indie sex, corporate lies, and digital videotape*
ANDREW DE WAARD & R. COLIN TATE

the cinema of TERRY GILLIAM: *it's a mad world*
JEFF BIRKENSTEIN, ANNA FROULA & KAREN RANDELL (eds)

the cinema of TAKESHI KITANO: *flowering blood*
SEAN REDMOND

the cinema of THE DARDENNE BROTHERS: *responsible realism*
PHILIP MOSLEY

the cinema of MICHAEL HANEKE: *europe utopia*
BEN McCANN & DAVID SORFA (eds)

the cinema of JAN SVANKMAJER: *dark alchemy*
PETER HAMES (ed.)

the cinema of LARS VON TRIER: *authenticity and artifice*
CAROLINE BAINBRIDGE

the cinema of WERNER HERZOG: *aesthetic ecstasy and truth*
BRAD PRAGER

the cinema of TERRENCE MALICK: *poetic visions of america (second edition)*
HANNAH PATTERSON (ed.)

the cinema of ANG LEE: *the other side of the screen (second edition)*
WHITNEY CROTHERS DILLEY

the cinema of TODD HAYNES: *all that heaven allows*
JAMES MORRISON (ed.)

the cinema of DAVID LYNCH: *american dreams, nightmare visions*
ERICA SHEEN & ANNETTE DAVISON (eds)

the cinema of KRZYSZTOF KIESLOWSKI: *variations on destiny and chance*
MAREK HALTOF

the cinema of GEORGE A. ROMERO: *knight of the living dead (second edition)*
TONY WILLIAMS

the cinema of KATHRYN BIGELOW: *hollywood transgressor*
DEBORAH JERMYN & SEAN REDMOND (eds)

the cinema of
WES ANDERSON

bringing nostalgia to life

whitney crothers dilley

 WALLFLOWER PRESS LONDON & NEW YORK

A Wallflower Press Book
Published by
Columbia University Press
Publishers Since 1893
New York • Chichester, West Sussex
cup.columbia.edu

Copyright © 2017 Columbia University Press
All rights reserved

Wallflower Press® is a registered trademark of Columbia University Press

A complete CIP record is available from the Library of Congress

ISBN 978-0-231-18068-9 (cloth : alk. paper)
ISBN 978-0-231-18069-6 (pbk. : alk. paper)
ISBN 978-0-231-54320-0 (e-book)

Columbia University Press books are printed on permanent
and durable acid-free paper.
Printed in the United States of America

Series design by Rob Bowden Design
Cover image of Wes Anderson from the set of *Fantastic Mr. Fox* (2009) © Fox Searchlight Pictures

CONTENTS

Acknowledgments vii

1. Introduction: Wes Anderson as Auteur – A History 1
2. Wes Anderson: His Position in American Cinema and Culture 33
3. Gender, Youth, and the Exploration of Masculinity in *Bottle Rocket* 60
4. "Sic Transit Gloria": Transgressing the Boundaries of Adolescence in *Rushmore* 78
5. The Interplay of Narrative Text, Language, and Film: Literary Influence and Intertextuality in *The Royal Tenenbaums* 97
6. Opposition and Resolution: The Dissonance of Celebrity in *The Life Aquatic with Steve Zissou* 121
7. Fragmentary Narratives/Incomplete Identities in *The Darjeeling Limited* 137
8. Adaptation and Homage: The World of Roald Dahl and *Fantastic Mr. Fox* 151
9. Reconstitution of the "Family" and Construction of Normalized Gender in *Moonrise Kingdom* 168
10. Literary Influence and Memory: Stefan Zweig and *The Grand Budapest Hotel* 183
11. Wes Anderson's Short Films and Commercial Work 200

Conclusion: Memory and Narrative in the Works of Wes Anderson 213

Filmography 224
Bibliography 228
Index 239

ACKNOWLEDGMENTS

The author wishes to thank Jennifer Crewe, Director of Columbia University Press, and Yoram Allon, Commissioning Editor and Editorial Director at Wallflower Press, for their invaluable support and counsel throughout the course of this volume's creation.

Thanks are also due to editor John Atkinson for his meticulous attention to detail, and to production manager Tom Cabot and the entire production team at Wallflower Press for applying their consummate professional skills to this project. Thanks to Meredith Howard at Columbia University Press for her assistance to the author, and to Kathryn Schell at Columbia for her early enthusiasm. And one more thank you to Yoram Allon at Wallflower Press for promoting and sustaining the project.

A debt of gratitude is owed to Michael Z. Newman for his excellent suggestions regarding the manuscript, as well as to two anonymous reviewers commissioned by Wallflower Press whose trenchant comments helped shape the early structure of the work.

The author would like to thank Morgan Everett, David Ludwig, and Jonathan Klassen for serving as readers for the manuscript in its various stages. In addition, the author is very grateful to Carol Brennan, Larry Dilley, Lisa Buxbaum, David Weiner, Stephen O'Rourke, Barbara Kline, Timothy Conkling, Lynne Sandsberry, and to Columbia University Press former senior manuscript editor Roy E. Thomas for directly and indirectly inspiring this book. Also, many thanks to Kevin Healam, who has continuously read the author's work and offered timely suggestions and support.

Much gratitude goes to colleagues at Shih Hsin University who have always enthusiastically supported the author's research projects, especially the chair of the English Department Yuan-Jung Cheng and departmental secretary Kelly Weng for their gracious warmth and care. Shih Hsin University generously awarded the author several research grants and a year's sabbatical leave to complete the manuscript and ready it for publication. Finally, the author owes a continued scholarly debt to Frederick P. Brandauer, Ching-hsien Wang, and R. Kent Guy at the University of Washington, Douglas Kellner at UCLA, and Jerome Silbergeld at Princeton for their unfailing brilliance, an inspiration always to the author.

For my family

CHAPTER ONE

Introduction: Wes Anderson as Auteur – A History

A close examination of the generic, aesthetic, and cultural significance of Wes Anderson's films, most prominently known for their whimsical, deadpan humor, deliberately and studiedly (and sometimes jarringly) unique filming techniques, extensive literary references, and interplay with historically significant literature and films (Truffaut, Welles, Lubitsch, etc.), reveals that Anderson's influence on American film culture and contemporary culture in general cannot be underestimated.[1] Thinking of Anderson's films, such as his early tour de force *Rushmore* (1998), one may immediately call to mind an extreme close-up shot of an actor, perfectly centered in the frame, displaying little to no emotion, or a vivid sense of nostalgia conjured by such signifiers as carefully curated furniture, costumes and scenery, paintings, photographs, and music that create an Andersonian "mood" for the film, or even Anderson's penchant for obsessively detailed diorama-like displays such as the cross sections of the boat in *The Life Aquatic with Steve Zissou* (2004) or the Bishop family home in *Moonrise Kingdom* (2012). Anderson's films can also be recalled in vividly powerful moments of "memory," e.g., the vision of blonde, kohl-eyed Margot (Gwyneth Paltrow) descending from a bus in *The Royal Tenenbaums* (2001), or the three estranged Whitman brothers, played by Owen Wilson, Adrien Brody, and Jason Schwartzman, chasing a train while slowly tossing away their vintage monogrammed luggage in *The Darjeeling Limited* (2007). Anderson memorably employs deliberate shooting techniques such as slow motion and God's-eye view to create his ordered cosmos; he bombards the viewer with constant reminders that what is being shown is a fiction, with pretentiously elaborate costumes and matching custom-made uniforms (e.g., yellow one-piece jumpsuits, red tracksuits, or blue mariners' outfits with red knit hats). He creates a nuanced importance for venerable old (fictional) institutions and mixes these with deeply significant historical moments of memory, a signature technique epitomized by Anderson's juxtaposition of the real and the artificial to create a sense of hyper-nostalgia in films such as *The Grand Budapest Hotel* (2014).

Wes Anderson has been characterized by critics such as Matt Zoller Seitz (2009) as the most influential American filmmaker of the post-Baby Boom generation.[2] His cinematic style has been credited with inspiring a new generation of indie films such as *Napoleon Dynamite* (2004), *Garden State* (2004), and *Juno* (2007).[3] With Anderson's work being so instantly identifiable, often even from a single frame, it is clear that, as postulated by Jeffrey Overstreet (2012), no American director, not even Woody Allen,[4] has a more recognizable aesthetic, a more consistent thematic style, or a stronger authorial voice.[5] Anderson is thus a classic example of a filmmaker that the *Cahiers du cinéma* critics would have labeled an auteur – an artist who imprints his personality and preoccupations on each work so strongly that he is considered the primary "author" of the film. Anderson's focus seems to be consumed with the way people fumble their way through life, the awkwardness of this fumbling, and the transcendent futility, and his characters are often misfits with a theme of alienation from the established order. Anderson displays an iconoclastic streak in his filmic choices, as well. *Fantastic Mr. Fox* (2009) is a classic example of his not following the trends of the moment: while most other directors were turning to CGI and 3D in pursuit of box-office success, Anderson chose stop-motion fur puppets for his first foray into animation. Moreover, while most contemporary filmmakers are shooting on HD film, Anderson still prefers traditional, old-fashioned filming techniques, many times deliberately borrowing his mise-en-scène from the French New Wave, Italian neorealism, and other subcultures and niche film traditions, such as 1970s American police dramas. Closely tied to this is the idea of using veteran actors reflectively to play upon their previous work from earlier film history, some in iconic roles from the 1970s, such as James Caan, Gene Hackman, Anjelica Huston, Willem Dafoe, Seymour Cassel, and Bud Cort. Anderson's distinct visual aesthetic, with its use of a color palette that evokes 1970s interiors (Anderson's films often have deliberate, carefully chosen color schemes – blues, yellows, reds, and oranges, a prominent use of plaids) and his lack of mainstream, traditional Hollywood tropes inspires a sometimes quite virulently negative response.

Wes Anderson's film career trajectory has been truly unique. While scholars such as Geoff King, Claire Molloy, and Yannis Tsioumakis (2013) prefer to classify his work as belonging to American "independent cinema," by the strictest definition of the word, this label has not been applicable since Anderson debuted his early black-and-white short "Bottle Rocket"[6] at the Sundance Film Festival in 1993. While Anderson's work retains the "sensibility" of independent art-house cinema, all of his films since that first short film "Bottle Rocket" have been financed by major studios. This has allowed Anderson the latitude to produce work that is as obsessively detailed and uniquely personal ("quirky") as what is commonly considered independent art-house cinema. His films are considered independent (or "indie") in style, but in an assessment of the books and existing research on American independent film, Anderson's body of work is not frequently mentioned – in other words, not all scholars agree that his oeuvre can be distinctly studied as belonging to the independent film movement specifically. Thus, Anderson's body of work stands in the center of an ongoing scholarly debate on what exactly constitutes independent art-house cinema. An analysis of his films not only helps determine Anderson's identity within the sphere of American independent cinema, or more specifically, "Indiewood" cinema as defined by Geoff King (2009), King, Molloy, and Tzioumakis (2013), and others, but also engages the aesthetics of independent film, particularly the notion of "quirk" first postulated by James MacDowell (2010), and the "indie" film culture explored by Michael Z. Newman (2011). Anderson's films will be analyzed and theorized here in a way that both examines his evolution as a director and demonstrates his engagement with the industry and aesthetics of American independent cinema; in particular, how Anderson's hyper-stylized "brand" engages with current scholarly debates on authenticity, irony, "new sincerity" filmmaking and the idea of "quirk."

In addition, there is a second contradictory facet to Anderson's work and reputation, and that is his status as a filmmaker, particularly the question of whether Anderson can be recognized as an auteur and how influential his work has been on American film culture and global culture in general. The *New Yorker* magazine film critic Richard Brody has written that "Anderson is one of the very few filmmakers whose images are instantly recognizable, whose name could even become adjectival."[7] Indeed, many critics and scholars of Anderson's oeuvre consider him to be one of the most important American directors in contemporary film today, as well as historically one of the most unique filmmakers of the twentieth century, whose work has had a profound influence on the growing independent film movement of the last twenty years; his work continues to grow in reputation and scope in contemporary cinema (for example, *The Grand Budapest Hotel* was nominated for nine Academy Awards in 2015, which placed it, along with *Birdman*, as one of the two most nominated films of that year).[8] However, objectively speaking, there are still many Americans who do not even recognize his name, and have not seen or heard of his most prominent early films, such as *Rushmore* and *The Royal Tenenbaums*. Indeed, the name "Wes Anderson" does not seem like the name of a famous director, as *New Yorker* film critic Pauline Kael notoriously pointed out in 1998 when meeting the young director at his own request (she then suggested that he change it).[9] Kael also famously said, upon screening *Rushmore*, that she "did not know what to make of it,"[10] suggesting that Anderson's "postmodern" style is too far removed from Kael's generation of filmmaking, as Jesse Mayshark (2007) has postulated in *Post-Pop Cinema*, because the breakthrough concerns of Kael's generation were the introduction of explicit sexuality and violence to film, and Anderson makes his films in a generation where these battles are "considered already won."[11]

Wes Anderson's signature style poses some contradictions as well, which naturally causes his work to have a somewhat turbulent reception. His films have been accused of being repetitive, small-minded, self-indulgent, devoid of deep meaning, and even racist.[12] At the same time, those who champion his work feel an ardent identification with Anderson's personal vision – he has an extremely loyal cult following that fiercely defends him on such websites as "Rushmore Academy," among others.[13] In order to fully appreciate Wes Anderson's work, it is helpful to have a broad familiarity with twentieth-century film history, notably the films of François Truffaut and the French New Wave, the films of Orson Welles, the work of Italian film directors Michelangelo Antonioni and Federico Fellini, and Indian filmmaker Satyajit Ray, while having also a broad exposure to the unique and sometimes obscure literary influences to which Anderson frequently alludes, such as the 1970 Roald Dahl children's story *Fantastic Mr. Fox*, or the literature of Stefan Zweig from the 1930s and 1940s that underlies the main thematic elements of *The Grand Budapest Hotel*. The "hiddenness" of Anderson's depth of knowledge beneath the superficial cleverness of his films has been deceptive, yet at the same time, Anderson himself subverts this deeper context by not drawing attention to it – instead, through playful jokes, non sequiturs, and his characters' own teasing or sharp put-downs, he creates a sense of an "in-joke" with the viewer. That Anderson's films are mainly produced using the same cinematographer, musical supervisor, and actors whom Anderson prefers to work with repeatedly, underscores this playful tone that suggests that his films are just one big "in-joke" among friends. Anderson reveals the inner workings of families, institutions, organizations, etc., and generously allows the viewer in on the joke. This is why films like *Rushmore*, detailing the misadventures of a tenth-grader at a prep school, or more recently, the thieving capers in *The Grand Budapest Hotel*, have such a madcap, conspiratorial feel that adds to their enjoyment.

Anderson tends to work again and again with a fixed set of friends and collaborators (his working methods with this extended "troupe" of artists have been compared by a number of critics to Orson Welles and his Mercury Theater players).[14] The Wilson brothers, Owen and Luke (along with their brother Andrew, who had small roles in Anderson's first three films), were the most significant of Anderson's early collaborators, along with Jason Schwartzman and Bill Murray (to whom Anderson gave roles that helped invigorate his second act as a world-weary middle-aged male, which then won him similar turns in works such as Sofia Coppola's *Lost in Translation* [2003] and Jim Jarmusch's *Broken Flowers* [2005]).[15] Bill Murray has appeared in (or lent his voice to) every one of Anderson's films since 1998, while Owen Wilson (as writer, actor, or both) has been involved in every film Anderson has made except for *Moonrise Kingdom*. Other actors that have appeared repeatedly in his later films include Anjelica Huston, Tilda Swinton, Edward Norton, Seymour Cassel, Willem Dafoe, Jeff Goldblum, Adrien Brody, Michael Gambon, Harvey Keitel, Wally Wolodarsky, and Bob Balaban, supplemented by newcomers like Jude Law and Ralph Fiennes. In addition to repeatedly gathering the same actors around him, Anderson has built an extended family of technical collaborators such as cinematographer Robert Yeoman, film composers Mark Mothersbaugh and Alexandre Desplat, and music supervisor Randall Poster. In addition, although Anderson has written (or adapted, in the case of Roald Dahl and Stefan Zweig) every one of the screenplays of his films, he also chooses to write with a partner – he clearly experiences writing as a synergetic process. His co-authors have included Owen Wilson (*Bottle Rocket, Rushmore, The Royal Tenenbaums*), Noah Baumbach (*The Life Aquatic with Steve Zissou, Fantastic Mr. Fox*), Jason Schwartzman (*The Darjeeling Limited*), and Roman Coppola (*The Darjeeling Limited, Moonrise Kingdom*). In fact, the only film for which Anderson did not have a co-author was *The Grand Budapest Hotel*, and for that film, although Hugo Guinness shared credit with Anderson for the story, Anderson alone received authorship credit for the screenplay, which was nominated for an Academy Award.

Anderson's work in general is defined by his obsession and fascination with family/intergenerational issues, and the majority of his films have revolved around the topic of parents, or parent-figures, and their children. Writing about Anderson's early work, Jesse Mayshark has observed that Anderson directed his first four films before he turned thirty-five, and "they feel like young-man's movies."[16] Wrestling with the topic of maturity/immaturity, Anderson's first four films deal with men of middle age (Herman Blume, Royal Tenenbaum, Steve Zissou) in varying degrees of arrested development, while "the more fully adult figures in these films ... tend to be women."[17] Women can be absent or remote as well in Anderson's work – or even, quite commonly, deceased. In his three early films, *Bottle Rocket*, *The Royal Tenenbaums*, and *The Life Aquatic with Steve Zissou*, there are four dead mothers represented. While women can seem to be somewhat underrepresented in Anderson's heavily masculine-centered works, he has nevertheless worked with some of the strongest female actors of his generation: Cate Blanchett, Gwyneth Paltrow, Tilda Swinton, Natalie Portman, Soairse Ronan, Lumi Cavazos (coming from her star turn in *Like Water for Chocolate*, 1992), Frances McDormand, Anjelica Huston, and even Meryl Streep. Writing about Anderson's early films, Mayshark characterizes his focus on both elitist (adult) snobbery and playful (childlike) precocity:

> Anderson seems interested in documenting a particular social niche – an eccentric, affluent precocious slice of America, self-absorbed and often immature, but not, on the whole, badly intentioned. It is a Salinger America, a *New Yorker* America, a Dorothy Parker and Truman Capote America. [...] The world of Anderson's is a distinct and coherent place, a mingling of eras and style – 1950s prep-school literature, 1960s rock'n'roll, 1970s television, all filtered through an early twentieth-century fondness for boys' adventure stories.[18]

The air of childlike wonder in Anderson's work translates to a playful sense of whimsy. Again and again, Anderson reaches back into childhood/boyhood with, for example, the sudden, unexpected appearance of stop-motion animation by Henry Selick, who designed the imaginary fish in *The Life Aquatic with Steve Zissou* (this fascination with stop-motion continued with Anderson's animated adaptation of *Fantastic Mr. Fox*), with his numerous references to the work of Charles M. Schulz in the comic strip *Peanuts* (1950–2000), and with boyhood fascinations in *Rushmore* (with its reverence for stamp collecting, Swiss Army knives and BB guns). In one sequence in *The Royal Tenenbaums*, Royal tries to teach his overly serious grandsons how to act like boys, taking them on a crash course across Manhattan that includes jaywalking through heavy traffic and shoplifting milk, in a montage set to Paul Simon's "Me and Julio Down by the School Yard," an upbeat paean to perennial boyishness and playful delinquency.

A Wes Anderson film in general defies categorization: it is not a romance, and not an action thriller, nor a mystery, nor science fiction, nor fantasy, nor horror. Instead, each of his films is what could be perceived as a somewhat outrageous combination of elements of satire, fantasy, comedy, tragedy, farce, and drama. The lack of traditional "genre" specifications and signifiers in Wes Anderson's films makes them difficult to categorize. Anderson's films are largely comedies, in that comedy is the dominant modality, but a film like *Bottle Rocket* presents a type of humor that does not depend on "jokes" as much as it does on character foibles, misunderstandings, and the characters' own obliviousness, while films such as *The Life Aquatic with Steve Zissou* and *The Grand Budapest Hotel* mix conventions of melodrama, tragedy, romance, heist film, screwball comedy, murder mystery, and (faux) historical documentary. *Bottle Rocket* and *Rushmore* draw on some familiar conventions from the genre of romantic comedy, but the myriad ways that Anderson's films deliberately depart from those conventions – such as *Rushmore*'s age-defying, and unsuccessful, central romance – are a key marker of their position in the cinematic spectrum that distinguishes them from the mainstream. Geoff King has explained the ways in which many "indie" and "Indiewood" features use genre frameworks as points of departure (or, at least, partial departure). Thus, genre conventions become familiar foundations upon which to build, and serve as marker points for degrees of variation from the Hollywood norm. According to King, maintaining a range of balance between use of familiar conventions and departure from them is a prominent characteristic of indie and Indiewood films.[19] Anderson's films both employ the conventions of the typical romantic comedy and subvert these elements by using them humorously or ironically. As King has postulated, for indie directors, this is a conscious act of positioning that claims a particular ("higher") cultural standing, showing the move of the film beyond the limitations of genre. King's assessment of Sofia Coppola's *Lost in Translation* as falling into the genre of "*Not* a Romantic Comedy" is as follows:

> *Not* a romantic comedy can be understood as a positive rather than merely negative signifier for a film marked quite conspicuously by the extent to which – despite its mobilizations of some core generic devices – it denies any full belonging to the genre as a key aspect of its claim to a more distinctive position.[20]

In other words, a film that falls outside of traditional genre specifications is assigned a more distinctive position – clearly Anderson's genre-stretching films fall into the category of "Not a Romantic Comedy," and Anderson's categorization as an Indiewood filmmaker is suitable in this generic sense.

Despite the fact that Anderson's films seem somewhat marginalized and deliberately out of step with modern culture, his influence can be found ubiquitously. According to Michael Z. Newman (2013), "Anderson is lionized (or chastised) not only for being the quintessential hipster auteur, but also for having inspired a wave of indie cinema that bears his influence, imitating his comic tone, visual sense, and narrative situations."[21] Newman cites the 2007 article in *The Onion A.V. Club*, which lists ten films heavily influenced by Wes Anderson, especially in their depiction of precocious young people in the style of "indie quirk." These films include *Napoleon Dynamite*, described as "a pale imitation of Anderson's most obvious mannerisms;"[22] *The Squid and the Whale* (2005) and *Rocket Science* (2007), each of which echoes the eclectic selection of pop songs on Anderson film soundtracks; *Garden State*, with Zach Braff playing "a stock

Anderson character;"[23] *Little Miss Sunshine* (2006), in which the offbeat family is represented, according to the authors, in a typically Andersonian style; and *Juno*, in which, as the authors argue, the clothing choices reflect inspiration from Anderson's approach to costuming his characters. Other films that have been compared to Wes Anderson's include *Tadpole* (2007), *Lars and the Real Girl* (2007), and Richard Ayoade's coming-of-age comedy *Submarine* (2010), which was quickly dubbed "the Welsh *Rushmore*"[24] on the festival circuit. Just as niche movies of the 1970s and other artistic relics of the past have influenced Anderson and his co-collaborators, Anderson's influence can be seen across modern media – his films such as *The Royal Tenenbaums* and *Fantastic Mr. Fox* radiate style, highbrow playfulness and eccentricity, and his influence pervades not only indie filmmaking but is referenced through quirky T.V. ads, as well as the current vogue for all things "authentic" and craft-related, retro, and analog; moreover, through characters such as Margot Tenenbaum and Suzy Bishop, his films even influence high fashion.[25] It is also significant that Anderson's own personal fashion sense is noticeably out of time with the modern era: he favors custom-made brown corduroy suits, with his choice of footwear revealing a penchant for Clarks Wallabees, and with his hair often photographed at a middle length that does not quite reflect hairstyle trends of the moment, while his unfailingly polite civility and his soft-spoken and sometimes childlike demeanor embodies the same zeitgeist as his films. Whether the audience embraces or rejects his work, Anderson's brand of off-beat, sad comedy remains remarkably unique, and his meta-nostalgic voice remains his own.

The Auteur: Anderson/Truffaut

A study of Anderson's cinematic oeuvre necessarily leads to a particular focus on how his films cohere around a set of formal devices of storytelling and visual style balancing artifice and realism, and the central thematic concerns about nostalgia, family, and loss. These coherent formal and thematic devices amount to a highly personal style of filmmaking that defines Anderson as a cinematic artist. While there is a widespread consensus among critics that Anderson is a modern-day auteur with a distinct directorial style (see Orgeron [2007], Browning [2011], Newman [2011], and MacDowell [2012], among others), the understanding of Anderson's auteurship necessitates an examination of those features of his work which aid in the classification of Anderson as an auteur. Accordingly, it is important to demonstrate how Anderson's aesthetic and stylistic continuity in his films, his original and highly personal voice, and how he flaunts the incorporation of various influences (literary, cinematic, more generally artistic), so that his personal style is marked by a prominent allusive quality – Anderson's work can best be appreciated in conversation with his influences – all conjoin to define Anderson as an auteur. The discussion of Anderson's status as an auteur must necessarily incorporate the latest scholarship in auteur theory, in which Truffaut fundamentally argued that the director is the focal point of organization and control and, through participation in all stages of the filmmaking process, is thus able to imprint upon the final product his own "worldview," and that a true auteur is the "author" of a corpus of work in which every film displays a recognizable style and a consistent personal vision. While critics such as Thomas Elsaesser (2012) have pointed out that the concept of auteur theory has been challenged in recent years,[26] Elsaesser himself still defends the use of the term and asserts that Wes Anderson falls into the category of "auteur" along with Gus Van Sant, Jim Jarmusch, Hal Hartley, Richard Linklater, Terrence Malick, John Waters, and Todd Haynes.[27] In recent critiques of auteur theory, the idea of the "auteur" has required a more nuanced approach, recognizing that a commercially produced film involves hundreds of industry professionals in its making. Yet Elsaesser still finds the concept of the "auteur" useful to describe a director who could manifest the skill, talent (genius), and creative control of an artist achieving a personal vision. Elsaesser considers auteurism as a conjunction of art and industry, most helpfully explained by Jon Lewis's 2007 essay on auteurism in *New Hollywood*, where Francis Ford Coppola and Martin Scorsese represent the first wave of "New Hollywood" (post-studio era) auteurs, who demonstrate their auteur status by establishing a personal style and a unique mise-en-scène, while George Lucas and Steven Spielberg are members of a "new wave of auteurs notable less for a signature style than a signature product."[28] Lewis also points out how Hollywood has embraced auteurism "as a marketing tool."[29]

An examination of Anderson's oeuvre naturally leads to the discussion of Anderson as an auteur, with his penchant for flaunting numerous literary and filmic influences. This study uses Harold Bloom's term "influences"[30] which was first theorized in literary studies in the 1960s, due to Anderson's own repeated allusions to his literary inspirations, and the fact that he himself authored each of his films' screenplays. Anderson frequently mentions his literary influences in interviews, referring, for example, to the underlying connections to J. D. Salinger and the Glass family in *The Royal Tenenbaums* (there is even a character with the closely-related name "Tannenbaum" in the Glass family), as well as the intertextuality between Holden Caulfield and Max Fischer in *Rushmore*. At the same time, due to his rich familiarity with cinematic history, Anderson's filmic references are equally prominent. He speaks repeatedly in interviews about the directors and the films he admires, praising films such as *The Graduate* (1967), *Harold and Maude* (1971), and *Le Souffle au coeur* (*Murmur of the Heart*, 1971), and directors like Hal Ashby, Mike Nichols, Robert Altman, Luis Buñuel, and Federico Fellini. He reserves particular admiration for the French directors Jean Renoir, Louis Malle, Jean-Luc Godard,[31] and particularly François Truffaut. His admiration for all of these directors and their films influences his filmmaking in terms of style, subject, character, and theme. For example, Anderson was inspired to set his train/road trip film *The Darjeeling Limited* in India because of the film *The River* (1951) by French film director Jean Renoir, the films of Indian director Satyajit Ray, and documentaries on India by French film director Louis Malle; Anderson also dedicates his film to Ray. Other Anderson films echo the work of 1930s and 1940s Mitteleuropean directors in Hollywood, and Anderson cites specifically filmmakers Michael Powell and Emeric Pressburger of *The Life and Death of Colonel Blimp* (1943) and Ernst Lubitsch of *The Shop Around the Corner* (1940), with his work on *The Grand Budapest Hotel*. In his films, Anderson quotes directly from the French films of Malle and Truffaut to pay homage to them. For example, the quote "I'm going to kill myself tomorrow" from *The*

Royal Tenenbaums is linked to the same quote in Malle's *Le Feu follet* (*The Fire Within*, 1963), but Anderson also casts his own tenor to the quote – Richie Tenenbaum does not wait until "tomorrow," but attempts suicide immediately. Seemingly to underscore his connection to the original "auteur," Anderson's narratives and themes parallel those in the films of Truffaut in particular, especially in his early films and his commercial work. Finally, what is most significant is the obvious deliberateness with which Anderson devotes himself/adheres/pays homage to the auteur concept developed in its most doctrinal form by the French New Wave directors in the late 1950s and in the 1960s.

Anderson's greatest feat of performance[32] has been his presentation of himself/performance of the "auteur" in his filmmaking. First of all, in presenting himself as a "brand," according to Timothy Corrigan's (2003) notion in *The Commerce of Auteurism*,[33] Anderson makes use of his outsized public persona in a 2007 American Express advertisement, "My Life, My Card," in which he exaggerates and dramatizes his artistic façade to enhance his status as an auteur in the tradition of Truffaut (more on this in chapter 11). Corrigan also suggests the interview as an example of the "contemporary auteur's construction and promotion of a self."[34] For example, an interview in *New York Magazine* notes that Anderson's appeal to studio executives is not only in his films but in his "persona of the eccentric auteur."[35] Both in the 2007 American Express commercial, and in his daily life, Anderson dresses the part of an auteur in anachronistic formalwear which helps determine his social identity; in one interview he is described as wearing "a bespoke two-piece suit in brown-and-tan herringbone tweed, and his initials, WWA (the second W stands for Wales), are stitched on his shirt pocket."[36] Devin Orgeron (2007) has also noted Anderson's use of DVD technology to promote his own highly self-aware authorial image, as well as appropriating the terminology "la camera crayola" (a reference to how, for the New Wave filmmakers and theorists, films were "written" with what Alexandre Astruc called "le camera stylo"). Finally, Tom Dorey (2012) expands on Orgeron's point on how Anderson has capitalized on the advancements of DVD technology, and demonstrates how Anderson's status as an auteur has an undeniable stamp of pedigree due to his films being represented in the Criterion Collection (notable for pioneering the "special edition" DVD concept, containing bonus materials such as trailers, behind-the-scenes documentaries, commentaries, deleted scenes, and scholarly essays in DVD booklets). Anderson cleverly crafts his authorial image through the director's commentaries and copious extra features promoted by the Criterion Collection, which provides Anderson with the opportunity to present a privileged reading on the film,[37] as well as "canonizing the director alongside auteurs previously included in the collection such as Fellini, Truffaut, Hitchcock, Godard, Kurosawa and Bergman."[38]

Anderson also uses intertextual references within his films to point to his auteurial filmic influences. In his first and second films, *Bottle Rocket* and *Rushmore*, Anderson deliberately included signifiers pointing to Truffaut (the progenitor "auteur"). With his third film, *The Royal Tenenbaums*, Anderson distinctly referenced (through echoes of titular similarity, as well as points of narrative) the second film of boy-genius filmmaker Orson Welles, who made *The Magnificent Ambersons* (1942) when he was just twenty-seven. Distinct signifiers to Truffaut included both scenes such as the "Anthony running away" scene, which references *Les Quatre cents coups* (also known as *The 400 Blows*, 1959; at the end, Antoine escapes an institution), and the schoolroom scene in *Rushmore*, which copies a pan of a classroom in Truffaut's first film. In *Rushmore*, the theme of a misunderstood adolescent also echoes *Les Quatre cents coups*, while the subplot of the love triangle in *Rushmore* echoes the central theme of Truffaut's third film *Jules et Jim* (1962). *Jules et Jim* is also deliberately referenced in *The Life Aquatic with Steve Zissou*, when Zissou warns his friend not to pursue a girl he has reserved for himself, by repeating the same line: "Not this one, Klaus"/ "Pas celle-là, Jim" ("Not this one, Jim"). Anderson pointed to these auteurs with his early work to establish his "brand" as a twenty-first-century American auteur, signifying/demarcating his own position in film history. In addition, however, Anderson brought his own fresh twenty-first-century sensibilities to the mix, adding an original and creative touch to the potpourri of film history influences at his disposal. With a sure hand, Anderson deliberately cast himself as a filmmaker in the auteur tradition: the breathless beginnings of *Rushmore* and *The Royal Tenenbaums* are also inspired by the lightning-fast narration at the beginning of *Jules et Jim*, which was in turn inspired by the narration at the opening of *The Magnificent Ambersons*. Thus, a comparison of these films makes clear that Anderson consciously imitates the work of Truffaut, both thematically and stylistically, in his first two films, and Orson Welles with his third.[39]

In 2002, as part of a *New York Times* series for directors, Rick Lyman invited Anderson to show and discuss a film of his choice. Anderson chose Truffaut's *L'Argent de poche* (*Small Change*, 1976), stating at the time that he was choosing to "brand" himself with this choice of Truffaut:

> The first Truffaut film I ever saw was "400 Blows," and that had a huge impact on me. But there's something about this one, too. And when you do something like this – pick a movie to watch for an article – you want to pick something that you want to proselytize about, in a way. And you're also picking a kind of *brand* to put on yourself. Oh, he's the guy who picked "Shane" to watch, or he's the one who watched a Roy Rogers movie. I was a little nervous to pick a French movie, because it can make you sound a little too, well, you know. It might not go over with some people.[40] (italics added)

There is no single story in *L'Argent de poche*, but instead a collection of stories, or a series of narratives attached to multiple characters. It becomes clear as the movie unfolds, drawing the viewer in and out of so many lives, that at least one reason that Anderson chose it was to revisit so many of the influences that Truffaut had on his work, beginning with the use of children (from birth to the threshold of adolescence) and continuing through the intricate ensemble structure. Anderson adds: "It almost looks like the kind of movie that would be projected on a 16-millimeter projector in a school library, or something like that. And also, there's something about the fact that I am about the exact age as a lot of the kids in the movie. Even though it's taking place in France and I grew up in Houston, it's my exact childhood period."[41] He continues:

Do kids in French villages really run to school in packs? I don't know, but it feels natural, doesn't it? There's something about these shirts and sneakers that the children are wearing. It's all the same kind of stuff that we were wearing right around the same time, in the mid-70's. Although our streets in Texas didn't look like this, obviously, the way they're dressed really reminds me of the way me and my brothers would have dressed back then. And I really like them running to school, you know? I like the feel of it. It could come across as a little precious, but it doesn't, does it?[42]

Anderson first saw Truffaut's *Les Quatre cents coups* when he was sixteen years old, on a Beta tape he discovered in a small video rental section at the back of a record store in Houston. Later when he was an undergraduate at the University of Texas, he found it in the library (Anderson also recalls to Lyman that as a college student he stumbled across a huge volume of Truffaut's scripts and letters in the University of Texas library, and he can still vividly recall many passages from memory).[43] At the end of his lengthy series of interviews for the book *The Wes Anderson Collection*, Anderson recalls his first viewing of *Les Quatre cents coups*:

> It's one of those films where you say, "*Not only did I just enjoy this experience, now I think I would like to model my future on this somehow.*" [...] There are a certain number of books and movies that you come in contact with that are the ones you can look to and feel like they are what you were trying to imitate. [...] One striking element is just the visuals – Paris at that time. The boy he cast, how vividly he portrayed this boy's life – because it was his own, sort of. It's set in his neighborhoods. Something about the combination of all this ends up being a very forceful, very powerful experience.[44] (italics added)

In a directorial career spanning twenty-nine years from 1954 to 1983, Truffaut made twenty-four films (twenty-one full-length feature films and three shorts), of which the most significant ones stand out immediately as the five that recount the childhood, adolescence, and early adult life of Antoine Doinel (Jean-Pierre Léaud, who acted as Truffaut's alter ego), especially the first in the series, *Les Quatre cents coups*.[45] Details of Truffaut's personal life, both daily minutiae and intimate psychological explorations, reappeared in his films. For example, "It's my mother, sir, she's dead," is the excuse for truancy used by fourteen-year-old Antoine in *Les Quatre cents coups* and in Truffaut's own troubled childhood to avoid punishment.[46] Throughout his career, Truffaut often depicted the lives of children, likely due to his own difficult childhood experiences (*Les Mistons* [*The Mischief Makers*, 1957], *Les Quatre cents coups*, *L'Enfant sauvage* [*The Wild Child*, 1969], *L'Argent de poche*). In *Les Quatre cents coups*, Antoine Doinel steals some milk to drink after spending the night away from home (the scene in *The Royal Tenenbaums* in which the brothers Uzi and Ari Tenenbaum shoplift milk references this). In addition, after stealing a typewriter from his stepfather's workplace, Antoine spends the night in jail (the chain-link fence behind which Antoine stands in jail is referenced by Owen Wilson's character in *Bottle Rocket*, and by a similar shot of the serious-faced young prep-school boy Dirk in *Rushmore*). Antoine's only solace comes from his friendship with his schoolmate and fellow troublemaker René – based on Truffaut's real-life friendship with his close lifelong friend Robert Lachenay – and the study of male friendship is an essential element of Truffaut's films. Thus, according to Diana Holmes and Robert Ingram, "Aspects of Truffaut's ... childhood and adolescence enter his films not at the level of narrative detail, but as that of underlying structures and themes, the significance of which goes well beyond the personal."[47] Similarly, in his adaptation of *Fantastic Mr. Fox*, a children's story which obviously resonated with the adult Anderson, as well as in his original works such as *Moonrise Kingdom* and *Rushmore*, Anderson covers those experiences, characters, ideas, and attitudes that resonate with his own childhood/maturity and suit his singular vision. In other words, all of Anderson's works, both his selected adaptations and his own authored films, share the common themes of childhood, adolescence, maturity, desire, friendship, male bonding, and the pleasure of telling stories and the many diverse ways in which they can be told (narratively through the physical page, visually through filmic images, theatrically through drama, and musically through sound), while vividly reaching back to the past through these nostalgic signifiers.

Genesis of Anderson as a Director

Wes Anderson was only twenty-three years old when he shot the 13-minute, 16-millimeter black-and-white short film "Bottle Rocket" in 1992, written with his college roommate Owen Wilson and shot in Dallas with the Wilson brothers, friends of his with no formal acting training, not long after Anderson's graduation from the University of Texas at Austin. The film gained some prominence when it was shown at the 1993 Sundance Film Festival, and this success led to the making of a feature-length version of the film (with the same actors in the leading roles) being financed by Columbia Pictures. (The short film was also shown in 1994 at the Dallas-based USA Film Festival.) The film drew attention for its visual continuities with French New Wave cinema, as well as its diverse musical soundtrack, such as the use of jazz (Sonny Rollins' "Old Devil Moon") and also Vince Guaraldi's "Snowflakes" from the television holiday special program *A Charlie Brown Christmas* (1965) based on the *Peanuts* comic-strip by Charles M. Schulz. The "voice" that Wes Anderson brought to the screen through his directorial choices was a new, fresh one, steeped in knowing references to the past, especially films from the 1960s and 1970s.

As with many auteurs before him, such as Truffaut and Godard, Anderson's work contains clear autobiographical content. Descended from Swedish and Norwegian ancestry, Wesley Wales Anderson was born on May 1, 1969, and grew up in Houston, Texas, a city he has described in an interview with Arnaud Desplechin as hot, humid, and full of mosquitoes.[48] Anderson has claimed that the single most traumatic event in his childhood was the divorce of his parents. He returns again and again to the motif of familial dysfunction, conflict, and pain, most overtly in *The Royal Tenenbaums*, which centers on a dysfunctional family, *The Life Aquatic with Steve Zissou*, particularly in the relationship between Zissou and the wounded manchild Ned Plimpton, *The Darjeeling*

Limited, in which three brothers seek closure among themselves and with their mother through a spiritual journey in India, as well as in *Fantastic Mr. Fox*, with its nuanced familial relationships, and *Moonrise Kingdom*, a film in which the two protagonists run away from a dysfunctional home life and find solace in each other. Both of these latter films have comparatively happier endings as well, especially *Moonrise Kingdom*, in which nature, in the form of a massive lightning storm, cooperates to bring about magically surreal events, while the orphan boy is adopted by a proper, loving father figure, and the girl's mother ends her affair which will restore a measure of stability to their family life.

Wes Anderson's mother, Texas Ann Burroughs, was formerly an archeologist, who sometimes took her children to her archeological digs (a prototype for Etheline in *The Royal Tenenbaums*),[49] and also worked as a real estate agent, while his father, Melver Leonard Anderson, ran an advertising and public relations firm.[50] The two were divorced when Wes, the middle child, was in the fourth grade; he was eight years old at the time. Anderson has said in interviews that the trauma of the divorce was a crucial turning point in his childhood for him and his two brothers, and that his parents' divorce affected him deeply.[51] He began acting up in school, and his fourth-grade teacher discovered that a technique for getting Anderson to behave in class was to allow him to produce his own plays.[52] At around the same time, for his eighth birthday, his father gave him a Yashica Super 8 video camera, and Anderson wrote, directed and shot his own Super 8 films, mostly one-reel shorts about three minutes long, using older brother Mel as a star and his younger brother Eric Chase Anderson as a frequent die-er in the films, with cardboard boxes serving as sets.[53] Significantly, the first story he filmed was based on a library book called *The Skateboard Four* (1976)[54] which was the story of four adolescent males in a skateboard club run by a leader, Morgan, who feels insecure and threatened when a new boy wants to join the group – a bildungsroman of young male bonding. This theme of masculine bonding and camaraderie, jockeying for position among friends (or brothers), and particularly the relationship between father and son or master and protégé, has continued to be a running motif in all of Anderson's work, beginning with his earliest feature-length film, *Bottle Rocket*.

As a child, Anderson displayed both precocious and imaginative qualities that would later be clearly reflected in his films. Once, with the help of his older brother, he cut a hole in the roof to see what it was like to enter the house from a different angle,[55] presaging his interest in unique frames of reference and unusual ways of viewing the world. In addition, when Anderson was a child, he filled sketchbooks with drawings of fancy houses: "There was this certain phase I went through where I was obsessed with being rich. So I was fairly interested in Rolls-Royces and mansions."[56] These tropes, the trappings of wealth and luxury, are also common aesthetic images in many of his films, such as *Rushmore* and *The Royal Tenenbaums*. Anderson's earliest ambition was to become an architect, and his dad bought him a drafting table when he was very young: "I always worked at a kind of, you know, tilted table like that. I think, you know, after that I wanted to be a writer and in a way, I guess, part of what I do with these movies is a bit of a combination of those things."[57] In other words, Anderson's films are a juxtaposition of these visual and verbal proclivities. Some of Anderson's own childhood experiences are transcribed directly into his films. For example, at the age of ten or eleven, Anderson and his older brother took part in a large-scale local production of Benjamin Britten's opera written for child performers, *Noye's Fludde* (*Noah's Flood*, 1958), wearing felt animal costumes and performing technically exacting music for the piece, an experience he has revisited obliquely through Suzy Bishop's participation in a similar performance in *Moonrise Kingdom*. (Benjamin Britten, like Anderson, has expressed that he liked writing for children; as performers, he liked their simplicity and intensity.) In addition, similar to Suzy Bishop in that film, he once found a pamphlet on the top of the refrigerator at home about "Coping with the Very Troubled Child," likely related to Anderson's difficulties in dealing with his parents' divorce – and he knew immediately that the title was describing him.[58] Also related to *Moonrise Kingdom*, Anderson fell in love at a young age with a girl in his class at school (he does not name her, although he vividly recalls where her desk was located in the layout of their classroom).[59] Although the object of his affection was unaware of his interest because he hardly dared to speak to her, he has claimed that *Moonrise Kingdom* is an expression of the love story/fantasy he would have dreamed up in his imagination at that age.[60]

When he was twelve years old, Anderson announced to his parents, using detailed informational handouts, that he felt everyone in the family would be better off if he moved to France and finished his studies there, pointing out in his made-up data that France had a better program in the sciences.[61] This construction of an alternative reality to convince his parents, and this devotion to clearly quantifying his imagined world – the way twelve-year-old Anderson imagined France to be – is similar to his future creations of worlds both imagined and real. Needless to say, his parents did not send him to France at that time, although since Anderson now lives mainly in Paris, it is intriguing to see how his future plans were already taking shape at age twelve. In eighth grade, Anderson graduated from his private day school and was forced to move, rather unhappily, to a public high school, where he continued to wear his private school blazer as a badge of honor (as Max Fischer does in *Rushmore*).[62] Anderson attended Westchester High School,[63] but later transferred to the private preparatory school St. John's (the inspiration and eventual setting for *Rushmore*). The young Anderson's early interest in films was sparked through a revival house cinema in Houston that played *The Pink Panther* (1963) films, as well as Hitchcock retrospectives, and Anderson remembers becoming a devoted fan of Hitchcock around ninth grade.[64] Anderson's family had a boxed set of Hitchcock films at home and Anderson noted his early surprise to find the director's name, "Alfred Hitchcock," occupying the central, dominant position on the box – the director's name was more important than any of his actors. Anderson also cites the films of Steven Spielberg, specifically the *Indiana Jones* series (1981–1989), and George Lucas' *Star Wars* (1977) as early influences.[65] He gives recognition to Pauline Kael as a strong motivation; he began reading her film reviews in the *New Yorker* magazines in his school library when he was in the tenth grade; soon after, he began collecting *New Yorker* magazines and kept them in bound collections at his home. He has called Kael his "favorite" and "probably the most influential movie critic of all time"[66] and claims that her books and reviews were always his main guide for finding the right movies to watch and learning about filmmakers. Anderson was also an avid reader who devoured the short stories of F. Scott Fitzgerald when he was in high school, particularly "The Captured Shadow" (1928) about the exploits of a romantic fifteen-year-old, Basil Lee, as he attempts to stage his own play at his prep school (as Max Fischer, the hero of *Rushmore*, later would).[67]

Anderson attended college at the University of Texas, where he majored in philosophy. There, he met his frequent leading actor and earliest screenwriting collaborator Owen Wilson at the age of eighteen (Wilson was majoring in English). Anderson and Wilson first encountered each other because they took the same playwriting course,[68] but never talked nor interacted with one another in the class itself (Anderson sat alone in the back of the room in a corner, and Wilson sat in an opposite corner).[69] After the course was over, one day on campus Wilson came up to Anderson in the corridor of Benedict, one of the buildings in English Department, and "suddenly started acting as if they were close friends,"[70] with Wilson asking Anderson's advice on which professors' courses to take:

> We were signing up for classes and [Owen] started asking me to help him figure out what he should do, as if we knew each other. As if we had ever spoken before or knew each other's names. I almost feel like he was taking it for granted that if we didn't know each other yet, soon we would.[71]

Some time later, Anderson and Wilson decided to become roommates, and Anderson wrote a paper for Wilson as part of a deal over who would get the better room. The paper, on Edgar Allan Poe's short story "The Cask of Amontillado," earned Wilson an A+.[72] While in college, Anderson also asked Wilson to star in *A Night in Tunisia*, a variation on Sam Shepard's sibling rivalry drama about two estranged brothers, *True West* (1980), written with two other students as co-authors with Anderson and Wilson as a group writing exercise. This marked the first time Anderson and Wilson had ever written anything together, as well as the first time Anderson directed Wilson. The University of Texas library at that time had a broad collection of film books and European arthouse films from the 1950s and 1960s (Truffaut, Godard, Antonioni, Bergman, and Fellini), and Anderson credits this collection, which he describes as "very sort of sixties ... and sort of out of time,"[73] as being instrumental in his film education. He also worked part-time as a film projectionist during his college years, which added to his broad-based knowledge of film.[74] Anderson and Wilson bonded over their love for classical Hollywood and art-cinema films, and engaged in many late-night conversations about their favorite directors: Cassavetes, Peckinpah, Scorsese, Altman, Malick, Huston. *Bottle Rocket* was inspired by Anderson and Wilson's experiences living in an apartment together in Austin, where they had a lengthy dispute with their landlord over several windows that were broken and could not be closed. Because the landlord did nothing to fix the windows, the two began hatching various schemes which escalated the feud. To prove to the landlord the dangerousness of the situation, the two broke into their own apartment, stole some of their own belongings, and then reported the break-in to the police. The landlord, unperturbed, still did not fix the windows, saying the break-in looked like an "inside job." Later Anderson and Wilson moved out in the middle of the night, only to be tracked down by a private investigator.[75] All of this proved to be valuable inspiration for their first film.

After graduating in 1991, Anderson moved to Dallas, where he again shared an apartment with Owen Wilson, as well as the other Wilson brothers and various friends (notoriously Andrew Wilson was the only one who had a job and was supporting them all). The original 13-minute short "Bottle Rocket" was filmed at various locations around Dallas after Anderson and Wilson each borrowed US$2000 from their fathers; they were intending to shoot it as a feature-length film, but when they ran out of money, it became a short.[76] After "Bottle Rocket" was shown at the Sundance Film Festival by the arrangement of Wilson family friend L. M. Kit Carson (who also shared it with another producer-friend, Barbara Boyle), it caught the eye of production designer Polly Platt, who had worked with producer-director James L. Brooks on *Terms of Endearment* (1983) and other films. Platt showed the short to Brooks, and both of them worked to convince Columbia Pictures to produce a feature-length version, working with the same amateur, no-name cast and novice director. Platt (who also championed the careers of Peter Bogdanovich, Garry Marshall, and other promising filmmakers early in their careers) summarized her reaction to Anderson and Wilson's first script as follows:

> Most scripts you read are pale imitations of films that have already been made, but I had never seen anything like their work. As a producer, you live for – you pray for – finding that kind of writing. It was unique, unhomogenized, brilliant.[77]

Brooks elaborated on his "dazzled" response to the short version of "Bottle Rocket":

> The possession of a real voice is always a marvel, an almost religious thing. When you have one, it not only means you see things from a slightly different perspective than the billions of other ants on the hill, but that you also necessarily possess such equally rare qualities as integrity and humility. It's part of the package of being a real voice, because when your voice is real, you can't screw around. The voice must be served; all other exit doors marked "expediency" or "solid career move" are sealed over and the only way out of your inner torment is genuine self-expression.[78]

Brooks set up an arrangement where Anderson and Wilson lived in Los Angeles for two years working as screenwriters to hone their *Bottle Rocket* screenplay. Most youth-oriented scripts at the time had hackneyed writing and formulaic plots, but Brooks describes the new voice of the Anderson/Wilson screenwriting team in the foreword to *Rushmore* in 1998: "If they weren't writing their scripts, nothing at all like those scripts would exist."[79]

Taking Off

The screenplay for *Rushmore* actually preceded *Bottle Rocket*; Anderson began working on the script while still an undergraduate at the University of Texas as an application to graduate school. Although he ultimately changed his mind about attending film school, he continued working on the script with Owen Wilson, writing most of the final screenplay in 1993 during a road trip through the desert on the way to Los Angeles to work with a production company on *Bottle Rocket*.[80] The character of Max Fischer was an amalgamation of Anderson and Wilson,[81] based on their own personal experiences and the anecdotes of experiences that they had heard from friends, with the addition of many personally significant references to art, including the photographs of Jacques-Henri Lartigue (Max's go-kart club shot was modeled on one of Lartigue's famous images), the portrait of the teenaged Ludovico Capponi (painted circa 1550–1555) by Italian Renaissance painter Agnolo Bronzino (1503–1572), as well as significant visual references to Truffaut's *Les Quatre cents coups*, literary references from Mark Twain to J. D. Salinger, and numerous references to Jacques Cousteau that foreshadow Anderson's future work in *The Life Aquatic with Steve Zissou*. The character of Max Fischer, who appears in almost every scene and whose unique charisma drives the film, was originally described in the script as "extremely skinny and pale."[82] Anderson auditioned over 1800 actors for the part, ultimately casting the seventeen-year-old Jason Schwartzman, son of Talia Shire,[83] who showed up for the audition wearing a school blazer onto which he had sewn his own custom-made "Rushmore" insignia patch. Although he looked nothing like the character Anderson had envisioned, Schwartzman got the part. *Rushmore* was produced and released by Disney specialty divisions Touchstone Pictures and Buena Vista Pictures on a reported US$20 million budget in 1998. (The budget for *Bottle Rocket* had been US$6 million, although the film ended up costing US$7 million.)

According to Anderson, the idea for his next film, *The Royal Tenenbaums*, came from a place, rather than a story.

> I wanted to make a New York film. I am from Texas, but there were so many New York movies and novels which were among my favorites and I didn't have an accurate idea of what New York was like. I wanted to create an exaggerated version of that imaginary New York.[84]

Anderson also had in mind the idea of a family of geniuses, because he wanted to explore their failure and their family's development. Interestingly, he went on to cast three actors from celebrity families who had grown up in the limelight of fame: Ben Stiller, Gwyneth Paltrow, and Anjelica Huston.[85] Owen Wilson had told Anderson he should write a screenplay about his parents' divorce, and this was Anderson's original intention as he set out to write the film; however, "As soon as Royal began to speak, his answers were nothing like the answers my father had given under similar circumstances with my brothers and I."[86] The more he wrote of Royal and the family, the less it became about his own experiences. The director also mentions on the commentary how the film did not really come together until they found the Tenenbaum house (on Convent Avenue at 144th Street in Harlem) – Anderson knew he could never create an authentic "home" feeling in a studio.

Tom McGeveran writes that Anderson, who lived on the Upper East Side of Manhattan during this period, spent months looking at different houses, because the at-the-time unfinished script evoked a distinctly New York location with references to "Archer Avenue," "the Valenzuela Bridge," "the 375th Street Y," and "the Lindbergh Palace Hotel." The script painted the family as intellectual, elite yet bohemian, living in grand surroundings that were nevertheless somewhat dated and anachronistic. Anderson said, "It needed to be a New York house that wasn't stereotypical … where you'd have a real strong sense of family history."[87]

Speaking to Gavin Smith and Kent Jones, Anderson said *The Royal Tenenbaums* was a "romantic-house movie … family intrigues in a house, like *Rules of the Game*"[88] (Jean Renoir's *La Règle du jeu* [*The Rules of the Game*, 1939]). In addition, in this film, Anderson continued to hint at personal details referencing his own life: "And Margot does these plays, too. I'm a middle child, and the middle-child dynamic is something I've always felt was significant. I also feel a connection with Eli, Owen's character, because there's this family that he wants to get himself adopted into."[89] The film became one of Anderson's most successful (made for US$28 million and earning US$71.4 million), and co-writers Anderson and Wilson received their first Academy Award recognition for this film, which was nominated for Best Original Screenplay.

Anderson traveled extensively in Europe doing press tours for *The Royal Tenenbaums*, and he decided he would make his next film there. In *The Life Aquatic with Steve Zissou*, Anderson realized his homage to Jacques Cousteau, whose work is a fascination he had hinted at as early as *Bottle Rocket* and *Rushmore*:

> I wrote a little short story when I was in college. It wasn't even a short story; it was like one paragraph that was just a description of this one character and Anjelica's character and the ship, *The Belafonte*, and just the setting. So, I had that but I didn't mean for it to be a movie. I was just trying to write a story and it never really got any further. It was actually Owen Wilson who kept bringing it up from time to time over the years and kept reminding me about it and got me into thinking about it some more. I remember one day on *The Royal Tenenbaums* seeing Anjelica and Bill Murray on the set together. All they had together was about 30 seconds but I felt there was a great rapport between the two of them that would be worth exploring.[90]

Anderson completed the full script with Noah Baumbauch, writing together mainly at Bar Pitti in New York.[91] In an engaging DVD feature entitled "Aquatic Life" included in a cluster of featurettes on production design, costumes and visual effects Anderson reveals how he was able to fully realize his oceanic fantasy world. The stop-motion animatronics used to portray the unusual marine life were a key element of the film for Anderson: "The stop-motion animation is related to the whole concept of a movie being about people who create their own world – it's about self-invention."[92] While

Anderson enjoyed filming at Cinecittà in Rome (the stage where the big cross-section set of the *Belafonte* was built is called "Fellini's stage"), the film went over schedule and over budget: scheduled for an eighty-day shoot, it shot for a hundred days, and the budget of US$52 million went $8 million over to cost a total of $60 million. A film made to explore the topic of failure itself became a financial failure and is generally considered the least well-received of Anderson's films.

Second Act

By the time he was finished promoting *The Life Aquatic* overseas, in the summer of 2005, Anderson decided that he needed a change, and that in order to be productive he should leave New York, where he had lived and worked for nearly a decade.[93] Jason Schwartzman invited him to Paris where he had been living while filming *Marie Antoinette* (2006), and shortly thereafter the two became roommates. For some years, Anderson had had an idea about brothers traveling together which came from *Husbands*, a 1970 John Cassavetes movie about three suburban husbands escaping to London, and Anderson first got the idea to shoot in India after Martin Scorsese introduced him to Jean Renoir's evocative 1951 film *The River*. Yet, the story was mainly born out of close friendship: "But my main idea was not the train, not India, not the brothers," Anderson has explained; "My main idea was, *I want to write with Roman and Jason*."[94] Schwartzman and Coppola quickly signed on, and the three of them set aside a month to travel through India by train. "I guess we went to India as research," says Anderson, "but the more precise-slash-romanticized description would be that we were trying to do the movie, trying to act it out. We were trying to be the movie before it existed."[95] This film became the most personal of Anderson's stories.[96]

Anderson met Roald Dahl's widow, Felicity ("Liccy") Dahl, in New York City just before he began work on *The Royal Tenenbaums*, and set into motion the long process of procuring the rights to make *Fantastic Mr. Fox*. Anderson was invited to visit Roald Dahl's studio in March of 2001, and he documented the visit in an article published in *The New York Times* in 2002. In the article and its accompanying photographs, Anderson warmly describes Dahl's home (named "Gipsy House"), and Dahl's writing hut on the property, in which a table can still be seen strewn with some of Dahl's favorite belongings, such as a ten-pound ball of chocolate wrappers.[97] Anderson and Noah Baumbach were again invited by Liccy to stay at Gipsy House for another two weeks while they wrote the screenplay, and when it was approved by the Dahl estate, Anderson began making the film in 2007.

The process of making a stop-motion film played on many of Anderson's filmmaking strengths, first of all, because he could work with an entire new team of specialists (led by chief animator Mark Gustafson) and learn new filmmaking disciplines and techniques for animation that included capturing 15,000 individual frames (the entire film is made up of beautifully framed stills) to create a persistence-of-vision effect when projected in succession (twelve individual images per second, which appeared twice and were projected at twenty-four images per second).[98] Moreover, since every single object that appears in the film had to be made by hand, Anderson was able to draw on his well-honed dollhouse sensibilities to design miniature objects, tiny props, and built-to-scale sets (with his sketchbooks, Anderson had been training for this role since childhood), as well as fabricated real-fur puppets (Anderson liked the imperfections created by using real fur, which moved each time the puppet was handled). A majority of Anderson's designs had a distinctly 1970s retro-style feel to them since many of the furnishings, such as chairs, tables, or lamps, had been based on furniture Anderson had observed at Gipsy House. Anderson also re-created many of Dahl's favorite belongings from the table in his writing hut (such as his pencil-holder, electric pencil-sharpener and ball of chocolate wrappers).[99] For a director who generally gives close, obsessive attention to detail, this film offered an entirely new level of possibility in that Anderson could reference the author Roald Dahl's life through these objects and sets, essentially putting Dahl into the film (indeed, the Farmer Bean puppet, voiced by Michael Gambon, was made to resemble Dahl himself).

Anderson's next film, *Moonrise Kingdom*, co-written with Roman Coppola in Rome, and shot in Rhode Island, was Anderson's fantasy pre-adolescent love story between two twelve-year-olds; Anderson credits Truffaut as being an inspiration as well for *Moonrise Kingdom*. "*Small Change* is one of the movies that made me want to make a movie about people this age in the first place; Sam and Suzy are the same age as those kids in *Small Change*."[100] The two leads, played by newcomers Jared Gilman and Kara Hayward, had never seen a typewriter before, and it was memorably Bill Murray who taught Jared Gilman how to tie a necktie. The film combines magical realism and a pseudo-historic setting in 1965 to bring to life the dream-like story of *l'amour fou*. Significantly, as a marker of Anderson's rising status, *Moonrise Kingdom* was chosen to open the Cannes Film Festival, which it did on May 16, 2012.

The idea for *The Grand Budapest Hotel* came to Anderson in two parts. First, serendipitously, he was rummaging through a bookstore in Paris when he came across a novel called *Beware of Pity*, by the almost forgotten Austrian writer Stefan Zweig – once one of the most celebrated authors in Europe – and was immediately captivated by the author's style. His interest in Zweig led him to another novel, *The Post Office Girl*, in which a young postal clerk is invited to visit her aunt in an opulent Swiss hotel, where she is transformed by the aunt into a socialite reminiscent of Shaw's *Pygmalion*. According to Anderson: "I loved the way Zweig often sets the stage for his stories by having his narrator meet a mysterious figure who goes on to tell him the whole novel. And I could feel a movie coming out of this."[101] Anderson, working with close friend Hugo Guinness, went on to compose a story taking deep inspiration from Zweig's life and novels, particularly the dandyistic social life of Zweig himself, which was forced to a tragic end by World War II. The confection that is *The Grand Budapest Hotel* conjures an evanescent atmosphere of civility that belies the underlying brutality of war and destruction, and the screwball comedy involving jailbreaks, funicular escapades, and bobsled chases mixes the hijinks of a classic Tintin adventure with the "long knives and longer shadows of a Fritz Lang thriller."[102]

Because of its March release, *The Grand Budapest Hotel* had not been expected to be a major awards contender, but despite the film's long period out of theaters, it garnered nine Academy Awards nominations, including bids for Best Picture and Best

Director for Anderson. Globally, *The Grand Budapest Hotel* earned $174.8 million, more than double Anderson's previous high-water mark of $71.4 million for *The Royal Tenenbaums*. Anderson's film was nominated for Best Picture, Best Director, Best Cinematography, Best Film Editing, and Best Original Screenplay, and the film won in the categories of Best Achievement in Costume Design, Best Achievement in Makeup and Hairstyling, Best Achievement in Production Design, and Best Original Score (for Alexandre Desplat).[103] *The Grand Budapest Hotel* also did very well critically throughout the awards season, winning the Jury Grand Prix (Silver Bear) at the Berlin International Film Festival. The film also led the BAFTA nominations, with 11 nominations that year, including Best Film and Best Director for Anderson, and Best Actor for Ralph Fiennes. The film won the Golden Globe Award for Best Motion Picture – Musical or Comedy and garnered three more Golden Globe Award nominations, including Best Director for Anderson.

New Territory

Anderson claims to have not deliberately moved around a lot, saying in 2009, "The difference between exile and nomadism is probably just your mood."[104] However, Anderson moved from Houston to Austin to Dallas, then California, then New York, where he lived for nearly a decade (he had always wanted to live in New York). Over the next couple of decades, Anderson's films would take him increasingly farther from the United States. He went to Italy and sailed the Mediterranean in *The Life Aquatic with Steve Zissou* (which was originally supposed to be shot in the United States until Anderson visited Rome while promoting *The Royal Tenenbaums* and fell in love with Europe). He shot *The Darjeeling Limited* mostly aboard a moving train in India. *Fantastic Mr. Fox* was shot in England, and Anderson briefly returned to the United States (specifically Rhode Island) for *Moonrise Kingdom*, then went to Eastern Europe and Germany for *The Grand Budapest Hotel*. At the time of writing, there are reports that his next feature, another stop-motion animated film, is a Japanese-themed story involving dogs.

In May 1998, when Wilson and Anderson were not yet thirty years old, as they completed work on their second feature film, Wilson stood outside Don's Barbershop in Houston on the set of *Rushmore* – he would be appearing in the blockbuster *Armageddon* that summer – and mused: "Sometimes I stop and think how strange this all is. Something that began as a little idea in Austin, that Wes and I just walked around talking about between ourselves, has turned into all this."[105] A few years later, in making *The Royal Tenenbaums*, despite the celebrity of the stars involved and the big-movie budget, Anderson still relied on the talents of his hometown friends, from his brother Eric's drawings, to the acting and writing of his old best friends from Texas, Owen and Luke Wilson, to the comic talents of a man named Kumar Pallana (as Pagoda, faithful servant and friend to Gene Hackman's quixotic Royal), former proprietor of the Cosmic Cup coffee shop on Oak Lawn Avenue in Dallas, where Anderson and Wilson used to idle away the hours as young men, with all the time in the world on their hands, endlessly sharing their stories and lives.

Notes

1. Particularly profound has been the influence of Anderson's films on post-twentieth-century millennial hipster culture, which will be explored in chapter 2.
2. Matt Zoller Seitz, "The Substance of Style, Part 1," *Moving Image Source*. March 30, 2009. http://www.movingimagesource.us/articles/the-substance-of-style-pt-1–20090330 (accessed November 7, 2014).
3. In 2005, Anderson personally contributed to the American independent filmmaking scene by serving as a producer on Noah Baumbach's *The Squid and The Whale*, which went on to win two Sundance awards. Anderson also served as executive producer on Peter Bogdanovich's *She's Funny That Way* (2014), and the 2017 documentary *Escapes* about actor and *Blade Runner* screenwriter Hampton Fancher.
4. For this comparison with Woody Allen, see Jeffrey Overstreet, "*Moonrise Kingdo*m and the Divine Symphony." *Patheos.com*. July 5, 2012. http://www.patheos.com/blogs/goodletters/2012/07/moonrise-kingdom-and-the-divine-symphony/ (accessed November 17, 2014).
5. Interestingly, both Wes Anderson and Woody Allen have taken on the challenge of portraying their own "nostalgic" version of New York City on film, Allen through the medium of black-and-white and a soundtrack of Gershwin for his vision of Manhattan that is "romanticized all out of proportion" in *Manhattan* (1979) and Anderson through a fantasy of gypsy cabs, uniformed elevator operators in a luxurious 1940s-style hotel, and an iconic brownstone mansion in *The Royal Tenenbaums*.
6. Although the titles of short films are usually italicized, the title of "Bottle Rocket" has been here (and throughout this book) rendered in quotation marks to distinguish it from the feature-length film title, which throughout is italicized as *Bottle Rocket*.
7. Richard Brody, "Loving Moonrise Kingdom for the Right Reasons," *NewYorker.com*. June 14, 2012. http://www.newyorker.com/culture/richard-brody/loving-moonrise-kingdom-for-the-right-reasons (accessed February 27, 2015).
8. Anderson films have been nominated for Academy Awards four times before 2015: in 2002 for Best Original Screenplay for *The Royal Tenenbaums* (losing to Julian Fellowes for *Gosford Park*), in 2010 for Best Animated Feature and Best Original Score for *Fantastic Mr. Fox* (losing to *Up* in both categories), and in 2013 for Best Original Screenplay for *Moonrise Kingdom* (losing to Quentin Tarantino's *Django Unchained*).
9. In his introduction to the *Rushmore* screenplay, Anderson recounts the story of the day he had a private screening of the film for Pauline Kael, fulfilling a childhood dream of his (he and Owen Wilson dedicated the printed volume of their screenplay to Kael). In the essay describing that day, Anderson writes: "Kael told me she thought I should change my name. 'Wes Anderson is a terrible name for a movie director.'" Wes Anderson, "Introduction," in Wes Anderson and Owen Wilson, *Rushmore* [screenplay] (New York: Faber and Faber, 1999), xv.

10 Ibid., xvi.
11 Jesse Mayshark, *Post-Pop Cinema: The Search for Meaning in New American Film* (Westport, CT: Praeger, 2007), 118.
12 For example, on June 19, 2015, Whoopi Goldberg criticized Anderson's failure to cast actors of color on the daytime talk show *The View*. See Anna Silman, "Whoopi Goldberg wants more people of color in Wes Anderson's movies: 'I would like to give you my resume.'" *Salon.com*. June 23, 2015. http://www.salon.com/2015/06/22/whoopi_goldberg_wants_more_people_of_color_in_wes_andersons_movies_i_would_like_to_give_you_my_resume/ (accessed June 25, 2015).
13 The "Rushmore Academy" website can be found at rushmoreacademy.com.
14 For a detailed depiction of Orson Welles's working methods with his Mercury Theater troupe, see Simon Callow, *Orson Welles, Volume 1: The Road to Xanadu* (New York: Penguin, 1995), 308–321.
15 Anderson's reinvigoration of Bill Murray's career is also noted by Geoff King in *Lost in Translation* (Edinburgh: Edinburgh University Press, 2010), 50, and Jesse Mayshark in *Post-Pop Cinema* (Westport, CT: Praeger, 2007), 116, as well as Donna Peberdy in "'I'm Just a Character in Your Film': Acting and Performance from Autism to Zissou," *New Review of Film and Television Studies* 10:1 (March 2012): 54.
16 Mayshark, 2007, 136. Writing about American directors (such as David O. Russell, Todd Haynes, Sofia Coppola) and one screenwriter (Charlie Kaufman), who are members of the "post-pop" or "post-post modernism school" of filmmakers, Mayshark has noted that Anderson is "a filmmaker in a generation that was defined early by its uncertainty about the future and inability to commit to relationships, jobs, and career paths," 14.
17 Mayshark writes: "Anderson's stories return again and again to overgrown man-boys, whose rashness and irresponsibility makes them both lovable and infuriating," ibid., 136. He singles out Henry Sherman, whose humility and dignity set him apart from Royal Tenenbaum, as a notable exception.
18 Ibid., 117. In addition, Mayshark points out that Anderson's films make prominent use of the typeface Futura bold, popular in the 1950s and 1960s, which was used regularly by Stanley Kubrick.
19 This is explored more fully in chapter 4 of Geoff King's *American Independent Cinema* (London: IB Tauris, 2005), 165–196.
20 Geoff King, *Lost in Translation* (Edinburgh: Edinburgh University Press, 2010), 67.
21 Michael Z. Newman, "Movies for Hipsters," in Geoff King, Claire Molloy, and Yannis Tzioumakis, eds., *American Independent Cinema: Indie, Indiewood, and Beyond* (London: Routledge, 2013), 73.
22 Stephen Hyden, Noel Murray, Keith Phipps, Nathan Rabin, and Scott Tobias, "10 Films that Couldn't Have Happened Without Wes Anderson," *A.V. Club.com*. October 9, 2007. http://www.avclub.com/article/10-films-that-couldnt-have-happened-without-wes-anderson (accessed November 20, 2014).
23 Ibid.

24. Katey Rich, "TIFF Review: *Submarine* is Much More Than Just the Welsh *Rushmore*," *Cinemablend.com*. September 18, 2010. http://www.cinemablend.com/new/TIFF-Review-Submarine-Much-More-Than-Just-Welsh-Rushmore-20717.html (accessed January 15, 2016).

25. According to a 2015 article by Lauren Cochrane, fashion's biggest designers including Prada, Miu Miu, Lacoste, and Vogue referenced Anderson's retro influence in their Winter 2015 collections. Also in 2015, Anderson designed a trendy bar in Milan for Prada, Bar Luce, with artistic details (echoing his short film *Castello Cavalcanti*) reminiscent of Italian popular culture and aesthetics from the 1950s and 1960s. Lauren Cochrane, "Fantastic Mr. Wes Anderson: How Tenenbaum Chic Took Over the Catwalks," *The Guardian*. August 24, 2015. https://www.theguardian.com/fashion/2015/aug/24/fantastic-mr-wes-anderson-how-tenenbaum-chic-took-over-the-catwalks (accessed September 29, 2016).

26. Studies of auteur theory include that of Andrew Sarris, who defines the theory as marked by two levels: an auteur must return to distinctive themes or issues across his entire body of work, and there must be the presence of distinctive formal traits recognizable as the director's "signature." Andrew Sarris, in John Caughie (ed.), *Theories of Authorship* (London: Routledge & Kegan Paul, 1981), 64. Auteurism can be marked not only by an eclectic departure from the mainstream, but also by a consistent repetition of distinctive formal traits within the dominant paradigm, as suggested by David Bordwell: the "classical" Hollywood style yields a number of options for formal devices that can be used to create particular effects, thereby allowing an individual auteur to forge an identity through consistent favoring of particular identifiable options within the normative mainstream. David Bordwell, "Part One: The Classical Hollywood Style, 1917–1960," in David Bordwell, Janet Staiger, and Kristin Thompson, *The Classical Hollywood Cinema: Film Style and Mode of Production to 1960* (London and New York: Routledge, 1985b), 77–82. A more recent resource is David A. Gerstner and Janet Staiger, eds., *Authorship and Film* (New York: Routledge, 2002).

27. Elsaesser groups Anderson in with this list of auteurs: "To these and other authors of independent American cinema most of the traditional criteria and definitions of the *auteur* apply, as they continue to be used in Europe and other parts of the world for art cinema directors or international festival directors." Thomas Elsaesser, "*Auteurism* Today: Signature Products, Concept-Authors and Access for All: *Avatar*," in *The Persistence of Hollywood* (New York: Routledge, 2012), 364 (chapter 21, footnote 5).

28. Elsaesser, 2012, 285. Lewis expands on this idea: "The first wave *auteurs* [Coppola, Scorsese] focused primarily on mise-en-scène and took pride and care in directing actors, set design and lighting, all things accomplished during the production phase. Lucas and Spielberg are almost exclusively post-production directors, experts in sound and special effects and action editing. Popular directors in Hollywood today are significantly cut from the second-wave cloth, for example: James Cameron, the director of the ultimate nineties blockbuster *Titanic* (1997) and *Avatar* (2009)." Jon Lewis, "The Perfect Money Machine(s): George Lucas,

Steven Spielberg, and Auteurism in the New Hollywood," in Eric Smoodin and Jon Lewis, eds., *Looking Past the Screen: Case Studies in American Film History and Method* (Durham, NC: Duke University Press, 2007), 61–86.

29 Lewis, 2007, 68.
30 This study uses the Bloomian term "influences" because of Anderson's films' close relationship with literature (i.e., using literary textual references as a visual signifier in his films), and his own authorial role in the creation of his screenplays.
31 The entire oeuvre of Wes Anderson can be viewed as one "giant" film, the way Susan Sontag described the 1960s work of Jean-Luc Godard. See Susan Sontag, "Godard's *Vivre Sa Vie*," in *Against Interpretation* (New York: Picador/Farrar, Straus, and Giroux, 2001 [c1966]), 196–208. Anderson's films are all connected through shared threads and characters, and if not literally one volume to the next, they comprise at least a shared universe.
32 Anderson's performance as auteur is understood through the principles of performance theory most commonly associated with the work of Victor W. Turner, in his book *The Anthropology of Performance* (New York: PAJ, 1988), and Richard Schechner's *Between Theatre and Anthropology* (Philadelphia: Pennsylvania University Press, 1985). These two authors draw attention to the performative nature of societies around the world, how events and rituals as well as daily life are all governed by a code of performance. Others such as Judith Butler in *Bodies That Matter: On the Discursive Limits of "Sex"* (New York: Routledge, 1993), and Jacques Derrida in *Limited Inc* (Paris: Éditions Galilée, 1990) have drawn attention to the way performances seek to reinforce and communicate social identities.
33 Corrigan argues that today's commercial practice of the auteur has resulted into the modern conception of the "auteur-star." This "auteur-star" is acknowledged as a brand name and integrated into the commercial infrastructure as a Hollywood marketing approach. Timothy Corrigan, "The Commerce of Auteurism" in Virginia Wright Wexman, ed., *Film and Authorship* (New Brunswick, NJ: Rutgers University Press, 2003), 105. For example, Anderson's "brand" is promoted by using the phrase "A Film by Wes Anderson" for publicity on posters and DVDs.
34 Corrigan, 2003, 107. Through interviews, the auteur can address his audience and critics, by appointing and diffusing his own organizing agency as an auteur, 108.
35 David Amsden, "The Life Obsessive with Wes Anderson." *New York Magazine*. September 24, 2007. http://nymag.com/movies/filmfestivals/newyork/2007/380 24/ (accessed September 30, 2014), 2.
36 Robbie Collin, "Wes Anderson Interview," *The Telegraph*. February 19, 2014. http://www.telegraph.co.uk/culture/film/starsandstories/10644172/Wes-Anderson-interview.html (accessed April 27, 2016). Anderson's unique and highly personal fashion sense is part of his directorial image; he claims to repeatedly wear the same corduroy in his favorite caramel shade: "My very favorite corduroy suit – in my favorite color I wear 200 days per year – is the same outfit we put on Mr. Fox." Chris Heath, "*GQ* Style: Wes Anderson's Highly Influential, Slightly Tweaked Take on Reality," *GQ*. October 27, 2014. http://www.gq.com/story/gq-style-fall-2014-influencer-wes-anderson (accessed March 26, 2016).

37 See more on the "privileged" reading of film in David Bordwell, *Narration in Fiction Film* (Madison: University of Wisconsin Press, 1985), 104.
38 Tom Dorey, "Fantastic Mr. Filmmaker: Paratexts and the Positioning of Wes Anderson as Roald Dahl's Cinematic Heir," *New Review of Film and Television Studies* 10:1 (2012): 180.
39 Interestingly, Anderson's precocious age at the time of filming his first feature corresponds to these two film prodigies: Truffaut made his first feature-length film at the age of twenty-seven, Welles made *Citizen Kane* when he was twenty-five and *The Magnificent Ambersons* when he was twenty-seven, and the similarly prodigious Anderson released his first feature-length film *Bottle Rocket* at the age of twenty-seven.
40 Rick Lyman, "From Centimes, A Wealth of Ideas (Watching Movies With: Wes Anderson)." *NYTimes.com*. January 11, 2002. http://www.nytimes.com/2002/01/11/movies/watching-movies-with-wes-anderson-from-centimes-a-wealth-of-ideas.html?_r=0 (accessed May 14, 2015).
41 Ibid.
42 Ibid.
43 Ibid.
44 Wes Anderson, in Matt Zoller Seitz's *The Wes Anderson Collection* (New York: Abrams, 2013a), 312.
45 Other striking similarities between Truffaut and Anderson include Truffaut's relationship with Jean-Pierre Léaud (he first cast the boy in *Les Quatre cents coups* when he was fourteen, and made many films with him over a twenty-year period), which is reminiscent of Anderson's relationship with the years-younger Jason Schwartzman (Anderson first cast Schwartzman in *Rushmore* when he was seventeen; there is a twelve-year age difference between Léaud and Truffaut, while the age difference between Schwartzman and Anderson is eleven years). Truffaut's films, especially *Les Quatre cents coups* and *L'Argent de poche*, often reflect the deep bonds of male friendship, especially among adolescent boys.
46 Robert Ingram, with Paul Duncan (ed.), *François Truffaut: Film Author, 1932–1984* (London: Taschen, 2004), 9.
47 Diana Holmes and Robert Ingram, *François Truffaut* (Manchester, UK: Manchester University Press, 1998), 11.
48 Wes Anderson, quoted in an interview with Arnaud Desplechin, "Wes Anderson," *Interview*. October 26, 2009. http://www.interviewmagazine.com/film/wes-anderson/ (accessed June 4, 2014).
49 Anderson had Anjelica Huston wear his mother's eyeglasses for the role of Etheline Tenenbaum, thus strengthening this connection.
50 Anderson has said in interviews that people often think he must have a terrible father because of the flawed father figures in his films (and because of the title "Bad Dads" given to the annual exhibit of artwork based on his films in a studio in San Francisco). However, in an interview with Olivier Zahm and Olympia Le-Tan, Anderson revealed that "Seymour Cassel's character [Max Fischer's father] in *Rushmore* is the most like my own father – especially the way that he treats his

son." Wes Anderson, in Olivier Zahm and Olympia Le-Tan's "Interview with Wes Anderson," *Purple.fr*. September 2008. http://www.purple.fr/magazine/ss-2008-issue-9/wes-anderson/ (accessed June 17, 2016).

51   Anderson characterized his response to his parents' divorce as follows: "At home I felt I think I felt angry. I do remember that. I was not – I was probably one of the grouchiest kids you could be around in the household. [...] We spent a lot of time with my father and my mother in our separate houses, but probably I was kind of acting out against something to do with not wanting to have a divorce. That was probably my way of refusing to accept what needed to happen." Terry Gross, "Wes Anderson: Creating a Singular 'Kingdom,'" *NPR.org*. May 29, 2012. http://www.npr.org/2012/05/29/153913922/wes-anderson-creating-a-singular-kingdom (accessed October 4, 2014).

52   Anderson elaborates: "I must've been some kind of troublemaker, because [my fourth-grade teacher] made this arrangement with me that each week that I did not get in a certain amount of trouble she was giving me some points. And when I added up enough points, she let me put on a play in our school because she knew I'd written this one little short play that we had done in our class and she let me kind of become a little 'theater person' at that age. And I did many of these five-minute plays over, you know, over that year. And I feel like in a way what I do now is vaguely, you know, continuing something from then that she kind of got me going on." Ibid.

53   Pamela Colloff, "The New Kids – Owen Wilson and Wes Anderson," *Texas Monthly*. May 1998. http://www.texasmonthly.com/articles/the-new-kids-wes-anderson-and-owen-wilson/ (accessed May 30, 2015). These cardboard-box sets for his early films are the prototype for the boxy compartmentalization and diorama-like display which characterizes his mature work.

54   Scott Feinberg, "Wes Anderson on His Life, Career and Biggest Success Yet, 'Moonrise Kingdom: Interview with Wes Anderson," *The Hollywood Reporter*. December 25, 2012. http://www.hollywoodreporter.com/race/wes-anderson-his-life-career-406295 (accessed October 3, 2014).

55   Wes Anderson, in Dave Calhoun, "Wes Anderson Interview: 'I Always Used to Have Two Desserts a Day; Now I Have Only One,'" *TimeOut.com*. March 4, 2014. http://www.timeout.com/newyork/film/wes-anderson-interview-i-always-used-to-have-at-least-two-desserts-a-day-now-i-have-only-one (accessed April 29, 2016). Anderson explains: "Well, at one point my older brother and I decided we wanted to make an entrance to our house through the roof. So we cut a hole in the roof and went into the attic. We had a plan for the whole thing, and it took days. Then my father saw it, and I don't ever remember seeing him like this. He couldn't believe it. It was unthinkable. We'd cut a hole in the roof of our house!" Such an action was a precursor to Anderson's trademark "God's-eye view" shots in his films.

56   Amy Wallace, "Bittersweet Dreamers," *Los Angeles Magazine*. December, 2001, 175.

57   Wes Anderson in an interview with Paul Holdengräber, "LIVE from the New York Public Library: Wes Anderson | Paul Holdengräber," *Nypl.org*. February

27, 2014. http://www.nypl.org/audiovideo/wes-anderson-paul-holdengraber (accessed August 14, 2014).

58 Anderson confirmed this was based on his personal experience: "I know I had – there's a thing in the movie where the girl finds this pamphlet on top of the refrigerator in her house. And the pamphlet says *Coping with the Very Troubled Child*. And she gathers that that's her. Well, I found that pamphlet, in fact, at about that same age and when I saw it – and it was literally on top of the refrigerator – and I know that if either of my brothers had found that pamphlet they both would've known it was me. No one was going to – they were never going to make a mistake and think it was themselves. I knew it was me. They would've known it was me." Wes Anderson, in Gross, 2012.

59 Ibid. Anderson elaborates: "You know, a girl two rows over and three seats up who was in my class for years, and I never really had much of a conversation with her."

60 Ibid. "[A French reporter] asked if the movie was a memory of a fantasy. And I thought – at first I wasn't quite sure what that meant. Then I realized that that is sort of exactly what the movie is. It's – I remember the emotion of feeling like I was falling in love at that age, twelve years old, and how powerful it was and sudden, and kind of inexplicable. And yet in this – you know, I – nothing happened in my case. But the – so the fantasy – so I think it's a fantasy that I would have had at that age, would have envisioned."

61 Anderson elaborates: "I had written out all these reasons: the science program in French schools was stronger, and so on. [...] Which I had made up. They had absolutely no basis in reality. I really knew nothing about the country, apart from what one of my classmates who had moved there had told me." Robbie Collin, "Wes Anderson Interview," *The Telegraph*. February 19, 2014. http://www.telegraph.co.uk/culture/film/starsandstories/10644172/Wes-Anderson-interview.html (accessed April 27, 2016).

62 Richard Brody, "Wild, Wild Wes," *NewYorker.com*. November 2, 2009. http://www.newyorker.com/magazine/2009/11/02/wild-wild-wes (accessed January 10, 2016).

63 Westchester High School was closed in 1985 due to decreases in enrollment, which forced the school board to close Westchester and relocate its former students to Memorial and Stratford High Schools.

64 Keith Phipps, "Interview: Wes Anderson," *The Onion A.V. Club*. February 10, 1999. http://www.avclub.com/article/wes-anderson-13580 (accessed April 22, 2016).

65 Feinberg, 2012. Anderson expresses his earliest conception of director as auteur when he says: "You know, Hitchcock and Spielberg were kind of the first two filmmakers where I was really aware, 'There is a guy who was behind of all of this who we're not seeing.'"

66 Wes Anderson, "Introduction," in Anderson and Wilson, 1999, xvi.

67 Brody, 2009.

68 The character Rosemary from the film *Rushmore* later takes a job at a girls' private school called "The Webster Smalley School for Girls." Webster L. Smalley was well

known for teaching playwriting at the University of Texas at Austin. Smalley died in 1996, two years before the release of *Rushmore*.

69 Susie Mackenzie, "Wes Anderson: Into the Deep," *The Guardian*. February 12, 2005. http://www.theguardian.com/film/2005/feb/12/features.weekend (accessed January 2, 2015).

70 Matt Zoller Seitz, "Seitz: 24 Things I Learned While Writing My Book About Wes Anderson," *Vulture*. October 23, 2013b. http://www.vulture.com/2013/10/wes-anderson-collection-24-tidbits-matt-zoller-seitz.html (accessed August 14, 2014).

71 Wes Anderson, quoted in ibid.

72 The professor commented that Anderson's paper on Edgar Allan Poe was "magnificent and droll." Anderson and Wilson then adopted this phrase to ironically describe anything and everything – ten years later, Wilson and Anderson still found pleasure in calling things "magnificent and droll." Wallace, 2001, 93–94.

73 Wes Anderson, in Holdengräber, 2014. In an interview with Jennifer Wachtell, Anderson elaborates about the viewing experience in the UT Austin library: "I saw this movie [*The Last Detail*] in the library of the University of Texas at Austin in 1988, long before the advent of the DVD. They had little booths, and you could check out the movie with your student ID, but it could not leave the building. You would walk by the other booths and look in a window at each person watching their VHS tape. They were looking at Fellini movies and Fassbinder movies and Antonioni movies and that kind of thing because that was all you could get in the library." Wes Anderson interviewed by Jennifer Wachtell in "The Director's Director." *Good*. June 20, 2008. http://magazine.good.is/articles/the-directors-director (accessed May 12, 2014).

74 Collin, 2014. Anderson also joined a cable-access channel in Houston so he could use the equipment there and made some video shorts.

75 Colloff, 1998.

76 Wes Anderson, interviewed in Feinberg, 2012.

77 Colloff, 1998.

78 James L. Brooks, "Foreword" to Wes Anderson and Owen Wilson's *Rushmore* [screenplay] (New York: Faber and Faber, 1999 [1998]), viii.

79 Ibid., xii. Brooks elaborated on Wes Anderson's persona and its reception in Hollywood when Anderson was in his young twenties: "No matter what they thought of him in the jock-infested world of his youth, here in Hollywood he was an intimidating presence. First off, he looked like a genius. There was some Einstein thing with his hair, and he was rickets-thin and shabbily dressed. When he looked at [Hollywood] agents and did that long think thing before saying any words at all, you could see the sweat staining the Egyptian cotton of the agents' shirts." Brooks, ix.

80 Iman Charania, "25 Years Later: Director Wes Anderson on Living, Filming *Rushmore*," *The Review: The Official Student Newspaper of St. John's School* 63:8 (2012): 6.

81 Ibid.
82 Anderson and Wilson, 1999, 4. This description of Max Fischer more closely matches his creator, much like Truffaut casting young alter ego Jean-Pierre Léaud.
83 Anderson originally wanted to cast an unknown (as he later did with Jared Gilman in *Moonlight Kingdom*). Instead, Schwartzman belongs to a Hollywood dynasty, the Coppola family; he is nephew to Francis Ford Coppola and cousin to Roman Coppola. However, at the time Anderson cast him, he was known chiefly as a drummer, not an actor, and *Rushmore* is Schwartzman's film debut.
84 Wes Anderson, in Alisa Pomeroy, "Interview with Wes Anderson for *The Royal Tenenbaums*," BBC.co.uk. February 27, 2002. http://www.bbc.co.uk/films/2002/02/27/wes_anderson_the_royal_tenebaums_interview.shtml (accessed October 2, 2015).
85 Ibid.
86 Anderson, quoted in the DVD director's commentary for *The Royal Tenebaums*.
87 Tom McGeveran, "Wes Anderson's Dream House." Observer.com. June 4, 2001. http://www.observer.com/2001/06/wes-andersons-dream-house/ (accessed July 2016). The first time Anderson walked through the house he knew exactly which rooms would match which character. Only the ballroom scenes and scenes in Etheline's studio were shot elsewhere; apart from that, the real house became the set where most of the film was shot for 22 days.
88 Wes Anderson, in an interview with Gavin Smith and Kent Jones, "At Home with The Royal Family: Wes Anderson Interviewed by Gavin Smith and Kent Jones," *Film Comment* 37, 29.
89 Ibid.
90 Wes Anderson, in Stella Papamichael, "Interview with Wes Anderson on *The Life Aquatic with Steve Zissou*." BBC.co.uk. February 15, 2005. http://www.bbc.co.uk/films/2005/02/15/wes_anderson_the_life_aquatic_interview.shtml (accessed August 30, 2015).
91 Zissou's homebase, called Pescespada Island, was named after the swordfish entrée on Bar Pitti's menu, Esteban was modeled after the restaurant's bald owner, Giovanni, and the three-legged dog Cody was named after a frequent customer at the restaurant. Baumbach and Anderson would meet at Bar Pitti between 1:00 and 1:30 every day, sit at a table and work on the screenplay, have two meals, and write together into the evening. According to Anderson, Owen Wilson was unable to cowrite the screenplay due to his increasing acting commitments. Wes Anderson, quoted on the director's commentary for *The Life Aquatic with Steve Zissou* DVD.
92 "Aquatic Life" featurette on *The Life Aquatic with Steve Zissou* DVD.
93 Amsden, 2007. http://nymag.com/movies/filmfestivals/newyork/2007/38024/ (accessed September 30, 2014), 3.
94 Ibid., 4.
95 Ibid.
96 In an article accompanying the DVD for the Criterion Collection, Richard Brody noted, "I was surprised to learn that Anderson's approach to his subject was both

documentary and personal from the outset. He had conceived of the film while staying in Paris with Schwartzman in 2005; the two strolled through the city at night, walking the actor's dog and talking, and Anderson had the idea that the stories and personal matters under discussion would make for a good film. Schwartzman recalled Anderson telling him, 'I think we should write a movie about three brothers in India. That's kind of all I have now, but the three of us will get together every night and we'll tell our stories. It will be the most personal thing we could possibly make – let's try to make it even *too* personal.'" Richard Brody, "Voyage to India," *The Darjeeling Limited*, liner notes for the Criterion Collection DVD, 2010.

97 The whole quotation reveals just how closely Anderson identified with Dahl, most particularly with the "found objects" Dahl left behind after his death. "Liccy showed me into Dahl's famous writing hut. There is part of a bone from his hip on the table next to his first metal hip replacement, which didn't take. There is a 10-pound ball of aluminum foil made from several years of Cadbury chocolate wrappers. There is a little surgical valve he invented that saved his son from hydrocephalus. That night Liccy left me to examine Dahl's manuscripts in an office next to the guest house. An archivist made me wash my hands twice with special soap and told me to close all the curtains and lock the door when I was finished. I was alone with dozens of handwritten drafts with Dahl's sketches in the margins, and I could see his whole process laid out in front of me. More than ever, I felt as if I were in his presence." Wes Anderson, "Welcome To the Dahl House." *The New York Times Sunday Magazine*. August 18, 2002, 46, 49.

98 Because it would normally take nine days to shoot several seconds of film (and a particularly complicated shot may take 18 days to film just a few seconds), Anderson had up to 29 different units filming at once. Anderson received criticism for not being present at the filming site every day, and for directing the film through emails sent from Paris. This controversy is covered in Tom Dorey's 2012 article "Fantastic Mr. Filmmaker: Paratexts and the Positioning of Wes Anderson as Roald Dahl's Cinematic Heir." *New Review of Film and Television Studies*, 10:1, 169–185.

99 The technique of voice recording for the film also offered Anderson unique flexibility – he claims that during the process of animating the movie, which lasted over two years (from the first recording until the movie was finished), he rewrote and rerecorded almost half the film. Wanting to capture authentic sounds of the outdoors, Anderson recorded actors at a farmhouse in Connecticut, in the woods, and at a lake (when the sound of a nearby boat threatened to ruin the best take, Anderson decided to animate an airplane flying overhead to incorporate the sound of the boat).

100 Wes Anderson, in Seitz, 2013a, 312.

101 Collin, 2014.

102 Ibid.

103 Desplat wrote five major film scores in 2014. His score for *The Imitation Game* was also nominated for the Academy Award, and his win therefore marked the first

time a composer had won against another of his own scores since John Williams won for *Star Wars* (beating *Close Encounters of the Third Kind*) in 1978, and only the seventh time overall (Alfred Newman, Bernard Herrmann, Max Steiner, Miklos Rozsa and Johnny Green are the only other composers to achieve this).

104 Wes Anderson, quoted in Desplechin, 2009.
105 Colloff, 1998.

CHAPTER TWO

Wes Anderson: His Position in American Cinema and Culture

In December 2016, the United States' National Film Registry, which selects up to twenty-five films each year that are considered of enduring importance to American culture for preservation by the Library of Congress, chose Wes Anderson's *Rushmore* as the most recent feature fiction film to be inducted into the Registry (only *The Matrix* [1999], which was inducted in 2012, is more recent). Under the National Film Preservation Act, movies are only eligible to be preserved under the Registry if they are at least a decade old and recognized in the National Film Preservation Board's view as "culturally, historically, or aesthetically significant."[1] This recognition of *Rushmore* as a cultural milestone confirmed Anderson as a major American filmmaker whose visual and narrative tone has both captured the contemporary zeitgeist and had a seminal influence on both mainstream and independent film culture. As explored in the opening chapter, Wes Anderson's signature style is instantly recognizable, and he returns again and again to the themes of loss, divorce, family dysfunction, etc., expressed through hyper-attention to detail, and through the juxtaposition of both real and highly artificial elements, combining both existing and invented narratives. The combination of Anderson's unique pop sensibilities and the wealth of personal detail from his biographical background has contributed to the emotional core of his films and served to create a signature style in his work, characterized by Anderson's overriding focus on honoring the past and paying homage to both filmic and historical influences with an almost meta-nostalgic attention to detail.

Academically, Anderson is considered a central figure in the growing scholarship on contemporary American independent cinema, and this "indie" profile is essential to his director-image. In the following chapter, Anderson's hyper-stylized "brand" will be considered in relation to the ongoing debates concerning authenticity, irony, the "smart" film, "new sincerity," and "quirk" in independent cinema studies. This chapter will engage the ideas of Emanuel Levy (1999), Kristin Thompson (2003), and David Bordwell (2003, 2007) on the tendency toward artifice and stylization in independent cinema, Geoff King (2005, 2009) and Yannis Tzioumakis (2006) on the definition of independent and "Indiewood" cinema, Michael Z. Newman's examination of how Wes Anderson films fit the "indie" aesthetic in *Indie: An American Film Culture* (2011), Alisa Perren's concerns regarding industry and marketing in *Indie, Inc.* (2013), and the King, Tzioumakis, and Molloy collection *American Independent Cinema: Indie, Indiewood and Beyond* (2013), as well as the treatment of Anderson in numerous essays and articles over the past decade in other film and cultural studies journals. These stylistic features will be examined in conjunction with the movement of "hipsterism" in American culture as it relates to Wes Anderson, as well as the changing Hollywood production scene from the rise of the Sundance era in the late 1980s to the gradual disbandment of Miramax and the closing of most independent film studios following the global economic crisis of 2008. While Anderson made his debut at the Sundance Film Festival, so that he has roots in the American independent cinema movement, his films will be considered mainly for their "independent" stylistic features in conjunction with the ongoing scholarly debates on what truly constitutes American independent cinema.

In recent years there has been a growing number of scholarly studies on the topic of the American independent film and "Indiewood" cinema (Levy 1999, Pribram 2002, King 2005, Tzioumakis 2006, King 2009, Newman 2011, Murray 2011, King, Molloy, and Tzioumakis 2013). These authors tend to periodize American independent cinema with slight variations amongst them, but all generally focus on the period of the 1990s and after as the legitimate starting point for the establishment of the movement of independent cinema. While some scholars look back to filmmakers such as Andy Warhol, Hal Ashby, John Cassavetes, and John Waters, or precursors in the 1980s such as David Lynch, John Sayles, and Jim Jarmusch (for example, Newman [2013] dates independent cinema from 1984 with *Stranger Than Paradise*), scholars generally agree that it can be accurately dated from the Miramax-Sundance era, beginning with the break-out success of *sex, lies, and videotape* at the Sundance Film Festival in 1989, which serves for most scholars as the pivotal moment in the mainstreaming of independent cinema.

These scholars have approached the topic of independent cinema from a range of perspectives. As Yannis Tzioumakis has argued, the notion of independence and the definition of independent cinema is a matter of continuing scholarly debate, and thus the idea of independent cinema can possibly best be articulated as a "discourse" that changes over time due to its continued redefinition and reformation by the forces of critical reception, audience response, and the industry itself.[2] At the same time, Geoff King has also documented the commercial and critical rise of "Indiewood" cinema. In his 2009 book *Indiewood, USA*, King employs the subtitle "Where Hollywood meets independent cinema," determining a name for the growing interrelationship between Hollywood and independent cinema since the 1990s.[3] These authors must grapple with the connotations of the "freedom" of artistic choice implied by the term "independent cinema" as a genre unconstrained by market forces. Thus, books produced on this subject, as well as a wide variety of journal articles and book chapters, approach the subject of independent cinema from the point of view of "true" artistic choices vs. "false" market forces, creative control vs. institutional control of the production process, the ideology of "independence" (i.e., "independence" is viewed as a positive quality, while the lack of independence is viewed negatively), the aesthetics of independent cinema, such as narrative, stylistic choice, subject matter, performance, music/sound, and the "tone" of independent cinema, which in the case of the hyper-stylized "brand" of Wes Anderson relates to ongoing debates around authenticity, artifice, irony, and "quirk" cultures.

James MacDowell (2012) theorizes the term "quirk" in film scholarship in articles such as "Wes Anderson, Tone, and the Quirky Sensibility." MacDowell explores the concepts of "irony" and "sincerity" in American independent film comedy and comedy-drama, and dates the independent film aesthetic movement toward "quirk" as a theoretical concept from Wes Anderson's *Bottle Rocket* in 1996. In his 2011 essay, MacDowell listed Jim Jarmusch, the Coen brothers, and Hal Hartley as important precursors who helped establish the tone of "quirky" in cinema. Moreover, in 2010, MacDowell provided an extensive discussion and definition of the conventions underlying the notion of "quirky" in Indiewood comedy and comedy-drama, which he summarizes as follows in his 2013 essay "Quirky: Buzzword or Sensibility?":

(1) A combination of varied comic styles such as deadpan, comedy-of-embarrassment and slapstick; (2) a type of "self-consciousness" in visual style which hints at a sense of surreal artificiality and/or fastidious neatness; (3) a thematic preoccupation with childhood and innocence; and perhaps most importantly, (4) a tone that is often concerned to create tensions between "ironic" distance from and "sincere" engagement with protagonists.[4]

Michael Z. Newman, who defines Anderson as the "quintessential hipster auteur,"[5] has defined indie films as a "film culture" and as feature films "that are not mainstream films."[6] Newman has productively studied the idea of the hipster from a historical standpoint, using John Leland's study *Hip: The History* (2004), to determine how "hip is a verdict, not an intention,"[7] noting that hipness tends to be a reaction against the mainstream, to *negate*, and, in particular, that there is a tendency by the hipster himself to reject hipsterism as inauthentic.[8] Yet Anderson's films do not negate normalcy; instead, they explore the world of the outsider or the misfit without condemning normalcy – in fact, many Anderson characters yearn for "normal" relationships, marriage, and family life, which they would hold up as an ideal (in *Moonlight Kingdom*, and to a lesser extent, *The Darjeeling Limited*, there is pursuit of a nostalgic innocence to be recovered, rather than a "norm" to be rejected, or to be considered inferior). As Newman details in his 2013 article "Movies for Hipsters," *The Hipster Handbook* (2003), *Stuff White People Like* (2008), and other works which appeared at the same cultural moment when the concept of the "hipster" was in its ascendancy, tend to detail how Anderson's films were first embraced by the hipster community, and then chastised as too hipster.⁹ Newman quotes Lorentzen's criticism of *The Life Aquatic with Steve Zissou* in *n+1* (2010):

> For a brief half decade or so, [Anderson] seemed the voice of our generation, the hipster messiah. He took the ethos of the subculture and made it the governing principle in his films' every detail – their sets, costumes, characters, and neato conceits (one might even say, their metaphysics).[10]

Newman also examines the typical audience for an "indie" film: "In contrast to Hollywood's youth audience or mass audience, the audience for independent cinema is generally mature, urban, college-educated, sophisticated and familiar with conventions of representation and reception in many various media and forms, high and low."[11] Newman notes that many indie films can be described as "postmodern," although "rather than conveying deep symbols for scholarly exegesis, these texts offer what poststructuralist theorists might call a 'play of signifiers.'"[12] These include such elements as exaggeration and incongruity, overly mannered performances, conventional elements of films being referenced and turned comical or grotesque, and especially "genre play" or the insertion into a generic framework of something that clearly does not belong. Newman cites the films of the Coen brothers as examples:

> The semi-ironic tone of the Coens' films, at once respectful of their cinematic predecessors and irreverent toward them, is also found among independent filmmakers ranging from Hal Hartley to Jim Jarmusch to Quentin Tarantino to Wes Anderson to Todd Haynes. All of them, and many others, combine exaggerated conventions with incongruous admixtures to similar results.[13]

In an article entitled "Irony, Nihilism, and the New American 'Smart' Film," Jeffrey Sconce (2002) also documents the phenomenon he labels "smart cinema" of the 1990s and early 2000s, identifying a trend in American specialty filmmaking which relies on irony and nihilism as a way of distinguishing itself and setting itself apart from the Hollywood mainstream, which he finds in the work of filmmakers such as Todd Solondz, Todd Haynes, Wes Anderson, and Richard Linklater.[14] However, although Sconce classifies Anderson as a "smart" filmmaker, James MacDowell sets "smart" films apart from the "quirk" of Wes Anderson. Jeffrey Sconce coined the term "smart film" as an often cynical, nihilistic, or disengaged kind of 90s/00s indie film typified by the early work of Neil Labute or Todd Solondz. To avoid overly emotional display, these films regularly filtered their dark subject matter through a lens of ironic dispassion. By contrast, quirky movies can usually be defined by a tone that balances ironic disaffection with a more generous and sincere engagement, as can be demonstrated by an examination of their comedy, style, and recurring themes.[15]

Paradoxically, other scholars have attempted to characterize Anderson's work as part of the "new sincerity" movement defined by Jim Collins in 1993 as a mode of filmmaking that "rejects any form of irony in its sanctimonious pursuit of lost purity."[16] The term "new sincerity" as a concept was adopted across a range of academic disciplines, and it has been loosely applied to film studies to refer to a lack of cynicism/irony in film. It is a testament to the complexity of Anderson's (anti)-heroes that scholars of Anderson's oeuvre fall into both camps: those who find his work ironic and those who wish to view it as straight or purely "sincere." Warren Buckland also takes up this argument in his 2012 article, "Wes Anderson: A 'Smart' Director of the New Sincerity?" which places Anderson in a larger movement of "new sincerity" dialectically synthesizing a slightly detached position of irony with genuine sentimental expression. Buckland offers a general assessment of recent criticism incorporating the ideas of Sconce and Collins, noting how recent critics such as Deborah J. Thomas (2012) have examined "how [Anderson's] irony distances spectators from characters but also how moments of affect encourage allegiance towards them,"[17] with her characterization of *Rushmore* as "melancomic" (a combination of the melancholy and the comic). Similarly John Gibbs (2012) argues that, in *The Life Aquatic with Steve Zissou*, "ironic and empathetic [i.e. sincere] elements clearly temper each other, ebbing and flowing across the movie,"[18] citing the meeting of the ironic, cynical, and world-weary Zissou with the innocent, naïve, and sincere Ned Plimpton. Buckland, Thomas, Gibbs, and MacDowell all produce scholarship which places Anderson along a spectrum between the "smart" film and the "new sincerity," and view Anderson's films within the context of this conflicted tone.

Wes Anderson's Audience and the Indie Aesthetic/Brand

Anderson's inclusion in 2003's *The Hipster Handbook* and Newman's definition of Anderson as "the quintessential hipster auteur"[19] draw strong connections between Anderson and his earliest audience, an audience whose aesthetic tastes his films arguably helped shape. A number of articles have attempted to define the "hipster" urban youth subculture in recent years. In a *Huffington Post* article entitled "Who's a Hipster?", Julia Plevin (2008) argues that the "hipster" culture, which began appearing in the early 2000s, can be vaguely defined by its "postmodern," and "anti-consumerist" tendencies; Plevin notes the difficulty of defining the "hipster" in that members of the subculture typically do not self-identify as hipsters.[20] In addition, Zeynep Arsel and Craig Thompson, drawing from Pierre Bourdieu's work (postulating that judgments of taste are related to social position, or more precisely, are themselves acts of social positioning), argue that in order to segment and co-opt the indie marketplace, mass media and marketers have engaged in commercial "mythmaking" and contributed to the formation of the contemporary discourse about hipsters.[21] Similarly, Mark Greif, a founder of n+1 and co-author of "What Was the Hipster?" (2010), states in a 2010 *New York Magazine* editorial that "hipster" is often used by youth from disparate economic backgrounds to jockey for social position. He questions the contradictory nature of the label, and the way that no one wants to be classified as a hipster, and reiterates the much-cited difficulty in analyzing the term. Like Arsel and Thompson, he draws from *La Distinction* by Pierre Bourdieu (1979) to conclude that the hipster subculture draws its "superiority" from converting real capital into "cultural capital." In other words, Greif's analysis places the term "hipster" into a socioeconomic framework rooted in the petit bourgeois tendencies of a youth generation unsure of their future social status. Thus, the cultural trend toward "hipsterism" is indicative of a social structure with heightened economic anxiety and lessened class mobility.[22]

In his 2014 article "Late-Modern Hipsters: New Tendencies in Popular Culture," Bjørn Schiermer Andersen draws on his background in sociological theory to discuss the issues of authenticity, imitation, individualization, irony, and nostalgia, defining the two key traits in hipster culture as "[1] its redemptive gesture toward the objects of the recent past and [2] its predilection for irony."[23] In particular, Schiermer Andersen points out that previous studies of the "hipster" tended to negate the subculture's contribution toward redeeming and giving fresh value to obsolete or forgotten objects of cultural history. While this reclamation is often intended to be ironic, the hipster does society a service in recognizing the value of previous cultural forms, i.e., the typewriter, vinyl albums, and hand-made craft items, reclaiming and re-legitimizing these items for the millennial generation.[24] The article seeks to analyze hipster culture and sociality in an ongoing dialogue with sociological theory in general and conventional ways of thinking about subculture in particular. Schiermer Andersen argues that the current hipster culture can be used as a kind of magnifying glass that helps highlight impending changes to the current conception of culture and of cultural development. According to Schiermer Andersen, the hipster movement is indicative of broader cultural and social changes: different relations among generations, new ways of relating to technology and media, new styles of community interaction, and new phenomenologies and sensibilities. Thus, Schiermer Andersen recognizes the importance of the social phenomenon of hipsterism, rather than negating it.[25]

Schiermer Andersen's take on hipster culture as redemptive of the past, and Mark Greif's characterization of hipsters as "collectors and connoisseurs,"[26] aligns with the nostalgic aspect of Anderson's work. As hipster culture has become a worldwide commercial and social phenomenon, including the cultural elitism implicit in gentrifying neighborhoods whose lifestyle and fashions now extend far beyond the borders of the places they originated in (for example, New York's Brooklyn, the 3rd Arrondissement in Paris, Shoreditch in London, Berlin's Kreuzberg and Prenzlauer Berg, and Södermalm in Stockholm), hipsterism has become a widely influential subculture on a global level. At the same time, Wes Anderson's films have also extended their reach, both alongside the growth of their original "hipster" audience, and beyond it. Anderson's meta-nostalgic style shares the hipster movement's reclamation of the past as defined by Schiermer Andersen, and also reflects the larger cultural shift toward the mainstreaming of this interest in historical and cultural reclamation. For example, *The Grand Budapest Hotel* has broken through to broader mainstream success as evidenced by its wider reception and numerous Academy Award nominations in 2015.

In January 2015, Peter Knegt reported on the *Indiewire* website that Wes Anderson's *The Grand Budapest Hotel* topped the list of "The 50 Highest-Grossing Indies of 2014." (The list is limited to North American grosses for specialty films – indie, foreign and/or documentary – that opened in limited release [initially under 500 screens] in 2014 and were released by an independent distributor or a studio specialty division. Anderson's *The Grand Budapest Hotel*, released by Fox Searchlight, topped the list with grosses of $59,076,019.)[27] The reception of Anderson's work has been aided by both the ascendancy of hipsterism as a cultural movement in the early 2000s, and by the cultural transformations within the independent "indie" film industry itself in the 1990s and early 2000s. Historically, as noted, the "indie" brand of filmmaking became popular in the 1990s with the commercial success of the Sundance Film Festival and of Miramax Films, a specialty distributor. After the phenomenal success of *sex, lies, and videotape* in 1989, the conventions of independent film started to be popularized by a number of films produced and distributed by Miramax. Following Miramax's successful formula, in 1995, Fox Searchlight was created by 20th Century Fox as a specialty film division designed to make "indie" films following the same conventions of independent film. Miramax was subsequently taken over by Disney after the spectacular box office success of several of its films, which meant that the entertainment conglomerates like Disney and Fox were now producing films that followed the conventions of "indie" films without actually meaning that the films were economically independent from major film companies. Thus, the label "indie" now suggests a particular type of film that adheres to a set of conventions, as well as a transformed "independent" cinema sector (now labeled "indie") that was driven by specialty companies, most belonging to major film companies like Disney, Fox, Paramount, and Universal. "Indie" cinema enjoyed a period of record growth until the economic crash of 2008, which led to the closing of most of these specialty studios. Ultimately, although film historians have employed the term "independent" to refer to the mode of financing and/or distributing films, this definition has proved too limiting. Instead, "independent"-style cinema or "indie" cinema can distinguish the film practice from the industrial facts. Geoff King's approach of looking at "(1) [the films'] industrial location, (2) the kinds of formal/aesthetic strategies they adopt and (3) their relationship to the broader social, cultural, political or ideological landscape"[28] has facilitated broader discussion of independent cinema. King and other scholars contend that the aesthetic concerns of indie film include certain conventions such as "quirky" or odd characters, dialogue for purposes other than advancing the plot, unique narrative techniques, and a demand for the viewer to seek an emotional and intellectual engagement with the film.

In *Indie Inc.*, Alisa Perren (2012) offers a historical analysis of shifting industrial practices and cultural discourses about "independence" and "mainstream" that influenced the conceptualization of Indiewood and Hollywood during the 1990s. Her analysis demonstrates how Miramax, under the powerful ownership of Disney, played a major role in transforming Hollywood in the 1990s by making "independence" more "mainstream," and paving the way for the more mainstream acceptance of films like *sex, lies, and videotape*, *Clerks* (1994), *Pulp Fiction* (1994), *Sling Blade* (1996), *Good Will Hunting* (1997), and *Life is Beautiful* (1998), peaking with the 1999 Best Picture Academy Award victory of *Shakespeare in Love* (1998). By the end of the 1990s, the Miramax-Disney relationship had helped alter the structure of the film industry and the marketing of low-budget and niche-targeted films, as well as motion picture aesthetics, creating a broader audience for independent or "indie" films. Thus, Wes Anderson's popularity was aided by the rise of "indie" filmmaking as mainstream in the 1990s and early 2000s, combined with the ascendancy of the hipster subculture in the early millennial generation (which arguably was also in part shaped by Anderson).

Wes Anderson's films are considered "indie" in style, but in an assessment of existing research on independent film, Anderson's body of work is not commonly cited. One of the reasons Anderson is not frequently discussed in broad academic studies of independent film is that his work is difficult to categorize using contemporary theory, labels, and trends. This is largely due to the fact that Anderson's oeuvre, with its "retro" style and deliberate conjuring of nostalgia, does not fit easily into contemporary academic debates, and therefore scholarly journals face difficulties in classifying him. Anderson's evoking of old Hollywood of the 1930s and 1940s, or police dramas from the 1970s, is sometimes viewed as racist or anti-feminist; for example, Rachel Dean-Ruzicka (2013) writes of Anderson's "perpetuation of white privilege"[29] in his use of old Hollywood tropes from the 1930s-40s. To counter this criticism, it has been noted that Anderson's work, rather than endorsing all the ideas of the era, is trying to evoke the ambience of earlier films. Similarly, Anderson can be accused (and has been accused) of being focused on the concerns of mainly privileged white men. However, in this he is also retro/nostalgic, in that the films to which he connects in the past, especially those from the 1970s (such as *The Godfather* [1972], *The Sting* [1973], *The French Connection* [1971], *Serpico* [1973], and *All the President's Men* [1976], to name a few examples) were also often focused on the concerns of men, with the casts of these films often being made up of and celebrated for their principally white male actors. Mark Browning's *Wes Anderson: Why His Movies Matter* (2011), the first academic monograph study of Anderson's films, also notes that scholars and academic journals have been very slow to respond to Anderson's work, but he offers no specific explanation for this, instead observing that the reactions of viewers to Anderson's work fall into the two extreme camps of either fierce loyalty or violent antipathy.[30] While some scholars consider Wes Anderson one of the most recognizable figures of American indie cinema, other scholars overlook him because although his first short film was shown at the Sundance Film Festival, and thus claims true "independent" origins, all of his feature-length films are produced by Hollywood studios, thus disqualifying him from "independent" status in the strictest sense of the word, as discussed above.

In earlier scholarship, Anderson was frequently grouped with other filmmakers in an attempt to classify and categorize his work, including Sharon Waxman's *Rebels on the Backlot: Six Maverick Directors and How They Conquered Hollywood* (2006), James Mottram's *The Sundance Kids: How the Mavericks Took Over Hollywood* (2006), and Derek Hill's *Charlie Kaufman and His Merry Band of Pranksters, Fabulists and Dreamers: An Excursion into the American New Wave* (2008). Anderson in these works is mentioned briefly in lists and seen as part of a group, and mainly discussed from the point of view of how these directors broke into the Hollywood system, rather than comparing the aesthetics of his work with other directors' films. More recently, Peter C. Kunze (2014) has collected essays about Anderson's films under the title *The Films of Wes Anderson: Critical Essays on an Indiewood Icon*, giving Anderson the hybrid label of "Indiewood" director, thus further bolstering Anderson's reputation as belonging to the classification of Indiewood directors, as defined by Geoff King.

An assessment of the difficulties in these attempts to categorize Anderson's oeuvre makes it clear that his films are best studied in comparison with other films within the body of Anderson's own work, for they alone share the same tone, stylistic choices, and authorial voice, which helps in defining them as a whole. Anderson's distinctive style links his films together and separates them from the work of others, creating the sense of Anderson's own unique world in his films. As the "author" of his screenplays, Anderson writes in a voice that makes his films resemble each other more than they resemble any other director's work. In addition, the granting of "auteur" status in the critical/analytical sense requires the identification of distinctive traits that mark out a body of work from the industrial norm. The following is a list of certain traits common to Anderson's films which contribute to the unique character of his work.

Characteristics of the Cinema of Wes Anderson

Artifice: A key feature of Wes Anderson's films is that they are overtly staged: the director is clearly creating a unique world, an enclosed cosmos, and the characters are operating within the rules of that world. In many of his films, this staging is explicit: for example, in *Rushmore*, the film is divided into chapter sections, or months, by the device of theater curtains opening. In *The Royal Tenenbaums*, the film is divided into chapter breaks, with illustrated book pages appearing on the screen. Other examples of artifice are related to technical presentation of the setting. For example, in *Moonrise Kingdom*, the Bishops' house is presented in a cross section cutaway so that it resembles a dollhouse, rather than a real house; the film invites the viewer into this dollhouse world. Similarly, in *The Grand Budapest Hotel*, Anderson deliberately employs an obvious miniature model of the hotel which becomes a visual signifier of a past world; he also uses pointedly outdated filming techniques that emphasize this artificiality and thus, the ephemeral appearance of the hotel in the past. Anderson's experiments with artificiality versus realism call to mind the filmmaking techniques of Federico Fellini. In Fellini's *And the Ship Sails On* (1983), there is a scene on a luxury liner where passengers admire a sunset from the deck. One passenger comments that the sunset is so beautiful, it looks painted. Then the camera draws back and reveals that it is an obviously painted sunset on a painted scenic backdrop, and the sea is created from polyethylene; thus, the appearance of artificiality is deliberate. Fellini also points out that in the end of the scene, he deliberately reveals the set, and even reveals himself as the director behind the camera.[31] In this scene from *And the Ship Sails On*, it is clear that Fellini wants the viewer to be aware of the artifice behind what he is seeing, that what is filmed is not "real"; instead, it is an enchantment created by the director. Fellini deliberately reveals his painted set, his "smoke and mirrors," and even his own presence as a filmmaker behind a camera, shattering the "fourth wall" and toying with the viewer's suspension of disbelief. As Fellini explains it, the truth can be revealed through outward artifice:

> Cinema vérité? I prefer 'cine-mendacity." A lie is always more interesting than the truth. Lies are the soul of showmanship and I adore shows. Fiction may

have a greater truth than every day, obvious reality. The things one shows need not be authentic. As a rule, they are better if they aren't. What must be authentic is the feeling one is trying to see and to express.[32]

Speaking about the completed miniature version of the Grand Budapest, filmed in front of a green screen for which tree-covered mountains would be added digitally in postproduction, Anderson echoes Fellini's idea:

> This is one of those situations where you say, well, I'm more interested in the thing that we can invent, the thing that's not trying to be completely realistic, the thing that's more a representation. Rather than trying to figure out a way to digitally composite all of these photorealistic things, which I think can limit your scope, I like to do something that's a painting and a miniature – and very clearly, that's what a lot of the stuff in the movie is: a painting or a miniature. That is exactly the world that I would like for the audience to be in. We can create whatever mood we want, and go further than any reality is going to let us.[33]

Anderson's penchant for old-fashioned filming techniques that reveal "how the trick is done" is deliberate. Like Fellini, Anderson uses artifice to bring the audience into his carefully created cosmos of "cine-mendacity" – a representation of reality rather than reality itself. Anderson prefers the handmade look of miniatures and cutaways because it communicates an old-fashioned, deliberately handcrafted atmosphere that brings the viewer beyond "reality" to a place of postmodernist nostalgia.

Fading Institutions: Anderson tends toward invention of respected, world-class institutions, such as the Society of the Crossed Keys,[34] Rushmore Academy, the Khaki Scouts of North America, etc., which he infuses with the elitist potency of "old-world" class and reputation. Anderson works hard to create the illusion of elitist superiority for these institutions. For example, Zero notes that the Grand Budapest Hotel is an "institution" respected for its worldwide renown, within an imaginary Mitteleropean country called Zubrowka, and Anderson even invents a currency for this nation: klubecks. The Tenenbaum family are themselves living on the memory of their previous glory, which reached its height in the 1970s and has since been dimming; likewise, the dwindling reputation of the once-famed oceanographer Steve Zissou and the rusting, fading glory of his boat, the *Belafonte*.[35] The *Darjeeling Limited* is based on the concept of nineteeth-century Indian Raj-era luxury trains (and their present-day counterparts, such as the "Palace on Wheels"); there is no train called "The Darjeeling Limited," but there are two Indian trains making up a route to Darjeeling (the "Darjeeling Mail" that operates between Sealdah and New Jalpaiguri, and the "Darjeeling Himalayan Railway" between New Jalpaiguri and Darjeeling), as well as the "20th Century Limited," a historically illustrious train catering to upper class travelers which ran between Chicago and New York from 1902 to 1967 (and the originator of the phrase "red-carpet treatment" – a crimson carpet the length of a football field would be rolled out for the New York evening departure – again evocative of old-world glamour). The Grand Budapest Hotel (loosely based on an early photochromic image of the Grandhotel Pupp in Karlsbad, Germany) is shown at various stages of its history, from its glorious zenith under M. Gustave's meticulous eye, to the decay and datedness of its appearance in the sequences from 1968, when very few guests visit any more. The Author himself writes of hoping to go back someday to reminisce and enjoy the memories of the Grand Budapest Hotel: "It *was* an enchanting old ruin, but I never managed to see it again."[36]

Familial Dysfunction: The adults in Anderson's world are always wrangling disappointment and nursing damaged dreams while wishing for an idyll, or longing for a panacea. Often the children act with more maturity than the adults (as in *Moonrise Kingdom*). In *Fantastic Mr. Fox*, the cousin Kristofferson arrives as an unaccompanied minor to live with his cousin Ash's family while his father recovers from an illness. Mr. Fox creates a seething jealousy in his son with his visible preference for Kristofferson. Anderson's fascination with the dynamics of familial dysfunction is one of the most prominent features in each of his films.

Male Bonding – Masculinity: Beginning with the three misfit burglars who team up and bond over a robbery in *Bottle Rocket*, Anderson's films consistently explore the relationships between men, which are often brotherly relationships, such as the brothers that go on a spiritual journey together in *The Darjeeling Limited*, or relationships between an older father figure and a younger protégé who looks up to the imperfect (often deeply flawed) older male character. Anderson's films have, each in its own way, dealt with the notion of masculine coming of age, from *Bottle Rocket* (in which men act like boys) to *Rushmore* (in which a young teenager acts like an adult male) through *The Royal Tenenbaums* (where an entire family's adult children are in a state of arrested development). In *The Life Aquatic with Steve Zissou*, the central character struggles with fatherhood and mortality, while in *The Darjeeling Limited*, immature boys are forced to grow into men upon effectively losing both parents. In *Fantastic Mr. Fox*, the two young cousins, Ash and Kristofferson, compete as rivals to win the admiration of a "fantastic" father figure. In *Moonrise Kingdom*, Edward Norton plays an adult boy scout, while two preteens enact a mature love story leading to a marriage. When Bill Murray's Mr. Bishop suspects that his wife is going to leave him, his childish "acting out" response is to go outside and chop down a tree. Similarly, when Sam finds a positive male role model in the form of Captain Sharp, he is finally able to settle down into a mature, stable home life. In *The Grand Budapest Hotel*, the character of the lobby "boy," literally named "Zero," is shown to mature into an admirable character under the mentorship of Gustave H.

R. W. Connell's groundbreaking conceptualizations of multiple masculinities (Connell, 1995, 2000) and hegemonic masculinity (Connell, 1987, 1995, 2000) have been adopted as central concepts in the sociology of gender and gender studies.[37] According to Connell's 1995 model, gender can be defined as the ways in which the "reproductive arena," which includes "bodily structures and processes of human reproduction,"[38] organizes practices at all levels of social organization from identities, to symbolic rituals, to large-scale institutions. Thus, the idea of masculinity, according to Connell, is made up of three components: masculinity is a social position, an identifiable set of practices, and the effects those collective practices have over space and time on groups, communities, and societies. For Connell, the central concept of "hegemonic masculinity" is the distribution of power in the form of authority in institutions (such as the school, the military, the workplace, and the state), peer groups, and societies.[39] Anderson's work continuously calls to mind Connell's idea of the interplay of masculine roles and masculine behavior in groups and hierarchies, for example, the troop of Khaki Scouts in *Moonrise Kingdom*, the clandestine organization of hoteliers called "The Society of the Crossed Keys" in *The Grand Budapest Hotel*, Team Zissou, the aquatic research team in *The Life Aquatic*, and the all-male preparatory school environment of *Rushmore*. Connell's research originated with a study of hegemonic masculinity which presents itself as a set of masculine behaviors in school environments as well as military organizations. In *Fantastic Mr. Fox*, there are allusions to military operations (such as trench warfare), and the title character leads military-style raids with a less than adequate motley crew of friends and neighbors. In this film, there are also hints of the social hierarchy of competitive team sports. Connell's exploration of masculinity is reflected by Anderson's continued exploration of jockeying for position and masculine dominance among brotherly relationships: in *Bottle Rocket*, with the heist friends in their identical yellow jumpsuits, in *The Royal Tenenbaums*, through Chas's brotherly rivalry with Richie, and most prominently in *The Darjeeling Limited*, which Anderson made specifically to explore the dynamics of the central three-brother relationship, thrown against the backdrop of a foreign culture to highlight their differences.

The centrality of masculinity in Anderson's work is obvious from his very first movie, the black-and-white short "Bottle Rocket," in which male signifiers dominate even this brief, 13-minute film. The competitive footrace, the male ogling of the waitress, the focus on the pinball game, and the film's central theme of male bonding through petty crime (the men grow closer as they recount their antics for one another with charismatic bravado) – these are clearly the essential elements of much of Anderson's future work, merely in different forms and plots. Related to Connell's concept of hegemonic masculinity, the film's early focus (during the home robbery) spends a particularly lengthy moment on an upstairs bedroom, the bedroom decorated like that of an adolescent boy, with sports pennants, championship medals, and toy soldiers (Anthony stoops down and gives the orderly lines of soldiers a long look – and in the feature film version, reaches out and straightens one of the soldiers into position) – all reflect typically masculine pursuits.

The Father Figure: The importance of father figures in Anderson's movies is notable. In *Rushmore*, the young Max Fischer attempts to ally and identify himself with a successful businessman as his protégé; in *The Royal Tenenbaums*, the film's central patriarch is an antagonistic character who has eschewed involvement with his family for decades and even stumbles in his attempt at self-redemption; and in *The Life Aquatic with Steve*

Zissou, a central subplot involves a character named Ned Plimpton trying to determine whether Zissou is his long-lost father (the film never clearly answers this question). The topic of the family patriarch in Anderson's first four films is the subject of a detailed study by Joshua Gooch (2007), in which Gooch concludes that Anderson's films are narratives about fatherhood structured by fatherhood, both in terms of technique and thematics, and that reading the films through the lens of Lacanian theory reveals the impact of castration upon Anderson's work. Gooch gives the example of the alteration of Margot's pink glove offering a playful image of this subjective castration.[40] Gooch followed this up in his 2014 article "Objects/Desire/Oedipus: Wes Anderson as Late-Capitalist Auteur," in which he examines how *The Darjeeling Limited* explores the absent-yet-present father, the title character in *Fantastic Mr. Fox* is emasculated by the loss of his tail when it is shot off by the three farmers (which Gooch compares to castration) and *Moonrise Kingdom* creates ties to the father figure by ending with Jared Gilman dressed in a miniature version of the police uniform identical to his adoptive father's clothes.[41] Finally, although there are no actual father/son relationships (except for the brief interaction between the writer-grandfather and his grandson) in *The Grand Budapest Hotel*, the elder Moustafa adopts a fatherly demeanor with the young writer (played by Jude Law), while the young Zero benefits from the tutelage of the semi-fatherly figure of M. Gustave. There is also a kind of paternal devotion expressed by the members of the Society of the Crossed Keys, here again represented by Bill Murray.

Flawed Heroes: The central characters in Wes Anderson's films are often deeply flawed characters who are unabashedly selfish, self-serving, and egotistical: Max Fischer in *Rushmore*, Royal Tenenbaum, Steve Zissou, Mr. Fox, and M. Gustave in *The Grand Budapest Hotel*. These characters all have their origin in Owen Wilson's astounding lack of self-awareness and ne'er-do-well charisma as Dignan in *Bottle Rocket*. Mainstream Hollywood audiences are generally accustomed to film heroes who are more purely heroic, and this idea of a perfect hero is alluded to with Anderson's references to the American folk hero Davy Crockett, through the use of the opening song in *Fantastic Mr. Fox* and the coonskin cap worn by the boy hero Sam Shakusky in *Moonrise Kingdom*. Yet Anderson subverts this perfect heroic image by imagining characters who are almost too flawed to be called heroes – his male leads are human beings with an amalgamation of irritating, all-too-human traits.

Generic Ambivalence: Another consideration worth exploring is the issue of generic innovation and hybridization employed by Anderson, and the different formats evident in his work: comedy, tragedy, romance, documentary. Due to the deliberate mixing of generic signifiers in his work, Anderson's films are often difficult to categorize into common groupings of genre: his films cannot be classified as romantic comedies, nor are they tragedies. A full examination of this aspect of Anderson's oeuvre demonstrates how, for example, his signature themes operate in diverse genres such as the documentary/romance hybrid *Moonrise Kingdom* and the stop-motion animation film *Fantastic Mr. Fox*. The generic disparities in *The Grand Budapest Hotel* make it an ideal example of Anderson's generic mixing in his work. *The Grand Budapest Hotel* combines elements of madcap, screwball comedy (an impossibly long ladder), dark comedy (the sudden slicing off of four fingers), historical drama (with suggested elements of film noir and war drama), murder mystery (mistaken identity, a hidden envelope containing a key legal document), and romance (the young love of a lobby boy and a local pastry girl).

Violence: The abundance of violence against pets in Anderson's films is questioned in a 2012 *New Yorker* blog post by Ian Crouch entitled "Does Wes Anderson Hate Dogs?"[42] There is violence shown against the lawyer's cat in *The Grand Budapest Hotel* ("Did he just throw my cat out the window?"[43]), against the dog Snoopy in *Moonrise Kingdom*, and against the dog Buckley in *The Royal Tenenbaums*. In *Fantastic Mr. Fox*, beagles are drugged with blueberries laced with sleeping powder. Steve Zissou is saddled with a three-legged dog left behind by Filipino pirates when they kidnap one of his men, and he names the dog Cody; later Alistair (Jeff Goldblum) harshly disciplines the whining dog by swatting it in the head with a rolled up newspaper. Zissou's cat, Marmalade, has also died from a poisonous snakebite. Unexpected violence occurs among many of Anderson's human characters as well. In *Rushmore*, when Max tells his actor not to change a single line of his play, punches are exchanged, and Max ends up with a bloody nose. Max is also beat up by Dirk and a gang of boys in Halloween costumes who throw rocks at him, while Magnus Buchan remains a constant threat because of his bullying. The *Lord of the Flies*-like violence among young boys is most apparent in *Moonrise Kingdom*, although in that work, the worst attack is carried out by a girl, who stabs another boy using lefty scissors. The fistfights and squabbles among the "gang" in *Bottle Rocket* is one of the chief obstacles to their being able to accomplish any of their plans; for example, Dignan levels Anthony in a field. It is just as shocking as when Mrs. Fox slaps Mr. Fox across the face, leaving a scratch that does not heal for the rest of the film. Blood rarely appears in Anderson's films, which invests it with powerful shock value when it does appear, most memorably in the scene where Sam pierces Suzy's ears in *Moonrise Kingdom* (many critics compare this to a metaphorical deflowering), in the suicide attempt in *The Royal Tenenbaums*, and in the outbreak of violence with the soldiers on the train in *The Grand Budapest Hotel* (itself a film that stands out for its unusually shocking violence, including the cutting-off of fingers and the viewing of a decapitated head). Though the violence in *The Grand Budapest Hotel* seems more expected because the film relates to wartime, it is still difficult to watch because of the carefully-maintained veneer of civility in Anderson's work. This is precisely the point: as with the sudden, unexpected deaths of Esteban and Ned in *The Life Aquatic with Steve Zissou*, violence intrudes into Anderson's filmic worlds to demonstrate that life is never "safe."

Repeated Use of the Same Actors/Use of Non-trained Actors: Anderson's tendency toward working repeatedly with the same actors reflects his interest in maintaining a core group of familiar collaborators. In addition, he regularly casts untrained actors as extras in his films. During the filming of *Rushmore*, Anderson cast students attending St. John's, the school which he was using as a filming location. Similarly, while scouting locations for *The Grand Budapest Hotel*, Anderson visited a hotel in Hamburg called the Atlantic, built in 1909, and later cast the Atlantic's concierge, Dirk Vassman, in a small role in the film because he was so taken with Vassman's "interesting face,"[44] along with two brothers-in-law from Budapest, Julius and Gino, whom Anderson met while location scouting. Since Anderson frequently casts children in large roles, he often auditions thousands of kids; frequently the children cast are not trained actors, such as Jared Gilman and Kara Hayward in *Moonrise Kingdom*. In addition, Anderson has often cast untrained actors who just happened to be friends of his at the time he was shooting the movie, i.e., Kumar Pallana and his son Dipak Pallana, who ran the coffee shop in Dallas frequented by Anderson, and of course college roommate Owen Wilson, and friends Luke Wilson, Andrew Wilson, Bob Musgrave, and childhood friends Stephen Dignan and Brian Tenenbaum. He also cast chef Mario Batali, and his friend Hugo Guinness, another non-actor, in *Fantastic Mr. Fox*.

Connections with Books/Literary References: Books play a singularly important role in Anderson's films. Some examples include the loving way that runaway Suzy Bishop has filled her suitcase with books in *Moonrise Kingdom*, the plot twist that involves Max Fisher borrowing a library book in *Rushmore*, Margot's library in *The Royal Tenenbaums*, etc. The book Max is reading at the beginning of *Rushmore* is *Diving for Sunken Treasure* by Jacques-Yves Cousteau, who was the main inspiration for Anderson›s later film, *The Life Aquatic with Steve Zissou*. In one of the most memorably romantic scenes from *The Grand Budapest Hotel*, Zero gives Agatha a book as a gift. In *Fantastic Mr. Fox*, Anderson takes the literary sensibilities of the characters a step further by having designed actual copy for the *Gazette* newspaper column "Fox About Town," written by Mr. Fox (with references to "English Wolves" and "Whack-Bat"), and an entire fox comic book "White Cape" starring the eponymous fox hero (designed by Christian De Vita) that is read by Fox's son Ash in the film.

Anderson talked with Paul Holdengräber about how he shares a love for books with François Truffaut in an interview at the New York Public Library in 2014:

> You know, the idea of a relationship between books and movies – this also, I think, can take us back to the Truffaut because with the exception of the Antoine Doinel movies and *Day for Night*, maybe there are one or two others, but almost every Truffaut movie is his adaptation of a book he loves, and his movies are full of books. Their physical presence is a part of so many of his movies and ... I share that affection for books.[45]

Juxtaposition of High and Low Culture: In *The Royal Tenenbaums*, there is a liberal use of expletives paired with the use of euphemistic or more tasteful terms such as "cuckold." Dignified and "civilized" behavior is juxtaposed with extremely undignified or cartoonish elements. Ridiculous and winsome turns of phrase pop up to surprise the viewer, like those uttered by Scoutmaster Ward in *Moonrise Kingdom*: "Jiminy Cricket! He flew the coop!" The use of Latin and French adds a layer of sophistication to films such as *Fantastic Mr. Fox*, such as when Mr. Fox uses the phrase "comme ci comme ça," or when Fox attempts to communicate with the Wolf using Latin ("Canis lupus," "Vulpes vulpes") and then trying French, asking the Wolf if he thinks it will be a hard winter ("Pensez-vous que l'hiver sera rude?"). Latin is also used in *Fantastic Mr. Fox* in the sequence where Fox reinvigorates the animals for battle by reminding them of their Latin names. In *Rushmore*, Miss Cross and Max bond over an exchange of Latin phrases (after some confusion about Miss Cross's thesis on Latin American economic policy): Miss Cross asks in somewhat imperfect Latin "Nihilo sanctum estne" ("Is nothing sacred?") and Max responds "Sic transit gloria" ("Glory fades"). The juxtaposition of high and low culture, and the whiplash back and forth, is especially clear in *The Grand Budapest Hotel*, where the tattooed felon is visibly pleased by M. Gustave's compliments about his well-drawn escape map, where the highbrow painting "Boy With Apple" by a fictional Dutch master is replaced by an erotic modernist painting of two nude women, and where M. Gustave liberally douses himself with his expensive cologne L'Air de Panache and recites poetic prose, but then frequently interrupts himself with expletives.

Multiple Beginnings/Multiple Endings: In most of Anderson's films, there are several different expositional, introductory scenes, and, congruently, often many closings. Anderson has claimed that there are at least three beginnings to *Rushmore*, including the fantasy math problem sequence, the chapel speech about "rich kids," and the clubs montage. The beginning of *The Royal Tenenbaums* is eleven minutes into the film; the story does not begin until the elaborate prologue introducing the family is concluded (marked by the conclusion of the musical arrangement of "Hey Jude"). The opening sequence of *The Life Aquatic with Steve Zissou* has several party scenes in a row, and the film has several distinct endings. In *The Darjeeling Limited*, there are at least three endings, with Jack reading the end of his short story "He would not be going to Italy," the brothers running for the train, and finally, on the train once more, each taking a proverbial bow by looking out a low window before going to have a drink and a cigarette (with Jack eating a "savoury snack"). The final shot is simply the train traveling through the countryside, filling up half the frame, while the landscape of India flows by. In *The Grand Budapest Hotel*, the central character of M. Gustave does not appear until nearly ten minutes into the film; instead, the film is couched in an elaborate set of flashbacks. When the film begins, it is the present day, and a young girl takes a key and hangs it on a famous author's statue as a tribute to him, and then sits on a cemetery bench to read his book. The film then shifts backwards in time to the 1980s, when that author (played in the 1980s sequence by Tom Wilkinson) is recording a filmed interview, interrupted repeatedly by his mischievous grandson. The film then steps back again in time to 1968 when the author (now played by Jude Law) first visits the Grand Budapest Hotel, which is in a state of disrepair: the lobby is dilapidated and nearly empty; the baths are murky and missing tiles. Here he meets the mysterious owner of the hotel, a man named Zero Moustafa (F. Murray Abraham), who will recount the whole story of the hotel over dinner. At last, the film moves back once more in time, to settle in 1932. At the end of the film, these time sequences are revisited in reverse.

The Cultural Outsider/The Foreigner: From Anthony's fling with the Paraguayan girl who speaks very little English in *Bottle Rocket* to the refugee Zero who becomes a lobby boy at the Grand Budapest, Anderson has been fascinated with the dialectic of outsider/insider and the humor created by this juxtaposition. While in cases like Inez, the character is actually from an entirely different background and speaks a different language – another example is the girl from the train, Rita, who has a relationship with Jason Schwartzman's character in *The Darjeeling Limited* – and there are many examples such as the lawyer Sanchez and the faithful Indian butler/servant Pagoda (Kumar Pallana) in *The Royal Tenebaums*, the gardener Mr. Littlejeans (also played by Kumar Pallana) in *Rushmore*, and Eli's drug accountability partner "Runs With Two Horses." Royal Tenenbaum is also lampooned for his insulting attempt to "talk jive" with his wife's African-American suitor, Henry Sherman. This fascination with filtering cultures through the lenses of other cultures reaches its zenith in *The Darjeeling Limited*, where the Americans are the ones on an unequal footing because the film is set in India. Thus the Americans become the "foreigners," and it is they who are thrown off-kilter.

Mark Browning's 2011 monograph on Anderson deals extensively with the topic of race and class in Anderson's films, particularly in how he deals with his non-white characters, his non-white female love interests for his white male characters (for example, Inez in *Bottle Rocket*, Margaret Yang in *Rushmore*, and Rita in *The Darjeeling Limited*), and Anderson's treatment of Indian culture in *The Darjeeling Limited*. Browning notes how Anderson repeatedly casts Waris Ahluwalia, and Dipak and Kumar Pallana, but that the nature of their roles, and even the names given to their characters, such as Mr. Littlejeans and Pagoda, may be construed as demeaning. Browning mentions that Dipak Pallana is cast as an advanced math teacher in *Rushmore*, Mr. Adams, but he then points out that this occurs during a highly unrealistic "absurd fantasy sequence,"[46] while he paradoxically downplays Dipak Pallana's casting as a medical doctor in *The Royal Tenenbaums*. In direct contradiction of his point, he notes Kumar Pallana's important role as an anachronistic faithful servant and friend of thirty years to Royal, and Waris Ahluwalia's (Vikram's) important role in the ensemble of *The Life Aquatic with Steve Zissou*. According to Browning, "It is not perhaps that Anderson's films condone overt racism but that in a series of films, non-white roles are often subordinate and for sexual/comic relief only."[47] (Browning's book was published before the second-largest role in *The Grand Budapest Hotel*, playing opposite Ralph Fiennes, was given to Tony Revolori.)

This issue is examined from another angle in 2014 by Jen Hedler Phillis in the article "'I Always Wanted to Be a Tenenbaum': Class Mobility as Neoliberal Fantasy in Wes Anderson's *The Royal Tenenbaums*." This article makes the case that Anderson's films often bring together characters across class lines (numerous examples include *Bottle Rocket*'s Anthony and Inez, steel magnate Herman Blume and barber's son Max Fisher, as well as Gustave H's unlikely bond with the young immigrant Zero Moustafa). Phillis suggests that this sustains an unrealistic, fairy-tale idea that such class lines can be easily bridged through bonding and friendship, an idea that Phillis claims appeals to Anderson's "neo-liberal" audience.

Use of Veteran Actors as Signifiers from Film History: Anderson frequently casts actors who may be considered "has-beens" by today's standards, and he deliberately casts these actors in roles that both reflect upon the work they have done before, largely from iconic roles in American films in the 1970s (such as the appearance of Bud Cort in *The Life Aquatic with Steve Zissou*, signaling his signature role in the 1971 "indie" film *Harold and Maude*), and to comment anew by both revisiting these nostalgic images and exploring new depths of character that add a multidimensionality to the person being portrayed. This is especially clear in the case of Gene Hackman's role as Royal Tenenbaum (a role written expressly for Hackman by Anderson and Owen Wilson), which reflects upon the character of Jimmy "Popeye" Doyle from *The French Connection* (1971), in which Hackman played an alcoholic, womanizing, seemingly almost heartless police officer prone to outbursts of violence and profanity, who was nevertheless very dedicated to his work. Knowledge of Hackman's acting history (he won a Best Actor Academy Award for *The French Connection*) adds another dimension to the seemingly almost heartless ("I'm dying/I'm not dying") womanizing Royal Tenenbaum in Anderson's film, with his wardrobe in the film also reflecting a 1970s film aesthetic.[48] Other actors used reflectively by Anderson to play upon their previous work from earlier film history include James Caan, Bill Murray, Anjelica Huston, Danny Glover, Willem Dafoe, and even Bruce Willis (playing against type as a gentle, sweet-natured police officer in *Moonrise Kingdom*, in contrast to the wisecracking, hard-edged action hero roles in which he was typically cast at the height of his career, such as the character John McClane in 1988's *Die Hard*).

Hotel Life/Itinerant Living: Anderson's films frequently feature scenes in hotels – often a glamorized, Hollywood version of hotel life with bellhops and lobby boys in crisp, tidy uniforms. Anderson seems particularly interested in the rhythms and routines of hotel life, even having Anthony follow Inez through her workday and helping her change sheets in *Bottle Rocket* (he first notices her and is attracted to her in her crisp maid's uniform as she is standing behind her hotel cart). In *Rushmore*, Herman Blume stays in an upscale hotel with a uniformed bellhop and a welcome card reading "Enjoy Your Stay" after his wife sues him for divorce, while in *The Royal Tenenbaums*, the disenfranchised Royal lives in a memorably beautiful 1940s-style hotel in New York City after leaving the family home. Finally, the two clearest examples of foregrounding hotel living are films in which the title also points to Anderson's focus: the short film *Hotel Chevalier* and, of course, *The Grand Budapest Hotel*. (*Hotel Chevalier* contains many cliché hotel elements, such as standard-issue fluffy white hotel towels, color-coordinated robes monogrammed with the name "Hotel Chevalier," matching chocolates with a "Hotel Chevalier" wrapper, the finely dressed hotel concierge and staff, and a room service meal brought in on a wheeled, table-clothed cart with elaborate presentation under rounded metal warming covers. This film reminds us that hotel culture is its own enclosed world of taste and class, with its own rituals and expected behaviors, and therefore, a hotel seems a particularly apt setting for a Wes Anderson film.) The other four of Anderson's feature films, while not specifically containing scenes in a hotel, are examples of itinerant living or picaresque journey in which the characters are constantly moving: Steve Zissou, the Whitman brothers, Mr. Fox's family under siege from the farmers and digging their way to safety, and finally, the two runaways in *Moonrise Kingdom*. All of these films metaphorically imply (whether through hotel living or picaresque journey) that Anderson's characters have been unable to find a true "home."

The Use of Paintings for Narrative and Meta-Narrative Purposes: Beginning with *Rushmore*, Anderson employed actual paintings as visual signifiers in his films. This is noticeable from the opening credits of *Rushmore*, which shows a formal portrait of Herman Blume with his family (the painting is also used in a flashback during a moment of Blume's psychological crisis in the swimming pool) – in the painting, Blume is set apart and distant from the other three people in the portrait, his wife and two sons, who are all redheads. Also in *Rushmore*, Max and the school headmaster Dr. Guggenheim scuffle over a set of compromising photographs while the camera suddenly shows Guggenheim's office portrait of Winston Churchill, giving an air of solemnity to their comical battle. The prominent paintings in *The Royal Tenenbaums* include the portrait of Royal's mother that hangs over Royal's chair, the many portraits of Margot scowling at the artist, Richie, over the pages of her book, and the comical yet menacing Calderon portraits in Eli's apartment that hint at Eli's darker side. In *The Life Aquatic with Steve Zissou*, three majestic painted portraits of Lord Mandrake, Steve Zissou, and Alistair Hennessey are displayed side by side in the Explorer's Club – the differing styles of the paintings expand on the characters' narratives. There are also paintings displayed on the walls of Zissou's home and even on his research vessel, suggesting his refined tastes (Hennessey's villa in Port-a-Patois also contains modern art, and photographs by Richard Avedon). Felicity Fox's bucolic pastoral landscapes, while aesthetically beautiful, hint at something darker with their prominent depiction of lightning bolts and tornadoes, demonstrating the unpredictable "wildness" of the natural world. *Moonrise Kingdom* and *The Grand Budapest Hotel* both integrate paintings fully as part of their plot – in *Moonrise Kingdom*, because the film ends with Sam capturing their memories in the titular painting of their secret cove, and in *The Grand Budapest Hotel*, because the theft of the painting "Boy With Apple" drives the plot.

Signature Filming Techniques: *Rushmore* was shot in anamorphic widescreen format by Bob Yeoman, the first of Anderson's films to be shot in this format (Anderson had wanted to shoot *Bottle Rocket* this way, too, but the studio turned the idea down because of budget limitations). Most of *Rushmore*, and all of the films after it except for *Fantastic Mr. Fox* and *Moonrise Kingdom*, have the same primo anamorphics (shot with exceptionally wide-angle anamorphic lenses that display considerable barrel distortion), while *The Grand Budapest Hotel* uses three different aspect ratios to reflect three different time periods. *Fantastic Mr. Fox* was shot with Nikon D3 digital cameras with Canon lenses, marking the only time Anderson has shot with digital cameras, and for *Moonrise Kingdom*, special hand-held Aaton cameras were used because they can more easily capture images at the height level of a twelve-year-old, and the filmmakers chose the smaller gauge Super-16 format, in part because the less-wide 1.85:1 aspect ratio seemed appropriate to the more vertically oriented woodland setting. Anderson's affinity for anamorphic widescreen format comes from his own preference for viewing films where the frame is larger, and also because he can easily frame three characters in one scene, and have an ideal closeness to them, without having to cut. The shape of the widescreen format also provides a great freedom in filming landscapes, and because this format allows Anderson additional space to add more objects/detail to the scene.[49] Anderson's choice is unusual because anamorphic widescreen is not usually used for comedies. *Rushmore* shows an increasing propensity toward what David Bordwell defines as "planimetric" shots, based on the definition of Heinrich Wölfflin, because that term suggests the rectangular geometry characterized by the shot. According to Bordwell, these kinds of shots were used occasionally by Antonioni and Godard in the 1960s, but their use proliferated in the 1970s due to the filmmakers' increasing reliance on long lenses. The planimetric shot is defined by David Bordwell as a frontal shot, which means that the camera is positioned perpendicular to the background, usually a wall, and stays straight in front of its subjects who stand on one plane in ordered lines, like a police lineup. Normally, mainstream filmmakers will avoid this type of shot because it appears flat and static, whereas mainstream Hollywood films tend to have depth and look dynamic, by using diagonals to enhance the sensation of depth in the image. While the planimetric shot has been used since the early days of filmmaking, Bordwell notes that the use of the dry, rectilinear planimetric shot has had a resurgence in American independent cinema since the 1990s, reflecting the influence of European "art" cinema:

> "In the 1990s US indie filmmakers adapted this staging strategy. In *Safe*, Todd Haynes uses it to suggest the hard-edged sterility of the wife's suburban life, which surrounds her with cubical furniture. Wes Anderson used the image schema occasionally in *Bottle Rocket* but came to rely on it more and more. [...] For Anderson, as for Keaton and Kitano, the static, geometrical frame can evoke a deadpan comic quality."[50]

Another common feature in the cinematography of Anderson is the tracking shot, which also adds a linear quality, as the camera dolly moves on a horizontal line from left to right, or sometimes vertically. Tracking shots are often paired with Anderson's use of cut-away sets. Anderson also frequently uses a "take/double take" whip-pan technique where he will show a character/action, quickly pan to another character/action, and then pan back (usually with a hand-held camera). Anderson is also known for his one take/shot scenes (very long, continuous filming of a scene without any cuts). Although these shots are more difficult to film because they have to be carefully planned and rehearsed (such as the scene on and around the fire truck during the aftermath of Eli's car crash at the end of *The Royal Tenenbaums*), Anderson feels that this adds a heightened sense of excitement and dramatic suspense to the scene (citing a drinking scene in *Raiders of the Lost Ark* [1981] as an example in which the absence of cuts adds to the scene's intensity) – because it often requires at least twelve takes to get every element of the scene right.[51] Another favorite technique of Anderson already noted is his frequent use of close-up shots of his characters motionless and facing the camera squarely, displaying little to no emotion, which creates an "insect under glass" effect, and this is often paired with Anderson's penchant for symmetry in his shots – characters are often framed or balanced by objects or detailed ornamentation displayed symmetrically on the screen; this adds to the Andersonian sense of an ordered cosmos and a hermetically sealed world. Use of symbolic, carefully selected color schemes also emphasizes the unique cultural signifiers in a Wes Anderson film – particularly noted has been his use of the yellow tent (Richie's tent in *The Royal Tenenbaums*, and the Khaki Scout tents in *Moonrise Kingdom*). Additionally, overhead shots or "God's-eye view" shots are used frequently to make it seem like the viewer is experiencing what the main character is doing or reading – books, letters, checks, laminated lists, even Richie's bleeding wrists. Montages set to music are a common feature, either as a device to advance the narrative or to recount activities such as Max Fisher's extracurricular activities and Margot Tenenbaum's love affairs. Finally, Anderson is well-known for his slow-motion shots. Almost all of his films use a slow-motion ending to deepen the impact of the final scene, notably the final dance at the Heaven and Hell Cotillion in *Rushmore*, and the Tenenbaum family's exit from the cemetery plot in *The Royal Tenenbaums*, ending with Pagoda closing the gate.

Other Art Forms and New Projects

Besides the aforementioned virtual community site "Rushmore Academy," there are numerous online blog analyses of Anderson's work, as well as YouTube film clip commentaries. For example, Matt Zoller Seitz's excellent five-part 2009 video essay, "Wes Anderson: The Substance of Style," was later adapted into a bestselling hardcover book: *The Wes Anderson Collection* (2013). On a broader cultural level, Anderson's film art continues to inspire and impact contemporary art and design with formidable signs of homage. For example, a *Saturday Night Live* parody aired on October 26, 2013 revealed how recognizable, significant, and influential Anderson's style had become among US audiences by pairing *The Royal Tenenbaum*'s narrator, Alec Baldwin, with *Moonrise Kingdom*'s and *The Grand Budapest Hotel*'s Edward Norton, starring as an Owen Wilson-type character, in a mock trailer for a nonexistent horror film entitled *The Midnight Coterie of Sinister Intruders*. This homage was the most high-profile sign of recognition of Anderson's work in popular media, indicating that his style was so identifiable that his filming techniques, mise-en-scène, color palettes, and choice of actors was recognizable on a national level. This parody takes its place among other YouTube parodies of Wes Anderson's film style applied to *The Shining, A Wes Anderson Porno*, and Anderson-style parodies of *Forrest Gump, X-Men,* and *The Amazing Spider-Man*, among others.

Also based on Anderson's work, the "Bad Dads" art exhibition, curated by Spoke Art Gallery in San Francisco, has continued to grow and progress as a dynamic group exhibition since its inaugural show in 2011, and has featured work from more than 400 artists from around the world, with artworks ranging from paintings to sculptures to limited-edition screen prints all related to Anderson's films. This fan-generated merchandise exemplifies what Henry Jenkins, in his book *Textual Poachers* (1992), called "participatory culture."[52] The "Bad Dads" exhibition became popular enough to generate its own title in *The Wes Anderson Collection* series, published in 2016 as *Bad Dads: Art Inspired by the Films of Wes Anderson*. Anderson writes in the introduction to the book: "For me, it is extremely encouraging to know that somebody-or-other somewhere is interested enough to make something-or-other new of their own inspired by something-or-other old of *my* own – that was in itself inspired by all sorts of other something-or-others somebody else invented before that."[53] It is notable that Anderson fully encourages this fan culture and speaks favorably of it without concern for his own personal copyrights; instead, he acknowledges his indebtedness to this shared aesthetic past from which his own films contain similar echoes and borrowings.

After the broad mainstream success of *The Grand Budapest Hotel*, there has been much curiosity regarding Anderson's next project. It is reported that he will return to the stop-motion animation format used in 2009 for *Fantastic Mr. Fox* for his next film, which will center around dogs – a pack of them – in a "Japanese-inspired"[54] film. Plot details have not been released, but the film, entitled *Isle of Dogs*, is in production and is slated for release in 2018. The cast will include Bill Murray (this will be Murray's eighth collaboration with Anderson), Jeff Goldblum, Bob Balaban, Edward Norton, Frances McDormand, Tilda Swinton, Harvey Keitel, and F. Murray Abraham, along with newer additions to Anderson's film troupe including Bryan Cranston, Kunichi Nomura, Scarlett Johansson, Mari Natsuki, Liev Schreiber, Greta Gerwig, Courtney B. Vance, Fisher Stevens, Akira Takayama, Akira Ito, Yojiro Noda, Frank Wood, and Yoko Ono. The expansion of Anderson's world to include "Japanese" cultural inspiration represents a logical progression for a filmmaker who continually expands outward to cross new borders and explore new terrain – from Houston, to Austin, to Dallas, to Los Angeles, to New York, to London and Paris, to Eastern Europe and India, and now, ever moving further outward, to cultural East Asia.

Notes

1 "Mission: National Film Preservation Board of the Library of Congress," *www.loc.gov*. December 1, 2016. https://www.loc.gov/programs/national-film-preservation-board/about-this-program/mission/ (accessed December 15, 2016).
2 Yannis Tzioumakis, *American Independent Cinema: An Introduction* (New Brunswick, NJ: Rutgers University Press, 2006), 11.
3 King has written about the films associated with Hollywood studios as "Indiewood" rather than independent cinema. This is because Miramax, New Line and Fine Line, Fox Searchlight, Sony Pictures Classics, Paramount Classics, and Focus Features are, or were, Hollywood companies, branch labels under the control of the entertainment conglomerates Disney, Time Warner, News Corp., Sony, Viacom, and NBC Universal.

4. James MacDowell, "Quirky: Buzzword or Sensibility?" in Geoff King, Claire Molloy, and Yannis Tzioumakis, eds., *American Independent Cinema: Indie, Indiewood, and Beyond* (London: Routledge, 2013), 54.
5. Michael Z. Newman, "Movies for Hipsters," in Geoff King, Claire Molloy, and Yannis Tzioumakis, eds., *American Independent Cinema: Indie, Indiewood, and Beyond* (London: Routledge, 2013), 71.
6. Michael Z. Newman, *Indie: An American Film Culture* (New York: Columbia University Press, 2011), 1–2. Newman writes: "The value of indie cinema is generally located in difference, resistance, opposition – in the virtue of alternative representations, audiovisual and storytelling styles, and systems of cultural circulation. [...] Indie film profits from its alterity, which sustains it and has the potential to be politically progressive and even counter-hegemonic. At the same time, this same culture functions to reproduce social class stratification by offering an elite, culturally legitimate alternative to the mass-market Hollywood offerings of the megaplex," 2.
7. John Leland, *Hip: The History* (New York: HarperCollins, 2004), 10.
8. According to Newman, "Negation of hipsterism and Anderson's hipsterish influence can be just as significant for the production of indie authenticity as affirmation, and so much of the discourse of indie hipsterism is negative that denial and de-authentication must be a key structuring principle of hipsterism as it is of indie culture more generally." In Newman, 2013, 73. This idea is explored more fully through a discussion of the backlash against the success of *Juno* in chapter 6 of Newman, 2011, 221–246.
9. Newman details the backlash against the popularity of Anderson's works, noting that *Rushmore* was put on a list of "movies hipsters need to get over," and concluding that "Negation feed hipsterism as overexposed, too-popular artifacts are left behind in a regular cycle of fashion and vanguardism," in Newman, 2013, 73.
10. Christian Lorentzen, "Captain Neato," in *n+1*, *nplusonemag.com*, April 23, 2010. https://nplusonemag.com/online-only/captain-neato/ (accessed February 7, 2016).
11. Newman, 2011, 38. This conception of the indie audience has also been denoted by Emmanuel Levy, *The Cinema of Outsiders: The Rise of American Independent Film* (New York: New York University Press, 1999), 28–29, and Alisa Perren, "Sex, Lies, and Marketing: Miramax and the Development of the Quality Indie Blockbuster," *Film Quarterly* 55:2 (2001): 30.
12. Ibid. For a thorough discussion of this, see "Postmodernism in the Arts," Steven Best and Douglas Kellner, *The Postmodern Turn* (New York: Guilford Press, 1997), 124–194.
13. Ibid., 39.
14. Jeffrey Sconce, "Irony, Nihilism, and the New American 'Smart' Film," *Screen* 43.4 (Winter 2002): 349–369. Sconce argues that a specific "smart" tone underlies the aesthetics of these filmmakers, and this ironic tone divides the audience into those who "get it" and those who do not.
15. James MacDowell, "Defining 'Quirky,'" *Alternate Takes*. March 28, 2011. http://www.alternatetakes.co.uk/?2011,3,250> (accessed May 20, 2015).

16 Jim Collins, "Genericity in the Nineties: Eclectic Irony and the New Sincerity," in Jim Collins, Hillary Radner, and Ava Preacher Collins, eds., *Film Theory Goes to the Movies* (New York: Routledge, 1993), 242–243.
17 Warren Buckland, "Wes Anderson: A 'Smart' Director of the New Sincerity?" *New Review of Film and Televisions Studies* 10.1 (March 2012): 2.
18 John Gibbs, "Balancing Act: Exploring the Tone of *The Life Aquatic with Steve Zissou*," *New Review of Film and Television Studies* 10:1 (March 2012): 132.
19 Newman, 2013, 71.
20 Julia Plevin, "Who's a Hipster?", *Huffingtonpost.com*. September 8, 2008. http://www.huffingtonpost.com/julia-plevin/whos-a-hipster_b_117383.html (accessed May 15, 2015).
21 See more on hipsters in Zeynep Arsel and Craig J. Thompson, "Demythologizing Consumption Practices: How Consumers Protect Their Field-Dependent Identity Investments from Devaluing Marketplace Myths," *Journal of Consumer Research* 37:5 (February 2011): 791–806.
22 Mark Greif, Kathleen Ross, and Dayna Tortorici, eds., *What was the Hipster? A Sociological Investigation* (Brooklyn, NY: n+1 Foundation, 2010), 4–9.
23 Bjørn Schiermer Andersen, "Late-Modern Hipsters: New Tendencies in Popular Culture," *Acta Sociologica* 57:2 (2014): 167.
24 Schiermer Andersen writes: "The hipster figure ushers in a new, sensuous awareness of the losses and sacrifices made by the previous generations at the altar of technological development. The hipster is no time traveller; rather, he actualizes what former generations fascinated by the latest technological developments have thoughtlessly relegated to the past. The hipster rediscovery of the vinyl disc record, the cassette tape, the travelling typewriter, the traditional offset printing technique, the conventional 'film' camera and the 'old-school' photograph development hides a sensuous and pleasure-seeking conservatism. Hipster culture saves sensibilities and 'experiences' inherent to certain media; from the warm scratching sound coming from the pickup in the groove to the yellowed ambience of the old Polaroid photographs." Ibid., 176.
25 Ibid., 169–170.
26 Greif *et al.*, 2010, 8.
27 Peter Knegt, "The 50 Highest-Grossing Indies of 2014," *Indiewire.com*. January 2, 2015. http://www.indiewire.com/2015/01/the-50-highest-grossing-indies-of-2014-66644/ (accessed August 25, 2015).
28 Geoff King, *American Independent Cinema* (London: IB Tauris, 2005), 2.
29 Rachel Dean-Ruzicka, "Themes of Privilege and Whiteness in the Films of Wes Anderson," *Quarterly Review of Film and Video*, 30:1 (2013): 27.
30 Mark Browning, *Wes Anderson: Why His Movies Matter* (Santa Barbara, CA: Praeger, 2011), xi.
31 Federico Fellini, *I, Fellini*, trans. Charlotte Chandler (New York: Cooper Square Press, 1995), 222.
32 Federico Fellini, *Fellini on Fellini* (London: Eyre Methuen, 1976), 100.

33 Matt Zoller Seitz, "Behind the Scenes at The Grand Budapest Hotel," *Telegraph.com*. February 19, 2015a. http://www.telegraph.co.uk/film/the-grand-budapest-hotel/behind-scenes-wes-anderson/ (accessed March 20, 2016).
34 The Society of the Crossed Keys is based on the "Clefs d'Or" guild of hotel concierges which had its beginnings in 1929 in Paris, and was formally consolidated as an international organization in 1952. Concierges who are members wear golden crossed-key "badges" on their lapels.
35 This is an indirect reference to Cousteau's ship, the *Calypso*, because the name *Belafonte* points to the singer Harry Belafonte, who was dubbed the "King of Calypso" for popularizing the Caribbean musical style with an international audience in the 1950s.
36 Wes Anderson (screenplay) and Hugo Guinness (story), *The Grand Budapest Hotel* (New York: Opus, 2014), 150.
37 For an extensive overview of theory and research on masculinities, see Michael Kimmel, Jeff Hearn, and R. W. Connell, eds., *Handbook of Studies on Men and Masculinities* (Thousand Oaks, CA: Sage, 2005); for a summary of critiques on the concept of hegemonic masculinity, see R. W. Connell and James W. Messerschmidt, "Hegemonic Masculinity: Rethinking the Concept." *Gender and Society* 19:6 (2005): 829-859.
38 R. W. Connell, *Masculinities* (Cambridge: Polity Press, 1995). It is important to clarify that, for Connell, the notion of masculinity is not reducible to individual experience or expression. Instead of possessing or having masculinity, individuals produce masculinity by engaging in masculine practices. Thus, masculinity can be defined as a specific, identifiable set of practices that occur over space and time and are moved through and enacted by groups, communities, and societies. Over time, according to Connell, these practices lead to the distribution of power in the form of authority ("cathexis," by which Connell refers to the arena of desire and sexuality), and the production of meaning and values.
39 In 2006, Victor J. Seidler published *Transforming Masculinities: Men, Cultures, Bodies, Power, Sex, and Love* (London: Routledge, 2006), in response to Connell's work, defending masculine sensitivities and broadening the field by focusing on masculinities at the global cultural level.
40 Joshua Gooch, "Making a Go of It: Paternity and Prohibition in the Films of Wes Anderson." *Cinema Journal* 47:1 (2007): 27.
41 Joshua Gooch, "Objects/Desire/Oedipus: Wes Anderson as Late-Capitalist Auteur," in Peter C. Kunze, ed., *The Films of Wes Anderson: Critical Essays on an Indiewood Icon* (New York: Palgrave Macmillan, 2014), 194–195.
42 Ian Crouch, "Does Wes Anderson Hate Dogs?" *NewYorker.com*. June 21, 2012. http://www.newyorker.com/culture/culture-desk/does-wes-anderson-hate-dogs (accessed July 16, 2015). Another article on the subject is C. Ryan Knight's "Who's to Say?": The Role of Pets in Wes Anderson's Films," in Peter C. Kunze, ed., *The Films of Wes Anderson: Critical Essays on an Indiewood Icon* (New York: Palgrave Macmillan, 2014), 65–75, although Knight does not specifically focus on the violence of the animals' deaths.

43 Anderson, with Guinness, 2014, 82.
44 Robbie Collin, "Wes Anderson Interview," *The Telegraph*. February 19, 2014. http://www.telegraph.co.uk/culture/film/starsandstories/10644172/Wes-Anderson-interview.html (accessed April 27, 2016). "The concierge of the Atlantic was cast in a small role ('his name is Dirk Vassman and he has such an interesting face,' Anderson says enthusiastically), as were two brothers-in-law from Budapest whom Anderson met while looking for somewhere to shoot. 'We met them at a … I don't want to say abandoned, but a vacant mental hospital on the outskirts of the city,' he says. 'We visited it to see if it could possibly be turned into our hotel, which it couldn't. But in this hospital we met these two caretakers, Julius and Gino, and we loved them, so they ended up coming to Germany and staying with us and being a part of the whole thing.'"
45 Wes Anderson in an interview with Paul Holdengräber, "LIVE from the New York Public Library: Wes Anderson | Paul Holdengräber." *www.nypl.org*. February 27, 2014. http://www.nypl.org/audiovideo/wes-anderson-paul-holdengraber (accessed August 14, 2014).
46 Browning, 2011, 122.
47 Ibid., 121. For Browning's full discussion of this topic, see chapter 8, "The Discreet Charm of the Bourgeoisie: Anderson's Portrayal of Race and Class," 117–130. For further critical discussion on the topic of race in Anderson's films, see Rachel Dean-Ruzicka, "Themes of Privilege and Whiteness in the Films of Wes Anderson," *Quarterly Review of Film and Video*, 30:1 (2013): 25–40.
48 Hackman was at first resistant to playing the role of Royal Tenenbaum, claiming that he didn't like to play roles other people had written for him. He retired permanently from acting three years (and three films) later, in 2004. In a 2011 *GQ* interview, when asked if he would ever come out of retirement and make another film, Hackman responded: "I don't know. If I could do it in my own house, maybe, without them disturbing anything and just one or two people." Michael Hainey, Interview with Gene Hackman, *GQ*. June 1, 2011. http://www.gq.com/story/gene-hackman-gq-june-2011-interview (accessed November 28, 2015).
49 Wes Anderson, interviewed in Matt Zoller Seitz, *The Wes Anderson Collection* (New York: Abrams, 2013a), 86–87.
50 David Bordwell, in Kristin Thompson and David Bordwell's "Observations on Film Art: Shot-Consciousness." January 16, 2007. http://www.davidbordwell.net/blog/2007/01/16/shot-consciousness/ (accessed October 28, 2015).
51 Wes Anderson, interviewed in Seitz, 2013a, 115–116.
52 Henry Jenkins, *Textual Poachers: Television Fans & Participatory Culture* (New York: Routledge, 1992), xxi.
53 Wes Anderson, "Introduction," in Ken Harman, Matt Zoller Seitz, and Wes Anderson, eds., *The Wes Anderson Collection: Bad Dads: Art Inspired by the Films of Wes Anderson* (New York: Abrams, 2016), 9.
54 In the DVD voice commentary to *Fantastic Mr. Fox*, Anderson spoke about his visit to Studio Ghibli Museum in Tokyo, a museum designed by Ghibli head Hayao Miyazaki, who produced *Sen to Chihiro no kamikakushi* (*Spirited Away*,

2001), and *Hauru no ugoku shiro* (*Howl's Moving Castle*, 2004), among others. Anderson was especially taken with a replica of the artist's office workspace.

55 Kunichi Nomura, Scarlett Johansson, and Bill Murray all appeared together in Sofia Coppola's Japan-set *Lost in Translation* in 2003. Anderson has also stated that his new film, *Isle of Dogs*, is heavily influenced by Japanese director Akira Kurasawa.

CHAPTER THREE

Gender, Youth, and the Exploration of Masculinity in Bottle Rocket

When the feature-length version of *Bottle Rocket* was released in 1996, few people understood it. This is because the idiom in which Anderson was working (and continues to work) was so unique that it had no precedent, and audiences simply did not understand the film's style of humor. *Bottle Rocket*'s disastrous test screening in Santa Monica has become notorious as one of the all-time worst test screenings for Columbia Pictures, with 85 walk-outs.[1] After that, the film was given a February 1996 release date; it was intended as a fall 1995 release, but after the catastrophic test screenings, Columbia Pictures decided unceremoniously to dump it. Released on only 40 screens in the whole of the United States, Anderson's first film was given very little exposure in cinemas, which could have resulted in the end of the director's career. This reaction by the studio and the first audiences is in some ways understandable because the world that Anderson and Wilson had invented was so unusual (atypical for either a romantic comedy or a road trip/buddy movie) that most viewers were uncertain how to respond to the film. Few people were drawn to this seemingly unimportant story of three Texas boys turned would-be criminals named Dignan (Owen Wilson), Anthony (Luke Wilson) and Bob (Robert Musgrave) who plan a bungled heist, in which the mastermind of the three is a nitwit with delusions of grandeur; his friend, the gentle Anthony, is recently rehabilitated from a mental institution (but seems the sanest of them all); and their friend Bob is hired as the get-away driver only because he owns a car.

Bottle Rocket was not only the feature debut for director Wes Anderson, but also the screen debut of Luke and Owen Wilson, and the first movie written by Owen Wilson and Anderson, who would later go on to co-author the screenplays for both *Rushmore* and *The Royal Tenenbaums*. While *Bottle Rocket* lacks the tight cohesion of these subsequent films, it is a distinctive prototype for Anderson's future work. In a way similar to *The Darjeeling Limited*, this is a meandering, character-driven story, as social rejects Anthony, Dignan and Bob attempt to assert themselves in the adult world by embarking on a well-structured but inevitably dysfunctional life of crime. The three main characters are harmless goofballs, but their emotional pain is real. As in other Anderson/Wilson collaborations, the characters lack a sense of belonging, but all they truly seem to need is a father figure – indeed, the three men seem happiest not when they are pulling their capers but when they have been adopted by James Caan's Mr. Henry character, who serves, for a short time, as the benevolent protector they so badly need. The unusual style of the humor in the film showcases the thoughtful and engaging complexity of Anderson's films – it is subtle, casual and true to the characters. There are no outright jokes; instead there are oddities, ironies, uncomfortable truths, malapropisms, mistranslations, distorted logic, and unexpected revelations, but at no point does any event in the movie prioritize a joke over story/character development.

As for the film's title, the bottle rocket[2] is a metaphor for the heists that the young men pull in the sense that fireworks and bottle rockets, although dangerous (and illegal in some states), are just another fun activity to do with friends to create a little excitement on a do-nothing day. This parallels the idea that although the men's heists might be dangerous, they carry them out because they have nothing better to do. The title *Bottle Rocket* is also a reference to the scene in the film when the boys blow their robbery loot on firecrackers, and Dignan sets them off from the passenger seat of Bob's car to the 1975 Oliver Onions' song "Zorro is Back." The bottle rocket is a juvenile noise-maker, a diversion, like the boys' foray into crime, and a fleeting sparkle, like the first movie of a young director – virtually still a boy himself – just beginning to reveal his trademark talents.

Origins of the Feature Film: The "Bottle Rocket" Short (1994)

Much of the genius of the feature-length film has its germination in the 13-minute original short. The film begins with a black screen, while Artie Shaw's quick-paced, energetic jazz tune "The Chant" plays, and the film's title, "Bottle Rocket," appears as stark white letters displayed statically on this black background. The conversation begins while the screen is still black – the viewer is thrust into the middle of a debate about an episode of the television series *Starsky and Hutch*, in which the ringleader, Dignan,[3] accuses his friend, Anthony, of dreaming the episode, trying to prove to him that what he says he saw on the episode was actually only in his imagination. Meanwhile, Anthony insists he saw the events he describes on the episode, even using details like Huggy Bear and phone conversations to prove his point. The two young men are making their way over backyard fences and through people's yards. Anthony wears a black shirt and has a backpack over his shoulders, while Dignan carries a large white tennis bag and wears a shirt with a vividly hideous pattern. Dignan's shirt is one of the early Wes Anderson wardrobe choices that point to Anderson's later use of costuming to help define and personalize his characters: Dignan's comically gaudy shirt helps clue the viewer in to understanding Dignan's complete lack of self-awareness – all of Dignan's ideas sound good to him, and he believes in himself with great earnestness, unaware of just how ridiculous he actually appears.

At just over a minute into the film, the two men enter a house by the front door and begin robbing it, each of them stuffing the numerous items he picks up into an empty white pillowcase. Some of these items – a coin collection, small knickknacks, a jewelry box – are recognizable in the thieves' hands before they disappear into the pillowcases. The house is a comfortable family home, and the items taken are not remarkable in value. The rooms are burgled one by one, the living room, an upstairs bedroom, a child's room with sports pennants displayed on the wall, trophies, and a marching band of toy soldiers arranged in a group on the shelf. When they leave the house, again through the front door, Dignan politely allows Anthony to go out first, holding the door for him. In the next scene, Dignan and Anthony are celebrating the success of their robbery while talking seated at the counter of a drugstore diner. Dignan compliments Anthony for filing down the window, which would have helped them as a backup plan in the robbery if the owners had changed the locks and the keys hadn't worked. Dignan praises Anthony for his ingenuity, as if it is an artistic touch to the master plan. He praises Anthony's mental prowess and engineering skills, like a master complimenting an apprentice. It is not revealed immediately that the house they robbed was, in fact, Anthony's own home.

The scenery in the diner is stereotypical: the white counter displays a bottle of ketchup, a small bottle of Tabasco sauce, a container of sugar, a straw dispenser, and a saltshaker. The two men leisurely finish off burgers and drinks. They receive the check from the waitress and comment on her attractiveness as she walks away. She is older than one would expect for her attractiveness to generate these comments from young men, and this adds a humorous levity to the scene. Except for the waitress, there are no other female roles in the short (besides extras shown browsing in the background at the bookshop), and this emphasis on male bonding demonstrates the early establishment of what would continue to be an essential focus of Anderson's feature film work. Dignan and Anthony play pinball (a nod to Truffaut's *Les Quatre cents coups*) while arguing about how much the coin collection they stole will be worth when they sell it. Later, out on the street, Anthony gets angry when he discovers Dignan stole "the earrings," because the earrings were "#3 on the list" of things they had agreed not to steal. It turns out that Anthony bought the earrings for his mother for her birthday. Dignan defends his actions, claiming that the burglary is professional, and that he was just doing his job.

A few more scenes that establish the main robbery set-up at the bookstore follow, some of which are repeated in the feature film, such as the scene when the boys purchase a gun, and the argument in the planning meeting at the house after the gun is purchased (more detail about the short film can be found in chapter 11). In a comic touch reflecting their youth, the boys are constantly eating, mainly at three separate hamburger joints, including "Goff's Hamburgers," with a take-out pizza box at the planning meeting. The crime itself is omitted – the screen goes to black, holding the blacked-out pause for several seconds, which ends with the sound of tires screeching. Next the boys are at "Mr. Charlie's Burger Factory" – they sit outside the burger stand in what appears to be a row of student desks with little attached tables, which adds a youthful "student" look to their appearance. They talk with great exhilaration about the highlights of their holdup: an armed robbery which only brought them $183, and yet, absurdly, they are pleased with their "success." The last scene shows the boys exiting a convenience store, over which the theme "Happiness Is" from Vince Guaraldi's "A Charlie Brown Suite" adds a melancholy atmosphere, but at the same time vividly casts a childlike quality over the scene.[4] Dignan gives Bob a warmhearted hug, and then a formal handshake, praising him with great charisma: "Man, that was a great driving. Seriously, that was a really good driving. Okay? One hundred and eighty-three dollars is a pretty good haul, Bob. Good driving." Bob walks away with a forlorn expression, growing distant from the camera. He carries a carton of milk. His departure feels very lonely. Dignan turns away, chewing bubble gum. These elements, the carton of milk, the chewing of bubble gum, and the youthful appearance of these childhood friends, all combine with the music to produce a feeling that they are impossibly young.

The last image before the credits is a shot of Anthony and Dignan sitting together outside the convenience store after Bob's departure, looking pensive and serious. Their slightly wistful look suggests the ending of Mike Nichols' *The Graduate* (1967) where the runaway couple on the bus together face an uncertain future. However, as the credits roll, it is daylight the next day, and the two men, after boredly flipping through a newspaper on the steps outdoors, challenge each other to a footrace after Anthony boasts that his shoes are superior to Dignan's. The last image is of Anthony and Dignan racing with childish competitiveness, and Anthony pulls ahead, clearly set to win. The shot of these two childhood friends racing emphasizes again that these are mere "boys," which is underscored by the credit which reads "Copyright Wes Anderson and Owen Wilson, 1992." In 1992, at the age of twenty-three, Anderson and Wilson in many ways still seemed like children themselves. The world of the young aspiring thieves in "Bottle Rocket" is not far removed from the world of boys, and this is a point that would be highlighted in the feature-length version of the film, which would contrast Anthony's conflicted movement toward maturity with Dignan's childlike fantasies of criminal derring-do.

The film is episodic, composed of vignettes from the lives of these two young men, played by brothers Owen and Luke Wilson. In many ways, the performance of Owen Wilson immediately suggests the unique persona by which he would come to be known as an actor: his spaciness, his neurotic outbursts, and his unusual charisma. The film comprises nine separate scenes in and around Dallas, where Anderson got permission from local businesses to film: a drugstore diner counter, a bookstore, a hamburger stand, a convenience store, etc. All of these locations are downscale and unattractive, reflecting urban sprawl. And yet, especially in the medium of black-and-white film, these commonplace public spaces are given a strange and ethereal beauty. The black-and-white short suggests strong ties to Truffaut's *Les Quatre cents coups*, which also dealt with the misadventures of a thieving youth who is condemned as a delinquent by the adults around him. One of the last shots from the feature-length film *Bottle Rocket* shows Owen Wilson behind a chain-link fence, an homage to Truffaut's hero Antoine Doinel, who is locked behind a similar fence and "criminalized." In addition, the pinball scene in both the short and feature versions of *Bottle Rocket* is modeled on a similar scene from *Les Quatre cents coups*, with techniques such as the tight cutting and the use of close-ups, strongly referencing the pinball scene from Truffaut's film. Both in setting (Truffaut's film was a striking black-and-white portrait of the Paris of his youth) and subject matter (a fundamentally "innocent" young male ends up on a path to delinquency), *Bottle Rocket* shares ties with Truffaut.

The short "Bottle Rocket," while in general seeming not at all stereotypical of his future work, nevertheless contains several elements that are prescient and foreshadow future directions in which Anderson's films will develop. Some examples include the wardrobe choices, including Dignan's tacky shirt, and the "I'm A Pepper" tee-shirt worn by the gun salesman. There is also the emphasis on male friendship, which is an essential part of this story of three disparate, aimless characters bonded together by the shared experiences of robbery. Third, there is the juxtaposition of naïveté and innocence with the more hardcore issues of crime and the harshness of reality, where Anthony suggests that Bob grow cinnamon instead of marijuana in his backyard, because "then you could have your own cinnamon toast." In addition, there is the germination of the Wes Anderson hyper-focus on the small detail, the object: the close-up focus on the toy soldiers in Anthony's room, the pinball machine with the ball in play, the books in the bookstore. This last detail suggests several of Anderson's key stylistic directions in the future. First, it is significant that the store the three young men choose to burglarize is a bookstore, a store that sells literature, because it is literature that Wes Anderson has regularly chosen to make the main focus of his films. In other words, this suggestion of "theft" from a literary establishment predicts in a prototypical way the future borrowing and influences from classic and contemporary literary works such as those of J. D. Salinger, F. Scott Fitzgerald, Jules Verne, Stefan Zweig, Roald Dahl, and even Mark Twain, Herman Melville, and Nathaniel Hawthorne. A second, very subtle presence is Anderson's focus in the bookstore on certain titles, such as those of the *Utne Reader* journal's story on "Money," as well as Scott Peck's *The Road Less Traveled* (1978) and Carol S. Pearson's *Awakening the Heroes Within* (1991) which both comment on the action (the film's main characters are drawn to titles involving money, while they also envision themselves as modern day heroes who are simply trying out an alternative career as petty thieves). This focus on book titles suggests the earliest incubation stage of Anderson's later predilection for putting chapter headings and annotations on the screen.

Finally, Anderson's use of music in this film already suggests the innovative way he will score his future films. For example, the film contains six jazz pieces, selections from Artie Shaw, Chet Baker, Duke Ellington and John Coltrane, as well as "Old Devil Moon" performed by Sonny Rollins, which add different moods to different scenes. In particular, the use of Artie Shaw's "The Chant," against a black screen in the beginning, is reminiscent of several Woody Allen films, which also begin with upbeat jazz pieces against a black screen, in particular, *Sleeper* (1973). However, it is the use of two pieces recorded by the Vince Guaraldi trio, taken from the Charlie Brown series of animated television specials, including "Skating," from *A Charlie Brown Christmas* (1965) and "Happiness Is," from the feature-length film *A Boy Named Charlie Brown* (1969) that suggest the childishness in this film that contains scenes of two boys fighting while playing pinball, ogling a waitress, and, in the final images, two pals racing each other.

Andersonian Film Techniques and the Presence of Women in the Feature Length Film

The feature-length version of *Bottle Rocket* begins with a very abbreviated title sequence, just like the short. Production company Columbia Pictures is listed, with the Columbia Pictures logo, then the title *Bottle Rocket* in the same distinctive font, and then a frame showing Luke Wilson's face. No mention is made of the director's name in the opening credits, and out of all of Wes Anderson's oeuvre, *Bottle Rocket* feels the least like a "Wes Anderson movie." The plotline, while out of the ordinary, does play on standard conventions and leads to a traditional ending. The film is light and breezy with many outdoor scenes, road scenes and sequences.[5] The relaxed, meandering pace of the film belies the future intensity and lightning-fast pacing of Anderson's future work, with very few jump cuts and none of the tracking shots Anderson is now known for. Nevertheless, it does share with his future films thoughtful writing and dialogue, a number of very memorable characters, and a well-chosen soundtrack. It also contains many tropes common to past heist films, especially over-the-top details like Dignan's boastful quote ("On the run from Johnny Law ... ain't no trip to Cleveland") even though the group only performed a very under-the-radar bookstore heist. "Going on the lam," having a "getaway car," stealing another car, having dealings with a crime figure or a local mob boss, Dignan, Anthony, and Bob have the trappings of what seems to them to be the "big time," but it is clear to the viewer that these boys are nothing but incompetent slackers. Life is not a heist flick, or a crime flick, and definitely not a drama or thriller – just ordinary day-to-day life. None of the boys' grandiose plans succeed, although Dignan never seems deterred by his lack of success, nor even seems to notice his pattern of failure. The group is also plagued by their own internal arguing – as young twenty-somethings, the boys argue and even get into physical brawls, which highlights the pointlessness of their conversations and further emphasizes their ineptitude.

The bright sunlight and broad outdoor vistas in *Bottle Rocket* are rare in Anderson's oeuvre; Anthony's (Luke Wilson) pool scene recalls the influence of artist David Hockney.

A few Anderson characteristics are already evident in this loping heist caper: the evocative use of montage and slow motion, the formation of an ad hoc family around a quixotic enterprise, and, in James Caan's Mr. Henry, the dynamic father figure who turns out to be needy, unreliable and in need of some fathering himself. The casting of Caan as a veteran to add weight from earlier American cinema history is relevant because he and Tak Kubota (Rowboat) previously appeared together in *The Killer Elite* (1975). In addition, Caan's Mr. Henry character in *Bottle Rocket* is a professional thief, drawing obvious connections with Caan's earlier performance of the title role in *Thief* (1981). These earlier roles are referenced as James Caan plays an over-the-top kung-fu-fighting crime boss. Caan's character also provides a jolt of energy to the film, as he is menacing and unpredictable, as well as puerile and childish (as a joke, Mr. Henry pours water on Dignan from the rooftop). The film shows an underdeveloped version of Wes Anderson's directorial proclivities, before he started making seriously stylized films. While *Bottle Rocket* is most definitely the most "real world" film of Anderson's catalogue, all of the characters, especially Dignan and Anthony, Mr. Henry, Rowboat, and Kumar (Kumar Pallana) are written to Anderson's type, surrounded by a normal universe.

While the short film was deeply masculine, the most striking thing about the feature-length film is its addition of several fully-drawn female characters. Three of these stand out: Grace (Shea Fowler), the younger sister of Anthony, who appears to be about twelve years old, Stacy Sinclair (Jenni Tooley), a friend of Bob's brother, who engages Anthony in a deeper discussion of his mental illness, and, most centrally, Inez (Lumi Cavazos), the hotel housekeeper Anthony begins dating while he and the boys hide out in a motel after their robbery. Grace is significant because this character reflects what will continue to develop in the style of Wes Anderson, the knowing, unflinchingly honest and serious-minded child that is followed so closely by the Tenenbaum children and the character of Suzy Bishop in *Moonrise Kingdom*. Already in the character of Grace there is a palpable sense of gravity, in the way she reprimands Anthony for drifting along and not having a plan for his life – in this way she seems more like a mother than a sister. Her steely-eyed gaze is formidably stern, and she seems to be the one truth-teller who calls out the boys for their immaturity, even warning Anthony to stay away from Dignan because he is a "liar." Grace's assessment of Dignan is sobering for the viewer because his charming idealism, including his "75-Year Plan," has been beguiling the audience since the beginning of the film. Grace also offers a ballast for Anthony – in the middle of the film, Anthony writes a letter to Grace while she is away at camp, in which he confesses the difficulties in his life, and he also offers her some practical advice, such as recommending that she take a foreign language at school, since his lack of knowledge of a foreign language has led to some lost opportunities for himself (his budding romance with Inez). The relationship between Anthony, the young adult who seems like a lost child, and Grace, who seems protective of Anthony like a mother (no actual parents to any of the characters are ever shown in the film, making it that much more like a "Peanuts" cosmos) is one of the most fascinating prototypical signals of Wes Anderson's further use of his child characters in his future work.

The second female character to hold the film's focus, albeit briefly, is the sorority girl Stacy Sinclair (Bob's brother's friend), whom Dignan and Anthony meet in Bob's backyard. While in the short, Dignan and Anthony were ogling an older waitress, here it is the young woman herself who seems to express a strong interest in Anthony (much to Dignan's exasperation, as he tries to win her attention for himself without success). When Anthony calmly asserts that he "went nuts," Stacy asks Anthony empathetically about his mental illness, even crouching down before his chair in order to show her interest in his story. When she asks Anthony about the circumstances that led to his stint in the psychiatric care facility, he replies:

One morning over at Elizabeth's beach house, she asked me if I'd rather go water-skiing or lay out. And I realized that not only did I not want to answer that question, but I never wanted to answer another water-sports question, or see any of these people again for the rest of my life.

Stacy sits listening patiently to him, and then sympathetically comments that he must be very complicated. Anthony counters this with the assertion that he tries not to be complicated, thus signaling that she has not understood him very well. The exchange shares affinities another film in which characters project profundity upon a very simple and uncomplicated man, Peter Sellers' Chance the Gardener in Hal Ashby's *Being There* (1979).[6]

The character of Inez reflects Anderson's fascination with the outsider, with "otherness," because Inez is a young hotel worker from Paraguay who has not yet learned to speak much English. Thus, mistakes and misunderstanding characterize Anthony's relationship with Inez. He wants to keep the tiny photo she carries in her locket as a memento, but finds out a moment later that it is a photo of her sister, not her. He touches her face and says it feels like "silk," but she does not understand the word. He becomes frustrated with the language barrier when she speaks animatedly with a young man at a bar. When he wants to tell Inez he loves her, he enlists the help of another hotel worker, Rocky (Donny Caicedo), to translate what he is saying into Spanish. He embarrasses Inez by having Rocky translate when Anthony wants to describe their lovemaking. Finally, when he proposes to stay at the hotel with her because he doesn't want to leave her behind, she calls him "paper," like a piece of paper blowing in the wind, which Rocky translates as "trash." Anthony is hurt, but Rocky insists that it doesn't sound bad in Spanish:

Rocky: (*translating for Inez*) You're like paper. You know, you're trash.
Anthony: Like trash?
Rocky: You know, you're like paper falling by, you know… It doesn't sound that bad in Spanish…

One final misunderstanding is when Inez tells Rocky to tell Dignan that she loves Anthony, then Rocky says "Tell Anthony I love him." Thus it appears to be a message that Rocky loves Anthony. This is made all the more comical because Dignan has been using the alias "Jerry" to hide his identity, so Inez says to Dignan, "Bye, Jerry."[7] The resolution of this misunderstanding leads to the reunion of the couple and the traditional happy ending of a male/female relationship restored.

The presence of females in the film heightens the emphasis on the youthfulness/childishness of the "boys" – the young men in their twenties who are in a period of post-adolescence. In a specific example, when he is robbing his own bedroom, Anthony pauses to straighten one of the toy soldiers that is out of place in the formation – the viewer can assume this is Anthony's old bedroom because his sister Grace is the only sibling mentioned. In a touch of irony, when Grace asks Anthony when he's going to come "home," Anthony replies in an irritated voice that lacks conviction that he cannot come home because he is now an "adult":

Grace: What's going to happen to you, Anthony? When are you coming home?
Anthony: I can't come home, Grace – I'm an adult.

In another carefully contrasting scene, the "boys" are dressed up and eating at Bob's country club with Mr. Henry like mature adults, and yet when they see Bob's older brother (nicknamed "Futureman," and played by the third Wilson brother, Andrew Wilson, as the perfect sadistic bully brother), the two brothers immediately regress to teasing and heckling one another until Mr. Henry, just as childishly, taunts Futureman until he backs down. (The name "Futureman" also points to the character's stunted growth and immaturity.) In the party scene,[8] Dignan tells Mr. Henry he would like to lead the heist alone, and Mr. Henry praises him like an approving father; Dignan, delighted by this paternal endorsement, puffs up like a proud son. Later, Dignan is staking out the crime scene while Anthony is writing in his notebook; the viewer assumes Anthony is taking notes in preparation for the heist until it is revealed that he is making a flip-page doodle of a pole-vaulting stick figure.

The final series of scenes also share this emphasis on childishness/immaturity. First, Anthony and Dignan argue about who will go back for their fallen comrade at the crime scene, Applejack (Jim Ponds), who apparently had a heart attack midway through the heist. Dignan makes his grand speech – "They can't catch me, because I am innocent" – and the Rolling Stones' "2000 Man" begins to play. Then the scene jumps to Mr. Henry, who turns out to be robbing Bob's house as the heist goes awry. Then, the police chase Dignan and he, in a comic touch, runs into a storage freezer marked "No Exit," where the police tell him to "freeze," capture him, beat him with their fists, and push him down into a pile of ice chips. In the next scene, as Bob and Anthony are seen entering a county jail (named Wasco Penitentiary after production designer David Wasco), the front door is festooned with a few skimpy decorations for Christmas, while the Christmas carol "Good King Wenceslas" plays. The paltry decorations cannot hide the cold institutionalization of the place; instead they make it seem all the more depressing and pathetic. The Christmas carol continues as the boys share a take-out lunch of burgers and fries wrapped in tinfoil, and Dignan gives to Anthony and Bob the belt buckles he made for them in jail. As the three men walk through the wintry jail yard before sitting on some bleachers at the far end of the field, Anderson makes a point of focusing the camera at ground-level so that the viewer can see the mud caked on their shoes, evoking the idea of little children who have been playing outside in puddles in the rain.

Just like the title of the film refers to the cheap fireworks that sparkle and then quickly fizzle out, Dignan's moment of glory, his much anticipated heist on Hinckley Cold Storage, leads him to ruin and jail time. However, there are still some small victories that lead to a happy ending for the film. For example, despite the fact that Bob's house was robbed by Mr. Henry, who took everything, including the grand piano, Bob explains that his relationship with Futureman has been better since the robbery – they bonded together while shopping for a new grand piano. Also, throughout the film, Anthony is able to achieve all of the traditional markers of adulthood: he forms a mature romantic relationship, he starts earning a living like a responsible adult (until he briefly gets involved in crime to help his friend feel better), and he becomes involved in his community by coaching youth soccer. Dignan, on the other hand, has not fully grown up (which is why he is in jail), but he has made big strides toward adulthood by taking responsibility for his friends (for example, he goes back for Applejack, he refuses to get mad at the people who betrayed him, etc.). Dignan also has not lost his spirit – he goads the other two into making them think he needs their help to break out of jail, only later admitting he is joking. *Bottle Rocket*, like many of Anderson's films, is about becoming a grown-up. Many of Anderson's adult characters are childish and immature people who, at the beginning of the film, do not act like adults. On the one hand, Anderson admires these "dreamers" in some sense: his characters retain a childlike innocence, as if they never really had to grow up. On the other hand, his films show the process by which people need to become responsible for their own sake, and for the sake of the people in their lives, as a true mark of maturity.

The Dialectic of Sanity/Insanity

In the last line of the film, Dignan alludes ruefully to the fact the Anthony was institutionalized for his mental health, and Dignan is now the one in an institution: "Isn't it funny how you used to be in the nuthouse and now I'm in jail?" The film contrasts the mental states of Anthony and Dignan, detailing how the characters swap mental positions, and highlighting the indistinct line between madness and sanity. The film starts with Anthony institutionalized and Dignan on the outside. Anthony agrees to go into a mental institution after a breakdown: he recognizes his mental ill health which, paradoxically, makes him healthy. Dignan does not recognize his own state of mental ill health; this is underscored by Dignan's early delusion that he must help Anthony "break out" of a voluntary psychiatric facility at the beginning of the film. This is given a further comic layer when Anthony "plays along" with Dignan's delusion, and climbs out of the window using a make-shift rope ladder made of bedsheets, just to placate his friend.

With Dignan, Anderson and Wilson created a very memorable character whose dreams of glory as an outlaw are almost noble. Dignan's careful organization, with his 75-Year Plan, and outfit coordination, with the gang's yellow jumpsuits,[9] show his unusual drive and unique creative force. At the beginning on the bus, Dignan seems to be the competent leader, telling Anthony, "We both respond to structure," and asking, "Driver, what's our ETA?" finally concluding that they are "on schedule" with an air of authority. Dignan is undone merely by his "shortcomings" as a thief: sensitivity, compassion, inclusiveness, and empathy. His natural kindness stands in the way of his becoming a ruthless criminal, and therein lies the great contradiction of this unusual character – his "fatal flaw" is that he is simply too nice. (This is the reason he ultimately takes the fall and sacrifices himself to go back for Applejack in the bungled heist.) Dignan is also naturally gracious. He tries to appear tough during the bookstore robbery, but after being reprimanded by the manager for his uncouth manners, he robs the bookstore politely, displaying a deferential manner toward his victim, even though he is robbing the man at gunpoint, and timidly asking for a larger bag "for atlases and dictionaries" to hold all of their stolen money. Wilson's unique charisma makes for a standout performance in the film. His performance is so heartfelt and sensitive, but also annoying and loony (his most distinct prototype may be the character of Corporal Klinger from the 1970s television series *M*A*S*H*). Not only that, but he reveals subtle clues pointing to his inner insecurities, which only make his character's hardcore criminal aspirations all the more humorous. For example, Dignan says "I'm not always as confident as I look," or "What, is it weird being into exercise? Does it sound weird to talk about it?" These statements demonstrate that Dignan is insecure and overly concerned about how he appears to others. Dignan's comment about his fifteen years of education also seems to imply that he flunked two grades.

Dignan's efforts to maintain a confident exterior are also revealed by his sensitivity toward discussions of Anthony's mental condition at the beginning of the film. As much as possible, Dignan avoids talking about mental health, quickly dismissing Anthony raising the topic with the words "Be sensitive to the fact that other people are not comfortable talking about emotional disturbances. … Put it behind you. You're out. You're better." Dignan's hypersensitivity toward this topic indicates deeper insecurities about his own mental health – there are hints throughout that Dignan, not Anthony, is the one close to insanity. This is made especially clear when Anthony and Dignan are arguing on the side of the road when their stolen car breaks down, and Anthony says to Dignan, "I thought I was supposed to be the one who's so crazy," upon which Dignan slashes Anthony in the face with a screwdriver. In addition to Dignan being overly sensitive about anything related to mental instability, he is also sensitive about his inferior economic status, hiding the fact that he was fired from his landscaping job with the Lawn Wranglers. Dignan is the least financially well-off among the three friends: Anthony's upper-middle-class home is shown during the robbery, while Bob's family is clearly the wealthiest because there is a pool in the backyard of his sprawling family home (Dignan fumes: "How does an asshole like Bob get such a great kitchen?"), and he and his family are members of a country club. In addition, Dignan seems stung by Anthony's jibe that they rob his house because "You know there's nothing to steal from my mom and Craig." The fact that Dignan gets defensive shows he is lacking a stable family life with a proper father at home, and this is further reason to explain why he wishes to view Mr. Henry as a father/mentor figure. Dignan looks forward to going home, to the wrong home ("Till we say: 'Mr. H., we are coming home!'"), and his idealized vision of Abe Henry as a father figure does not materialize. In place of "home," Dignan is proud of being in jail ("We did it though, didn't we?"), but at the end when Anthony is staring at Dignan walking back into prison, the look on his face reflects a fearful thought: "Will he be okay?" This film also features the first of many great Wes Anderson final shots, reminiscent of the final shot in Truffaut's *Les Quatre cents coups*: in both films, Antoine/Dignan turn back to face the camera with an ambivalent facial expression, reflecting an uncertainty about the future.

The Heist Film Genre and Literary Influences

While *Bottle Rocket* features a strange and unreliable main character, the film also departs from formula in its storyline. *Bottle Rocket* is the opposite of a slick "heist" film, a genre in which the master plan works without a single hitch and the heist artists get away scot-free – the expected narrative of a standard heist film. *Bottle Rocket* plays with this idea; nothing ever goes quite right, and anything that can go wrong does. The group is plagued by infighting and disagreements, and their planning meetings frequently devolve into fistfights; at several points the "gang" itself is threatened with dissolution:

> Dignan: (*points to Bob*) He's out. (*points to Anthony*) And you're out, too. And I don't think I'm in, either. No gang![10]

Other aspects of their crimes go awry as well, and it is these realistic touches that add humor to the film. During their attempt to burglarize Hinckley Cold Storage, the safecracker, Kumar, turns out to be slightly senile ("Who's that man?" "Kumar, that's Applejack!") and gets lost in the freezer. Their other accomplice, Applejack, apparently has a heart attack midway through the crime. The gang can't see out of their masks and feel suffocated by them, their smoke bomb sets off the fire alarm, adding to their confusion and making them cough, as well as further limiting their visibility. They fail to factor in the human element when three workers suddenly enter the scene of the robbery:

> Dignan: What are you doing here?
> Worker: We work here!
> Dignan: You're always at lunch now!
> Worker: Not always.
> Dignan: Yes, always!

One of the prototypical "heist" elements of this film is the use of the binocular-shaped matte screen in the first scene where Dignan is looking through binoculars at Anthony, while reflecting light with a mirror with his other hand. This early placement of binoculars signaled the beginning of a trend in Anderson's work which continued with the use of the binocular-shaped screen in *Rushmore*, as well as the very significant use of binoculars which are associated with the character of Suzy Bishop in *Moonrise Kingdom*. The film's satiric view of the "heist" film genre is also reminiscent of several Woody Allen films, especially *Take the Money and Run* (1969), in which the incompetent petty criminal Virgil Starkwell (played by Allen himself) memorably thwarts his own robbery by giving the bank tellers a note in illegible handwriting. Later in Anderson's oeuvre, over-the-top elements in the "crime-caper" film reappear in *The Grand Budapest Hotel* – the reading of the will, the hidden envelope, the jail break scene, and even the prison gruel.

In addition to these, there is also a small hint of Anderson's future references to literary classics through the inclusion of several telling details that point to J. D. Salinger's *The Catcher in the Rye*. First, a further dimension is added to the relationship between Anthony and Grace when it is compared to Holden Caulfield's relationship with his sister Phoebe. Holden's secret visit to his younger sister in their Manhattan apartment in order not to be detected by their parents is similar to Anthony's visit to Grace in the yard of her school. Phoebe's presence, and her adult-like incisiveness, is an anchor and a corrective to Holden in the same way Grace is a bracing presence for Anthony. Other signifiers pointing to *The Catcher in the Rye* include both Holden and Dignan ordering a "Tom Collins" as an alcoholic drink, Anthony's red pullover and its symbolic similarity with Holden Caulfield's red hunting hat, and the presence in both stories of a character named "Bernice." In addition, both narratives deal with the themes of innocence versus adulthood, and madness vis-à-vis sanity. Holden Caulfield, who thinks of himself as a runaway and a hardened adolescent who cannily lies to people about his identity, is obsessively concerned with protecting the innocence of children, even envisioning himself as "the catcher in the rye," a protector of children from going over a "cliff" into adulthood. Similarly, Dignan and Anthony (who each embody various aspects of Holden's personality) are caught on the cusp between the worlds of childhood and adulthood; their dreams of becoming master criminals are thwarted by their childish naïveté, impractical plans, and the fact that they can barely have a meeting to plan their crimes without childishly breaking down into bickering and fistfights. In addition, Holden Caulfield and the three young men in *Bottle Rocket* are all social misfits; thus, the film and the book are both concerned with a male protagonist finding his place in society. Finally, both narratives are a meditation on what it means to be "crazy" versus what it means to be sane – Anthony "escapes" from a mental institution at the beginning of *Bottle Rocket*, while in *The Catcher in the Rye*, it is implied that Holden is narrating his first-person account as a flashback, while taking a "rest" in a mental institution. Because Salinger's book is written from Holden Caulfield's point of view, the reader sympathizes with his off-kilter perspective and sees the world through Holden's eyes. Similarly, the viewer is invited into the gang of misfits in *Bottle Rocket*, and likewise encounters an off-kilter world, a Texas that is not a true Texas, but seen through the eyes of love, and the motives from which the three friends in *Bottle Rocket* operate are all the true bonds of friendship, loyalty, and love. Although hardened and cynical, Holden Caulfield is earnest and well-meaning in his desire to protect children and in his love for Phoebe, especially in one of the final scenes of the novel when Holden expresses his true happiness for the first time, so happy that he's "damn near bawling" while watching his little sister ride a carousel in the park ("It was just that she looked so damn *nice*, going around and around in her blue coat and all"[11]), and this same earnestness underlies the characters in *Bottle Rocket*.

In one of the final scenes, the lyrics to the Rolling Stones' song "2000 Man" illustrate a man so caught up in elements of the future, technology, and his career that he loses sight of his own humanity – family, children, etc. The song suggests how new technology from the "space race" and onwards in time has led to dehumanization of culture on a global scale through the obsessive pursuit of achievement and financial gain, as well as predicting the abstraction of individual identity that can be seen now in today's corporate environment: specialized jobs, cubicles, name tags and badges, etc. Dignan is now "just a number" in jail. According to the *The Royal Tenenbaums* DVD director's commentary, Anderson wanted the final scene to be set to Bob Dylan's "Billy (Main Title Theme)" from Dylan's score to *Pat Garrett & Billy the Kid* (1973), but could not afford the rights to use it. (Anderson later used the song in *The Royal Tenenbaums* in the scene where Royal is kicked out of the house.) This song expresses the isolation of a criminal, who can trust no one, and who is lost, weary, alienated, alone, and far from home. *Bottle Rocket* is less about a botched crime than it is about inescapable pasts, impossible love, and unending childhoods.

Reception of the Feature-Length Bottle Rocket

In interviews about *Bottle Rocket*, Anderson has stated he was never more confident than when the film was finished, and never as confident again after the disaster of the film's test screenings.[12] Producer James L. Brooks described not only the devastating response of audiences to the test previews, but also the startlingly cruel rejection of the film by the Sundance Film Festival – the very festival that had premiered "Bottle Rocket" in their Sundance Shorts Program – which refused to admit the feature-length film into its competition in 1996. Thus, this "indie"-style film opened without the benefit of a festival showing, opening on no more than 40 screens in the U.S.[13] Only last-minute reprieves like Kenneth Turan's laudatory *Los Angeles Times* review kept the film from complete obscurity:

> *Bottle Rocket* has just what its characters lack; an exact sense of itself. [...] Unlike most lost generation tales, this one never loses its way. Inexplicably, almost criminally turned down by the Sundance Film Festival, *Bottle Rocket* is especially exciting because it was put together by a core group of under-thirties, all of whom are new to features. [...] Here's hoping there are others out there this fresh and this bright.[14]

Anderson describes *Bottle Rocket*'s initial failure and subsequent reappraisal as follows:

> The first screening we had was just absolutely atrocious. And every screening we had after that, until about 10 years after the movie happened, was awful. We

had very bad numbers, and hundreds of walk-outs. We lost half an audience at the first screening. But I did come out of the experience with reason to be happy. It was like film school for me, and we had these amazing professors. And some people in the business liked the movie, like Joe Roth, who ended up green-lighting the next movie we did, *Rushmore*. People like Mike De Luca and Scott Rudin took notice of this flop. So even though the movie was a disaster from the point of view of the box office, it actually put us into the movie business anyway.[15]

In 2012, Anderson was interviewed by Mike Fleming, Jr., and asked what Hollywood should do differently to nurture young directors who have the potential to develop a distinctive voice, as Anderson did with *Bottle Rocket*. Anderson's reply is worth quoting in full:

Well, that movie was probably just a complete fluke. We had every reason in the world where it would have been impossible for us to get that movie done then, and it's probably physically impossible to get it done now. I don't think there is any conceivable business motive for how to make the movie. One big part of the business model that was flawed was, that movie cost seven million dollars, and it probably should have been made for around 750,000 dollars. Then, it could have probably made more money if it had been approached differently. At the same time it wasn't like we showed it to all the film festivals and they all said let's put this into the system. We got turned down by all of the film festivals! We didn't have any place to show it. I don't really know what anyone could have done differently with that one. Except just wait.[16]

After the failure of *Bottle Rocket*, Owen Wilson was so discouraged that he almost quit acting and considered joining the Marines. In time, through word-of-mouth, the film gradually gained status as a cult favorite, and was ultimately named #7 on Martin Scorsese's list of the Top Ten Films of the 1990s. For all of its lightness, *Bottle Rocket* is now considered by critics to be one of the very best films of its year, on a par with the much-acclaimed *Fargo* (1996). Over time, the film was aided by appearing on various critical Ten Best lists, and it was notably championed by Scorsese, who referred to Anderson as "the next Martin Scorsese"[17] in an interview with *Esquire*. (Meanwhile, Peter Bogdanovich has compared Wes Anderson to Orson Welles, quoting Howard Hawks: "It's nice to see a smart kid for a change."[18]) In a prescient move of recognition, Wes Anderson was voted the 1996 Best New Filmmaker at the MTV Movie Awards for *Bottle Rocket* – it is fitting that the younger, cutting-edge generation of people working for MTV would be among the first to recognize Anderson's voice, being closest to him in age.

Anderson has often publicly expressed his gratitude to producers Polly Platt and James Brooks for making it possible for him to direct his first feature film. Brooks tells the story of how he had to suggest to Anderson and Wilson that they read the script aloud. "They were so raw and new at writing and directing that it had never occurred to them to read the script aloud even though practically the entire cast lived in the same [apartment] and was never unavailable."[19] Not long afterward, Wes Anderson and Owen Wilson were brought to Hollywood and given offices on the Sony Studios lot. They were still in their early twenties and they had a script deal in Hollywood.

It is all the more poignant that the film had such humble beginnings, just a group of friends making a movie, as Anderson has observed:

> You know, when we made *Bottle Rocket*, the cast was just my friends, Owen and Luke and our friend Bob, and their brother Andrew.[20]

Bottle Rocket is about brotherhood, camaraderie, and male bonding – and even though this film contains some strong female characters, the ties that bind these men together are indestructible. Dignan and Anthony are brothers in all respects save blood, and this is interesting because although they simply play close friends in the film, the two actors are actual brothers. Friends in the film are played by actual real-life friends, brothers, and roommates, all of whom were living together in the same apartment in Houston when they first wrote the film.

Although *Bottle Rocket* was not a commercial success, it was celebrated and embraced by a core group of devoted fans, and the film can be viewed as a catalyst that launched three careers. Considering the major roles that Luke and Owen Wilson began to play in subsequent films,[21] in time, the Anderson/Wilson team would, in a subtle way, change the face of American comedy.

Notes

1 Anderson elaborates: "The darkest hour was the evening of our first test screening, in Santa Monica, at which we had 85 walkouts. The head of the studio said, 'Congratulations. Seriously.' [My agent] Jim Berkus said that our goal for the next screening should be for someone to say 'congratulations' without having to say 'seriously' afterward. And then later that night, my girlfriend broke up with me." Anderson, quoted by Leonard Maltin in "Wes Anderson," on the *Turner Classic Movies* website, from an interview in *Premiere* magazine, March 1999. TCM.com. http://www.tcm.com/tcmdb/person/514940%7C0/Wes-Anderson/ (accessed December 5, 2015).
2 A bottle rocket is a type of firework attached to a stabilizing stick, which the user can place in an empty glass bottle (hence the name), and ignite the rocket engine; the mouth of the bottle guides the stick, stabilizing the rocket in its first moments of flight, so that it will explode high in the air.
3 Dignan is named after Wes Anderson's childhood friend Stephen Dignan, who appears in *Rushmore* as the deejay at the "Heaven and Hell Cotillion," and plays "Rob" in this film. Brian Tenenbaum also appears as "H. Clay Murchison." Bob Mapplethorpe is named after the controversial American photographer Robert Mapplethorpe, who died in 1989.
4 The sound of the music creates an instinctive Proustian rush of childhood

memories for those who grew up with the "Charlie Brown" series of animated holiday specials on television.

5. The sunlit, shiny quality of the outdoor scenes, especially of Anthony in the hotel pool, suggest the work of David Hockney. Anderson notes, "I can't think of any books that would affect my visual style, but maybe there are some. I remember when we were doing *Bottle Rocket*, there was a book of Hockney's body of work up to that point. That had quite an effect on *Bottle Rocket* somehow." Anderson quoted in Jacob Weisberg's "The World According to Wes," *Slate.com*. May 25, 2012. http://www.slate.com/articles/podcasts/conversations_with_slate/2012/05/wes_anderson_the_complete_slate_interview_.html (accessed September 3, 2015).

6. Mark Browning, *Wes Anderson: Why His Movies Matter* (Santa Barbara, CA: Praeger, 2011), 9.

7. Dignan introduces himself and Bob to Inez in the hotel room using the aliases Jerry and Cornelius, respectively. Jerry Cornelius is a character from Michael Moorcock's books such as *The Final Program* (1968) and *A Cure for Cancer* (1971).

8. In a detail foreshadowing Anderson's fourth film, there is a black-and-white portrait by Richard Avedon of Jacques Cousteau hanging on the wall during the party.

9. One of the most memorable images from the film is this set of yellow jumpsuits worn by Dignan and his heist crew, which Jason Davids Scott has identified as evocative of the late-1970s New Wave band Devo, in Jason Davids Scott, "'American Empirical' Time and Space: The (In) Visibility of Popular Culture in the films of Wes Anderson," in Peter C. Kunze, ed., *The Films of Wes Anderson: Critical Essays on an Indiewood Icon* (New York: Palgrave Macmillan, 2014), 87.

10. The idea of the three boys, Dignan, Anthony, and Bob (just because he owns a car) forming a "gang" with Dignan as the ringleader, relates to the first film Anderson ever made, about the children's book *The Skateboard Four* by Eve Bunting.

11. J. D. Salinger, *The Catcher in the Rye* (New York: Little, Brown, and Company, 1951), 213.

12. Kevin Conroy Scott, *Screenwriters' Masterclass: Screenwriters Discuss their Greatest Films* (New York: Faber and Faber, 2005), 115.

13. James L. Brooks, "Foreword" to Wes Anderson and Owen Wilson's *Rushmore* [screenplay] (New York: Faber and Faber, 1999 [1998]), xi-xii.

14. Kenneth Turan, "The Gang That Couldn't Shoot, or Think, Straight," *LATimes.com*. February 21, 1996. http://articles.latimes.com/1996-02-21/entertainment/ca-38140_1_bottle-rocket (accessed October 14, 2015).

15. Anderson in Mike Fleming, Jr., "Fleming Q&A's 'Moonrise Kingdom' Director Wes Anderson," *Deadline.com*. December 30, 2012. http://deadline.com/2012/12/fleming-qas-moonrise-kingdom-director-wes-anderson-394927/ (accessed May 25, 2015).

16. Ibid.

17. Martin Scorsese, "Wes Anderson," *Esquire*. January 29, 2007 [2000]. http://www.esquire.com/news-politics/a1608/wes-anderson-0300 (accessed September 18, 2015).

18. In Hawks' *Rio Bravo* (1959), John Wayne uses this line to show how impressed he is by the young Ricky Nelson's professionalism. Peter Bogdanovich, "Introduction," in Wes Anderson and Owen Wilson's *The Royal Tenenbaums* (New York: Faber and Faber, 2001), ix.
19. James L. Brooks, in Anderson and Wilson, 1999, viii.
20. Scott Feinberg, "Wes Anderson on His Life, Career and Biggest Success Yet, 'Moonrise Kingdom: Interview with Wes Anderson," *The Hollywood Reporter*. December 25, 2012. http://www.hollywoodreporter.com/race/wes-anderson-his-life-career-406295 (accessed October 3, 2014).
21. From this first performance, before which neither Owen Wilson nor Luke Wilson had ever acted in a film and had no formal training, the two men have gone on to become highly paid actors with Owen Wilson taking roles in more than seventy films (including *Marley and Me* [2008], *Midnight in Paris* [2011], and several successful franchises including the *Night at the Museum* franchise [2006–2009-2014]) and Luke Wilson appearing in over sixty films (including *Legally Blonde* [2001], *Old School* [2003], and *Idiocracy* [2006]). In their childhood, the brothers had some (minimal) experience in front of a camera lens; their mother, Laura Wilson, is a celebrated still photographer who has worked with Richard Avedon. Their father, Bob Wilson, was the longtime chief executive of KERA Channel 13, a public-access television channel in Texas.

CHAPTER FOUR

"Sic Transit Gloria": Transgressing the Boundaries of Adolescence in Rushmore

Filmed in his own hometown of Houston, Texas, *Rushmore*, Wes Anderson's second feature-length film, is a potent combination of coming-of-age story, French New Wave homage, and black comedy dealing with darker themes of grief and depression, set to the classic rebellious strains of 1960s British Invasion music. The film is a significant example of Anderson's auteuristic voice, both because he authored the film (with co-writer Owen Wilson), and because, as previously mentioned, *Rushmore* demonstrates a singular connection with auteur theorist François Truffaut's 1959 film *Les Quatre cents coups*,[1] considered a masterpiece of the French New Wave, in which Truffaut told the tale of Antoine Doinel based on his own misunderstood teenage years. *Rushmore*, which traces the first half of an academic school year in the life of tenth-grader Max Fischer (from September 1997 to January 1998, marked month by month on the screen), is similarly filled with strongly autobiographical elements.[2] *Rushmore* seemed to spring forth organically from Anderson's own experiences at St. John's School in Houston, Texas.[3] Similar to Max Fischer, Anderson staged his own plays in the school auditorium, ambitious epics and action-filled dramas with names like "The Five Maseratis" and "The Battle of the Alamo."[4] Anderson's own experiences as a precocious teenage boy are lovingly – and even breathlessly – presented with all the driving force of youthful passion and exuberance paired with adolescent devil-may-care insouciance and derring-do. This film is a comedy about interpersonal relationships at an elite academic institution, but it is also testament to Anderson's own driving, almost relentless intellect and irrepressible energy. As Anderson's sophomore effort, the film could have been burdened by posturing or overreaching. Instead, the film's scenes are precisely written, and astonishingly clean and fast, unencumbered, even reckless. The dialogue is fine-tuned to present exactly what Anderson and Wilson wanted to communicate, and nothing more – not a word is wasted in this lean, 93-minute film (88 minutes without the ending credits).

Early on, the viewer is shown a montage of all the school clubs and societies run by Max Fischer (Jason Schwartzman) – he is editor of the school newspaper, captain of the debate team, manager of the lacrosse team, president of the calligraphy club, founder of the astronomy society, captain of the fencing team, founder of the bombardment society, founder of the trap and skeet club, president of the Rushmore beekeepers, and director of the "Max Fischer Players," as well as an alternate on the wrestling team. It is clear that Max is an unusual character. He runs an excessive number of extracurricular clubs because he can get away with it, and competes for an older teacher's affections because he is challenged by it. Max is a celebration of intellectual oddity, whimsicality, and uniqueness. His wholehearted devotion to his less than noble causes – he is a prodigy with failing grades who lives with the constant threat of expulsion hanging over his head – is what makes him so endearing. Max is also a creative force – this is demonstrated by his devotion to his artistic endeavors such as the elaborate plays he stages at school, especially when he comes out with guns literally blazing in the final production of his play "Heaven and Hell" (for which the audience is given advance warning to wear safety glasses and earplugs). The play's ambitious scope seems out of reach for a high schooler, and almost comically doomed to failure. Likewise, Max's romantic pursuit of a teacher out of his age range seems comical but at the same time poignant because of his doomed devotion. Max is a dreamer, and he is seduced into believing his beautiful, fantastical visions. The same might be said of Anderson, who seems to be equally obsessively caught up in creating worlds and microcosms – each of his films is driven by his own astonishing ambitions.

In addition, the film sets up a dialectical framework between the overachieving Max, on one hand, and the staid world of an academic preparatory institution on the other. The world of Rushmore Academy, as in all preparatory institutions, is a restrained, conservative one in which things are done in a particular way – at a certain time in a certain manner – behavior is regulated by time-honored rules and traditions. Max presents a contradiction to this established order. He represents an antithesis – a creative and imaginative force – that sets itself in opposition to the hubris of a preparatory school environment. Not only that, but he presents himself at quixotic full tilt with his good-hearted but reckless schemes, flying in the face of the established order. This is what makes his relationship with successful business magnate, Herman Blume (Bill Murray[5]) such a delightful juxtaposition. They are literally rivals in romance, for the attention of Miss Cross (Olivia Willams). But they also stand as polar opposites – Max, the young upstart, and Herman, a jaded, bored-to-death steel tycoon, who laments his own lackadaisical, non-gifted offspring ("Never in my wildest imagination did I ever dream I would have sons like these"[6]) but over time develops a father-son dynamic with Max. Ironically, it is Max's youthful exuberance that serves to awaken the world-weary Blume from his mid-life near-comatose state. The relationship between the two is tender at moments when the viewer sees that Max can serve as not only a student at the school, but as a mentor to the adults who have lost their passion:

Blume: What's the secret, Max?

> Max: The secret?
> Blume: Yeah. You look like you've got it all figured out.
> Max: I don't know. I think you just got to find something you love to do, then do it for the rest of your life. (*shrugs*) For me, it's going to Rushmore.[7]

This exquisite tenderness carries over into the other relationships in the film as well. For example, when Max climbs through the young teacher's bedroom window with blood on his face, claiming to have been hit by a car while riding his bicycle, the audience is somehow truly rooting for him to not be caught in this lie. When the lie is discovered, the viewer is somehow just as crushed as Max. Furthermore, when Max and his friend Margaret Yang (Sara Tanaka) have a misunderstanding, the pain is very acute. This argument is mirrored somewhat in the argument/resolution between Sam and Suzy in *Moonrise Kingdom*, when Sam inadvertently hurts Suzy by laughing at her in her psychological distress over being labeled a "problem child." In both cases, the young male does not intend to wound with his words, and in fact is likely unaware at the time that his behavior is insensitive. Anderson does a remarkable job of reflecting this dynamic in a male/female relationship, and his insightful writing stands out in both films. The resolution of the argument is also very true-to-life:

> Margaret: You were a real jerk to me.
> Max: I know. I'm sorry, Margaret.
> Margaret: Well. Anyway. Nice to see you.[8]

This is also similar to the Sam/Suzy resolution where Sam perceives that restitution needs to be made, and makes the beautiful speech, "I'm on your side." In the case of Margaret and Max, when Margaret points out that Max was a "jerk," and Max says he is sorry, it helps ease the tension in their friendship – Margaret will not tolerate Max's insensitive treatment of her. This admonishment wakes Max up to self-awareness. It is right after this pivotal kite-flying scene, and Max's reconciliation with both Dirk Calloway (Mason Gamble), and Margaret, that he begins to formulate his ideas for a new club.[9]

The Character of Max Fischer and the Elite Preparatory Institution

The character of Max Fischer was created by Anderson and Owen Wilson for what they originally referred to as their "school movie," in a screenplay written even earlier than *Bottle Rocket*. The screenplay reflects their own school experiences in several distinct ways. For example, Owen Wilson was expelled from his prep school, St. Mark's School, in the tenth grade,[10] while Wes Anderson attended St. John's School for the last few years of his high school education until he graduated in 1987. According to the school's website, St. John's School was established in 1946. Famous graduates include former US Ambassador to the United Kingdom (2001–2004) William Stamps Farish III, who graduated in the Class of 1957, and Anderson himself, while former President George W. Bush was famously rejected from St. John's and went on to attend Philips Academy Andover.[11] St. John's offers a strict curriculum providing high-caliber academic training for students from kindergarten through grade 12. Students at St. John's are required to wear uniforms, blazers and khaki pants similar to the outfit worn by Max. The student body is currently 87% Caucasian, with 1,225 students and 200 faculty, with a student/teacher ratio of 7:1. It is likely that Anderson attended the school because he craved more intellectual stimulation than a regular public school can normally offer, similar to the prodigiously talented Max Fischer.

Preparatory institutions have historically been viewed as upper-crust, snobbish, and elitist, catering to students bent on acceptance to an Ivy League university, and perhaps this overemphasis on academics throughout childhood may produce a certain social dysfunctionality (Max Fischer epitomizes this when he boasts to Miss Cross: "My top schools where I want to apply are Oxford and the Sorbonne. But my safety is Harvard."[12]) In addition, being viewed as "gifted" academically often leads to arrogance and narcissism – this is due both to the societal expectations placed on students as they are expected to hold to the high standards of the school's elite reputation, and the child's own experience of difference and alienation from his academically "normal" peers. This situation may lead a gifted child to feel intense loneliness and isolation, and in extreme cases, may lead to suicidal tendencies (such as those displayed by Luke Wilson's character, Richie, in *The Royal Tenenbaums*), but in the case of Max Fischer, this "difference" becomes a kind of exuberant, freewheeling strength of personality. Some modern-day filmic counterparts are Ferris Bueller, the charmingly above average schemer in *Ferris Bueller's Day Off* (1986) played by Matthew Broderick in the film by John Hughes, which enjoyed immense popularity during Anderson's own high school years, and Harold (Bud Cort) from Hal Ashby's *Harold and Maude* (1971), whose different and "special" hobbies and talents originally ostracize him from society, but through the help of Maude, become a source of mutual celebration and humor. Max, like all uniquely gifted people, thrives in the presence of like-minded friends and intellectual equals – people who can spar with him at the same level, "get" his jokes, and become worthy adversaries (such as Dr. Guggenheim [Seymour Cassel]) and friends (such as Herman Blume). This points to something essential in Anderson himself, and helps explain why Anderson tends to repeatedly make films with the same group of collaborators. It also explains the poignancy of the end of the film, where all of the characters, even those previously wronged by Max, find solidarity in Max's play (even Max's nemesis, the foreign exchange student Magnus Buchan [Stephen McCole], has a part in the play).

Early in the film, it is established that Max Fischer does not come from the same privileged background that the other Rushmore students do. In a conversation with the headmaster, Dr. Guggenheim, it is revealed that Max began attending Rushmore after writing a play about the Watergate scandal and winning a scholarship to the school. This is obviously a sensitive point for Max, because he hides his lower-income background, claiming that his father is a neurosurgeon rather than a barber. During an early scene, class differences at *Rushmore* are brought to the fore by Herman Blume's chapel speech:

You guys have it real easy. I never had it like this where I grew up. But I send my kids here. Because the fact is, whether you deserve it or not, you go to one of the best schools in the country: Rushmore. Now, for some of you it doesn't matter. You were born rich and you're going to stay rich. But here's my advice to the rest of you: Take dead aim on the rich boys. Get them in the crosshairs. And *take them down*. Just remember: they can buy anything. But they can't buy backbone. Don't let them forget it. Thank you.[13]

Max gives Herman Blume a standing ovation, due to his honest description of the school's class differences. Max also takes notes on the speech: "Rushmore – best school in country. Rich kids – bad?"[14] Max is galvanized by Herman Blume's speech because Blume does not gloss over the glaring class differences in a private school atmosphere. Additionally, although he is now a rich businessman, Blume makes it clear that he did not come from a privileged background himself, and this is what initially draws Max to him.

Rushmore is also used as a metaphorical concept, representing a prized goal. These lines capture the rivalry between Max and Herman Blume over Rosemary Cross:

Blume: She's my Rushmore, Max.
Max: Yeah, I know. She was mine too.[15]

Max considers his attendance at Rushmore central to his life, almost a life-giving force. It is clear that when Max is kicked out of Rushmore, he struggles to fit into the non-elite, public school environment of Grover Cleveland High School. When he offers to start a fencing team at his new school and then is overrun in the gym by the school's basketball team, it becomes obvious that Max's unique skills do not easily translate to a public school environment.

Literary and Cinematic References in Rushmore

In his introductory essay on *Rushmore* that accompanied the film's Criterion Collection release, Dave Kehr, contributing editor of *Film Comment*, sets the narrative of *Rushmore* firmly in the classic American literary tradition of Mark Twain and his tales of resourceful, clever young male protagonists, particularly in *The Adventures of Tom Sawyer* (1876) and its sequel, *Adventures of Huckleberry Finn* (1885). Kehr calls *Rushmore* "a profoundly American comedy in the direct tradition of *Huckleberry Finn*,"[16] postulating that Anderson's work not only reflects Twain's focus on class division and societal stratification, but also the essential character of the American boy-hero:

Mark Twain used his adolescent hero to provide an outsider's viewpoint on a rapidly stratifying American society, a republican dream pulling apart into divisions of age, income, and race. *Rushmore* is also about class divisions – Max, the son of the local barber, is attending the exclusive school on a scholarship – but Anderson and co-writer Owen Wilson, more wishful thinkers than Twain, use comedy to imagine the healing of those divisions, the reweaving of relationships across the lines of class and generation.[17]

According to Kehr, while Twain's work uses satiric and comedic elements to point out profound inconsistencies in American society, Anderson and Wilson take this one step further to bring about a longed-for healing of these divisions. This contributes to the profoundly hopeful and satisfying conclusion of Anderson's simultaneously deeply sad film. In addition, the character of Max Fischer embodies the conflicts deeply inherent in Twain's young male protagonist Huck Finn, the "character flaw" of the "American dreamer" which Kehr points out in Max: this is Max's "refusal to allow reality to limit his aspirations,"[18] both in Max's doomed romantic ideals and in his overreaching extracurricular ambitions. Max's desire to achieve great things in every realm of possibility is in direct contradiction with his status as the worst student in school who is, in reality, on academic probation because of his poor grades, and even on the road to expulsion.

The character of Max Fischer and the setting of Rushmore Academy draw on tropes that have been famously dealt with in films and novels such as J. D. Salinger's *The Catcher in the Rye* (1951), Peter Weir's *Dead Poets Society* (1989), and, as mentioned above, *Ferris Bueller's Day Off*. Salinger's literary classic chronicles Holden Caulfield's notorious escape from "Pencey Prep," an exclusive educational institution in Pennsylvania, and his subsequent odyssey of "adult" adventures over the course of three days in New York City. While Holden is disgusted by Pencey's false advertising in magazines featuring a picture of "some hot-shot guy on a horse … like as if all you ever did at Pencey was play polo all the time"[19] (and the school motto: "Since 1888 we have been molding boys into splendid, clear-thinking young men"[20]), Holden views the school as a corrupt system designed by privileged adults catering to wealthy young boys who wish to someday join their ranks. However, he is equally set adrift in New York, where his interactions with the adult world leave him floundering for meaning. These encounters with the adult world include his attendance at a club where he meets and tries to charm three older women from Seattle, his reluctantly agreeing to the visit of a prostitute (the young girl Sunny in the green dress), only to inform her when she arrives that he simply wants to talk, as well as his disillusioning encounter with his former English teacher Mr. Antolini, who offers Holden guidance and a place to stay the night (although later Holden wakes up to Mr. Antolini patting his head in a way that makes the boy feel uncomfortable) – all of these "fish out of water" experiences suggest similarities with the iconoclastic character of Max Fischer. Similarly, just as the death of Max's mother has set him adrift in grief, Holden's brother Allie's death three years before (Allie died from leukemia at the Caulfields' summer home in Maine on July 18, 1946, when he was eleven years old and Holden was thirteen) has been a profound loss for Holden. Holden's protective affection for his red hunting cap, a somewhat ridiculous-looking accessory with a long bill and ear flaps, is also mirrored by Max's odd collection of outfits, including his own Russian *ushanka* (fur hat with ear flaps), his penchant for wearing his Rushmore blazer, or the green velvet suit he dons for the evening of his play performance. Both Salinger's and Anderson's created characters are iconic because of their strong personalities and stubborn individualism which stands in resistance against "the Establishment" represented by adult conformity (Holden Caulfied labels the adult world as "phony"[21]). In Peter Weir's film *Dead Poets Society*, set in the late 1950s, pride in the long-standing traditions of another all-boys preparatory school, the elite Welton Academy, stands in opposition to the spirited teaching of "Carpe diem," educational exploration, and the questioning of authority suggested by English teacher John Keating (Robin Williams). Keating inspires the young high school boys in his charge, including Neil Perry (Robert Sean Leonard), who longs to pursue a career as a thespian, in opposition to his strict father's wishes for him to become a doctor. Both *The Catcher in the Rye* and *Dead Poets Society* tell a darker tale than *Rushmore*, as Holden Caulfield ends up being committed to a psychiatric hospital and the father/son conflict in *Dead Poets Society* ends in the son's suicide. By contrast, although Max's character is in some ways just as anarchic and recklessly self-sabotaging as Holden, and much more so than Neil Perry (Max certainly breaks rules with an astonishing insouciance), *Rushmore* has one of the happiest endings of Wes Anderson's films.

Rushmore succeeds at reaching its bucolic conclusion because the darkness of the adult world is kept at bay, or relegated to the outskirts, by the film's heightened tone. The presence of death is muted because Max's mother Eloise and Miss Cross's husband Edward Appleby have already passed away at the time of the narrative's events, so Max's bereavement is apparent only through his visits to his mother's gravestone and Miss Cross's through the beloved mementos she preserves in her deceased husband's old bedroom. Divorce does play a role in the film, but the subject is dealt with in a humorous light by the tragicomic presence of Bill Murray's Blume (who is shown to be unhappily married in any case). Even the film's central conflict of unrequited love is resolved at the end by Max's more age-appropriate blossoming romance with his school friend. The film ends with one of the most exuberant, joyous scenes in all of Anderson's oeuvre, Max's triumphant production of the hit play "Heaven and Hell," where nearly the film's entire cast is reunited in the audience, even Coach Beck (Andrew Wilson), Mr. Littlejeans (Kumar Pallana), and the police officers who arrested Max earlier in the film, brought together again for one final overwhelming display of friendship, forgiveness, and solidarity. Even Miss Cross's friend Dr. Peter Flynn (Luke Wilson) has been invited, the same man whom Max had humiliated earlier at a dinner date after the "Serpico" play. Later, at the "Heaven and Hell Cotillion," the song "Ooh La La" by the Faces is played while Max dances with Miss Cross, and Mr. Blume dances with Margaret. The film is so lighthearted overall that its sad moments definitely stand out in high relief. One of the most heartbreaking moments of the film may be when Herman Blume finds out that Max's father is really a barber, not a neurosurgeon as he had been led to believe by Max. The response on Bill Murray's face is a masterful job of understated acting as he lets it sink in that all of Max's stories about his dad are untrue. The levity of *Rushmore's* tone and the madcap hijinks in the film match the lighthearted playfulness of *Ferris Bueller's Day Off.* In that film, John Hughes' screenplay captures a high school boy who plays hooky from school for the day, devising ever more perilous and daring plans to outwit his school principal, borrow his friend's dad's expensive sports car, and acquire reservations at an upscale restaurant by assuming someone else's identity. By comparison, Max tries to outwit his school headmaster, becomes leader or head of every club in his school, and tries to get funding for an aquarium. Max's success with his final "Heaven and Hell" play brings him a touch of glory similar to the glory experienced by Ferris Bueller when he dominates the city streets of Chicago while performing "Twist and Shout" from atop a parade float.

Max begins the evening of his grand opus by standing in front of the red curtains in his green velvet suit and making a dedication to Miss Cross's husband and to his own deceased mother. Both Miss Cross and Max's father Bert are visibly moved by Max's dedication. One of Max's greatest successes of the evening is the bringing together of Miss Cross and Mr. Blume, whom he has seated next to one another at the performance. While they at first treat each other with some distance, they are given a tender moment during their reunion at the play, in a conversation they have during the play's intermission:

> Miss Cross: So, what do you think of Max's latest opus?
> (*Mr. Blume gives a thumbs-up and stares out into the snow.*)
> Mr. Blume: Let's just hope it's got a happy ending.
> (*Miss Cross smiles. She smooths her hand across Mr. Blume's hair. He looks into her eyes. She links arms with him gently, and they drink their coffees together.*)[22]

Max has also written a final love scene into his play, giving a happy ending to himself and Margaret:

> (*Max looks into Margaret Yang's eyes.*)
> Max: Marry me, Le-Chahn.
> Margaret: (*instantly*) You bet I will.[23]

The laughing, exuberant response at the end of "Heaven and Hell" includes Kumar Pallana as Mr. Littlejeans giving his enthusiastic review: "Best play ever, man."[24]

Aquatic Themes in Rushmore

One of the most striking things about the *Rushmore* screenplay is the repeated references to oceanography and water that neatly foreshadow Anderson's future take on the theme in *The Life Aquatic with Steve Zissou*, which he would not fully explore until after he had finished making *The Royal Tenenbaums*. The most obvious hints foreshadowing this future obsession of Anderson's are both direct references to Jacques Cousteau, first in the form of a library book that sets the hero on a quest early in the film, and later in the film, a photograph of Cousteau on the wall of Edward Appleby's room. Max and Dirk also take notes while watching the Cousteau film *The Living Ocean Part 2: Exploring the Reef*. In addition to these direct references, there are a number of further water or sea-related images or references, including Rosemary's reading of the Robert Louis Stevenson works *Kidnapped* and *Treasure Island*. (It is highly unusual that Rosemary Cross would be reading the novel *Kidnapped*, a bildungsroman which follows the growth of David Balfour from a naive young boy to a heroic, experienced man, to seven-year-olds, but this is the novel she is shown to be reading to her first grade class when Max first sees her.) The book that Miss Cross is reading when she meets Max for the first time is Jules Verne's *Twenty Thousand Leagues Under the Sea*. Moreover, when Miss Cross and Max meet for the second time, she invites Max to help her feed the classroom fish. While Max is feeding them, Miss Cross refers to her "husband" (it is not yet clear that she is a widow), and Max, in shock, drops the entire food container into the tank and needs to fish it out. His name, after all, is Fischer. (This scene has subtle ties to the early fish tank scene in *The Graduate*, where Mrs. Robinson [Anne Bancroft] asks Benjamin Braddock [Dustin Hoffman] for a ride home, and then casually tosses Ben's car keys into the aquarium behind him, so that the boy has to fish the keys out of the glass tank to drive her home.) Moreover, when Max sees the excitement on Miss Cross's face as she tells him about the fish that were just born in her classroom fish tank, he decides to have an aquarium built for her on the Rushmore campus (which he names the Cousteau-Blume Marine Observatory). The original copy of the Jacques Cousteau book *Diving for Sunken Treasure* (1971) was a present from Edward Appleby to Rosemary in seventh grade, a precocious age to be reading about Jacques Cousteau. The quote that Miss Cross writes in the book, next to a photo of Cousteau laughing uproariously, is "When one person, for whatever reason, has the chance to lead an extraordinary life, he has no business keeping it to himself – Jacques Cousteau."[25] Toward the end of the film, it is revealed that Miss Cross's husband died in a drowning accident, indicating that Rosemary's deceased husband possibly took sea-related risks similar to his hero.

Finally, in another direct reference to *The Graduate*,[26] Herman Blume is seen in a long shot underwater in his family pool, similar to Benjamin Braddock wearing the scuba gear his father is showing off to friends when he sinks to the bottom of the family pool. Both scenes indicate that the characters feel that they are "drowning" or "out of their depth." In the screenplay, Blume makes several references to a "natatorium," from the Latin word used to describe a building containing a swimming pool. When Blume checks into his hotel for an indefinite stay after his wife sues him for divorce, he immediately asks where the pool is located (it's on the roof). In another scene from the screenplay, a group of Rushmore fourth graders file past a painting in a museum on a class field trip; the piece is described as a depiction of a ship caught in a storm. In the scene where Miss Cross wears a large men's shirt backwards as a smock while teaching a painting class outdoors, when Blume asks one of her young pupils what he is painting, the boy answers that it is "a jellyfish" (again a reference to a sea creature; in the screenplay, the boy "makes a swimming gesture" and responds: "It's a little swimming snake"[27]). Miss Cross has an improbably large number of fish tanks in her classroom, and the characters in the film are often shot in or around the tanks, or looking through them. A conversation between Max and his father also relates the sea to the idea of depression and loss:

> Max: You think I'm spending too much of my time starting up clubs and putting on plays?
> Mr. Fischer: I don't know. It's possible.

Max: I should probably be trying harder to score chicks. That's the only thing anybody really cares about. (*sighs deeply*) But it's not my forte, unfortunately.
Mr. Fischer: It'll happen, Max. It's just. You're like one of those clipper ship captains. You're married to the sea.
Max: Yes, that's true. (*pause*) But I've been out to sea for a long time.[28]

Here the idea of being "out to sea" is related to Max's feeling of loss and depression. Max's father recognizes that his son is different and unique, but that he is being true to his "calling" as someone who is "married to the sea" like a clipper ship captain, or some other lone figure devoted to his craft. This conversation shows how deeply Max is understood by his father.

The Music of Rushmore: From the British Invasion to "A Charlie Brown Christmas"

The music in *Rushmore* is often recognized as an integral element in bringing an authentic tone of teenage angst and rebellion to the story. Anderson's original idea was to score the film entirely with songs by the Kinks ("They're in blazers but they're more sort of lunatics, which is also our character [of Max Fischer]"),[29] and indeed, the Kinks are represented in the score by the song "Nothin' in the World Can Stop Me Worryin' 'Bout that Girl." British Invasion songs were selected for the soundtrack because Anderson felt that they captured the energy, rebellion, and anarchy of the tenth-grade Max Fischer. The song "I Am Waiting," written by Mick Jagger and Keith Richards for the Rolling Stones album *Aftermath* (1966), is filled with the anger and despair caused by Cold War sensibilities and the threat of nuclear apocalypse that hung over the younger generation – the idea that the young people were powerless to affect their political realities, and were in a state of "waiting" hopelessly for their annihilation in a nuclear holocaust (the song speaks of truth being censored, suggestive of brainwashing, and future escalation of the nuclear threat filling the waiting youth with bone-piercing fear because they are sitting ducks waiting for the bombs to start dropping). This song is thus one of the seminal pieces of Cold War commentary in pop music, written at the start of the counterculture revolution, in the midst of the anti-nuclear war movement, precisely capturing the atomic anxiety of the era. Likewise, the use of the Who song, "A Quick One While He's Away," adds a driving, rebellious beat of Who drummer Keith Moon during the montage where Mr. Blume and Max sabotage each other's bicycle and car, respectively.

The use of Vince Guaraldi's "Hark the Herald Angels Sing" from the animated television special *A Charlie Brown Christmas* (1965) by animator Bill Melendez, based on the comic strip by Charles M. Schulz, draws attention to the strong allusions between Max and the lead character of the Peanuts comic strip. One obvious comparison is that Charlie Brown's father is a barber, just as Max's father is in the film. Matt Zoller Seitz (2013) also notes the similarity of Max's winter jacket sporting an orange zig-zag stripe with Charlie Brown's iconic yellow shirt with the black zig-zag stripe, as well as the similarity of the scene where Max is carrying Margaret's little plant to the scene in *A Charlie Brown Christmas* where Charlie Brown carries the small, spindly Christmas

The curtain closes on the "Heaven and Hell Cotillion" marking the end of the story and conjuring questions of artifice and "theater" in *Rushmore*. Anderson has related this scene to the Peanuts gang all joining together for a spontaneous dance onstage during a rehearsal for the Christmas play, in Bill Melendez's 1965 made-for-TV special, *A Charlie Brown Christmas*.

tree that he took pity on and bought for Christmas.[30] Even the final dance scene at the "Heaven and Hell Cotillion" at the end of *Rushmore* replicates in spirit the joyous free-for-all as all the Peanuts characters dance together onstage in the *Charlie Brown Christmas* special – the scene gathers all of the beloved characters onstage at once, each shown to be enjoying his or her own unique dancing talents, notably Snoopy, dancing and simultaneously playing a red guitar, and Pigpen playing the stand-up bass while emitting clouds of dust; this resembles Anderson's ensemble of characters appearing in a joyful dance as the curtain closes on their "stage" at the end of the film.

Anderson artfully employs Cat Stevens' music, namely "Here Comes My Baby," and "The Wind." The use of Cat Stevens songs in *Rushmore* serves as a clear homage to 1971's early "indie" film *Harold and Maude* directed by Hal Ashby (a study of Hal Ashby's films as precursors of the independent cinema movement was completed by Philip Drake in 2013). *Rushmore* unmistakably references the pacing and tone of *Harold and Maude*, with its dark, edgy humor, and its direct, unsentimental treatment of the topic of depression. Even the love songs used in *Rushmore*, including Stevens' "Here Comes My Baby" and John Lennon's "Oh Yoko" from his *Imagine* album in 1971, are both upbeat-sounding songs that belie an underlying sense of heartache – the song "Here Comes My Baby" talks about the lover's experience of seeing his beloved walk by with another man, and how such a love is always out of his own reach, while "Oh Yoko" is written as a love song to Yoko Ono despite the tumultuous circumstances at the time it was written (another song on the *Imagine* album, "How Do You Sleep," reveals Lennon's resentment toward McCartney following the breakup of the Beatles, for which Ono is often blamed) and the complex and volatile relationship between them (with Lennon even taking a mistress, May Pang, at Ono's suggestion in the years 1973–75, for a period of eighteen months in what Lennon later referred to as his "lost weekend" period). The soundtrack of *Rushmore* does not restrict itself to easy emotion, but rather points at the complexities and the true hardships and heartaches of a love relationship. The French song "Rue St. Vincent" that Max brings along and pops into the tape player by Miss Cross's bed to provide a romantic atmosphere for his visit after the faked "bicycle accident" is also a song about the loss of a love, this time a beautiful and innocent girl who falls in love with the wrong type of fellow and is stabbed and killed by him, performed by celebrated Franco-Italian singer Yves Montand, known for his love ballads in the 1950s and 1960s. And finally, the song highlighted most clearly in the film is "Ooh La La" by the Faces – the song chosen by Max for his final dance with Miss Cross at the "Heaven and Hell Cotillion" after the successful performance of his play (Max makes a gesture to the DJ at the dance, a pre-arranged signal indicating that it is time to play his special song). "Ooh La La" is written from the point of view of a grandfather giving advice on women to his grandson, and cautioning him to avoid heartbreak. However, ultimately, the grandfather in the song knows that the young boy will have to learn these lessons on his own, through harsh life experiences. The older man expresses the universal truth of adult maturity that he wishes he had learned at a tender age what he knows now, and that heartbreak can only be tempered by wisdom gained over time. The instrumental pieces provided by frequent Anderson collaborator Mark Mothersbaugh, create a sprightly feel to the opening of the film with Mothersbaugh's use of unusual instruments such as mandolin, guitar, glockenspiel, contra bass, bells, an organ-type keyboard, drum set, and a flute.[31]

Trangressing Time and Genre

Rushmore was set in 1997, and Max is shown to be a student who would have graduated in the year 2001. Despite the time period being clearly spelled out by annotations in the film (the Swiss army knife that Dirk gives Max as a present reads "Rushmore Yankee 1985–1997,"[32] marking 1997 as the year Max is expelled from *Rushmore*), and despite the film being released in 1998 thus making the film apparently set in the "present day" when it was released, like all Wes Anderson films, the time period is kept deliberately ambiguous. The pace of the film evokes the French New Wave, and the film is filled with anachronistic signifiers such as the British Invasion period music, the use of a pay phone, Max's 1950s hair style, the screenplay's description of Max's house as "an Archie Bunker-type house,"[33] the "retro" appearance of Max's father's barbershop, Max's interest in Jacques Cousteau, his interest in Watergate (he is reading David Halberstam's *The Powers That Be*, a 1979 book about Watergate and the American media, when he introduces himself to Miss Cross), some of Max's club activities, as well as Max's plays, which are focused on the interest stories of the 1960s and 1970s (for example, his "Serpico" play, based on the film *Serpico* from 1973, which was also made into a television series from 1976–1977, and "Heaven and Hell," which incorporates elements from the Oliver Stone film *Heaven and Earth* of 1993 and the Francis Ford Coppola film *Apocalypse Now* from 1979). The film also contains numerous homages to French culture, in addition to the French New Wave, including Max's French beret outfit for the French club, and Max's choice of an Yves Montand song to aid in his attempt at seduction, while the yearbook photo of Max as president of the Yankee Racers Go-Kart Club is a reference to the work of early twentieth century French photographer Jacques-Henri Lartigue (there are also four Lartigue photos symmetrically hung on the wall behind Max in his classroom at the beginning of *Rushmore*). These touches are deliberate by Anderson to invite the viewer into a nostalgic view of the past, especially because Lartigue's photographs are both elegant and whimsical, with meticulous composition similar to Anderson's work. *Rushmore* was released in 1998, prior to the Y2K crisis, and prior to the events of 9/11, as well as preceding by nearly a decade the explosion of social media technology. It was a more innocent time, before the Internet began to permeate American lives, a time when an adolescent's personal problems did seem as if they could dominate an entire year, and a time when self-introspection ("navel-gazing") was perhaps more common to the adolescent world than the present-day posting and tweeting. Anderson demonstrated with this film that he could luxuriate in the details of telling a story, and take a leisurely amount of time doing so – he could film Max Fischer reading the *Wall Street Journal*, slowly standing up, buttoning his blazer, and taking a sip from a cup of coffee before solving the world's hardest geometry problem.[34]

Just as *Rushmore* takes the viewer out of fixed chronological time by obscuring and disrupting the time period, the film also transgresses its genre as a bildungsroman, or coming-of-age story, by subverting the normal timeline of maturity. At the start of the film, Max is more of an "adult," exemplified by his affinity for Mr. Blume and his romantic pursuit of Miss Cross. Max's relationships with both Blume and Miss Cross somewhat exceed the boundaries of adolescence, and in that lies both the humor of the film – his interactions with them are as equals, rather than minor-to-adult – but also its touching and melancholy aspects, since Max must face the fact that he is a minor, essentially still a child, and that he cannot have a romantic/sexual relationship with Miss Cross. Throughout the film, Max has been adopting the façade of maturity and authority, which comes across as comically pretentious. Ultimately, the film's conclusion demonstrates that Max has been the protagonist in a reverse coming-of-age story – he grows down (into childhood) instead of up, and through doing so, he grows into maturity, honestly embracing his identity by introducing his father as a barber and building a new relationship with Margaret. Just as Margaret explains her failed science experiment by confessing to Max that she "faked" the results ("I thought it would [work], but it didn't"[35]), Max is forced to the same conclusion. *Rushmore* is a transgressive coming-of-age story because the lead character transforms from an "adult" to a "child."

Innovative Filmmaking Techniques/Homages in Rushmore

Rushmore represents Anderson's first use of symmetrical widescreen compositions, which give the film a gentle touch of stylization, of heightened reality – a technique that would become more prevalent in his future works. This is also the first appearance of many increasingly "Andersonian" filming techniques, including the increasingly prevalent use of intertitles (in this film, introducing Max's many club activities), the long tracking shot, quick pans back and forth between characters to display reactions, and unique divisions with the story that resemble book chapters – this time done with the names of the months September to January projected onto curtains parting, to add an air of heightened theatricality to the story.

Matt Zoller Seitz explains the significance – and serendipity – of Anderson's first tracking shot in *Rushmore*:

> Anderson's first elaborately choreographed tracking shot is the aquarium groundbreaking in *Rushmore*. It was originally meant to be a more subdued shot facing the athletic field. The day before shooting there was a torrential rain that turned the field to mud. Anderson turned the camera around and shot toward the bleachers instead, and compensated for the less attractive background by moving the camera in an intricate pattern and filling the background and foreground with action. Anderson liked the result so much that "after that, I kept doing it. More and more, I'd say, 'I'd like to do this on a train track.'"[36]

Rushmore has also frequently been recognized for its nod to the work of Truffaut, especially the deliberate imitations of actual frames in Truffaut's *Les Quatre cents coups* which are simulated both in the classroom scenes, where rows of adolescent boys are shot from behind, and the famous shot of Truffaut's young adolescent behind a chain-link fence, which is matched by a shot of Max's chapel partner Dirk with his hands grasping a similar fence in *Rushmore*. These distinct visual references to *Les Quatre cents coups* serve as an homage, as discussed in chapter 1, to Anderson's direct inspiration from Truffaut, and how Truffaut's semi-autobiographical Antoine Doinel character – a misunderstood adolescent believed by the adults in his life to be headed on a path to delinquency – is a kind of prototype for "troublemaker" Max Fischer. The love triangle between Mr. Blume, Miss Cross, and Max is also faintly evocative of Truffaut's third film *Jules et Jim*, which deals with the two titular characters who are fascinated with the same woman. The other Truffaut film that could be connected to *Rushmore* is *L'Argent de poche*, due to its focus on life of children in a school in Thiers, a provincial town in France. Truffaut used many actors who were citizens of the town, and many unknown actors, all dressed in the clothing of that time period (the film was shot during summer holidays in 1975). Although the film purportedly portrays the local life of the children of Thiers in 1975, Truffaut's vision is actually an anachronistic view that relates more clearly to childhood in France of the 1940s and 1950s. *Rushmore* is similarly anachronistic as it refers both to the present while it is filled with somewhat improbable references to the 1960s and 1970s.

For *Rushmore*, Anderson credits Michael Powell and Emeric Pressburger films, particularly *The Life and Death of Colonel Blimp*, as inspiring how this film looks. As noted by Matt Zoller Seitz, another intertextual aspect of the film is Anderson's and Wilson's references to Elia Kazan's 1954 film *On the Waterfront*, and the 1995 film *Heat*, from which certain scenes are referenced, such as the scene where Max orders dynamite. The scene where Max reveals Mr. Blume's affair to Mrs. Blume in a private meeting where he first offers her a choice of sandwiches is a direct reference to the scene in *On the Waterfront* where Marlon Brando, as Terry Malloy, imparts previously concealed information to Edie Doyle (Eva Marie Saint); the actual moment of Max's revelation is drowned out by the noise of city traffic, just the way the words between the two characters in *On the Waterfront* are obscured by a steam whistle. As mentioned, *Rushmore* also marks Anderson's first use of extensive annotations on the screen. This use of words on the screen was necessary for rapidly describing Max's various club activities, 18 clubs in 65 seconds, allowing Anderson to condense a great amount of information to be delivered to the viewer.[37] Anderson's use of annotations on the screen, all in Futura font, is a feature he would increasingly enjoy experimenting with in his later work (the *Rushmore* DVD commentary also notes that Anderson was paying homage to how Futura was commonly used for credits in European films in the 1950s and 1960s). Anderson credits Jean-Luc Godard as a director who puts many words on the screen in his films, as well as citing graphic designer Saul Bass' work with Alfred Hitchcock, and the films of Charles and Ray Eames.[38] *Rushmore* is also the first film that made use of the distinctive Wes Anderson close-up – a character is shot in widescreen format facing the camera, and may be looking straight into the lens or slightly off to the side, with his/her face framed in the center (a feature common to Jonathan Demme's work, for example with 1986's *Something Wild*, or 1991's *The Silence of the Lambs*).[39] With an Anderson close-up, the character often displays little to no emotion which results in a very formal, stylized shot.

Finally, Anderson originally faced opposition toward his unusual choice in *Rushmore* to film the name of the month ("September") against a curtain that resembles a stage curtain. Anderson's agent questioned this as possibly being too gimmicky for the film – because they are actual people in an actual story, not characters behind a theater curtain as is possibly implied. Anderson wanted to communicate the name of the month, and the "mood" of that segment (for example, "October" is projected onto a blue curtain). The opening of the curtain is intended to launch the viewer into the next "chapter" of the film – the viewer can go "through" the curtain and enter into the story. Naturally, these curtain chapter breaks also provide a short interval or pause, a restful moment in a highly antic film. Anderson was questioned by his agent on the use of the curtain, out of fear that this "special effect" would be distracting and take the viewer out of the story:

> For me, often what might take somebody else out of [the story] is what I think is just the most beautiful thing, and I'd rather have that. I remember Mike Nichols saying something like, "Whatever movies are best at – well, they're not best at being reserved." [...] The most exciting movies have always been the ones with people who attack it.[40]

The opening and closing of curtains is a pronounced structural feature of *Rushmore*, which indicates a live performance, and also suggests that the entire story resembles/could be one of Max's plays. Max, of course, plays a starring role in the movie – it begins with his fantasy of solving a near-impossible math problem, and receiving the cheers and adulation of all, and Max appears in nearly every scene. In addition, the use of curtains to mark the months divides the action into a series of mini-plays. Within those mini-plays, there is also the "scene" acted out by Max when he visits

Miss Cross in Edward Appleby's old bedroom (he even brings the musical selection, the Yves Montand song which he pops into the tape-player by the bed), and sets the "scene" with theatrical fake blood, and the "prop" of his smashed bicycle. At the end of the performance, when Max has been found out, he climbs out the window again in disgrace, and Miss Cross closes the window curtain – signaling the end of Max's "performance." In addition, when Margaret goes to visit Max to say hello and find out how he is doing, Max, in his depression, closes the curtain on himself. This signifies a sad defeat for the star "actor" – he no longer feels like participating as a player on his life's stage.

In an interview on *Rushmore* with Matt Zoller Seitz, Anderson spoke on the storytelling techniques of both Federico Fellini and Roald Dahl:

> You know, if you look at Fellini's movies, there's this progression – the earliest Fellini movies are kind of neorealist. But then with each one that comes along, you've got more and more Fellini, and then you reach the point where it's at *Roma*, which is – you know, I don't think there *is* a story in *Roma*. *Roma* is just, let's go through his city with him, and it's just entirely of his invention ... I read some of Roald Dahl's notebooks and journals and things, and he would have a sentence that says, "Idea for story where a husband's cheating," and it lays it out, and you see there's a whole story there. I've never had *any* of those. I don't have any gift for that. Every movie I've done is this accumulation of information about these characters and who they are and what their world is, and slowly figuring out what's going to happen to them.[41]

Anderson and Wilson have claimed they wanted *Rushmore* to present a slightly heightened reality, like a children's story, specifically pointing to the work of Roald Dahl, which Anderson would eventually go on to adapt and direct in *Fantastic Mr. Fox*. He takes his character's humanity as a starting point for discovery, finding humor in human fumblings, in absurd juxtapositions, filling a frame with a spectacle of information and detail, but these things are not meant to be silly or irrelevant. Instead, Anderson shows the world through Max's eyes as one rife with possibility. That the film is slightly overwhelming is because he sees the world as a young child sees it – as if viewing something for the first time – stunning, thrilling, vivid. While dipping into the darker topics of grief and depression, *Rushmore* resounds with a great burst of revitalizing hope, reflecting perfectly the moodiness of high school adolescent years.

Notes

1   Commonly rendered as "The 400 Blows" in English; the correct translation of the film's title is a more colloquial French expression which accurately reflects the adolescent rebellion in the film: "faire les quatre cents coups" means "to raise hell," or to live a wild, undisciplined life, as Truffaut's misunderstood teenage protagonist Antoine Doinel does in the film. This also has its counterpart in Max Fischer's uniquely undisciplined behavior in *Rushmore* (Max's rebellions include

petitioning to save the Latin program and fundraising to build a marine aquarium on campus).

2. Anderson has called this film "personal." He elaborates about co-writing the film with Owen Wilson in the director's commentary on the *Rushmore* DVD: "It's got so many things that connect to our own lives. The characters come from people that we've known, and little aspects of ourselves. The setting is so familiar to us, and then there's the thematic stuff that is personal to us." Included in his definition of personal thematic material is the idea of Max Fischer as someone in high school who is not "cool" and is, in fact, a failure at a great many things, but succeeds in some way that is important, due to his drive and "resilience."

3. Anderson scouted locations as far as private schools in the UK to capture the look he wanted for his Rushmore Academy campus, but ultimately returned to his own alma mater to stage scenes in the familiar places from his own high school memories.

4. Dave Kehr, DVD Booklet Introductory Essay on *Rushmore*, Criterion Collection DVD, 1999 [1998], 1.

5. According to Anderson in his interview on *Rushmore*, Murray was paid a total of no more than US$9,000 (the Screen Actors Guild minimum) for his work on the film. When Disney refused to pay for the rental of a helicopter for the montage to "A Quick One While He's Away," Murray also generously wrote a check to cover the amount for the helicopter rental (US$25,000) but the chopper scene was cut before they used the money. Anderson still has Murray's uncashed check. Wes Anderson, interviewed in Matt Zoller Seitz, *The Wes Anderson Collection* (New York: Abrams, 2013a), 83.

6. Not in the original screenplay, the line is a direct quote from Bob Wilson, Owen and Luke Wilson's father.

7. Wes Anderson and Owen Wilson, *Rushmore* [screenplay] (New York: Faber and Faber, 1999), 16.

8. Ibid., 108.

9. The kite-flying scene is reminiscent of Charles M. Schulz's comic strips because of the notorious "kite-eating tree" which plagues Charlie Brown and Linus.

10. Like Max Fischer, Wilson was kicked out of St. Mark's School of Texas in the tenth grade, much to the embarrassment of his father, who was on the board of trustees. Wilson had taken a teacher's math textbook and copied from the book's answer key to hand in assignments for extra credit. "Even though I was the worst geometry student," he says, "I was handing in extra credit – 50 lines of complicated theorems and proofs that I'd taken from the teacher's edition." Wilson continued his high school education at Thomas Jefferson High School, followed by New Mexico Military Institute. Alan Peppard, "Dossier Dallas: Owen Wilson," *The Dallas Morning News*. September 29, 2012. http://www.dallasnews.com/entertainment/celebrity-news/headlines/20120929-dossier-dallas-owen-wilson.ece (accessed June 28, 2015).

11. Abigail Jones, "America's Elite Prep Schools," *Forbes*. April 6, 2009. http://www.forbes.com/2009/04/06/america-elite-schools-leadership-prep.html (accessed

June 28, 2015). Jones lists St. John's as one of the most prestigious preparatory high schools in America alongside Choate Rosemary Hall, Phillips Exeter Academy, and others.
12 Anderson and Wilson, 1999, 24.
13 Ibid., 5–6.
14 Ibid., 6.
15 Ibid., 89.
16 Kehr, 1999, 1.
17 Ibid. Taking Kehr's idea a step further, Twain's narrative friendship between the young teenager Huck and the adult runaway slave Jim can be seen as a literary precursor to the odd-couple pairing of schoolboy Max Fischer and steel magnate Herman Blume. Huck, a boy of thirteen or fourteen, was brought up with no (known) mother by his abusive father, the town drunk, and now has difficulty fitting into society, despite a kindly Christian widow's attempts to "civilize" him.
18 Ibid.
19 J. D. Salinger, *The Catcher in the Rye* (New York: Little, Brown, 1951), 4.
20 Ibid.
21 Ibid., 6. Another similarity between the two characters is their tendency to distort the truth when it suits them. The scene in the car where Max talks with Dirk's mother is similar to the conversation Holden has with an attractive older woman sitting next to him on the train to New York, who turns out to be the mother of his classmate, Ernest Morrow. Holden dislikes Ernest immensely but tells extravagant lies about him to his mother, claiming that he is the most popular boy on campus and would have been elected class president if he had only allowed the other boys to nominate him. Holden tells her his own name is Rudolph Schmidt, which is actually the school janitor's name. When she asks why he is leaving Pencey early, Holden claims to be returning to New York for a brain tumor operation. Holden's spirited falsehoods are mirrored by Max's forceful manipulations, such as his feigning being hit by a car (after applying fake blood to his forehead) in order to get sympathy from Miss Cross.
22 Anderson and Wilson, 1999, 122.
23 Ibid., 123.
24 The line in the screenplay is "Best play all year, man." Anderson and Wilson, 1999, 125.
25 Ibid., 12.
26 Yet another reference to Mike Nichols' *The Graduate* is the famous final scene where Ben and Elaine ride away from the church in the back seat of a city bus, with Elaine still in her wedding dress, with ambivalent looks on their faces. This scene is mirrored in *The Royal Tenenbaums* when Richie escapes from the hospital after his suicide attempt and also rides in the back row of a city bus. Both scenes emphasize that the riders are heading into an uncertain future.
27 Anderson and Wilson, 1999, 49.
28 Ibid., 21–22.
29 Seitz, 2013a, 79.

30 Ibid., 101.
31 Mark Mothersbaugh is one of the main composers for the late-1970s new wave/punk band Devo, and he is one of two members who have been a part of Devo throughout the band's history. According to the *Rushmore* commentary, Anderson was drawn to Motherbaugh's music because he considered it "eccentric." Wes Anderson, interviewed for the Director's Commentary on the "Special Features – Director's Commentary" for the *Rushmore* DVD, *Rushmore*, Criterion DVD, 1998.
32 "Yankee" is an inside joke referring to the mascot of St. John's at the time of Anderson's attendance being the controversial "Johnny Reb," a symbol of the Confederacy. The Rushmore "Yankees" are a counterpoint to the "Rebels" of Anderson's youth. The school permanently changed its team nickname to the "Mavericks" in 2004 to discontinue any association with the Confederacy.
33 Anderson and Wilson, 1999, 21.
34 Other details that indicate Anderson's languorous, detailed approach to storytelling include stage directions in the screenplay that never appear in the final film. These include the description of Dirk holding a hamster in his hands as he waits outside the meeting room to hear about Max's expulsion, Margaret's plane exploding in a fireball before her departure in the kite-flying scene, and the slow-paced scene which lingers on Bill Murray eating the carrot offered to him by Miss Cross: "Mr. Blume takes another bite out of his carrot and throws the rest of it into the yard. Miss Cross laughs." Anderson and Wilson, 1999, 68. Another noticeable cut is this detail immediately following Max's final play: "Mrs. Guggenheim looks on in amazement as Dr. Guggenheim stands up out of his wheelchair and leads the ovation. The rest of the audience quickly follows suit" (123). Although these details add even more intricate richness to the screenplay, they were presumably trimmed out to keep any distraction away from the film's focus on the main action of the narrative.
35 Anderson and Wilson, 1999, 107.
36 Matt Zoller Seitz, "Seitz: 24 Things I Learned While Writing My Book About Wes Anderson," *Vulture*. October 23, 2013b. http://www.vulture.com/2013/10/wes-anderson-collection-24-tidbits-matt-zoller-seitz.html (accessed August 14, 2014).
37 Anderson elaborates: ""So that's a lot of things, and how do you get all that information across? It must have been just in the process of that sort of thinking. You know: 'I'll just *write it* up there.'" Seitz, 2013a, 88.
38 Ibid.
39 Ibid., 92.
40 Ibid.
41 Ibid., 95–96.

CHAPTER FIVE

The Interplay of Narrative Text, Language, and Film: Literary Influence and Intertextuality in The Royal Tenenbaums

The Royal Tenenbaums further hones Wes Anderson's voice and visual style, with its fastidiously curated images, unforgettable details, stylized sets, and foregrounded artifice, harmony from discordant elements, and pretense revealing a deeper reality in Anderson's exploration of a uniquely dysfunctional family. This film's appearance captured the quintessential Andersonian ethos, which suggests a Victorian curio chest full of specimens from exotic locations – preserved animals, horns, tusks, skeletons, minerals – as well as other interesting man-made objects such as sculptures that were unusually old, or unusually small, as well as simultaneously recalling children's storybook illustrations, Color Forms, puppet shows, school project dioramas, and community theatre productions. The award-winning screenplay by Wes Anderson and Owen Wilson was chiefly inspired by J. D. Salinger's novella *Franny and Zooey* (1961) and the Glass family stories, but other sources of significant importance to Anderson included the Orson Welles film *The Magnificent Ambersons*, based on the eponymous novel by Booth Tarkington dealing with the faded glory of a once-great family, and George Cukor's *The Royal Family of Broadway* (1930), modelled on the Barrymore family, where the mother is the dominant authority figure (based on Ethyl Barrymore) and the son is a roguish actor (based on John Barrymore) played by Fredric March. Another obvious inspiration is the George S. Kaufman and Moss Hart play *You Can't Take It with You* (made into a Frank Capra film in 1938), a comedy in which each character in the family is portrayed as uniquely eccentric. Anderson wrote the part of Royal Tenenbaum specifically for Gene Hackman, and presented a vision of New York that is an amalgamation of stylistic features from 1970s-era films such as *The French Connection* (1971) and *Midnight Cowboy* (1969, with Eli Cash's wardrobe suggesting *Midnight Cowboy*'s Joe Buck) and musical cues from the 1970s: The Rolling Stones, Paul Simon, Jackson Browne, and Van Morrison. Anderson also references his debt to

French New Wave, explaining in the DVD commentary how his guiding principle was to have only tracking shots in a nod to Jacques Demy's exuberant and heartbreaking musical film, *Les Parapluies de Cherbourg* (*The Umbrellas of Cherbourg*, 1964) which floats with tracking/dolly shots.[1]

The film's opening title shot is the image of a library-bound copy of a novel entitled *The Royal Tenenbaums*. On the director's commentary for the film, Anderson notes: "One of the initial ideas for this movie was that it would be based on a book, a book that doesn't actually exist."[2] He also mentions that this opening title shot is a reference to Michael Powell and Emeric Pressburger's opening titles, particularly that of *The Red Shoes* (1948), in which a copy of Hans Christian Andersen's 1845 book of fairy tales is shown to reference the inspiration for the story. On the dust jacket of the *The Royal Tenenbaums*, there is an illustration of a cream-colored note card that strongly resembles, according to Anderson and Wilson's screenplay, "a wedding invitation."[3] The book is taken up by a pair of hands (belonging to director Wes Anderson) and stamped to be checked out for borrowing (by the viewer). These opening images are striking for several reasons. First, the film notably begins with a formal "invitation," which seems to offer entrance into a world of privilege, or has bestowed upon the viewer a position of honor. This idea of inclusion by invitation is also present in *The Grand Budapest Hotel*, in which the main narrative is revealed only following a formal invitation to dine. As in *The Grand Budapest Hotel*, the invitation on the front cover of *The Royal Tenenbaums* volume leads to the unfolding of the narrative – in a structure where the invitation leads to revelation, or, in other words, the honor of an exclusive invitation leads to shared intimacy and the pooling together of secrets. This initiating of the story by formal invitation adds a conspiratorial air to the film, as if the viewer were being selected on an exclusive basis, to be included among the privileged few.

In addition, similar to many of Anderson's works, this film has as its centerpiece a work of literature, and although the book is an imaginary work of fiction, the film that follows purports to be an adaptation of this make-believe narrative. In fact, the next page of the book says "Chapter One," and as the film shifts after its introductory section to the family after the children are grown, there is another shot of the book, reminding the viewer that this film is following a written narrative. The screenplay directions say "Insert: Page 22 of *The Royal Tenenbaums*. It says Chapter Two."[4] Such repeated references to the original textual source of the story (albeit imaginary) are continued throughout the film in these references to the book's individual chapters. Anderson thus takes elaborate measures to remind the viewer that the film is based on a literary work, and faithfully follows this imaginary volume's structure, including chapter breaks. This emphasis on the literary textuality of the film closely imitates the opening title sequence of Truffaut's *Les Deux anglaises et le continent* (*Two English Girls*, 1971), in which the opening image is the white book cover of Henri Pierre Roché's *Deux anglaises et le continent*, which fills the screen. This opening sequence, over which the credits of the film are superimposed, teaches the viewer how to "read" the film: Truffaut films the volume open to various chapters (the book even contains Truffaut's handwritten notes to himself in the book's margins about the plans he has for the filmic adaptation of the text – interestingly, some of these notes intrude into the text itself, covering some of Roché's original words, which metaphorically suggests how Truffaut will take the work of Roché's authorship and superimpose his own ideas on it). The book's cover is shown repeatedly, then it is displayed as many identical book covers of *Deux anglaises et le continent*, which cover the screen like a mosaic (this image is later replicated by a "mosaic" of book covers that fill the screen in *The Royal Tenenbaums*). Thus, Truffaut (and Anderson) highlight the literary sources of their films by flaunting the physical text of the book – celebrating rather than hiding their literary, textual sources.

The narrative of *The Royal Tenenbaums* describes the rise and fall of a grand New York family and shares close literary and filmic ties with the 1918 Pulitzer prize-winning Booth Tarkington novel (and the Orson Welles adaptation) of *The Magnificent Ambersons*, beginning with the titular similarities, i.e., the adjectival descriptor ("royal/magnificent"), followed by a surname ("Tenenbaums/Ambersons"). The narratives are both centered around the vagaries of fortune that befall the children of the families, born into wealth, whose talent/lack of talent plays off against the fickle fortune and faded glory of their present-day lives. The Tenenbaum children are born to the successful litigator Royal Tenenbaum (Hackman), and their talents are so astonishing that they are invited to hold press conferences as children after their mother Etheline (Anjelica Huston) publishes a bestselling book on their accomplishments entitled *Family of Geniuses*. Young Chas Tenenbaum (played as a child by Aram Aslanian-Persico) "started buying real estate in his early teens and seemed to have an almost preternatural understanding of international finance;"[5] Margot Tenenbaum (played as a child by Irina Gorovaia), "a playwright, won a Braverman Grant of $50,000 in the ninth grade;"[6] and Richie Tenenbaum (played as a child by Amedeo Turturro) "had been a champion tennis player since the third grade ... turned pro at seventeen and won the U.S. Nationals three years in a row. [He also] kept a studio in the corner of the ballroom, but had failed to develop as a painter."[7] This information is presented with rapid-fire speed of narration in a prologue that Derek Hill (2008) has compared to the opening introduction to the titular characters of the Truffaut film *Jules et Jim*.[8]

The chief subject of Tarkington's *The Magnificent Ambersons* (and Welles's film adaptation) is the spoiled adult child of Isabel Amberson (Dolores Costello), George Amberson-Minafer (Tim Holt), whose life is chronicled from childhood to adulthood in the novel and the film, where he grows from a spoiled little "princely terror" known for calling others "riff-raff" and imperiously telling the Reverend Malloch Smith (Jack Baxley) to go to hell, causing all the adults in the town to long for his "comeuppance." Indeed, the decline of his family fortunes and his own inability to adapt to the changing economic realities of his day (his professional aspiration is to be "a yachtsman") do lead to his sobering fall from grace. The narratives are thus parallel in their presentations of the unique talents and failures of a set of extraordinarily privileged children. The opening line of *The Royal Tenenbaums* is also matched perfectly by the line that opens Tarkington's novel, demonstrating the strong textual influence of the original Tarkington story on Anderson's and Wilson's screenplay. In the source text of *The Magnificent Ambersons*, the opening line of Tarkington's novel is as follows:

Major Amberson had "made a fortune" in 1873, when other people were losing fortunes, and the magnificence of the Ambersons began then.[9]

In *The Royal Tenenbaums* screenplay, the opening line read by the narrator (Alec Baldwin) seems to imitate in tone and substance the opening line in the Booth Tarkington novel:

Royal Tenenbaum bought the house on Archer Avenue in the winter of his thirty-fifth year.[10]

Thus, both narratives begin with a line suggesting early promise. In addition, the family patriarchs are contrasted: business tycoon Major Amberson's (Richard Bennett) fortune establishes him comfortably as the elite family of the small town, while Royal Tenenbaum's wealth as a successful litigator has allowed him to purchase a large mansion in Manhattan. However, despite this early promise and sense of financial security, both families are undone over time, and thus a central theme of both works is precisely this faded glory.

The theme of divorce is immediately presented by the narrator of *The Royal Tenenbaums* in the second line of the film. "Over the next decade, he and his wife had three children, and then they separated."[11] The third line of the film reiterates this idea, when in the first line of spoken dialogue after the narration, the young Margot asks "Are you getting divorced?"[12] This leads into the scene in which the family members, sitting around a table, react to the announcement that the parents are separating. The description in the screenplay is as follows:

Chas is twelve, with curly hair, dressed in a black suit and tie. Margot is ten, with a barrette in her hair, wearing a knitted Lacoste dress and penny loafers. Richie is eight, with long hair, parted on the side, dressed in a Bjorn Borg-style tennis outfit and a headband.
Chas wears a blank expression, Margot looks as if she is about to cry, and Richie has tears all over his face.[13]

The clothes that the children are wearing in this scene are significant because these are the same outfits they will continue to appear in as adults, as if the trauma of this moment has frozen them in time. The children's shocked and tearful reactions show their devastation at the loss of their family as an intact unit; the crumbling of their harmonious world takes a greater toll on them than can be measured at that moment, and the destructive fallout from this decision plays out through the rest of the film.

This prominent theme of divorce is the focal point of trouble for the Tenenbaum family, while the Amberson family is also rocked by its own affair of the heart: the longstanding love between Isabel Amberson and Eugene Morgan (Joseph Cotton) is blocked by Isabel's sullen adult son, George. Although Isabel's first husband has passed away and she and Eugene have waited a respectable time to rekindle their feelings for one another, George Minafer will not allow for a romance between them because he believes it is unseemly for the Amberson family, and that the town will gossip about them. He reminds his mother, "You're an Amberson," as if to seal her identity. This is similar to a line in *The Royal Tenenbaums* screenplay when Royal reminds Margot of her identity to shame her into ending her own extramarital affair: "It isn't right, dammit. You used to be a genius."[14] Ultimately, the repressed love that Isabel Amberson has for Eugene Morgan leads to her early death. Similarly, the theme of the *The Royal Tenenbaums* is summed up in the pivotal line by the narrator after Royal ruins Margot's eleventh birthday party by criticizing her first play:

> In fact, virtually all memory of the brilliance of the young Tenenbaums had been erased by two decades of betrayal, failure, and disaster.[15]

This "disaster" has resulted in the star tennis player, Richie (played as an adult by Luke Wilson), suffering a breakdown during a match and subsequently abandoning tennis: he travels around the world aimlessly in an ocean liner called the Côte d'Ivoire visiting both poles, five oceans, the Amazon and the Nile. Likewise, Margot (Gwyneth Paltrow) has abandoned her writing career, and now spends up to six hours a day soaking in a bathtub, watching television and chain-smoking. Finally, Chas (Ben Stiller) has been struggling with the death of his wife Rachael (Jennifer Wachtell),[16] and the shock has closed him down emotionally – he now spends his days fretting about his boys' safety and having them maintain a strict exercise regimen and helping with administrative tasks in his office. The only success is the Tenenbaums' childhood friend Eli Cash (Owen Wilson), whose first novel won him critical acclaim – but now that is threatened by the poor reception of his second novel as well as his raging drug addiction.

Welles's film *The Magnificent Ambersons* and Anderson's *The Royal Tenenbaums* share many obvious connections. The two films are both examinations of the fading fortunes of two families over time, but their productions are separated by exactly sixty years, and their settings by several hundred geographic miles; the former is based in an Indianapolis suburb at the turn of the twentieth century, the latter in a mythically timeless uptown Manhattan. The opening scenes of both films show the house that serves as the family abode, and both houses are large manors with remarkably similar exteriors (both have tall spires rising at the right). In addition, both films center around a storyline involving a "dysfunctional" family due to imperfect marriage, which in the case of *The Royal Tenenbaums* has ended in divorce. Finally, the family partriarchs are contrasted: Major Amberson, business tycoon who made his money before the turn of the century, experiences a loss of dignity in the film as he ages and becomes befuddled about his dwindling fortunes (brought on by the changing of the times and the rise of the automotive industry, which his grandson unwisely refuses to recognize as the wave of the future), while Royal Tenenbaum, a once-successful lawyer, has also fallen from grace. The highly educated but spoiled son of Isabel, George Amberson-Minafer, is matched by the diversely talented but troubled offspring of Royal and Etheline, because the dysfunctionality of their broken home has instilled anguished insecurity and restlessness in their children.

The two films also share technical similarities: *The Royal Tenebaums* begins with a shot of its "source" book, while Welles's *The Magnificent Ambersons* ends with a shot of Booth Tarkington's novel. Another noticeable similarity between the films is in the presentation of the actors in the cast: *The Magnificent Ambersons* ends with a dramatis personae roll call, while *The Royal Tenenbaums* begins with one. Welles made his film seem more personal by introducing his actors (and some of the important film technicians) by name, finishing the roll call of the ending credits with the statement that "I wrote the script and directed it. My name is Orson Welles." This presentation of the dramatis personae is mirrored at the beginning of *The Royal Tenenbaums*, where the actors are presented one by one in an introduction that also serves to create intimacy between the viewer and the characters. In addition, much of Welles's opening narration in the *The Magnificent Ambersons* was focused on the changing clothing fashions of the different periods, while Anderson is known for his attention to his characters' wardrobes, and especially the specialized clothing choices in *The Royal Tenenbaums* which are used to highlight how out of step with the times the Tenenbaum children are, seemingly caught in a time warp with their fashion choices dating back to several decades prior to the present day.

Booth Tarkington, who was born in Indianapolis, Indiana in 1869 and watched as his small midwestern town grew and modernized into a city, is a nostalgic voice for the turn-of-the-century civility that characterized small-town America before the modernizing forces of urbanization and industrialization. Tarkington begins his novel with a lengthy reminiscence about the disappearance of certain high-class civilities from American culture, capturing this "vanishing" culture in astonishing detail, involving references to changes in clothing styles, hair grooming, social customs, architecture, and, most notably, transportation, with the invention of the automobile. This is also referenced in Welles's film, which provides loving images of the "boot jack," the "stove-pipe" hat, and the changing length of men's overcoats. Tarkington looks back upon this lost culture, particularly the loss of the horse-drawn carriage, with a bittersweet longing:

> The stables have been transformed into other likenesses, or swept away, like the woodsheds where were kept the stove-wood and kindling that the "girl" and the "hired-man" always quarreled over: who should fetch it. Horse and stable and woodshed, and the whole tribe of the "hired-man," all are gone. They went quickly, yet so silently that we whom they served have not yet really noticed that they are vanished. [17]

Tarkington describes other "vanishings," including this passage about the unhurried civility of the mule-drawn streetcar, also reproduced in Welles's film ("In those days they had time for everything"):

> The car was genially accommodating: a lady could whistle to it from an upstairs window, and the car would halt at once and wait for her while she shut the window, put on her hat and cloak, went downstairs, found an umbrella, told

the "girl" what to have for dinner, and came forth from the house. [...] In good weather the mule pulled the car a mile in a little less than twenty minutes, unless the stops were too long; but when the trolley-car came, doing its mile in five minutes and better, it would wait for nobody. Nor could its passengers have endured such a thing, because the faster they were carried the less time they had to spare! In the days before deathly contrivances hustled them through their lives, and when they had no telephones – another ancient vacancy profoundly responsible for leisure – they had time for everything: time to think, to talk, time to read, time to wait for a lady! [18]

There is an essential connection between the writing of Tarkington and the nostalgia portrayed in both films – both Welles and Anderson interact intimately with literary traditions. Tarkington condenses the massive shifts recently undergone within America's national industry, and the related human difficulties, into the arrogance and eventual comeuppance of a single downwardly mobile rich boy, George Amberson-Minafer. George is unable to understand that a great revolution is taking place around him, that the lifestyle he has always known is soon to become anachronistic as people with talent and a little capital will soon surpass him in wealth and prestige. As the Amberson family compound becomes surrounded with factories and apartment buidlings, the bucolic existence of the Amberson family is threatened by mechanical innovation, and the Amberson wealth, frivolity, and upper-crust lifestyle is becoming irrelevant in the face of this fast-paced new urban society.

Similarly, *The Royal Tenenbaums* depicts a New York City as it was, or might have been, in a bygone era steeped in literary history, conjured in the pages of *The New Yorker* magazine by the eccentricities of the literary personalities of Joseph Mitchell, A. J. Liebling, Lillian Ross, J. D. Salinger, John O' Hara, E. B. White, James Thurber, and others. Moss Hart's autobiography *Act One*, as well as Hart and Kaufman themselves are also influences, as are stories by F. Scott Fitzgerald, such as "Babylon Revisted" and "May Day," and the plays and journalism of S. N. Berhman. The film's literary origins and influences are strongly suggested, as noted above, by the opening scene in which an unseen library patron checks out a novel entitled *The Royal Tenenbaums*. Margot, Eli, Raleigh (Bill Murray), Etheline, and Henry Sherman (Danny Glover) are all published authors. The appropriations and misappropriations of language (the Tenenbaums have many words but only in rare moments have honest communication) are also a central focus of the story. Margot as a child reads Anton Chekhov's *The Cherry Orchard* (1904) and Eugene O'Neill's *The Iceman Cometh* (1939), foreshadowing her later career as a playwright (the failed aristocratic family of *The Cherry Orchard* also parallels the Tenenbaums' slow decline, while *The Iceman Cometh* depicts the lives of a group of alcoholics who wish to relive their better days in the past). A little later, Richie reads an *Atlas of the World*, foreshadowing his future travels on the Côte d'Ivoire, while Chas as a child has bound collections of business journals such as *Forbes*. Meanwhile, Eli Cash as a child lives in a run-down two-room apartment with his aunt and sleeps on a fold-out couch, in a building across the street from the Tenenbaum's mansion. On a Tenenbaum family trip to their summer house on Eagle Island (likely a nuanced reference to F. Scott Fitzgerald's West Egg), Eli wears Apache warpaint, foreshadowing his future career as a cowboy professor interested in Custer and The Battle of Little Bighorn. Eli's[19] writing style is a parody of Cormac McCarthy, the Pulitzer Prize-winning author of such books as *No Country for Old Men* (2005) and *Blood Meridian* (1985):

> The crickets and the rust-beetles scuttled among the nettles of the sagethicket. "Vámonos, amigos," he whispered, and threw the busted leather flintcraw over the loose weave of the saddlecock. And they rode on in the friscalating dusklight.[20]

Just as this text is from a non-existent book and uses several invented words, *The Royal Tenenbaums* uses inventive interplay with existing and fictional literary works to conjure the ambience of a faded past. Through *The Royal Tenenbaums* screenplay's intertextuality with literary works from the past, Anderson and Wilson capture evocative eras of American history, and the evanescent world of various "vanished" pasts in New York City. A greater range of these literary sources will be explored further in the chapter.

The Use of Language in The Royal Tenenbaums

Anderson brings out some unique aspects of language in his screenplay for *The Royal Tenenbaums*. First, while the language is elevated, seemingly borrowed from a bygone, arcanely bookish era ("You've made a cuckold of me"[21]), there is the mixture of high and low culture, of genteel expressions mixed with more casual – or even vulgar – language rooted in popular idiom, that makes the film so strikingly unique (for example, when Royal says jauntily: "Well, we can swing by her grave, too"[22]). In particular, language offers a hint of what Etheline sees in Royal that drew them together in the first place, in a moment in the screenplay when the two of them really talk honestly to each other. When Etheline asks Royal why he was never really committed to the family, and why he didn't help her raise their children, Royal admits he is ashamed of himself, and adds, "I'll tell you one thing, though. You've got more grit, and fire, and guts than any woman I've ever known ... You're true blue, Ethel."[23] Etheline laughs, and Royal asks her what is funny. She replies, "Nothing. Just these little expressions of yours."[24] This brief exchange makes it clear that Etheline at one time was in love with Royal's wild and unpredictable nature, which is so different from her own character. He uses language in a rough-shod, arrogant, humorous way that she finds attractive.

Another unusual use of language in the film is the parodic use of medical or legal professional jargon for comic effect. In the scene where Royal pretends to be dying of stomach cancer in a hospice bed in the Tenenbaum mansion, in the original screenplay this is paired with the comic visual effect (paying homage to Marx-brothers-type movies) where Royal's pretend doctor, Dusty (Seymour Cassel), is dressed in a white lab coat and elevator operator pants with a red stripe down the side – in actuality, anyone can see he is not a real doctor, but this humorously escapes the notice of his family, who watch in silence as Dusty takes Royal's pulse. His medical advice has the right pedantic tone: "His condition is stable. The attack was just a side effect. I recommend that you push fluids and continue the stomach cancer medication,"[25] and insists that Royal absolutely cannot be moved. When Chas asks if his father is going to be all right, Dusty (as the doctor) replies, "That depends. Is he a fighter?"[26] Again, this is a parodic imitation of medical scenes in movies, a tired cliché made funny by its use by Dusty in the scene. The ruse of Royal Tenenbaum's fake illness becomes genuinely moving due to the sincere concern of his children; at the same time, because of the privileged viewpoint of the viewer, coupled with the fact that the fake doctor's play-acting is so baldly apparent, it is also absurd. This is one of numerous examples of Anderson spoofing stodgy professionalism, or robbing a potentially serious moment of its gravitas. Anderson deliberately throws absurdity into painful situations and fakery into very real pain, serving as a jarring reminder to viewers that reality is many-layered, and real life is rarely as simple and one-dimensional as film clichés tend to make it look.

A second example of this comic use of professional-level jargon is the scene in which Henry proposes to Etheline, using tax codes and legalities as a warm-up to his proposal:

> Apropos of my question re: I-40 slash I-9 adjustments ... it would probably be advantageous for your marital status to be legally established as single, in light of the circumstances.[27]

Henry continues to insist that he is making this suggestion that Etheline be legally divorced for tax purposes, while, at the same time, Etheline is recognizing that Henry is referring to something deeper than a tax issue. Henry is proposing marriage in the language that is most comfortable and natural for him to use: the legalese of taxation law. Later in the film, after Eli has crashed his car into the Tenenbaum mansion, Henry is also the one who assesses the damage from a legal perspective. When his son Walter notes: "But these aren't structure-bearing elements, Dad," Henry replies, "It doesn't matter. It's still best to file it under force majeure and recoup the deductible."[28] Henry's consistent use of legal terminology shows his character to be quite opposite to Royal's – he is a law-abiding, honest citizen. Henry is also the one who calls out Royal for faking his stomach cancer: in a bittersweet twist, it is revealed that Henry's wife died from the same disease. In a final example, legalese is used when Royal formally offers to sign the divorce papers with Etheline as a gift to her, to free her to marry Henry: "If you'll just sign here, please, Ethel ... And here ... And initial here."[29] Here, as in other memorable moments in his films, Anderson deflects the sharpest, most painful emotional punch through the incongruity of using formal language in an emotional situation. He uses the elements of comic language and heavy cliché to help soften the experience of his characters' suffering.

Another creative use of language in *The Royal Tenenbaums* screenplay is the British English used to comic effect in the speech of Raleigh St. Clair (even the name is deliberately elitist-sounding), originally scripted to be an Oliver Sacks–like neurologist in the film. Raleigh has written a book entitled *The Peculiar Neurodegenerative Inhabitants of the Kazawa Atoll*, and he is researching a fictional disease called "Heinsbergen Syndrome" (marked by "amnesia dyslexia, color blindness, and a highly acute sense of hearing"[30]) through his young test subject, Dudley (Stephen Lea Sheppard). Raleigh St. Clair's character was originally written to have an English accent with a lisp to provide yet another intentionally humorous effect – his Britishisms make him sound stuffy and removed from the other characters; he is an outsider. For example, when the private detective asks Raleigh and Richie if they would like to examine the report of Margot's clandestine affairs, Raleigh replies with genteel British reserve: "We would, rather. Yes."[31] This is matched by Raleigh's question to Margot as she is moving out of their home and relocating to the house on Archer Avenue: "But why is this bloody necessary?"[32] In another example of accented English used for comic purposes, the use of Indian-accented English by the character Pagoda in this film is a device employed by Anderson to again provide a humorous, softening effect to dull the edge of painful truths, such as when Pagoda says, "He has the cancer,"[33] or this exchange after Royal is kicked out of the family and must rent a room at the 375th Street Y:

Royal: How much money you got?
Pagoda: I don't have.[34]

The most potentially controversial use of language in the screenplay is the scene where Royal taunts Henry by saying he is going to "talk jive." The humor here is supposed to come from the fact that Royal doesn't know how talk jive, and in fact says and does things that are ridiculous and make no sense. He acts completely childish in this scene, showing how offensive and annoying he can be. Such behavior is common to many of Anderson's works, where the characters demean themselves by descending into childish language, or silly taunting. This is also an instance of Royal, being exceptionally manipulative and very cagey, improvising a racial "slur" to try to get a rise out of Henry. Wes Anderson carefully sidesteps the charged issue by having Royal be obnoxious with a made-up slur that sounds offensive but really is not (and which later Royal denies having said at all, in a childishly awkward exchange).[35]

In many of the Tenenbaums' conversations, no meaning at all is exchanged – there is a distinct lack of content, of self-revelation. For example, when Raleigh directly asks Margot if she doesn't love him anymore, she replies, "I do, kind of. I can't explain it right now."[36] Later, when he asks her if she is seeing someone else, she parries with this response: "I couldn't begin to even think about knowing how to answer that question."[37] In both of the conversations, the answer given by Margot is so unclear as to be practically meaningless; Raleigh is no more enlightened than he was before he asked the question. Throughout the film, characters talk from behind windows, stand still with their backs to one another, speak on the staircase from different floors of the house, and discuss failed romance while on two different overhead footbridges, all the while demonstrating the chasms between them. Characters walk out of the room in anger, slamming the door behind them; characters are walled off in tents, hidden behind clothes in closets, and literally disappearing over walls. Margot, the most secretive of all the characters (for example, lying about and concealing her smoking habit for 22 years) is often removed from the family in spatial arrangements; she lingers in doorways. There are African masks on the walls, often shown surrounding Margot. Her dark eyeshadow in some ways resembles a mask, giving her an inscrutable expression. Similarly, Richie wears sunglasses almost constantly, which is especially noticeable indoors. Chas snaps off the light in the closet where he and Royal are speaking, and walks out, leaving his father alone in the dark. In another scene, Chas switches the lights off on Royal while he is reading. When Etheline and Henry lean toward one another for a hug at the hospital, Dudley quickly snaps down his flip sunglasses, shutting himself off from them. Very little is communicated in conversations – the film is less about what is said than about what is communicated through silence. Words are few, and those that are used are chosen deliberately and carefully, but their meaning somehow gets obfuscated. Sometimes, the dialogue expresses directly how futile and meaningless their attempts to communicate are, such as this exchange between Richie and Eli:

> Eli: What'd you say?
> Richie: (*pause*) Hm?
> Eli: What?
> Richie: I didn't say anything.
> Eli: When? Right now? (*pause*) I'm sorry. Don't listen to me. (*barely audible*) I'm on mescaline. I've been spaced out all day.
> (*Eli pours himself another glass of wine.*)
> Richie: Did you say you're on mescaline?
> Eli: (*nods*) I did, indeed. Very much so.[38]

In this conversation, Richie and Eli are both searching for answers and explanations from one another, but their communication is barely coherent – Eli even says "Don't listen to me." This lack of communication is taken to its extreme in Richie's suicide note, which he writes after his suicide attempt (thus, if he had succeeded in killing himself, there would have been no words left in explanation), and then refuses to let anyone read.

An important aspect of *The Royal Tenenbaums* is the idea of public versus private personas, and the representation of people's fame, through headstones (Royal orders a headstone with false information on it for his epitaph, to give himself a noble, heroic death), magazine articles (Richie's meltdown on the tennis court captured on a magazine cover rendered to look like *Sports Illustrated*), television interviews (Eli is interviewed on a talk show in which he brags that he grew up with the Tenenbaum family and, by this close association with them, he vicariously enjoys their glory, whereupon the interviewer points out that the Tenenbaum family is not what it once was, that the fame and glamour of the Tenenbaums is a relic of the past), plaques, trophies, framed posters, even the stuffed and mounted javelina head that Royal hangs boastfully over the grand staircase. The characters in the film are shown reading each other's books: Richie reads *Three Plays by Margot Tenenbaum*, Etheline reads a Sunday magazine cover story on Eli entitled "Where the Wild Things Are," and Margot reads

Henry's book *Accounting for Everything*. Presumably the characters can come to a deeper understanding of one another through reading each other's books. Richie's public renown for his former greatness is evident in the film; he is constantly being recognized and greeted as "the Baumer" from his glory days as a star athlete; he is asked to pose for pictures with strangers, and others call to him fondly in recognition of who he once was. Similarly, Eli is repeatedly asked for autographs for his novel, and a police inspector who is questioning Eli interrupts his interrogation to say, "I love your work."[39] These public recognitions of greatness contrast sharply with the reality of Richie's depressive suicide attempt, Eli's serious drug addiction, and, of course, Royal's true identity as a former felon who is now jobless and broke. Margot discusses the word "genius" saying she doesn't use that word lightly, and later, when Royal points out Margot's identity as a genius, Margot insists she wasn't, while Royal reminds her that "people" said she was.

The Significance of Animals and Plants in The Royal Tenenbaums

The Royal Tenenbaums is the first Wes Anderson film to give a central role to animals in the narrative, a subject explored in C. Ryan Knight's 2014 article "'Who's to Say?': The Role of Pets in Wes Anderson's Films," in which Knight's central argument is that the pets in Anderson's films move the characters forward on their journeys toward maturity, and help bring them back into community.[40] In *Rushmore*, the only animals to appear in the film were two dogs, Nicholas and Copernicus, belonging to the headmaster, Dr. Guggenheim (Brian Cox), and they were limited to brief appearances (Knight also counts Miss Cross's classroom fish as pets, expressing how they bring Max and Miss Cross together, and how Max increases their number by buying more fish for Miss Cross as a gift). *The Royal Tenenbaums* is a story primarily about a family, and about childhood; thus, the childhood pets have a strong psychological presence in the film. The film's most significant pets are Buckley, an aging beagle, Mordecai, the falcon kept in a coop on the roof by the young Richie, and Sparkplug, the Dalmatian bought by Royal, as well as an unnamed pet turtle belonging to Ari and Uzi. Buckley[41] is first introduced during the grievously poor fire drill practice, when Chas, who has become obsessed with safety issues since his wife died, has his young sons practice vacating their apartment as quickly as possible in preparation for a possible emergency. In the haste of the fire drill, Buckley is left behind, forgotten in the terror of the moment, sleeping on his plaid dog-bed pillow with his name monogrammed on it. Buckley is given a detailed physical description in the screenplay, characterized as looking very old (presumably he was the family dog before the boys were even born) with white fur around his eyes, and a wheezy breathing pattern. Throughout the film, Buckley troops gamely along on his leash, going wherever the family goes, but it is clear that his days are numbered – according to the screenplay, he often has a cold and a cough.[42] The idea of holding on to this beloved family pet as he ages is a tender point – Buckley represents the former happy times when Chas's wife Rachael was still living, a memory of an intact family. No one is willing to break that up, even though the dog is clearly showing signs of strain.

Another pet that is repeatedly mentioned in the screenplay is Ari and Uzi's pet turtle. This pet is first mentioned in the initial description of Ari and Uzi's bedroom:

> It is perfectly neat and organized like a military barracks. There are night lights in every socket. There are two fire extinguishers and a large first-aid kit mounted on the wall. There is a turtle in a fish tank in the corner. Ari and Uzi are sound asleep in their bunk beds.[43]

Although when the film was made, this scene was not filmed as described in the screenplay (one of the main differences being that the boys sleep in separate bedrooms in their apartment in the film), from this description, it is clear that Chas's obsessive need to control his life, and to limit the likelihood of future accidents like the plane crash that killed his wife, has driven him to organize and control his boys' lives in a stifling and unhealthy way. Chas has a neurotic need to keep the boys safe – psychologically, he is unable to handle any possible risk or danger. The one concession to normalcy seems to be the presence, in the boys' room, of the pet turtle. During the fire drill, Ari grabs the turtle out of the aquarium and carries it down to the street outside their building, "rescuing" it from the fire. When the boys move with their father back into his family home on Archer Avenue, the turtle in its tank is one of the items highlighted in the screenplay: "Pagoda carries the fish tank with the turtle in it. Buckley follows them."[44] The boys are uncomfortable away from home, and feeling unsettled, so their father has brought their pets along to help them feel a sense of normalcy in the chaotic circumstances of the move.

The falcon raised by Richie as a pet, named Mordecai (an interesting name choice, "Mordecai" is the name of a heroic Jewish man who averts a holocaust in the Old Testament Book of Esther), is also a powerful symbol in the film. When the child Richie is struggling with his grief after his parents announce their separation, Richie sets the bird free. He takes the falcon to the edge of the roof, and urges it to fly freely, symbolizing Richie's despair: Richie is pushing away one of his most treasured friends, his beloved pet. The bird flies away into the sky, representing Richie's deep loss. Later on, when Richie returns to his parental home as an adult, he lets the bird go (the narrator explains that Richie no longer feels that birds should be kept in cages) presumably forever, irretrievably lost. Later in the screenplay, when Richie experiences a kind of restoration through a healing conversation with his father on the hotel roof, the bird suddenly returns to him. It is a wonderful cliché, yet still moving even for being so heavy-handed; but then Richie interrupts the moment to say that he is not sure this bird is Mordecai, because his neck feathers look different. Royal tries to reassure him that this bird is the same bird, that it just looks different because it is molting, but Richie does not seem completely convinced. This is the kind of ambivalent reality that Anderson tends to highlight in his films – neither the characters nor the viewer can be absolutely certain. When Richie says "I'm not so sure this is Mordecai,"[45] this is significant because it does not have to be Mordecai – Anderson's point is that there is no need for it to be exactly the same bird. The bird that "returns" does not have to be Mordecai because, in fact, since everyone has gotten older, and since everything has changed and all the relationships among the characters are being reconfigured, the bird can be a different bird; this also means that it is all right for Richie to change – he can be both "the same" and also be changed permanently. This unresolved ambivalence over Mordecai highlights one of the central themes of the film, which is that each of the adult children of the Tenebaum family must come to terms with the fact that they are not what they once were.

The accident that happens to Buckley, when Eli's careening car hits and kills the dog, is wholly unexpected, making it one of the most climactic moments in the film, and ultimately leading to a catharsis for the characters, because it brings a psychological release. Chas had been "stuck" in his grief, and his crazed anger at Eli after the accident helps him to realize that he needs to stop trying to be so isolated and alone in his grief. In a way, the death of the dog symbolizes that Chas, Ari, and Uzi, can finally let go of the past and properly grieve the loss of their wife and mother. The elderly, hobbled, wheezing dog had represented the grief that Chas would not share and couldn't let go – this scene demonstrates how much he needed to do so. After the dog is killed, Royal has a funeral for Buckley in the backyard. The narrator's voice suddenly comes back into the film after a long hiatus, indicating the film's denouement, pointing out that it is Royal who dug the hole for Buckley, in his ongoing efforts to set things right with his family. Royal is also the one who purchases a new dog for the family, a fireman's Dalmatian named Sparkplug. This process of burial (Buckley, representing the past), and renewal (the new dog, whose name, "Sparkplug," also indicates a sign of reinvigorated life) represents Royal's own journey as he has learned how to be a better, more personally invested member of the family. It is significant, too, that the family's adoption of a Dalmatian has ties to Chas's childhood invention, the Dalmatian mice. This continuity reflects the new forgiveness and understanding between Chas and his father.

Finally, the presence of the Japanese bonsai trees in the scene where Chas and Eli admit they both need help (after Buckley is killed) is heavily symbolic. The bonsai is representative of longevity, for the tree, if properly cared for, can live for hundreds of years, outlasting many generations of a family; also, the bonsai tree is often handed down as a living legacy of beauty from generation to generation. The bonsai is also a symbol of peace and harmony, and of old age achieved after weathering the storms of life; this is the harmony so desperately lacking in the Tenenbaum family. The bonsai's heavy-handed symbolism is a gentle touch of humor in this scene, for the symbolism of the bonsai has been a staple in the American consciousness since *The Karate Kid* films of the 1980s (1984, 1986, and 1989), in which Mr. Miyagi (Pat Morita) uses the pruning of a bonsai tree to pass on wisdom to his pupil, Daniel Russo (Ralph Macchio). Another notable use of a plant by Anderson is the scene in *Rushmore* in which Max carries Margaret's plant out to put on his mother's grave, symbolizing the connection between Margaret and Max's mother, who both understand Max intuitively. At first, Max is resistant to what Margaret offers, but his acceptance of this gift represents a new beginning and a way out of his despair, motivating him to jump the fence between his home and the graveyard bordering it, in order to visit his mother's grave and reconnect with his past, which ultimately brings him new life as well.

Other Literary References in The Royal Tenenbaums

Like *Bottle Rocket* and *Rushmore*, the screenplay of *Royal Tenenbaums* is influenced by both the subject matter and tone of J.D. Salinger's writings, particularly *The Catcher in the Rye, Nine Stories, Franny and Zooey*, and *Raise High the Roof Beam, Carpenters/ Seymour: An Introduction*. Both the film – and the Glass family stories – are about child prodigies who find it difficult to adjust to adult life. Beatrice "Boo Boo" Glass, who is the central character in "Down at the Dinghy" in *Nine Stories*, takes the name of her husband, Tannenbaum, setting up the connection that the New York-based Glass family was a source of inspiration for the Tenenbaum family. Another specific parallel is in Salinger's *Franny and Zooey*, in which a character lies in the bathtub, smoking, for an extended period. However, this is Zooey, who is male. Similar to *The Royal Tenenbaums*, the Glass family children also are unusually talented: the seven precocious Glass children become famous for their participation in a television game show for child geniuses called "It's a Wise Child." This early promise ends as the children grow up; similar to Anderson's sadly comic vision of adult siblings who share a sort of social deficiency, the Glass children are so smart and well-read, and such deep thinkers, that they have trouble fitting in with ordinary people. In the Glass family, the ever-looming scandal is a suicide: the oldest sibling, Seymour, eventually takes his own life. "A Perfect Day for Bananafish" (included in *Nine Stories*) describes the event, which comes at the very end of the story and is described ambiguously.

The connection between Salinger's *Franny and Zooey* and *The Royal Tenenbaums* is made quite clearly in the opening section entitled "Franny," in which Salinger's Franny Glass descends from a train to meet her college boyfriend, Lane, for a weekend Yale football game. The scene where Margot descends from the Green Line bus seems to be at least partially inspired by Salinger's writing.

> Franny was among the first of the girls to get off the train, from a car at the far northern end of the platform. Lane spotted her immediately, and despite whatever it was he was trying to do with his face, his arm that shot up into the air was the whole truth. Franny saw him, and waved extravagantly back. She was wearing a sheared raccoon coat, and Lane, walking toward her quickly but with a slow face, reasoned to himself, with suppressed excitement, that he was the only one on the platform who really *knew* Franny's coat. He remembered that once, in a borrowed car, after kissing Franny for a half hour or so, he had kissed her coat lapel, as though it were a perfectly desirable, organic extension of the person herself.[46]

Like Franny, Margot is dressed in a fur coat, which seems like an organic extension of her – she has been wearing a fur coat since she began smoking at the age of twelve, as is seen in a flashback. Franny also smokes incessantly. The following description of Franny could easily be a description of Margot as well:

There were half circles under her eyes, and other, subtler signs that mark an acutely troubled young girl, but nonetheless no one could have missed seeing that she was a first-class beauty. Her skin was lovely, and her features were delicate and most distinctive.[47]

The circles under Margot's eyes are achieved through her kohl eyeliner, while the effect of the heavy makeup accentuates Gwyneth Paltrow's pale skin and fine features, matching the look of Franny as described by Salinger. After Franny and Lane hail a cab and begin heading to a fashionable restaurant, there is a further example of intertextuality between the novel and screenplay, this time echoing a similarity to what Franny says to Lane:

"I've missed you." The words were no sooner out than she realized that she didn't mean them at all.[48]

This line is quite similar to the line of Royal's after he is kicked out of the Tenenbaum house, where Royal says: "The last six days have been, probably, the best six days of my life." The Narrator then echoes Salinger's prose by saying "Immediately after making this statement, Royal realized it was true."[49] Comparing these lines from *Franny and Zooey* with Anderson's film calls attention to the distinct intertextuality between Salinger's writing and Anderson's vision for *The Royal Tenenbaums*, demonstrating that Salinger's writing shares the same overall tone and style as Anderson's film.

The scene where Margot and Richie run away to the Public Archives is a direct reference to E. L. Konigsburg's *From the Mixed-Up Files of Mrs. Basil E. Frankweiler* (1967), which merits further examination because of its tonal and thematic similarities with *The Royal Tenenbaums*. With her mischievous and wise heroine, six-grader Claudia Kincaid, who runs away from home with her nine-year-old brother Jamie, Konigsburg paints a glorious picture of Manhattan through the eyes of two child runaways. Claudia's voice is unusually precocious, like that of the Tenenbaum children:

Claudia knew that she could never pull off the old-fashioned kind of running away. That is, running away in the heat of anger with a knapsack on her back. She didn't like discomfort; even picnics were untidy and inconvenient: all those insects and sun melting the icing on the cupcakes. Therefore, she decided that her leaving home would not be just running from somewhere but would be running to somewhere. To a large place, a comfortable place, an indoor place, and preferably a beautiful place. And that's why she decided upon the Metropolitan Museum of Art in New York City.[50]

Claudia Kincaid is a young sophisticate, planning her journey with expertise, and judiciously selecting her younger brother as a traveling companion because he is better at saving money. After hiding in their school bus, and making a train commute (its price is equivalent to the cost of three weeks' worth of hot fudge sundaes), with their clothes stuffed into their violin and trumpet cases, they take advantage of the museum's free admission, and their adventures begin. Each night, when the museum guards lock up for the day, they hide in bathroom stalls, only coming out when they are certain it is safe. At night, when the museum empties, Claudia and Jamie have the run of the place, playing and sleeping among antiques and paintings. They hide Claudia's violin case in a sarcophagus, make an "income" from the wishing coins in the museum fountain, where they also bathe among dolphins sculpted in bronze, drying themselves with paper towels from the museum's bathrooms. The two have the good sense to join school tours, and generally revel in the exhibitions, marveling at the treasures around them, and ultimately solving a mystery involving a statue by Michelangelo.

Claudia and Jamie spend the first day deciding which antique display to sleep in, and they finally choose one in the English Renaissance Hall, a sixteenth-century, ornately-carved canopy bed, which makes Claudia feel like royalty:

> She lay there in the great quiet of the museum next to the warm quiet of her brother and allowed the soft stillness to settle around them: a comforter of quiet. The silence seeped from their heads to their soles and into their souls. They stretched out and relaxed. Instead of oxygen and stress, Claudia thought now of hushed and quiet words: glide, fur, banana, peace. Even the footsteps of the night watchman added only an accented quarter-note to the silence that had become a hum, a lullaby.[51]

This scene echoes the episode in *The Royal Tenenbaums* where Margot and Richie run away to African Wing of the Public Archives, and Margot reads *The Sharks of North American Waters* by flashlight while Richie sleeps on his camp-out sleeping bag at her side – they sleep under a viewing bench while a janitor tidies up within a few meters of them. Margot's reason for running away is not articulated in the film, while Konigsburg notes that Claudia's boredom drove her from her home and family: she is bored being "straight-A's Claudia Kincaid," bored with arguing about whose turn it is to choose the Sunday night television show, and tired of the monotony of everything. Margot, like Claudia, is a precocious child who is bored within the confines of her childhood, and she uses her theater interests to escape from the monotony of her daily life. However, when she produces her first play, for her eleventh birthday party, her father criticizes the play for not being "believable." The play, with Margot, Richie and Chas dressed as a zebra, a leopard, and a bear on a set that looks like an ocean liner (a play about animals on a boat lightly connects to the Noah story dramatized by Benjamin Britten that would later figure prominently in *Moonrise Kingdom*), is criticized by Royal for not having well-developed characters but instead just children dressed up in animal costumes.

These scenes are seminal to the meaning of Richie's suicide attempt, his self-inflicted wounds foreshadowed by his smashing his hand through a window in Mordecai's roof cage when he hears about Margot's affair. While the rest of the film uses "warm" color tones, especially pink, to evoke the "rose-colored glasses" of memory, Richie's suicide attempt is shot in icy blue. Richie enters the bathroom at Raleigh's house, and begins to shear off his hair and shave his beard, representing that the character, who was previously hidden behind dark sunglasses, a thick beard, and a long 70s-style Bjorn Borg hairstyle, has essentially stripped himself naked, baring himself physically and psychologically, wishing to make a complete break with the past; meanwhile Elliot Smith's "Needle in the Hay," which has already been playing in the previous scene, grows louder on the soundtrack. Looking straight into the camera/mirror, Richie whispers "I'm going to kill myself tomorrow."[52] (In Louis Malle's film *Le Feu follet*, where this line originated, the main character Alain Leroy finishes reading *The Great Gatsby* to the last page just before taking his life.) Richie's hands are shown as he removes the blade from the razor. The next six seconds is a rapid montage of eighteen images, many of them representing significant moments from Richie's life. There is now also a faint, atonal hum, and Anderson explains on the DVD commentary that this humming montage was a "flashback in [Richie's] mind, kind of an electrical thing."

At the beginning of the montage, there are several shots of Mordecai, with and without his blinder on, standing in for Richie (the shots show their heads deliberately lined up in similar positions). Following that, there are the two most significant images: Margot descending from the Green Line bus, and Mordecai, approaching from afar, against an empty gray sky. These are the two images repeated again and again throughout the montage, interspersed with shots from Richie's memories, almost all of which feature Margot: a shot of Royal sitting at the head of the dining room table, from the moment in the introduction when he informs the children that he and their mother are separating; a shot of a smiling young Richie, standing in front of a school bus, when he and Margot ran away to the Public Archives; a shot of the young Margot standing on the steps of the Public Archives and taking a picture; and a shot of young Margot and Richie sharing a sleeping bag under the bench in the Public Archives. The everpresent "hum" builds in volume and turns into more of a burning sound, which matches the next shot of Etheline holding a cake with lit candles at Margot's eleventh birthday, on the night of Margot's debut as a playwright, the last time that Royal was invited to the house. Finally, the last image of the six-second sequence is of Margot again, the longest take (at one full second) of her leaving the bus. It is significant that Richie does not have a flashback to his defeat at the U.S. Nationals; instead, his pain is bound up intricately with Margot's pain. Richie's suicide attempt also connects to Salinger's Glass family, where Seymour's suicide is a defining event in the family; likewise, Richie's attempted suicide ultimately brings more unity and clarity to the family.

Music in The Royal Tenenbaums

The soundtrack of *The Royal Tenenbaums* is often singled out as an integral part of the film, with a marriage of music and image that borders on the sublime, and that has even been called "absolution"[53] by Carol Lyn Piechota in a 2006 article analyzing the grace-giving aspects of the film's songs. Once again used here as it was in *Rushmore*, the music of Vince Guaraldi ("Christmastime Is Here") from *A Charlie Brown Christmas* provides a melancholy theme strongly associated with the depressive Margot, especially in the final reconciliation scene between Margot and Royal in the ornate ice cream

The scene where Richie Tenenbaum observes Margot (Gwyneth Paltrow) stepping off the Green Line bus was one of the few scenes Anderson had written down in a notebook a number of years before he even wrote the screenplay.

parlor, which is filled with other tables of daughters out on dates with their dads. The use of selections from "A Charlie Brown Christmas" also brings to mind those Charles M. Schulz "Peanuts" children whose parents never appear in the comic strip, and who wear the same outfits every day, outfits that have come to be associated with each child's persona, just as they are in Anderson's film (for example, Richie's Bjorn Borg headband, and Margot's Lacoste dress and penny loafers). Here again, as in *Rushmore*, there is a selection of musical cues from the 1960s and 1970s, especially Mark Mothersbaugh's cover of the Beatles' "Hey Jude," which plays throughout the opening sequence of the film.[54] Because "Hey Jude" is known to have been written by Paul McCartney for John Lennon's son Julian to help him deal with his parents' (John and Cynthia Lennon's) divorce, the song has special resonance as it is played when the Tenenbaum children react to their own parents' divorce.

Another notable selection from the film is Nico's cover of Jackson Browne's "These Days" which memorably accompanies the iconic scene of Margot (who strongly resembles Nico) descending from the Green Line bus and walking toward Richie. Browne's lyrics reflect the fear of missed opportunities, with an equally heavy fear of taking risks: taking a lover, dreaming of the future, or even simply sharing and connecting with someone else. Nico's voice perfectly captures Margot's self-isolation through its jaded, world-weary tone, and icy, mannered, lower-register vocals (Nico's German accent and slightly atonal singing also contribute to the alienated feeling of the song, which sounds almost as if it were sung underwater, the intensity of the emotion suggesting someone "drowning" in depression). This song contains lyrics about not wishing to be reminded of one's mistakes, which reflects Margot's desire to cleanse herself (represented by her long, depressive soaks in the bathtub) and free herself from the past. While the three titles of Margot's early plays all include sexual references, *Nakedness Tonight*, *Erotic Transference*, and *Static Electricity*, the play that Margot writes at the end of the film, *The Levinsons in the Trees*, is instead a thinly-veiled autobiographical account of her family life, indicating that she is now able to face and deal with her past, and move forward onto new possibilities.

In addition to these pieces, selections of classical music are used by Anderson in this film for the first time in his work. Notable among them are selections by Maurice Ravel, Antonio Vivaldi, Erik Satie, and twentieth-century classical composer George Enescu. The string quartet by Ravel is significant because Anderson has stated that listening to Ravel's "String Quartet in F Major" after a chance purchase of a Ravel CD in college was the catalyst that inspired the film in its earliest idea stage. Anderson reportedly fantasized about "an F. Scott Fitzgerald-type New York story"[55] to be likely set in the 1960s. The second movement of the Ravel piece is used in the film's early display of the actor's credits. The Rolling Stones are again used to great effect in this film: especially evocative of Margot's hidden depths are the songs "She Smiled Sweetly" and "Ruby Tuesday," which she plays on a record player in the tent scene with Richie. Finally, the film contains a memorable use of Elliott Smith's "Needle in the Hay," which hauntingly accompanies Richie's suicide attempt. In a widely reported historical connection, the composer Elliott Smith, long troubled by addiction and depression, committed suicide by stabbing himself in early 2004, three years after the film's release. "Fly" by Nick Drake is used in the scene after Richie leaves the hospital.[56]

The Father/The Denouement

Toward the end of *The Royal Tenenbaums*, Royal offers counsel to Richie on the roof of the Lindbergh Hotel (during which Mordecai returns, thus tying together the main images from the suicide montage), that he later acts on by confessing his feelings to Margot. This event is what truly starts to bring the family together. Royal is notably the only person in the audience laughing with pleasure at the performance of Margot's new play, reflecting a reconciliation and a new understanding between them. Chas also forgives Royal, and is the last person to see Royal alive when he rides in the ambulance taking Royal to the hospital after a heart attack. Thus Royal is given a sympathetic end in the film.

Yet as Stella Bruzzi has demonstrated in the book *Bringing Up Daddy* (2005), an ambivalence toward the father has been a recurring theme in many contemporary Hollywood films. Chris Robé (2012) explores this further in an analysis of masculinity and the crisis of the patriarch in all of Anderson's films, including *The Royal Tenenbaums*:

> What distinguished Anderson's films from the rest is their consistent emphasis on this ambiguity [toward the role of the father] without ultimately resolving into a pro or con stance. They identify the complex cultural matrices that surround twenty-first-century entitled masculinity and the traditional father, exposing how even within their critiques an aura of nostalgia slips through.[57]

Robé points out the irony in this clichéd World War II epitaph shown on Royal's tombstone in the final shot of the film:

> Royal O'Reilly Tenenbaum
> died tragically rescuing his
> family from the wreckage of a
> destroyed sinking battleship [58]

According to Robé, this honorable epitaph rings hollow because Royal was known to be a bad father who inflicted suffering on his family. However, the epitaph also has an element of truth to it: the "wreckage of the destroyed sinking battleship" was the state of the family as it imploded after the parents' divorce, but ultimately Royal earns a kind of redemptive honor because, as the film's denouement shows, he did bring his family together, rescuing them from psychological wreckage and loneliness. In addition, there is a kernel of truth to the epitaph at the meta-nostalgic level: the viewer may recollect that Royal's epitaph is a nod to *The Poseidon Adventure* (1972) in which Gene Hackman's character does indeed die tragically saving a group of passengers from a sinking ship.

The Royal Tenenbaums is a complex film because it works simultaneously on many narrative levels. Royal's epitaph, representing a story wrapped in nostalgia that makes it both true and not true, reflects the larger structure of the film, which is based on a book that does not exist, and told by a narrator who may not be entirely reliable, using locations that are entirely invented (the Lindbergh Palace Hotel, or the 375th Street Y) to represent a New York that may never have existed, or exists only in memory. Anderson deliberately avoided including recognizable landmarks, at one point having Kumar Pallana stand directly in front of the Statue of Liberty to block it in the background of a scene he was filming with Gene Hackman. Moreover, the city's name of "New York" is not mentioned once throughout the film. Just as Royal's epitaph describes a fictional event of invented heroism, all the New York locations in the film (e.g. Archer Avenue) are inventions, which is in line with the contention that the film is an echo of the now lost literary New York. Anderson was reaching back to a literary New York of the past represented by the writings of Salinger and F. Scott Fitzgerald, deliberately choosing a tone, style, and subject matter that call classic New York authors to mind, but at the same time, he was creating an entirely fictional place of memory and nostalgia, a New York that never really existed.

Notes

1   Anderson, quoted in the DVD director's commentary for *The Royal Tenebaums*. In other filmic homages, the line "I know you, asshole," that Royal screams at Eli Cash as he escapes from the house is the same line that Harrison Ford's character says to Danny Glover's character in the film *Witness* (1985). "Wind's blowin' up a gale today" is an improvised line which Owen Wilson also used in his film *Behind Enemy Lines* (2001).
2   Anderson, quoted in the DVD director's commentary for *The Royal Tenenbaums*.
3   Wes Anderson and Owen Wilson, *The Royal Tenenbaums* (New York: Faber and Faber, 2001), 3.

4   Ibid., 18.
5   Ibid., 8.
6   Ibid., 11.
7   Ibid., 12–13.
8   Derek Hill, *Charlie Kaufman and His Merry Band of Pranksters, Fabulists and Dreamers: An Excursion into the American New Wave* (Harpenden: Kamera Books, 2008), 86.
9   Booth Tarkington, *The Magnificent Ambersons* (New York: Modern Library, 1998), 3.
10 Anderson and Wilson, 2001, 3.
11 Ibid.
12 Ibid., 4.
13 Ibid.
14 Ibid., 83.
15 Ibid., 16.
16 Jennifer Wachtell, Anderson's girlfriend at the time, appears as Rachael in a photograph in a slideshow watched by Chas.
17 Booth Tarkington, *The Magnificent Ambersons* (New York: Modern Library, 1998), 6.
18 Ibid., 6–7
19 The character of Eli Cash is also modelled on 1980s celebrity author Jay McInerney.
20 Anderson and Wilson, 2001, 20–21.
21 Ibid., 113.
22 Ibid., 49.
23 Ibid., 90–91.
24 Ibid., 91.
25 Ibid., 77.
26 Ibid., 78.
27 Ibid., 29.
28 Ibid., 142.
29 Ibid., 131.
30 Ibid., 25.
31 Ibid., 107.
32 Ibid., 39.
33 Ibid., 99.
34 Ibid., 104.
35 Another example of childish language in the film is when Eli tells Margot: "You're in love with Richie. Which is sick and gross." Ibid., 106.
36 Ibid., 39.
37 Ibid., 83.
38 Ibid., 70.
39 Ibid., 141.
40 C. Ryan Knight, "Who's to Say?": The Role of Pets in Wes Anderson's Films," in Peter C. Kunze, ed., *The Films of Wes Anderson: Critical Essays on an Indiewood Icon* (New York: Palgrave Macmillan, 2014), 74.

41 Buckley is named after Wes Anderson's childhood friend, Jeff Buckley. Anderson notes on the director's commentary for *The Royal Tenenbaums* that having Buckley be a beagle was a direct reference to Snoopy of the "Peanuts" comic strip, Wes Anderson, "Director's Commentary," *The Royal Tenenbaums* DVD, 2001.
42 According to Anderson, the production team tried to get it across that Buckley was sick and dying, and they even considered including coughing sounds from the dog (mentioned in the screenplay), but this idea was dropped due to it being too cartoonish. The dog's illness was intended to prepare the audience for the later accident in which Buckley is run over by the car.
43 Anderson and Wilson, 2001, 26.
44 Ibid., 33.
45 Ibid., 125. The falcon used to play Mordecai flew away during the shoot and was held for "ransom" by a New Jersey resident who wanted money to return it, so the crew had to use a different bird for the later scenes in the film. Nevertheless, the line about Mordecai having more white feathers was already in the script, and it was just a coincidence that the replacement bird did.
46 J. D. Salinger, "Franny," in *Franny and Zooey* (New York: Little, Brown, 1961), 6.
47 Ibid., 82.
48 Ibid., 6.
49 Anderson and Wilson, 2001, 101.
50 E. L. Konigsburg, *From the Mixed-up Files of Mrs. Basil E. Frankweiler* (New York: Atheneum, 1967), 5.
51 Ibid., 41.
52 The Malle line from *Le Feu follet* suggests other Malle films that have incest as an element to them, such as *Le Souffle au coeur*, and *Damage* (1992), in which a brother kills himself after being unable to overcome his incestuous love for his sister. The semi-incestuous subplot is also Anderson's nod to director Jean-Pierre Melville's 1950 film *Les Enfants terribles* about a similar relationship between a brother and sister.
53 Carol Lyn Piechota, "Give Me a Second Grace: Music as Absolution in *The Royal Tenenbaums*." *Senses of Cinema*. February, 2006. http://sensesofcinema.com/2006/on-movies-musicians-and-soundtracks/music_tenenbaums (accessed August 17, 2013). "Music often supplants other elements of mise-en-scène in the expression of intense or complicated emotion in Anderson's films. For instance, the most sophisticated articulation of Richie's and Margot's grief and longing are expressed through the lyrical content, instrumentation and associated imagery of three specific songs ... by Nico, Elliott Smith and Nick Drake, respectively."
54 The opening of the film originally used the real version of the Beatles' "Hey Jude" (not the Mark Mothersbaugh version) and the end was originally scored to their *Rubber Soul* track, "I'm Looking Through You" (instead of Van Morrison's "Everyone" which is what was eventually used), but Anderson was unable to procure licensing rights to the Beatles songs, complicated by George Harrison's failing health prior to his death in 2001.

55 Anderson fantasized about using Ravel's quartet in "the scene where Margot is coming off the bus, and the tennis court scene where Richie has his meltdown." Ultimately Anderson used the second movement to accompany the introduction of the lead actors in the nod to Orson Welles's similar cast list at the end of *The Magnificent Ambersons*. Matt Zoller Seitz, "Seitz: 24 Things I Learned While Writing My Book About Wes Anderson," *Vulture*. October 23, 2013b. http://www.vulture.com/2013/10/wes-anderson-collection-24-tidbits-matt-zoller-seitz.html (accessed August 14, 2014).
56 In another historic parallel with the film connected to Richie's suicide attempt, Nick Drake committed suicide in 1974, at the age of 26.
57 Chris Robé, "'Because I Hate Fathers, and I Never Wanted to Be One': Wes Anderson, Entitled Masculinity, and the Crisis of the Patriarch," in Timothy Shary, ed., *Millenial Masculinity: Men in Contemporary American Cinema* (Detroit, MI: Wayne State University Press, 2012), 118.
58 Anderson and Wilson, 2001, 150.

CHAPTER SIX

Opposition and Resolution: The Dissonance of Celebrity in The Life Aquatic with Steve Zissou

> Twenty-seven years ago, I wanted to keep an eye permanently open into the oceans, so I equipped the bow of my new ship *Calypso* with an underwater observation chamber. At that time, I was convinced that the oceans were immense, teeming with life, rich in resources of all kinds; during the long crossings in the Indian Ocean or in the Atlantic, I spent many hours, day and night, looking through my undersea portholes, dreaming of Captain Nemo in the *Nautilus*.[1]
>
> Jacques Cousteau, *The Ocean World*, 1985

When he was still in college at the University of Texas, Wes Anderson wrote a short story based on the life of Jacques Cousteau, fourteen years before the film *The Life Aquatic with Steve Zissou* was made in 2004. The story was just a bare-bones treatment of a male protagonist (who would eventually become Steve Zissou) and the character of his ex-wife (the estranged wife in the film, Eleanor, who would be played by Anjelica Huston), along with a description of the ship, the *Belafonte*, and the story's main setting. Anderson reworked the story obsessively in college, and it was Owen Wilson who goaded him into turning the ever-unfinished story into a screenplay. Anderson was intrigued by the figure of Jacques Cousteau (to whom he dedicated the film), not only because of Cousteau's boundless energy and drive – he had worked with the French Resistance during World War II; he had invented various submersibles; he had built a successful empire on oceanography research – but also because of Cousteau's experience with nearly unprecedented international fame. (Cousteau's lasting fame even affected the film's dedication in the credits; according to Anderson, he simply wanted to dedicate the film to Cousteau, but the wording of the dedication was changed by Cousteau's company to add a disclaimer disavowing any connection to the film: "In memory of Jacques-Yves Cousteau and with gratitude to the Cousteau Society which was not involved in the making of this film.") The character of Zissou was originally supposed to be named "Steve Cousteau," and besides being an oceanographer-documentarian like the fictitious Zissou, Cousteau also had a research vessel named the *Calypso* which, like Zissou's *Belafonte*, had a mini-submarine, a gyrocopter, and a research balloon; Cousteau's crew were similarly costumed in red knit caps and uniforms; and Cousteau's son Philippe was tragically killed in a plane crash while piloting the Cousteau amphibious *Flying Calypso* seaplane.[2] The film was shot in the studios at Cinecittà near Rome where Federico Fellini made many of his most famous films, and it shares its film-within-a-film structure with Fellini's *8½* (1963), along with its portrayal of the lonely helmsman's problems of finding inspiration and financial backing; at the same time, Murray's Zissou is colored with the melancholy of *8½*'s Fellini alter ego Guido Anselmi (Marcello Mastroianni). According to Anderson, Steve Zissou is an amalgamation of Mastroianni's character in *8½*, Cousteau, and Murray himself.[3]

The screenplay by Anderson and Noah Baumbach opens with a description of a film festival showing of one of Zissou's films:

An immense movie palace with gilded carvings and three balconies. It looks like an opera house. The members of the audience excitedly take their seats. They are dressed in black tie and evening clothes. Flashbulbs go off, the lights dim, and a spotlight shines on a dark, thin man with glasses. He says in Italian (subtitled in English):

Festival Director: Ladies and gentlemen, we are very pleased to welcome you to the world premiere of Part 1 of the newest film from a great favorite of ours here at Loquasto, Mr. Steve Zissou. A brief Q and A will immediately follow the screening. Thank you very much.[4]

This scene is self-reflexive since the screening of a world premiere is a common experience for Anderson himself. The film is shown at the fictitious Loquasto Film Festival, and the film's title is displayed as *The Life Aquatic with Steve Zissou: Adventure No. 12, "The Jaguar Shark" (Part 1)*. Interestingly, this is a film about a fictitious film, much the same way *The Royal Tenenbaums* was a film about a fictitious book. However, in both cases, Anderson is also playing off existing tropes, and combining artifice with reality, specifically common or even cliché signifiers for fame such as flashbulbs popping, black tie dress, and elegant premieres at foreign film festivals, in an "Anderson" world where a hit documentary would be shown at an Italian opera house. Anderson would later do this again with the eponymous fictional book in *The Grand Budapest Hotel*, where he conjured a cult of loyal followers for the unnamed "writer" whose bust is on display in the cemetery, and whose followers go to hang a key from the statue in tribute to him. This creation of the atmosphere of devotion to fictitious people or works of art is an Anderson trademark, but specifically Anderson likes to create an atmosphere of reverence that is tastefully done, the recognition of elite tastes rather than mere sensationalism. Through his films, Anderson wishes to explore the meaning of fame and "success" from every angle and in every incarnation. This is the essential question in *The Life Aquatic* and it is this film that allows Anderson his very personal and yet, perhaps for that reason, his most disjointed exploration of this topic.[5]

In the opening scene of the fictitious film "The Jaguar Shark" (shot by Anderson on Ektachrome film to suggest the grainy, dated, highly saturated appearance of an old-fashioned Cousteau-era documentary), Bill Murray's character is introduced as he watches a flock of seagulls flying overhead – representing perhaps the fleetingness of life. This is how Zissou chooses to represent himself on film. As he introduces the topic of the film, the shots are very controlled and static, with Zissou standing stiffly and reading his lines in a rehearsed, pseudo-professorial way. This film is a comment on fame and image, artifice versus reality – the artificial media presence of Steve Zissou versus his true personality, which is revealed to be rather less savory than the respected oceanographer portrayed in "The Jaguar Shark." Past his prime at fifty-two, with waning credibility as an explorer and filmmaker, rusting equipment, marital troubles, and without a hit film in nine years, the character of Steve Zissou is arrogant, controlling, jealous, petty, and self-absorbed – in short, he is marred with all-too-human traits that are masked by his media personality: the filmmaker attempts to control – and even airbrush – his own image. It is revealed that Steve has lost his bearings after the sudden death of his closest friend and business partner, Esteban. Esteban was devoured by what Zissou names a "jaguar shark," and Steve, without money or a plan, sets out on a new project: to exact revenge on the shark that killed his partner. (There is a spiritual connection suggested between the two men; for example, Esteban is a variant on the name Steve, and during the scene outside the film festival, when Zissou touches a T.V. monitor's broadcast of Esteban, a spark flies between Steve and the image of Esteban onscreen. Steve's fate is thus inextricably tied up with his response to Esteban's death, which in some ways represents Steve's own death.)

This film also displays an interesting juxtaposition of sameness and uniformity with difference/otherness. Anderson dresses the members of Team Zissou in costumes that stand out as memorable even among Anderson's usual eclectic costume choices. These costumes are carefully described in Anderson and Baumbach's final draft of the screenplay: "The crew of the *Belafonte* sets to work on-board the ship. They wear pale blue swimsuits with navy stripes down the sides, long-sleeved aquamarine polyester shirts with epaulets and Team Zissou logos on them, and red knitted caps."[6] Yet, although identically dressed in blue uniforms, the crew introduced is from wildly diverse nationalities and backgrounds: for example, Klaus Daimler (Willem Dafoe) from Germany, Vikram Ray (Waris Ahluwalia) from India, Bobby Ogata (Niels Koizumi) from Japan, Pelé dos Santos (Seu Jorge) from Brazil, Vladimir Wolodarsky (Noah Taylor), and the American script girl Anne-Marie Sakowitz (Robyn Cohen). Team Zissou's sound man, Renzo Pietro, is played by the film's actual sound mixer Pawel Wdowczak (who in many scenes is carrying a live microphone to capture real-time audio from each take). Also included in the crew is Matthew Gray Gubler (who previously served as an actual intern of Anderson's), typecast as Intern #1, one of the research vessel's interns from the University of Alaska.

Another aspect of fame is dissected by the audience's reaction to the famous figure. In one of the final questions of the question-and-answer session hosted by the festival director (Antonio Monda) after the film, Zissou is asked about the accident that led to his friend Esteban's death.

> Festival Director: Was it a deliberate choice never to show the jaguar shark?
> Zissou: No, I dropped the camera.
> (*The audience laughs. The director of the festival translates Zissou's answer into Italian, and the audience laughs again.*)
> Zissou: Why are they laughing?[7]

Here there is a touching juxtaposition of Zissou's sincerity with the audience's expectation that he is making a joke. Zissou answers honestly that he dropped the camera. It has already been made clear that this was an event of extreme personal tragedy and the loss of Zissou's best friend, underscored by the dark, sunken look in his eyes and his hollow expression of despair as he watches the film in the premiere audience. When Zissou admits he dropped the camera, he is sharing this information in an unguarded moment – his eyes are devoid of any sarcasm as he answers the question. Yet, the audience interprets his response as a joke, their laughter clearly wounding Zissou.

Another observation about fame that comes directly from Anderson's personal experience is portrayed in a conversation between the hapless Zissou and Antonia Cook (Isabella Blow, described only as "Pale Woman" in the screenplay), the new head of the film commission, who accidentally delivers a backhanded compliment to Zissou as he is exiting the premiere:

> Pale Woman: You must be so excited!
> Zissou: (*distracted*) I hope so. You think it went OK?
> Pale Woman: No. Congratulations. Seriously.
> Zissou: Thanks. I wish it didn't need the seriously, but –
> Pale Woman: Hm? (*suddenly pensive*) Well, I just don't think they knew what to make of it.[8]

This film's tone is diffident, cynical, with a dark humor, and, like the blood spilled in the very opening scenes, visceral. The film is similar to Woody Allen's critical failure *Stardust Memories* (1980), when Allen committed to the screen all the distasteful and paltry aspects of fame, with a seeming hostility toward the critical community and indeed toward the movie-going public. At the age of thirty-five, Anderson seemed too young to be making a film about this subject. Coming off of his first three films, the last two being huge critical successes, and being nominated for awards, he was lampooning his own experiences with fame, but the bitter tone of Zissou's cynicism seemed excessive for a director so young and successful. Anderson intended the film to be darkly comic, but in many scenes it comes across as sour, the biting, cynical humor of an old man who is already washed up. This film is lacking much of the usual hope and sweetness that underscores and "saves" Anderson's films from their own dark topics. This dynamic is demonstrated clearly by the scene where Klaus introduces his nephew, Werner (Leonardo Giovannelli), a ten-year-old blonde German boy wearing lederhosen, and says "Steve, this is my little nephew, Werner. He wanted to meet you."[9] When Zissou starts to give the boy a lackluster greeting, Werner surprises him by offering him a present – a rainbow-colored seahorse ("crayon pony-fish") in a plastic bag. Zissou is visibly moved by this kindness. The presence of the child, and the kind, innocent gesture of warmth he provides by offering Zissou an unexpected gift, stands in sharp contrast with the slick deal-making and one-upmanship that is going on with various attempts at fundraising and networking following the premiere, as well as the somewhat seedy confrontation between Zissou's African lover and his present wife, Eleanor. Anderson's use of children in his films has always brought softness and equilibrium to the darkness and harshness of the adult word. Anderson uses the sincerity of childhood to balance the phoniness of the adult world, similar again to the writings of J. D. Salinger.

On the same evening, at the premiere's after-party, Steve is suddenly visited by Ned Plimpton (Owen Wilson), a genteel southern pilot for Air Kentucky (he wears a Colonel Sanders-type black string tie and speaks with a Civil War-era southern accent), who may or may not be his biological son. Ned's polite and naïve manner, and his enthusiasm for Steve (he had written Steve a fan letter as a child), echo the sort of child-like hero worship and good-natured admiration of which Steve would love to believe himself worthy. Thus, although Werner is the only actual child represented in the film, Ned is a stand-in for this attitude of hero-worship and idolization of the documentarian-oceanographer that Steve yearns for. At the same time, Ned is looking to understand whether Steve is his father, and this unleashes a wave of confusing and conflicting emotions in Steve, who takes a moment to walk alone to the prow of the boat to the strains of David Bowie's "Life on Mars" expressing Steve's disequilibrium. Anderson says, "Zissou sees himself, and wants to be, the kind of person who gives kids secret messages in cereal boxes, and that's an inspiration for him. The movie's about this real person [dealing with marital strife, crew jealousy, financial woes, possible fatherhood]; he's inspired by the fantasy version of himself, the red caps and uniforms."[10] The film explores how Zissou has to deal with his own past, and the toll his career has taken on him, and get back in touch with his own humanity.

The film is also about the cult of celebrity. Ned wants to know if Steve is his real father, and the film is a comment on how people's cinematic idols may become, in some cases, like surrogate fathers to them, as someone to look up to and to live vicariously through. Anderson plays with the idea of what happens when someone actually meets his idol, and how the reality is always different from the cherished idol in the imagination. Baumbach comments: "Cousteau was always an interesting figure to us [Wes and I], because as kids we idolized him, and watched his shows, but he was one of those characters who seemed just like a star incarnate, in some way: Cousteau, Evel Knievel, and Bill Murray. What was fun for us in writing it is Zissou is sort of a kid's idea of what an adult is, or what a celebrity is."[11] In some ways, the film is best understood as a fantasy dreamed up by twelve-year-old Ned: a touchingly cliché daydream in which a boy grows up to find out his boyhood hero is actually his own father. This conceptualization of the film also explains the over-the-top elements of the narrative as boyish flights of imagination: the fantastical animated marine life, the narrow escapes, the childish infighting and petty jealousies between Ned and Klaus, and even Steve's triumphant-underdog action scene in which he improbably chews through his bindings and singlehandedly fights off a gang of murderous pirates wearing nothing but a striped Speedo, a bathrobe, and flip-flops. Steve's heroism is on display again when he performs a dramatic rescue of the bond company stooge Bill Ubell (Bud Cort) at the Hotel Citroën in the Ping Islands, outwitting the same pirates in another equally improbable victory.

The cult of celebrity is also explored in other ways. Steve has a whole set of Zissou action figures and a Zissou pinball machine from when Steve's brand was in its prime, and there was the merchandising of the Zissou name; he also tries on a pair of high-performance Adidas Zissou sneakers he claims are from 1987, before the company terminated his sponsorship. He also has special correspondence stock stationery, which he uses to "name" Ned – changing his name to "Kingsley (Ned) Zissou." Cate Blanchett's character Jane Winslett-Richardson, a reporter for *Oceanographic Explorer* magazine who comes to interview Steve Zissou, was modeled after primatologist and anthropologist Jane Goodall.[12] According to Anderson, this character evokes "a world of the past that doesn't actually exist anymore, but is remembered by an earlier generation: these wild-life documentarian-scientist stars, which are rare now. There was a time when there were a number of them: Marlon Perkins, Jane Goodall, Carl Sagan."[13] The backstory for Jane's pregnancy – she had an affair with her married editor – is barely touched on, but the fact that Jane is reading Marcel Proust's *À la recherche du temps perdu* (*Remembrance of Things Past*, a multi-volume novel published from 1913 to 1927) to her unborn baby also points to a nostalgia for former times. Similarly, the crew bonds together with Ned over the tape of an early television episode of "The Life Aquatic" in which the *Belafonte* is trapped in a polar ice floe and Zissou does a flip off the ship's prow into a glacial spring and then rescues wild snow mongoose pups. History is also evoked through the silver-nitrate photograph and portrait of Zissou's mentor, the fictional Lord Mandrake, based on the likeness of photographer Jacques-Henri Lartigue. Throughout the film, there is also continual discussion of the Team Zissou flag and who the symbols represent (e.g., Steve, Klaus, Esteban, Ned, and even a "B," presumably for Bill, the bond company stooge). Ned also imitates Zissou's classic pose from the official publicity still, leaning against the *Belafonte*'s railing, looking out at the sunset, and pointing to the horizon.

The Life Aquatic plays with the idea of performance – Zissou is deliberately presenting a media image that is a heightened and more pleasing personality than his own, and he orchestrates emotional moments and lines of dialogue that will represent himself in the best light:

Zissou: Klaus, move into a two-shot of me and Ned.

(*Zissou stands next to Ned. Klaus points the camera at the two of them. Zissou puts his hand on Ned's shoulder and says with heightened significance*):
Zissou: Would you like to join my crew?
(*Klaus looks horrified. Ned hesitates.*)
Ned: What do you mean?
Zissou: I want you on Team Zissou.
(*Ned looks surprised and moved. Klaus cuts the camera. Ned says reluctantly*):
Ned: I don't think I can do that.
Zissou: (*thrown*) Why not?
Ned: Well, for one thing, it's not my field. I don't have the background for it.
Zissou: No one here does. Klaus used to be a bus driver. Wolodarsky was a high school substitute teacher ... We're all a pack of strays. Don't you get it?
Ned: I'm not even that strong a swimmer, Steve.
(*Zissou stares at Ned with a blank expression. Ned says suddenly*):
Ned: The answer's yes.
Zissou: Well, it's got to be. I'll order you a red cap and a Speedo.
(*Zissou hugs Ned. Ned seems overwhelmed. Zissou turns to Klaus.*)
Zissou: Cut.[14]

The cult of celebrity is explored through Ned's longing to legitimize Steve as his surrogate father. Ned asks if he may address Zissou as "Dad," but Steve says no. In another scene, Steve explains: "[It's] because I hate fathers, and never wanted to be one."[15] Klaus also wants Steve to be his surrogate father, and competes with Ned for this position, even though Klaus is closer to Steve's age than Ned's. Anderson plays with the conventions of the standard father-son relationship story: when Ned seeks out Zissou, the story is less about Ned trying to discover his own identity and more about how Ned's arrival forces Zissou to face himself. The quest is not to find the father, but to make Zissou into one. That is why Jane says later "I need to find a baby for this father,"[16] a Freudian slip that implies that the father must be somehow created. Up to this point, Zissou has held the adult world at bay, refusing to grow up and accept responsibility. He enjoys Ned's adulation of him but is essentially unwilling to become a father, or to accept the responsibilities of adult life. Zissou's life cannot be normal because he is more concerned about getting everything shot with the right sound rather than living it; Zissou's documentaries cannot be legitimate because they are cobbled together from staged shots and hosted by someone without a clear grasp of the science behind what is being filmed (i.e. Zissou mistakes the illuminated marine creatures for "electric jellyfish" when Jane correctly refers to them as Viet Cong man-of-wars, prompting Zissou to hastily suggest a correction by relooping the sound).

Literary References in The Life Aquatic with Steve Zissou

Steve Zissou's character evokes Captain Nemo from Jules Verne's 1870 novel *Twenty Thousand Leagues Under the Sea*. Verne (1828–1906), the French author regarded by many scholars as the father of science fiction, commonly referred to his own works as falling into the self-invented genre of "scientific romances" – a description which perfectly captures the blending of extravagant and sumptuous tales of intrigue artfully laden with precise scientific and geographical details which lend a convincing air of reality for the reader. This effective bonding of fantasy and reality could also be used to describe *The Life Aquatic*, and indeed all of Anderson's work: he invests his own self-invented and often lavish imaginary worlds with precise details that root them in reality, such as the use of title cards with (invented) place names and specific dates, and the citation of convincing-sounding measurements and maps. One particularly notable correlation between Anderson's film and Verne's novel is the fabulous vessel that serves as the centerpiece in both works. The interior of Verne's fantastical *Nautilus* is as luxurious as an imperial palace; Nemo's sumptuous dining room is described as follows:

> High oaken sideboards, inlaid with ebony, stood at the two extremities of the room, and upon their shelves glittered china, porcelain, and glass of inestimable value. The plate on the table sparkled in the rays which the luminous ceiling shed around, while the light was tempered and softened by exquisite paintings.[17]

This description of the *Nautilus* calls to mind the elaborate floor plan and the extensive rooms (including a sauna room and library) in the *Belafonte*. Captain Nemo's fantastic machine is first described as "an enormous thing" and mistaken for a sea creature, with its impenetrable interlocking scales. It is described as "a long object, spindle shaped, occasionally phosphorescent, and infinitely larger and more rapid in its movements than a whale."[18] Anderson's creation is also enormous and similarly "larger-than-life": when Zissou's ship is introduced to Ned, the camera moves across a wooden cross section of a boat, from room to room, without trying to hide the obvious artificiality of the set. On the DVD commentary track, Anderson says that this visual "was inspired by World Book Encyclopedia and Time-Life Books, elementary school books with fold-outs."[19] Anderson uses this theatrical staging as part of the narration, reminding the audience of the film's artificiality as well as questioning the relationship maintained between the subject and the representation. The sauna room in Zissou's *Belafonte* "designed by an engineer from the Chinese space program"[20] recalls the sumptuous extravagance of the *Nautilus*, whose library of 12,000 volumes is matched by the *Belafonte*'s "top-notch research library … with a complete first-edition set of the 'Life Aquatic' companion series,"[21] while the walls of the *Nautilus*' drawing room display the art of Raphael, da Vinci, Titian, and Rubens, among others.[22] Verne's description of wonder at the scenery viewed through the large undersea windows, and the 1954 Disney film version's special effects display of these "windows," were both clear influences on Anderson:

> Suddenly light broke at each side of the saloon [room], through two oblong openings. The liquid mass appeared vividly lit up by the electric gleam. Two crystal plates separated us from the sea. At first I trembled at the thought that this frail partition might break, but strong bands of copper bound them, giving an almost infinite power of resistance. The sea was distinctly visible for a mile all around the *Nautilus*. What a spectacle! What pen can describe it?[23]

"Let me tell you about my boat": *The Life Aquatic with Steve Zissou* was inspired by a single visual image Anderson had of seeing the inner workings of a boat cut in half.

Captain Nemo is an intensely complex character, arguably a villain or an anti-hero, with an intense desire for revenge against the killing of his wife and family in a backstory kept deliberately vague by Verne (in the initial draft of the novel, Nemo was a Polish noble who sought revenge against the Russians for killing his family during the Polish uprising against the Russians of 1863–64, but Verne's publisher, Pierre-Jules Hetzel, persuaded Verne to remove these details out of fear over offending the Russians, who were allies of France at the time; later, in *The Mysterious Island*, Verne hints at Nemo's origins as an Indian prince). The Latin translation for Nemo is "No One," and indeed, Captain Nemo seeks to build a world of his own apart from other people, constructing his *Nautilus* as a floating world of his own making, cut off from the rest of humanity. In Verne's story, there is also a character named Ned Land, a simple harpooner who seems out of place on the wondrous ship (from whom Ned Plimpton gets his name).

According to Dyalan Govender's 2008 essay for *Literature/Film Quarterly*, Herman Melville's *Moby Dick* (1851) and Anderson and Baumbach's screenplay for *The Life Aquatic with Steve Zissou* also share several striking similarities, which illuminate one another. Although Anderson and Baumbach claim never to have read *Moby Dick*,[24] both the film and the novel share an overarching plot centered on the vengeful hunt of a large sea creature, while their central characters are both domineering captains with powerful personalities; moreover, according to Govender "at times, the style of *The Life Aquatic* is reminiscent of the encyclopedic digressions of *Moby Dick*."[25] Both Melville's novel and Anderson's film share the same general plotline, and they both reflect a certain textual disregard for that plotline. Both texts are a broad depiction of a man's quest for revenge; both Ahab and Zissou chase a large sea creature across oceans, while in both cases their crews suffer severe losses along the way. Finally, upon eventually finding the creature, neither can destroy it, though unlike Ahab, Zissou is not even capable of attempting to destroy it, while Ahab is strangled/drowned by his own harpoon's rope wrapping around his neck in his final attempt to harpoon the beast, and his ship, *The Pequod*, sinks.

Music in The Life Aquatic with Steve Zissou

Mark Mothersbaugh served again as this film's composer, and the original song "Let Me Tell You About My Boat," which plays over the cutaway shot of the *Belafonte*, is actually the melody of "Scrapping and Yelling," which Mothersbaugh wrote for *The Royal Tenenbaums*, played backwards as a "musical palindrome."[26] Anderson requested that the action scenes be scored with Moog synthesizers and other period instruments to give it a distinctly dated Casio electronic keyboard sound (inspired by the 1970s proto-electro duo Suicide). The use of the Moog synthesizer also recalls Wendy Carlos' *Switched-On Bach*, released in October 1968, and it is interesting that all of the classical tracks in *The Life Aquatic* were Bach pieces.[27] Despite Mothersbaugh scoring all of Anderson's films up to and including *The Life Aquatic*, it is the only one of Anderson's films to include a song by Mothersbaugh's band, Devo, "Gut Feeling" (1978). *The Life Aquatic* is also the first Wes Anderson film (of his initial four) not to include a song from the Rolling Stones on the soundtrack. The song played during the emotional highlight of the interaction with the shark is "Starálfur" ("Staring Elf") by Sigur Rós, about an imaginary scene that the singer experiences deep in the night, and upon waking up has some doubt about what is real and what is imaginary. The song "The Way I Feel Inside" (1965) by the British pop/rock band the Zombies was used in the scenes after the helicopter crash when Zissou carries Ned's body onto the beach, and Ned's funeral.[28]

Much of the soundtrack in the film is made up of Seu Jorge, as Team Zissou member Pelé dos Santos, playing cover versions of David Bowie songs on acoustic guitar, highlighting the emotional thrust of the scene like a Greek chorus. Seu Jorge was a rising young Brazilian star, known for his role in the 2002 film *City of God*, when he caught the attention of Anderson, who cast him in the role of a troubadour deckhand. He performs several of David Bowie's songs in the film, including "Rebel, Rebel," "Life on Mars" and "Starman." But in a twist, he performed the songs in Portuguese, accompanying himself simply with acoustic guitar in bossa nova-inflected versions, and later re-recorded the songs, plus an original, "Team Zissou," for the album *The Life Aquatic Studio Versions Featuring Seu Jorge*.[29] Bowie's own version of "Life on Mars" is perfectly chosen to echo the themes of *The Life Aquatic*; this song is all about how modern-day entertainment (e.g., movies, music, television) has become so all-encompassing and central to human life that people have unconsciously begun to mimic it – that there remains little distinction between "entertainment" and "reality."

Filmic References

Anderson generally quotes other films to form a referential text, and in the director's commentary for the DVD *The Life Aquatic*, Anderson and Baumbach spoke mainly about Fellini's *8½* as their source of inspiration for this film. In the same way that *8½* reflected Fellini's frustration, stagnation, search for inspiration, and generally commented on the essence of filmmaking, *The Life Aquatic* also reflected Anderson's comment on filmmaking:

We often talk about the movies that have influenced us, and the different inspirations. But for this movie, for me, in the end, a lot of it has to do with my own feeling about making films, and just the luck of being able to do it, the situation of being able to make some movies, and how, for me, that's just the central event in my life, just getting [the chance] to do this. And that's part of what the movie is about – somebody who is getting together a group of people to go make these things. There's something kind of magical about movies, to me.[30]

Anderson's film reflects this concept because the final product is his vision of a loyal, rag-tag gang on a boat making a film about a loyal, rag-tag gang on a boat. According to Anderson, the beginning of the film is inspired by *8½*, as Zissou is faced with all the people in his life and all the issues and problems laid out before him: "A film festival … can be the most awkward thing. You're in the midst of all these people watching, and in this case, this character is exposing all these different problems that he has in his life that are just laid up in front of him in one miserable evening."[31] Baumbach continues: "We had talked about *8½* as a sort of inspiration for this, the Guido character Marcello Mastroianni plays because … that movie opens in a dream, but at the spa he's faced with all these people from his life. Here it's less surreal."[32] This film has an obvious reference to Truffaut, as mentioned in chapter 1, with its line, "Not this one, Klaus," mirroring a line said by Jules to Jim about Catherine in Truffaut's third feature. There is also a very explicit homage to Max Ophuls' *Lola Montès* (1955), also about the cult of celebrity, in which Lola is the brand, a product (in a cage) marketed by Peter Ustinov. *Lola Montès* is referenced in *The Life Aquatic* in the scene where Murray holds out a fish over a pool and a killer whale leaps up, like a dolphin, to take it out of his hand. Moreover Peter Ustinov was supposed to play the producer Oseary Drakoulias,[33] but when he died Michael Gambon took the role. Gambon's role is modeled on Italian producer Dino De Laurentiis, and his unique hexagonal eyeglass-frames are modeled on those of Sergio Leone. Werner is likely named for director Werner Herzog. Eleanor leaves at one point, saying "I don't want to be a part of whatever's going to happen out there,"[34] which is similar to the reason Etta (Katharine Ross) gives for her departure in *Butch Cassidy and the Sundance Kid* (1969). For using a single scene with a rocking motion to establish that his characters are on a boat (for the boat's interior scenes), Anderson cites *The Black Stallion* (1979), for its single use of a swaying camera in a scene to suggest the rocking of a boat. The Team Zissou flag is inspired by the samurai flag in *The Seven Samurai* (1954). Finally, the ending of the film with the entire crew joining Zissou as he is walking along the docks is a homage to the end credits of *The Adventures of Buckaroo Banzai Across the 8th Dimension* (1984).

Anderson explains that there are a number of personal letters in *The Life Aquatic*, and he points to the influence of Godard on his work: "Pauline Kael talks about how Godard's films are literary, they are filled with words: there are titles on the screen, there are letters, there is writing everywhere, and there are people quoting, people reciting from books."[35] Ned's letter, to which Zissou sent a response that was "dictated but not read," perfectly captures the child's voice of innocence and admiration, and this letter is displayed in its entirety toward the end of the film:

> Dear Captain Zissou.
> I am 12 years old and live in Jawbone, Kentucky. A creek runs behind our house where I live with my mother (she met you once some years ago), and I collect and catalogue amphibians, reptiles, and insects. I don't know what this one is called, so I named it myself:
>
> *[There is a drawing in pencil of a gnat named Kentucky Zissou Fly.]*
>
> You are probably my one of if not *the* favorite person I have ever studied. I plan to be either:
>
> a) an oceanographer.
> b) an architect.
> c) a pilot.
>
> Thank you very much for your good work.
>
> Sincerely,
> Ned Plimpton
> Blue Star Cadet, Zissou Society
>
> P.S. Do you ever wish you could breathe underwater?[36]

This letter represents the kind of life-giving properties of Zissou's celebrity; the pure admiration that Ned expresses in the letter sets up the purity and simplicity of emotion that prepare for the film's denouement.

Climax and Ending of The Life Aquatic

In the climactic sequence of *The Life Aquatic*, after Ned is killed in the helicopter crash, Zissou and his crew go diving in the "Deep Search" minisub to finally encounter face-to-face the elusive jaguar shark that killed Esteban. This results in a memorable image from the film in which Eleanor, Jane, Klaus, Vikram, Drakoulias, Bill Ubell, Pelé, Ogata, Wolodarsky, Intern # 1, and Renzo Pietro, and others surround Zissou in the tiny vessel designed for a maximum occupancy of six. When the enormous shark swims into view, Eleanor affirms to Steve that the shark is beautiful, and Steve muses "I wonder if it remembers me,"[37] and then his eyes fill with tears. This scene reflects Zissou remembering why he and his partner became oceanographers and explorers in the first place: they were trying to show the world the wonders it had within it. Esteban died in pursuit of that goal, and Zissou initially sought revenge, rather than giving himself the chance to mourn his friend. In this scene, Zissou lets go of his need for revenge because the world has too much beauty in it to be worth hating. In a way, the jaguar shark also represents Zissou himself: by deciding to allow the shark to live, he is letting go of his self-hatred. As he sits, weeping, in the darkness of Deep Search, watching the beautiful shark swim by, everyone lays their hands on him, signifying not only their understanding of what is transpiring, but their forgiveness. With their eyes on the breath-taking shark that looks like something dreamed up in Zissou's imagination, everyone finally sees what Zissou sees (his personal perspective, his approach to life) and is with him – their touch expresses their solidarity with him. Zissou reaches out to Jane and puts his hand on her stomach, and Jane remarks that in twelve years, her baby boy will be eleven and a half. Zissou replies that this was his "favorite age." This is significant because Ned was twelve when he wrote his first letter to Steve; similarly, it is suggested that Jane's son represents the twelve-year-old Ned still present with them, with all the enthusiasm and wonder toward marine life that were encapsulated in Ned.

In the final sequence, Zissou's finished film is again screened at the Loquasto Film Festival. It shows Ned practicing Zissou's famous pose, pointing his finger out at the horizon, and Ned's redesigned Team Zissou flag, which sports his own initial. The film is dedicated to "Ned Kingsley Plimpton Zissou." In the audience, Jane holds her baby, who is wearing a red knit Zissou cap. Zissou is shown sitting alone on the steps outside of the festival with a gold-plated award statuette of a barracuda sitting beside him, as described in the final draft of the screenplay:

> *The sound of applause is heard from inside.*
> *Klaus' nephew, Werner comes out and sits next to Zissou. Zissou looks at him. Pause.*
>   *Zissou reaches into his pocket and takes out Ned's Team Zissou ring. He gives it*
>   *to Werner. Werner examines it and puts it onto his finger.*
> *Zissou makes a little flick of the wrist and says quietly:*
> Zissou: Ho.
> *Werner looks up at Zissou. He nods.*
> Werner: Ho.
> *Strings of lights flicker over Zissou and Werner's heads. Zissou says wearily with*
>   *hope and regret:*
> Zissou: This is an adventure.[38]

Zissou and Werner's interaction has symbolic importance in this scene. Zissou sits with Werner on one side, and a newly won trophy on the other. Werner idolizes Zissou, just as Ned did as a child. Zissou hands Werner a very special gift – Ned's old Zissou Society ring – and they exchange the special "Ho" greeting that serves as a kind of secret password into the Society. It is clear from Zissou's next actions that he is a changed man. Prestige no longer drives him; celebrity no longer has a hold on him. When Zissou stands, he leaves the trophy behind and picks up the small child, whom he carries on his shoulders.

When at the very end of the film, Bill Murray, playing Zissou, says the last line, "This is an adventure," he essentially provides the final postscript for all of the characters previously introduced in the Wes Anderson world – Dignan and Anthony with their 75-year Plan as master criminals in *Bottle Rocket*, Max Fischer with his obsessive and auteuristic theatrical ambitions in *Rushmore*, and the Tenenbaum children with their various pursuits as child-prodigy geniuses. Anderson articulates Steve Zissou's fatal flaw: "He's more interested in making a film about something than he is in the thing itself. That's the comic idea of him, to some degree, and it's the sad thing about him. It's his weakness ... He's after any material that can bring him back to life."[39] In Zissou's ongoing adventures with red caps, Glocks, and Speedos onboard the *Belafonte*, with his dominating and imposing personality and obsessively controlling nature (he obsessively edits and rewrites "reality" through the final product of his documentaries) he ultimately brings life not only to himself, but to his extensive troupe of surrounding players. In the finale, as Zissou walks down the dock and the entire team comes and joins him, Werner is now part of the team (dressed in blue lederhosen), and Eleanor takes Werner's hand in a maternal way. There is a phantom figure at the top of the *Belafonte* waiting silently and apparently smoking a pipe – this is Ned's lasting presence with Zissou. Anderson creates a family out of his players, with the *Belafonte* as home.

The Life Aquatic with Steve Zissou was originally condemned as a massive critical and commercial failure (it cost twice as much as *The Royal Tenenbaums*, and performed half as well), with scathingly critical reviews accusing Anderson of self-parody. Over time, however, the film has experienced its own kind of redemption, and it is now recognized as a film of surprising depth – a midlife crisis film about failure, legacy, and death, made by a filmmaker just in his early thirties. In 2014, Anderson summed up his experience with the film: "I remember a friend said, 'It's going to be ten years before people appreciate [*The Life Aquatic*]. And she was kind of right. They did a screening of it in New York recently and it was a great night. Like *The Royal Tenenbaums* – we opened it at the New York Film Festival and it was fine, but we screened it again ten years later and I was like, where were these people ten years ago? It was the exact same room but a completely different experience. So I wouldn't mind only seeing my movies ten years after they come out."[40] It is clear that Anderson's film releases are out of step with their time, and, as this quote seems to suggest, his films are possibly ahead of their time.

Notes

1. Jacques-Yves Cousteau, "Introduction," *The Ocean World* (New York: Abradale Press/Abrams, Inc., 1985 [1979]), 12.
2. Philippe Cousteau died at age thirty-eight in 1979 as he was attempting to land the Cousteau PBY Catalina flying boat and crashed in the Tagus River in Portugal. All seven others onboard with him survived the crash.
3. Wes Anderson, DVD Commentary for *The Life Aquatic with Steve Zissou*, Criterion Collection, 2005.
4. Wes Anderson and Noah Baumbach, *The Life Aquatic with Steve Zissou*, [Final Draft] (Burbank, CA: Touchstone Pictures, n.d.), 1.

5   It is interesting that this film, an exploration of fame and professional burnout, would be accused of being Anderson's film where he burned out – it was *The Life Aquatic with Steve Zissou* that brought Anderson his harshest criticism for being self-indulgent and solipsistic with his films, which were accused of having "style without substance." Anderson was accused of having nothing new to say, that he'd lost direction, the very subject which is explored in this film.
6   Anderson and Baumbach, n.d., 2–3.
7   Note the similarity in tone to the question/answer session in Woody Allen's *Stardust Memories* (1980):
    Question: Some people have claimed that your films are narcissistic.
    Sandy Bates: Yes, many people have said that about me over the years, but I don't think it's true. If I were to say which Greek God I take after, I would definitely not say Narcissus.
    Question: Who would you say?
    Sandy Bates: Zeus.
8   Anderson and Baumbach, n.d., 9. Anderson's personal experience with the test screening of his first film, *Bottle Rocket*, is captured in this dialogue.
9   Ibid., 13.
10 Wes Anderson, quoted on *The Life Aquatic with Steve Zissou* Criterion Collection DVD director's commentary, 2005.
11 Noah Baumbach, quoted on *The Life Aquatic with Steve Zissou* Criterion Collection DVD director's commentary, 2005.
12 The name "Winslett-Richardson" evokes the names of two of Britain's most prominent actresses, although Kate Winslet's name only has a single "t."
13 Wes Anderson, quoted on *The Life Aquatic with Steve Zissou* Criterion Collection DVD director's commentary, 2005.
14 Anderson and Baumbach, n.d., 32–33.
15 Ibid., 45.
16 Ibid., 91.
17 Jules Verne, *Twenty Thousand Leagues Under the Sea* (London: Wordsworth Editions, 1992), 42.
18 Ibid., 1.
19 Wes Anderson, quoted on *The Life Aquatic with Steve Zissou* Criterion Collection DVD director's commentary. The ship's cross section deliberately resembles a large set from a play, with all the actors on set in their compartments. Anderson had been imagining this visual since he had first conceived the story fourteen years earlier.
20 Anderson and Baumbach, n.d., 23.
21 Ibid., 24.
22 Zissou's home displays a number of tasteful artworks, such as a painting by Francesco Clemente of his wife, Alma.
23 Verne, 1992, 59.
24 Wes Anderson, interview with Antonio Monda, on *The Life Aquatic with Steve Zissou* Criterion Collection DVD "Mondo Monda" featurette, 2005.

25 Dyalan Govender, "Wes Anderson's *The Life Aquatic with Steve Zissou* and Melville's *Moby Dick*: A Comparative Study," *Literature/Film Quarterly* 36:1 (January 2008): 61.
26 Mark Mothersbaugh, *The Life Aquatic with Steve Zissou* Criterion Collection DVD 19-minute interview with Mark Mothersbaugh
27 For *Rushmore*, Anderson and Mothersbaugh looked to Vivaldi, for *The Royal Tenenbaums* it was French impressionism and Ravel, and for *The Life Aquatic*, it was Bach. Mark Mothersbaugh, *The Life Aquatic with Steve Zissou* Criterion Collection DVD 19-minute interview with Mark Mothersbaugh featurette, 2005.
28 In a nuanced detail, Ned's casket is attended by three Air Kentucky pilots, who are played by Owen Wilson's father, Bob; Bob Wilson's college roommate, Don McKinnon; and Eric Chase Anderson, who are all very close to Owen Wilson. Anderson felt that intimacy would come through in the scene.
29 Seu Jorge's Portuguese adaptations of Bowie's songs were controversial because Jorge admitted to having liberally changed the lyrics in many instances. However, in the liner notes to the album *The Life Aquatic Studio Versions Featuring Seu Jorge*, Bowie himself gave this project his stamp of approval: "Had Seu Jorge not recorded my songs in Portuguese, I would never have heard this new level of beauty which he has imbued them with." David Bowie, quoted in the liner notes for *The Life Aquatic Studio Versions Featuring Seu Jorge*, produced by Wes Anderson and Randall Poster, Rome, Italy, Hollywood Records, 2005.
30 Wes Anderson, quoted on *The Life Aquatic with Steve Zissou* Criterion Collection DVD director's commentary, 2005.
31 Ibid., 2005.
32 Ibid., 2005.
33 The character Oseary Drakoulias is a reference to Anderson's friend, music producer and music supervisor George Drakoulias, and Guy Oseary.
34 Anderson and Baumbach, n.d., 56.
35 Wes Anderson, quoted on *The Life Aquatic with Steve Zissou* Criterion Collection DVD director's commentary, 2005.
36 Anderson and Baumbach, n.d., 136–137.
37 Ibid., 145.
38 Ibid., 147.
39 Wes Anderson, interviewed in Matt Zoller Seitz, *The Wes Anderson Collection* (New York: Abrams, 2013a), 176.
40 Wes Anderson, quoted in Dorian Lynskey, "Film by Film: Wes Anderson on Wes Anderson," *Empireonline.com*. March 4, 2014. http://www.empireonline.com/movies/features/wes-anderson/ (accessed April 25, 2016).

CHAPTER SEVEN

Fragmentary Narratives/Incomplete Identities in The Darjeeling Limited

With *The Darjeeling Limited*, Wes Anderson answers the call of his critics with his most profound and personal film yet. The picaresque journey of *The Darjeeling Limited* has the atmosphere of a lark, of a digressive adventure, one in which insight is gained: the setting in India points to the idea of enlightenment, and the film contains moments of startling transcendence, as well as retaining a wonderfully rambling quality. The train posing as the "Darjeeling Limited" was created for the film from ten rail cars and a locomotive purchased from the Northwestern Railways Company and elaborately decorated by production designer Mark Friedberg, and the film's shoot took cast and crew from Jodhpur to Jaisalmer and through the Thar desert, and ultimately to the Himalayas. *The Darjeeling Limited* has a beautiful, intricately ornamented surface typical of an Anderson film, with a dazzling color palette (the train is yet another dollhouse-style enclosed set), yet beneath this impeccably designed surface is the complexity of multicultural influences, such as the films of Satyajit Ray, Jean Renoir, and Louis Malle, and musical cues from early Merchant-Ivory films set in India, as well as an interlocking box of stories about the past.

The film begins with a man running to catch a train, which has left the station. The metaphorical implications of a man "missing the train" are suggested here, and this is poignantly acted by Bill Murray (known only as "The Businessman" in the script), neatly dressed in a suit and classic 50s-style gray fedora and carrying two tannish-brown 1970s-style hard shell suitcases. The first two lines of the film are "That's my train!" and shortly later, as he runs along the platform, "Wait! – Wait!" The Businessman's train is leaving him behind; life, in the form of the "Darjeeling Limited" train, is moving on without him. However, at this point, a second story is suddenly juxtaposed with the first. At the last moment, Peter (Adrien Brody), who is supposed to be on the same train, appears on the platform, running side-by-side with The Businessman, and then runs past him, but not before doing a double take. Peter is able to hoist himself onto the moving train, leaving the well-dressed older man, now slowing down in defeat, behind on the platform. After Peter jumps aboard the train, he pauses to take a long look back at the familiar apparition of the man he has left behind. His mouth drops open slightly in seeming disbelief – could it really be him? He lifts up the pair of sunglasses he is wearing – which turn out to be his father's – to try to see more clearly, and for a moment smiles wryly at the man with a sense of familiarity. But then the truth hits him afresh – this man, who reminds him of his father, is now out of reach – and Peter turns away, his face clouded with sadness. The young Indian man standing beside the train's back door, who has observed the entire exchange, looks at Peter without expression, while Peter meets his eyes searchingly – as one traveling abroad might try to engage with the new culture – but then, receiving no comment or response, Peter lowers his eyes and picks up his luggage. The young man continues staring at Peter as he heads inside the darkened train.

Because the film begins with its focus zooming in on The Businessman rushing to catch his train (he is first shown racing through an Indian town in a taxi, and the zooms and camera angles suggest the infamous car chase from *The French Connection*), the viewer is temporarily given the impression that Bill Murray will again have a central role in the film. Anderson does this deliberately to draw on the paternal nostalgia associated with Murray's former roles in his work, especially his leading role in Anderson's previous film, *The Life Aquatic with Steve Zissou*. However, *The Darjeeling Limited* turns out to be about the three Whitman brothers, Francis, Peter and Jack,[1] who meet on the train that gives the film its title. It is slowly revealed that the brothers' father has died, their mother is gone, and they have divided up their father's beautiful luggage among themselves, prodigal sons dividing up a hefty inheritance of Louis Vuitton luggage designed by Marc Jacobs – the most attractive and expensive baggage. The face of one brother – Francis (Owen Wilson) – is heavily bandaged after a motorcycle accident: it is a visual expression of his unhealed inner pain. Francis is the most well-to-do of the three brothers, and has planned the trip through India as a spiritual journey and a chance for the brothers to bond. Francis is wearing $3000 shoes and a $6000 belt, and traveling with a laminating machine and a personal assistant named Brendan (Wally Wolodarsky) – his assistant wears a hat with the logo "Francis Whitman Industries" – who helps make laminated schedules for their journey that begin with pedestrian activities like waking and showering, scheduled to the minute. Francis has an obsessive need to schedule every moment for optimum spiritual betterment, planning his brothers' days right down to their breaks for meditation.

The second brother, Peter, is expecting a baby with his wife Alice (Camilla Ruther) and is nervous about it – although he is six weeks away from becoming a father himself, he goes to India without telling her and he is using the trip as an escape from responsibility. Peter also appropriates objects – eyeglasses, keys, shaving razor – belonging to their father that Peter absorbs into his own life, suggesting memory, grief, and entitlement. Peter borrows Francis's belongings without asking, too. (Francis: "Is that my belt?" Peter: "Can I borrow it?") The youngest brother, Jack

(Jason Schwartzman), is attracted to a female train server, Rita (Amara Karan), but he is also haunted by his former girlfriend (an unnamed role played by Natalie Portman[2]). The brothers have never developed healthy boundaries; they all struggle with distrust and pain and resentment. Some of the resentment regards the older brother Francis's usurpation of patriarchal authority, or the keeping of secrets (and objects) by Peter, or the revelation of family secrets by Jack in his autobiographical short stories. It becomes apparent that these brothers – children of privilege – are nevertheless floundering in the void left by their father. They drink, smoke, and pass narcotics and cough syrup bottles back and forth. The train becomes a scene of screwball comedy, with a tall, disapproving Chief Steward (Waris Ahluwalia) who struggles to keep the brothers in line, stops them from smoking in their compartment, takes away Peter's new poisonous snake, and eventually throws the brothers off the train after they have a brawl.

The opening scene is also a eulogy for Steve Zissou (the image of the older actor Bill Murray missing the train is full of pathos) and a farewell to the former film that was the culmination of everything Anderson had been trying to say in his work. After his difficulties making *The Life Aquatic with Steve Zissou*, Anderson wanted to go back to simplicity with *The Darjeeling Limited*. Regardless of whether it is true that Anderson was reflecting his own mental state with the image of a young man holed up in a hotel hiding from the world in his short *Hotel Chevalier* (see chapter 11), he was clearly making a break from the heavily over-budget experience of his previous film. With *The Darjeeling Limited*, Anderson pared back by taking a small group of actors to India, with no trailers, no blocking off of streets for filming, and having the actors do their own makeup each day before showing up at the set, while each actor's costume was equipped with a microphone to simplify sound recording. The actors joked that they had to arrive on time each day or the set – a moving train – would be gone. The train was outfitted with an identical compartment set on either side, allowing for continuous filming in the morning and afternoon; the actors basically lived on the train for a month. While Anderson's *Zissou* had such enormous sets and challenging work conditions, now there was a compact set keeping everyone in place. In *The Darjeeling Limited* Anderson also pared back from his usual cast size: with the focus being on three brothers, and the second set of three young Indian brothers (no mother is shown for them) whose father is played by Irrfan Khan; the only other characters in the primary cast are The Businessman, Brendan, Rita, the Chief Steward, Patricia Whitman, Peter's wife Alice, and the German mechanic from Luftwaffe Auto (Barbet Schroeder). Kumar Pallana also appears in a non-speaking role.

The focus of the story on three brothers is significant because of Anderson's own history as a middle child among three brothers (and it is arguably Peter who faces the strongest emotional struggles in the film, as also the one on whom their father's death takes its greatest toll, which is made especially clear by his frenetic behavior during the flashback sequence in New York). Anderson wrote the story with two men he is very close to, Roman Coppola and Jason Schwartzman, two cousins who grew up together and know one another like brothers. Roman Coppola describes their relationship: "Jason and I have known each other forever, and Wes and I have known each other for many years, and Jason and Wes have their own separate relationship and friendship, so right off the bat there was something that resembled three brothers and history and that was the beginning of the project."[3] As Francis says, "I want us to become brothers again, like we used to be." There is a pull to looking back, to nostalgia, and to renewal, to an elliptical process of bringing what was dead back to life.

While the focus of the film is again strongly masculine because of the dominant role of the three brothers, this film is unusual for Anderson's oeuvre because the central patriarch is deceased, leaving the three younger men to sort out their relationships chiefly with their mother and other female characters who are uniquely represented in the film. The Whitman brothers' conflict with their mother begins before the film and before their father's death, and it is the acceptance of their mother that leads to a more peaceful performance of the feather ceremony at the film's resolution. Patricia abandoned the family, most likely divorced her husband, and has been living away from them and out of contact for an unspecified amount of time. The men's "abandonment" by their mother has affected them in different ways, but the mother denies any fault on her part by saying "It's over," to which Francis replies, "Not for us." It is to his mother that Francis first confesses that his motorcycle "accident" was deliberate – and this is possibly implicating her with some of the blame. Meanwhile, Peter's unwillingness to face the fact that his wife will be having a baby in six weeks – he attributes his lack of interest in having children to a fear that he always thought he would get a divorce – again seems related to the damage his mother's abandonment caused him. Finally, the youngest son Jack obviously has difficult relationships with women, presumably due to his mother's abandonment and her unsuitability as a role model for a healthy relationship. The fact that Patricia "abandons" them yet again when they go to visit her at the convent (she provides them breakfast – she decides the breakfast foods for each of her sons, and thus, it is easy to see where Francis gets his habit of ordering food for others – leaving it on the table and disappearing before they wake up in the morning, claiming to be needed by someone else) is the catalyst that propels them out of their stasis in self-pity – they know their mother will never change, so, to continue to heal, they must accept her as she is, with all of her faults and idiosyncrasies. It is interesting to note that Patricia thinks that others "need" her more than her own children do, and this basic neglect of them has wounded them from an early age. It is also apparent that Francis, as the oldest child, is the one most similar to his mother, because his obsessive need to maintain control and make lists of "agreements" (i.e. "We will not splinter into factions…") is echoed by his mother's own list of conditions that she mandates when they come to visit. From even this short time with Patricia, it is easy to see where Francis gets his controlling nature. She then abandons them, again. However, when they wake up in morning and leave their cornflakes and mango and porridge to run to the top of the hill to complete the peacock feather ritual at last, they all seem to have made peace with the past, and they can face the future unencumbered.

Jack begins a relationship with a train server named Rita (nicknamed "Sweet Lime" for the drink she offers the thirsty travelers in the train). Like Jack's ex-girlfriend, Rita remains an enigmatic presence – she has her own hardships, but the viewer is never given more than a glimpse of them. Jack's relationship with Rita is unhealthy in that he seems to be projecting some of his needs onto her; he states: "I feel like you may be very important to me in my life" – Jack is writing a narrative in his head and tries to pull Rita into that story. However, they have no chance to know each other deeply – instead Jack and Rita's stories begin to clash, when Rita admits she has a boyfriend (who turns out to be the Chief Steward), and that she is planning to break up with him. Jack and Rita's relationship abruptly ends when the three brothers, after spraying one another with mace, are kicked off the train. Jack sees Rita's tears and asks "Oh, were you maced, too?" Rita answers that she is actually crying, and states, "I've got to get off of this train." She and Jack have one final exchange in which Jack says, "Thank you for using me," and Rita replies, "You're welcome," thus showing that Rita is the one in control of her decisions and has her own agency; i.e., she admits she is unhappy with her boyfriend, is sick of the train, and has to deal with the personal pain her actions have caused her.

Other female characters of central importance in the narrative are Peter's wife, Alice (although it is difficult to get to know much about Alice from her brief screen appearances, other than that, like Miss Cross from *Rushmore*, she has a British accent, and that she appears much more levelheaded and capable than the hapless brothers), and Jack's unnamed ex-girlfriend, about whom little can be known, even to Jack, who monitors her answering machine. Peter, upon discovering that Jack's ex-girlfriend left her perfume in his suitcase, asks "Could she be gaslighting you?" whereupon Jack replies, "What's gaslighting?" Both Peter's suspicion and Jack's clueless response demonstrate just how little the brothers understand Jack's ex-girlfriend; they can only dimly guess at her motives. Another interesting set of female roles in the film is that of the German tourists, first seen in the train's dining car at a table opposite the brothers. The two middle-aged tourists whisper to each other when the brothers take out all their medications, asking in German "Did you see what they have on the table?" and giving the brothers disapproving looks. Later in the scene, the two women are loudly arguing with one another until Peter says, "Those Germans are bothering me," and says to them "Ladies, will you please keep it down?" When the brothers are kicked off the "Darjeeling Limited," the two German tourists are there, watching them from the train window, admonishing them with the words "Shame on you." The women in *The Darjeeling Limited* represent a kind of opposition and also a comic foil to the men which enriches the narrative.

Influences/Inspirations

It is important to understand Anderson's inspirations behind this film – primarily Jean Renoir and Satyajit Ray – in reflecting and presenting the complex diversity of the surrounding world. The director of the films *Boudu Saved from Drowning* (1932), *Grand Illusion* (1937), *The Rules of the Game* (1939), *The Southerner* (1945), and *The Golden Coach* (1953), Jean Renoir (1894–1979), the son of painter Pierre-Auguste Renoir, had a sense of complexity and of truth; and while he sometimes depicted the middle and upper classes in his films, he did so without false admiration or pretension: he was more likely to offer critique or satire. The great Indian filmmaker Satyajit Ray

(1921–1992) made about twenty-nine feature films, not counting documentaries or short films; Ray gained his earliest recognition as the maker of *The Apu Trilogy – Pather Panchali* or *Song of the Little Road* (1955); *Aparajito* or *The Unvanquished* (1956); and *Apur Sansar* or *The World of Apu* (1959) – a series of films about the youth, education, and marriage of a poor Bengali boy. Both Renoir and Ray have a grasp of a certain fundamental human dimension – the feeling beneath looks and gestures – in addition to the beauty of their photography or the drama of their scenarios. Viewers may be distracted by the surface beauty and control of Wes Anderson's formidable technique so that they miss the fact that his work similarly plumbs the depths of the complicated – contrary, deep, vexing – human heart. Finally, Anderson has also pointed to Howard Hawks' *Twentieth Century* (1934), with John Barrymore and Carole Lombard, and Preston Sturges' *The Palm Beach Story* (1942) with Claudette Colbert, screwball comedies in which train journeys play a part, as inspirations. A book Anderson cites as an inspiration is *The Photographs of Chachaji* (1980) by Ved Mehta (a writer whose work Anderson had seen in *The New Yorker*).

The eastern world has long been visited by westerners, the encounters recorded in memoirs and stories; and literary works, from Rudyard Kipling's *Kim* (1901) and E.M. Forster's *A Passage to India* (1924) to the fiction and essays of V.S. Naipaul and Salman Rushdie, have captured the attraction and tensions. While Edward Said's *Orientalism* (1978) has been the critical authority on that school of thought in which Said views Orientalism as permeated with condescending, exploitative and colonialist attitudes, the historian J. J. Clarke has written on enlightenment in the eastern world, and how westerners have perceived it. In *Oriental Enlightenment* (1997), Clarke argues that India and other eastern countries and their cultures have represented a positive alternative to western values. Often in these works, the eastern world has represented both ancient tradition and modern change for westerners, and Anderson's film references this idea by setting the brothers' spiritual journey in India, where their lives are indeed impacted by the culture and the people they meet. In an appreciative and thoughtful consideration of *The Darjeeling Limited*, the Canadian writer and religious studies professor Barry Stephenson (2011) examines community and ritual in the work of Wes Anderson: the pilgrimage of the three privileged but damaged brothers offers the possibility of healing – beginning with the recognition that there is something needing to be healed. Stephenson writes that the western mourning process is inadequate – commercialized, shallow, rushed – and that India and its mourning tradition is presented as something more genuine (the Indian funeral is tactile, with the hands on the body; grief is openly expressed, time is stilled): in mourning for a little Indian boy who Peter couldn't save on the river, the brothers were able, also, to mourn for their own father. The Indian boy's funeral becomes the objective correlative of the father's. Stephenson even emphasizes the repetitive cinematic style of Anderson as a type of "ritual." Stephenson writes: "If ritual is bound up with the rhythm of repetition, ritual is a tacit force informing Anderson's work. He returns, again and again, to a consistent style, and to work and rework the prima materia of family strife, angst, and a sorrow without a source. Form and content conspire in reflecting and projecting Wes's World."[4] The film also subtly suggests the visit to India of another group of

This shot of the three Whitman brothers walking in profile recalls the iconic 1969 *Abbey Road* album cover photo with a barefoot Paul McCartney; the film's drug-fueled spiritual journey suggests undercurrents of the Beatles' visit to the Maharishi Mahesh Yogi in Rishikesh, India in 1968.

westerners, the Beatles, who famously traveled to Rishikesh, India for a workshop on Transcendental Meditation with the Maharishi Mahesh Yogi in 1968. *The Darjeeling Limited* is richly textured with references to the Beatles: first, Schwartzman's thick mustache makes him look like a Beatle, and later, when the group walks single-file with Schwartzman barefooted, it calls to mind the Beatles' famous cover shot on *Abbey Road* (with the barefoot Schwartzman as Paul McCartney).[5] According to Anderson, the group traveled to Rishikesh at Schwartzman's urging, deliberately adding an extra dimension to the journey of making the film.[6]

Just as *The Royal Tenenbaums* had been set in an imaginary, hyperstylized version of New York City, Anderson based *The Darjeeling Limited* on an imaginary version of India derived from films about India he had seen when he was younger – especially the original two parts of Satyajit Ray's *Teen Kanya* (*Three Daughters*, 1961, an omnibus film based on three unrelated short stories by Nobel Prize winner Rabindranath Tagore) which Anderson discovered in one of the Sound Warehouse video sections in Houston as a teenager[7] – a younger man's imagined India. The films he had in mind were mostly made in the 1950s and 1960s, such as Jean Renoir's *The River* (1951), Ray's early *Apu* trilogy, *Teen Kanya*, and *Charulata* (*The Lonely Wife*, 1964), and the India documentaries made by Louis Malle (*Phantom India*, and *Calcutta*, 1969). Satyajit Ray himself was influenced by Italian neorealist films like *Ladri de biciclette* (*Bicycle Thieves*, 1948). He was first exposed to filmmaking through his friendship with Jean Renoir during Renoir's production of *The River*, and later became India's most internationally acclaimed filmmaker, working on films like *Pather Panchali* (1955), the first film of the *Apu* trilogy, that portrayed poverty, but not hopelessness (*Pather Panchali* contains scenes such as a joyous greeting of the rain with waterbugs skating on a river, and two children running toward the vision of modernity and prosperity of a train), films that speak to people across the boundaries of culture.

Viewers often remember the music of Ray's films as clearly as the visuals, especially music by the legendary Ravi Shankar, as well as Ray's original compositions for his own films and others. The music used in *The Darjeeling Limited* includes three songs by the Kinks ("This Time Tomorrow," "Strangers," and "Powerman," all from the 1970 album *Lola versus Powerman and the Moneygoround, Part One*), the Rolling Stones' "Play With Fire," and Beethoven's "Symphony No. 7 in A (Op 92) Allegro Con Brio" and Debussy's "Suite Bergamasque: 3. Clair de Lune." Other song choices play with the idea of cultural ambiguity, such as Joe Dassin's "Les Champs-Élysées" (originally a British song, "Waterloo Road," that was translated/adapted by Dassin in 1969), and "Praise Him" a traditional Christian Sunday School song similarly transplanted to India and sung in heavily accented English by the "Udaipur Convent School Nuns and Students." The majority of the soundtrack is an eclectic compilation of pieces drawn from various India-related film sources, including early Merchant-Ivory productions filmed in India, such as *The Householder* (1963), *Shakespeare Wallah* (1965), with "The Deserted Ballroom" theme composed by Satyajit Ray, *The Guru* (1969), and *Bombay Talkie* (1970), from which the film's song "Typewriter, Tip, Tip" and the opening credits theme were used. The music from Ray's *Jalsaghar* (*The Music Room*, 1958) is used for the opening sequence in *The Darjeeling Limited* where The Businessman is on a wild taxi ride to the train station; this music, which is set to a swinging chandelier in the opening of Ray's film, is related to The Businessman/father figure because Ray's film is the story of an aging, formerly wealthy landowner who has become stubborn and prideful in his old age trying to uphold his family's former prestige even when faced with changing fortunes, clinging to crumbling traditions and nostalgic for lost times of the past (this is also related to the father of the Whitman boys).

Ray's heroes, especially those played by Soumitra Chatterjee as Apu in *Apur Sansar* and Amal in *Charulata*, are often writers or men of great literary talent; this is reflected in *The Darjeeling Limited* by Jack, who is a published author (and whose father never got to read his book, significantly titled *Invisible Ink and Other Stories*, which he finds in an unopened manila envelope in the trunk of his father's Porsche). Jack shares portions of his short stories with his brothers throughout their journey. In *Apur Sansar*, Apu shares the pages of his manuscript with his friend Pulu, who tells him it is great, while in *Charulata*, the sharing of writing and manuscripts between a wife and her husband's visiting cousin leads to their bonding over a shared love of literature. While Jack is constantly deflecting the suggestion that his stories are autobiographical ("the characters are all fictional"), in the end he stops himself midway through the denial, and his face looks peaceful with the acceptance that he is telling his own version of the truth (this final exchange is sparked by Peter's comment, "I like how mean you are," to which Jack starts to respond with his third denial, "The characters are all fict... Thank you"). Richard Brody (2010) agrees that this reflects Wes Anderson's role in making the film – that the film actually provides the viewer insight into the writer/director's own personal experience.[8]

The influence of Satyajit Ray extends to the way Anderson uses objects in the film. In a 2012 article analyzing Anderson's focus on objects in *The Darjeeling Limited*, Stefano Baschiera claims, "The cinema of Wes Anderson is a cinema of objects. [...] Objects are not a mere element of décor in his films; they are central to the development of the narrative, and consequently, to the meaning of the film, to the extent that the cinema of Wes Anderson overcomes the separation between subjects and objects."[9] In other words, objects and physicality externalize what is internal about the characters. What is seen on the screen is what Anderson wishes to say, with the same simplicity and clarity of a Satyajit Ray story. One obvious example is the visual humor created by the brothers' constant struggle to carry their father's baggage, which in the end they toss away. A second example is the relationship between Alice and her handmade pots – Alice's pots haunt the film, both in the train car and in the convent. When Patricia first sees Alice's pot, she says it is ugly, but when she learns from Peter that Alice made it, she lies and says to Peter that she likes it. Another example is Francis's shoes – one Italian leather shoe is stolen by a shoeshine boy, so he grabs one of the Indian slipper-shoes Peter had just purchased at the market, and wears one western shoe and one Indian slipper-shoe throughout the rest of the trip. The fact that he steals this shoe from Peter (just as Peter has been stealing/borrowing from him) reveals something about his character, while on another level, the comical image of Francis walking around with one foot in an expensive leather shoe and the other in an Indian slipper shows that he feels comfortable in neither place.[10]

Renoir's *The River* is based on Rumer Godden's 1946 semi-autobiographical account of her childhood in India at the turn of the century as her father worked for the Bengal Steamship Company. The now-adult Harriet narrates the story and looks back on her coming-of-age as a teenage girl in a large British family living in colonial India. Like Anderson's film, it also involves a cobra (the family's young son, Bogey, is killed by a cobra when he tries to learn to charm it with a flute). There is also a funeral service in which his coffin is carried to the water in a somber procession, which leads to catharsis for the other characters. Harriet, overwhelmed by her brother's death and feeling partly to blame, goes out on the river alone in a skiff at night, and thus puts herself in danger of dying in a serious water accident – another connection to Anderson's story. However, Harriet is rescued, and there is a sense of cyclical "rebirth" in the film when a new baby is born to the family at the end of the movie. In Ray's *Charulata*, the wife uses binoculars to magnify her lover (in a binocular-shaped frame similar to Suzy's enhanced vision in *Moonrise Kingdom*). In its portrayal of India, Ray's film *Sonar Kella (The Golden Fortress,* 1974) stands out for its extraordinary, larger than life depiction of the state of Rajasthan (almost like a character in itself) with its unique natural beauty and romanticism, characterized by deserts, camels, forts, peacocks, steam engines, vibrant colors and mysterious goings-on; Anderson's scenes filmed in Rajasthan similarly make use of many of these elements. Rumer Godden's 1939 novel *Black Narcissus* was made into a 1947 Technicolor religious drama film by the British writer-producer-director team of Michael Powell and Emeric Pressburger. It is a psychological drama about the emotional tensions of jealousy and lust within a convent of nuns in an isolated area in the foothills of the Himalayas. The significant communication by letter in the opening of *Black Narcissus* whereby the nuns are invited to a convent in India mirrors Francis's attempts to communicate with his distant mother (also in a convent) by letter and telegram. Patricia's return letter seems to deliberately create a distancing effect rather than a welcoming one; she ends her letter with a lengthy blessing that masks the fact that she is rejecting her sons' visit: "God Bless You and keep you with Mary's benevolent guidance in the light of Christ's enduring grace. All my love, Your Mother, Sister Patricia Whitman." This effusive language of blessing hides the mother's selfishness in rejecting her sons.

The Luftwaffe Automotive Flashback

The "Luftwaffe Automotive" scene is the only flashback in a film otherwise notable for its simplicity and orderly chronological time sequence (unlike the complicated flashbacks and story-within-a-story plotlines common to Anderson's other films). The flashback occurs in a single prolonged unit, breaking into the narrative at a visually symmetrical point – in both cases, the brothers are on their way to a funeral – in one shot, dressed in white, and in the other dressed in black (Francis's bandages disappear, Jack's mustache is gone, and suddenly Peter's wife Alice is sitting across from them in the funeral car). "Luftwaffe Automotive" is the name of a short story Jack shows to his brothers during their first meal together on the train (Peter weeps while reading it alone in the train bathroom), and this is a foreshadowing of this important event (shown in flashback) in the Whitman brothers' life. The short story is typed on "Hotel Chevalier – Guest In Residence" stationery stamped with the name "Jack Whitman" and secured with a paperclip that has since rusted, demonstrating that Jack wrote the story quite some time earlier. The story begins, "He had been killed suddenly, struck buy [sic] a cab while crossing the street. A service was scheduled for the following week and family members flew or drove into town. I was in a rented funeral car with my brothers and…" This excerpt is the flash of the short story's text as it appears in the film. When Jack shows it to his brothers, Francis asks "How long is it?" as if he does not have time to read even a short story, which hurts Jack's feelings. Peter seems eager to read it, although he critiques it saying "I'm not too crazy about the part where I start screaming at the mechanic – that never happened," and Jack assures Peter that the characters in the story are "all fictional."

Anderson has said on the director's commentary for *The Darjeeling Limited* that the "Luftwaffe Automotive" short story is inspired by and a stand-in for J. D. Salinger's own short story "Raise High the Roof Beam, Carpenters" (1955), in which Seymour Glass is about to be married to his fiancée, Muriel, but he does not show up – instead, Buddy Glass is the only Glass family member able to attend his older brother's non-wedding. The connection with Salinger's story makes sense because of the absence of Seymour Glass from a story that ends up being completely revealing about him, first through the conversation of the five disparate characters thrust together in a limousine, and second through excerpts from Seymour's diary found in his apartment, which Buddy hides in a laundry hamper to protect from further discovery about his brother. Except for his central role in "A Perfect Day for Bananafish" (the earliest "Glass family" Salinger story, written in 1948, the account of the last day of Seymour's life, on vacation with his now-wife, Muriel, in Florida), Seymour does not physically appear in most of the stories about him, including the oft-paired novellas "Raise High the Roof Beam, Carpenters," and "Seymour: An Introduction" (1959). In this way, Seymour is always perceived through his absence; he can be understood only by being refracted through the impressions of his younger brother and other characters. The father figure is similarly elusive in *The Darjeeling Limited*. While Bill Murray's character provides a brief stand-in for the father, the viewer comes to know the father only through the conversations and impressions of others – including those among the Whitman brothers in the similar limousine/funeral car on their way to the funeral (which is ultimately missed by the brothers in the same way Seymour's wedding was "missed" by all of the guests because it did not take place). The viewer also comes to know the father through "found" objects scattered throughout the film – his glasses, his razor, his keys, his luggage, and his car. In "Raise High the Roof Beam, Carpenters," the reader gets to know Seymour through excerpts from his diary, but Salinger wrote "Seymour: An Introduction" partially to prove the impossibility of truly capturing the life and essence of someone absent and already deceased. Seymour's brother, Buddy, is purportedly writing the story but although he presents anecdotes and even reproduces Seymour's own writing, Seymour cannot be "brought back" or reproduced on the page. In the Luftwaffe Automotive scene, the viewer feels a pull to know the father through his car, and through his German mechanic friend at the auto shop (whose red-rimmed eyes reveal that he is clearly distraught over the loss of the Whitman father).

The setting of Luftwaffe Automotive in New York City (specifically Queens) on a nondescript street in a downscale neighborhood makes a striking contrast with the brightness and visually appealing sights that the film revealed as the brothers traveled through India in the film up to this point. Anderson set this section in New York City as a parallel to the story "Raise High the Roof Beam, Carpenters" (which also takes place in New York City, largely in a limousine caught in city traffic) but he also found a visual antonym to India's vibrancy in the cold, empty streets of this colorless neighborhood in Queens. In "Raise High," the wedding guests in the limousine speak unkindly and gossip about Seymour in front of Buddy (Buddy has been hiding the fact he is Seymour's brother), and this is reflected by Peter's first line: "I can't believe you just said that." While the brothers on the whole have found themselves treated with kindness by the people they encounter in India, their experience in New York City is quite different: the car is not ready, the part is still not available, the car which has been in the shop for months is still not driveable, and, to emphasize the coldness of the city, when they move the car into the street a large tow truck nearly crashes into them, followed by angry yelling, cursing, and threats of bodily harm. The "Luftwaffe Automotive" scene was also filmed on an extremely cold day, which adds to the numbness and emotional distance of the brothers – when they speak, their breath briefly fogs up the cold outdoor air, again in contrast to the warmth of India. New York's coldness, and the grays and blacks of the New York street on an overcast day, contrast with the vibrant colors and bright sunshine that was so palpable in the scenes shot in India, marking a visceral shift in tone for the New York segment.

The brothers unite to try to jump-start their father's car, clearly demonstrating a desire to bring their father back to life, and an inability to accept his death. Jack checks to see if his father ever noticed his literary dedication "For J. L. W.," (the name "Whitman" suggests literary greatness), while Peter manically grabs the keys for this hopeless venture – the car simply has to be rolled back into the garage and left there.

It is a pathetic end to their poorly-planned idea, and moreover, by engaging in this useless gesture, they miss their father's funeral.

Unfinished Business

The scene in the garage is an odd flashback, especially since the expectation would be that since the film has a flashback to the past, the most logical reference point would be a flashback to the funeral itself. Instead, the viewer is treated to a rushed, frenetic scene about what happened on the way to the funeral – it is a scene about missing a funeral. The three brothers want to claim their father's car from the shop, because they share a vision of attending his funeral by driving there together in their father's car, being present at the funeral, and then leaving together in the car – a tangible part of their father. However, the car is "not ready": there is a part missing. This points to the focus of the film on unfinished business. One way this is symbolized is through the characters' smoking of cigarettes: not one cigarette is ever smoked to the end – instead it is tossed away or stubbed out half-done. *The Darjeeling Limited* is filled with references to unfinished events: the journey on the "Darjeeling Limited" itself has begun already by the time Peter (and the viewer) joins it, and it ends up unfinished (when the brothers are kicked off the train). The film ends without the conclusion of the journey – ultimately the characters end up on a new train, signaling a new beginning for them – but the viewer does not get to see where it leads. Francis has been healing from his motorcycle accident, but the healing process is not yet finished; Peter is going to be a father, but the baby is not yet born; Jack is writing a new story, and he wrote the ending, but he does not yet know the beginning. The flashback to Luftwaffe Automotive is also the "middle" of a story – presented without an introduction or a conclusion. Anderson points out that the only event that the brothers experience completely, from beginning to end, is their entrance into the lives of strangers in India after they are bound together by the tragic death. It is the only time in the entire narrative that they connect to people and go through an experience with them, which is seen through to completion (in fact, they are on the bus and almost miss the funeral, but they are asked by the family and the villagers to come back and attend). Anderson states:

> The one thing that they go through, that they *do* complete, is that they enter into these strangers' lives, for the one time in the whole story that they actually connect to these people, and they go through this experience with them. And that we see from its start to its finish. But everything else is in the middle.[11]

The film is about spiritual change and the human condition. For example, at the beginning of the film, the brothers go to what Francis describes as "one of the most spiritual places in the world," and the first thing they do there is to go shopping at the marketplace, trying to buy a power adapter, shoes, and pepper spray. Searching truths about life are expressed simply by the line "We haven't located us yet" (said when the train gets onto the wrong track). Later in the film, the brothers reflect more commitment to spiritual growth and change, as Anderson describes:

They go through quite a lot, theoretically. They've had quite a year, and these things have an impact on them. But I don't know if somebody can make a 180-degree turn; I think it's just little, incremental changes. But certainly, there's a moment before they go to their mother when they keep finding different places to simulate rituals, and they're doing what people do when people go into a church: They're saying, "What's happening, and how do I deal with it? And what am I supposed to do next? And can I interpret somehow why I feel this way, and why have I done these things, and what's next? Can I be better?" That's what's happening to them in those moments. They're still the same people who sprayed each other with mace. But they're trying.[12]

The Darjeeling Limited is filled with repeated actions and rituals that come to have meaning as they are reinforced throughout the film. One of the repeated rituals in the film is the peacock feather ceremony: the first time, the feather ceremony goes awry as no one follows Francis's instructions (Peter keeps his feather, and Jack's feather blows away in the wind). In the second feather ceremony scene on top of the rock (filmed, according to Anderson, on Christmas Day), the brothers perform the feather ritual together correctly, with a sense of great peace and well-being, a symbol of true change. Second, there is the repeated "giving" of Francis's belt to Peter – offered and rescinded several times. When Francis finally bestows the belt on Peter permanently, it is a symbol that Francis himself is happy with the new memories he has been making with his brothers, and is ready to release the old object of security he was clinging to. Related to this is the boys' final decision to let Francis keep ahold of their passports for the rest of the trip, signifying their acceptance of Francis in the more fatherly role of protector. There is also the repeated ritual of greeting and welcome on the train by the Chief Steward (who checks the tickets) and the female server (who serves sweet lime and paints a bindi dot on the forehead of each of the brothers as they begin their train journey). The second time the brothers go through this ritual, they show that they are feeling more at home in India (they drink their sweet lime immediately, and one brother paints a bindi dot on his own forehead), and this reflects another theme of the film, the idea of feeling "at home": the film is about getting used to a culture and feeling comfortable there.

One of the film's most remarkable scenes is a detailed sequence displaying a series of cutaway train cars carrying various members of the cast in the middle of their own activities in their own personal spaces. This imaginary train sequence reflects the subconscious thoughts and wishes of the brothers and their mother as they talk "without words." This sequence is a broad vision of the film's characters, metaphorically stuck on that train called Life, relentlessly moving forward while not sure what exactly is going on in their own cars, let alone having the time to figure out what is rushing by them outside their closed perspectives. In the last car, The Businessman turns around to see death calmly staring him in the face in the form of a man-eating tiger, lurking quietly in the back of the train, ready to pounce whenever it feels compelled to come for its next victim. The film is ultimately about death,[13] and how difficult it is to reconcile it with the unfinished business of life.

Notes

1. According to the directors' commentary, the three are actually named in homage to Francis Ford Coppola, Peter Bogdanovich, and Jack Nicholson.
2. Natalie Portman, who appeared in a cameo, traveled to the film's location in Jodhpur, India, to shoot for about half an hour. Afterward, she spent ten days exploring India.
3. Michael Guillén, "2007 MVFF30: *The Darjeeling Limited* – Interview with Wes Anderson, Jason Schwartzman, and Roman Coppola," *Screenanarchy.com*. October 10, 2007. http://screenanarchy.com/2007/10/2007-mvff30-the-darjeeling-limited-interview-with-wes-anderson-jason-schwart.html#ixzz453AMLFwl (accessed November 8, 2015).
4. Barry Stephenson, "'Filled with Ritual': Wes Anderson's *The Darjeeling Limited*," *Brightlightsfilm.com*. October 31, 2011. http://brightlightsfilm.com/filled-with-ritual-wes-andersons-the-darjeeling-limited/# (accessed November 10, 2015).
5. According to Anderson, Schwartzman's character is barefoot throughout the film because he was barefoot in the hotel room in the short *Hotel Chevalier*.
6. Guillén, 2007.
7. Matt Zoller Seitz in *The Wes Anderson Collection* (New York: Abrams, 2013a), 203.
8. Richard Brody, "Voyage to India," *The Darjeeling Limited*, liner notes essay for the Criterion Collection DVD, 2010.
9. Stefano Baschiera, "Nostalgically Man Dwells on This Earth: Objects and Domestic Space in *The Royal Tenenbaums* and *The Darjeeling Ltd.*," *New Review of Film and Television Studies* 10:1 (March 2012): 118–131.
10. Owen Wilson gave his character a trademark limp by putting a lime in his shoe.
11. Anderson, quoted in Seitz, 2013a, 227.
12. Ibid.
13. A few months after shooting, before the final cutting of the film, Owen Wilson's suicide attempt in his Santa Monica home on August 26, 2007 made the haunting sense of death in the fictive world of the film all too real. Given awareness of Wilson's troubles, the dismaying state of his Francis enhances the poignancy of the brothers' predicaments beyond what was foreseen and scripted, scoring the film with an intensity beyond what the filmmaker could have imagined.

CHAPTER EIGHT

Adaptation and Homage: The World of Roald Dahl and Fantastic Mr. Fox

Fantastic Mr. Fox opens with a childlike limerick (later sung by children's voices in the film) taken from the fifth paragraph of Roald Dahl's original story, in a style and meter strongly suggesting a nursery rhyme:

> Boggis and Bunce and Bean,
> one fat, one short, one lean.
> These horrible crooks
> so different in looks
> were none the less equally mean.[1]

Thus, the very start of the film sounds like a nursery rhyme, and only then do the typical credits begin to appear: "20th Century Fox Presents..." The nursery rhyme-like words are printed on the screen like the opening lines to a fairy tale, immediately creating an illusion of fantasy, an invitation into a world of make-believe. After the initial credits, the viewer is shown a library copy (there is a Dewey Decimal tag on the side) of the book *Fantastic Mr. Fox* (1970) by Roald Dahl, held up by an animated human arm – this presumably suggests a person has borrowed the book from a library. The cover looks like a reproduction of an authentic cover of Dahl's book, with a design of Mr. Fox leaning jauntily against a tree. The cover, a burnished orange color, seems to date from the 1970s; however, this is not the original cover at all, but one designed for the film, with a promotional tag line that reads "Now a Major Motion Picture from American Empirical." (The authentic original cover of the early edition, illustrated by Donald Chaffin, was obviously the source of inspiration since it also shows Fox in a fancy brown suit leaning against a tree, but it is not nearly as beautifully drawn as the one designed for the film). The scene then transforms to a stop-motion film set identical to the cover of the book, where Mr. Fox is in the same position under the tree. He jogs in place, chews a piece of straw, picks an apple, wipes it on his double-breasted suit jacket, takes a bite out of it and spits out the seeds, all while the soundtrack plays the Wellingtons' "The Ballad of Davy Crockett" (1954). It is quickly revealed that the music is coming from the Walkman-like "Walk-sonic" attached to Fox's jacket pocket. This transformation from library book to look-alike film set once again underscores the literary origins of the film: Anderson does not hide the fact that his film is based on a story; instead, he goes out of his way to create a film trick that will highlight this idea. (Anderson used a similar technique with a fictional book in *The Royal Tenenbaums*.) This "coming to life" strongly communicates that the film literally "comes from" the story – the image on the book cover becomes animated and "real" – as if a daydreaming child, while staring at a cover of a book too long, willed the book into life. At the same time, it underscores the idea of Anderson as Dahl's literary/filmic heir, a somewhat contested notion that will be explored further in the chapter.

In the opening scene, the orange, autumnal tones of the sky[2] and wind-blown tree leaves, as well as the simplicity of the main character's actions (doing exercise and eating an apple), along with the peaceful, upbeat song from the 1950s, suggest an idyllic, homespun tale in a bucolic setting. Dahl's and Anderson's love for pastoral scenery and country living are captured in this homespun tale, which immediately centers on the husband-and-wife relationship. In the opening scene, Mrs. Fox, who is wearing a headband and a hippie-style shirt, comes up the hill as Mr. Fox – in the first line of the film – shows his concern for her by asking her about her visit to the doctor, and what the doctor said. Mrs. Fox downplays her doctors' visit, saying it was just a 24-hour bug, and the two then discuss whether to take the short cut or the scenic route to their destination. In this scene, the viewer gets an initial glimpse into the charming and rascally ways of Mr. Fox, who talks his wife into taking the scenic route with him, rather than giving in to her wishes of taking the short cut. He stops as they leave and chivalrously picks her an orange-colored flower, which she is still holding in the next scene. He continues his charming talk in the next scene (as the Beach Boys song "Heroes and Villains" plays on the soundtrack), announcing to her that she is so pretty that she appears to be glowing (in a comic touch by Anderson, the character is lit from within so that she does, indeed, glow). This scene ends with the serious turn of events in which the couple, "hunting" on a farm, are captured by a cage falling on top of them and trapping them, after which Mrs. Fox announces that she is pregnant (revealing the true purpose of her doctors' visit, plus the source of the glowing), and that she expects, if they survive this incident, that her husband will find another job (in place of raiding henhouses and squab farms). He agrees to this, reluctantly, thus leading into the central conflict of the film and story, which is that Mr. Fox longs to break out of his compromising domesticity and be as "wild" as his instincts call him to be.

There is much suggested by the happy stereotypes of the 1950s-style couple in the first scene at the Fox "home" (announced by a title card to be twelve fox-years after the incident of capture at the farm) where Mrs. Fox skillfully makes a pancake breakfast and pours coffee, all while wearing an apron with pockets full of utensils and tools such scissors, and conversing with her husband, while he, wearing a white short-sleeve button-down shirt and tie, reads his newspaper. The couple they resemble most are Lucille Ball and Desi Arnaz in the 1950s television series *I Love Lucy* (1951–1957), considered one of the most influential and widely-viewed programs in American history. Although in the television series, Lucy, played by Lucille Ball, is the one who gets into mischief and Ricky, played by Arnaz, is the straight man, they are the stereotypical 1950s picture of wedded bliss in the American consciousness (even having a young son, "Little Ricky" in the television series). This representation of domestic gender stereotypes grounds the film in an image of 1950s marital bliss that belies the struggle Mr. Fox hides from his wife – his desire for a life of greater excitement and risk-taking. Domestic details are lovingly presented in the film by Anderson, with typical flourishes such as the Fox family's address (which appears on an address label attached to the newspaper delivered to their home): "Fox, #1 Bramble-on-Shrub." It is also charming that the viewer gets to spot the header for Mr. Fox's newspaper column, "'Fox About Town' With Mr. Fox." Even the label on the manufactured cage that entraps Mr. and Mrs. Fox in the first scene has a twisted homespun charm: "Butler and Son – Wild Animal Destruction." Everything is labeled and civilized, and the outward orderliness of the domestic world hides the deeper struggle suggested by Dahl and Anderson – man's greed, selfishness, and hatred that threaten the bucolic world of nature, and how these worlds may coexist.

Congruency Between Anderson and Dahl's Art

It is fitting that Wes Anderson would be drawn to the work of Roald Dahl, whose children's stories are remarkable due to several factors. Dahl, born in 1916, was writing at a time in the twentieth century when the idea of "Children's Literature" was still largely undefined/unregulated, and "Young Adult (YA) Literature" did not yet exist as a genre category. Thus, Dahl's stories, while written for children, are not "safe," or sanitized for children's tastes as dictated by adults – instead, real-world violence, adult dissension, anger, and strife, war, separation, loneliness, and death are continuously intruding into his child protagonist's world. (Dahl's macabre adult short stories, such as those compiled in *Kiss Kiss* (1960), are even more terrifying and are as difficult to forget.) There are numerous examples of violence and trauma in Dahl's stories. The sudden orphaning of the child James in *James and the Giant Peach* (1961), whose parents are killed by an escaped rhinoceros, occurs in the book's second paragraph, thus forcing James to live with his ghastly, cruel aunts Spiker and Sponge. It is unsettling for a child to read about the sudden death of parents within the first few pages of a story (this also happens in *The Secret Garden*, another pre-"child-safe" story written by Frances Hodgson Burnett [1911]), but Dahl's story is even more disturbing because of its violent description of Spiker and Sponge being crushed by the giant peach when it falls from the tree in their yard and rolls over them – thus leaving the young boy completely without guardians except for his giant insect friends.[3] In another memorably traumatic series of events from Roald Dahl's best-known children's book, *Charlie and the Chocolate Factory* (1964), the children themselves are the ones to suffer violence.

Veruca Salt is dispatched by trained squirrels for being a "bad nut" and disappears down the garbage chute, while Violet Beauregarde is transformed into a blueberry after insisting on chewing the still-experimental "three-course dinner"[4] gum invented by Willy Wonka: her face turns purplish-blue, her body puffs up, and she is rolled away to be juiced. The corpulent Augustus Gloop takes a drink from Wonka's chocolate river, disregarding the adults who implore him not to, and falls in, getting sucked into a pipe and nearly turned into fudge, while Mike Teavee is physically shrunk after being transported by television airwaves. At the end of the book, when the glass elevator rockets up out of the factory, Charlie sees the other children leaving the factory with their candy prizes. The children are "okay" in a sense; Augustus is now skinny (from being squeezed in the pipe), Violet is purple, Veruca and her father are covered in garbage, and Mike is stretched out tall and thin from a gum-stretching machine. If this is a happy ending, it still has plenty of creepiness to it; Roald Dahl's diabolically ingenious works generally do have a macabre side to them.

Dahl's worldview, with its casual intrusion of violence, thus finds a sympathetic counterpart in Wes Anderson's invented cosmos: the bizarre airplane crash in which everyone in Chas's family miraculously survives except Chas's wife in *The Royal Tenenbaums*, the startling death of the dog Snoopy in *Moonrise Kingdom*, the brutal intrusion of war and murder in *The Grand Budapest Hotel* (which originally suggests itself to be a film about trifles, in which the main character is a model of civility), and *Fantastic Mr. Fox* itself, where the hero is repeatedly threatened with annihilation in "missions" and "battles" that are tainted with the violent trauma experienced by Dahl as a fighter pilot in World War II. (The holes dug also suggest foxholes, in which the soldiers of the war needed to lie down to preserve their own lives, as well as the warrens of trenches behind the front lines in which the soldiers had to live, often starving and uncomfortable, more like animals than human beings.) *Fantastic Mr. Fox* also presents as one of its themes the idea of man vs. nature, in which the effects of the Industrial Revolution continued to resonate in the English countryside in the mid-twentieth century when Dahl was writing, and this theme is terrifyingly presented by the digging bulldozers, described in the book as "two enormous caterpillar tractors with mechanical shovels on their front ends,"[5] that tear at the earth and shatter the bucolic peace of Mr. and Mrs. Fox's home, utterly destroying it (the hole dug in some ways suggests the absolute destruction left after the dropping of a bomb). Dahl employs ominous-sounding adjectives to describe the machines such as "clanking," "black," and "murderous, brutal-looking monsters."[6] These descriptions make them sound like weapons or war machinery, and Dahl's account of the farmers trapping the animals without food or resources is like a siege. This destruction of the natural world was of deep concern to Dahl, and Anderson's film, with its beautiful vistas (as well as the stunning natural landscapes painted by Mrs. Fox, especially the large mural she paints of the farms and their surrounding environs), also clearly reflects Dahl's love of nature.

When Anderson was asked why he chose Dahl's story to be the one piece of children's fiction he wanted to bring to the screen, his reply demonstrated a true appreciation of Dahl's unique talent for capturing the imagination of his audience, as well as a certain artistic kinship with him:

It's that [Roald Dahl] really did have a knack for seeing from a child's point of view. The details he focuses on and vividly describes are just the ones that might most fully and directly capture a child's attention and inspire a child's imagination. Or it might be that his books show a true interest in the things that make children laugh and frighten them. He never particularly held himself back from the extremely scary or disgusting things. He had such a broad imagination and would turn some real-life inspiration into something fabulous.[7]

Anderson's explanation of Dahl's particular genius focuses on both his penchant for disturbing turns of plot and his tendency to draw from real life experiences, both of which are features common to his own films. Clearly both Dahl and Anderson share a certain sensibility toward how they dramatize the human condition in their art, evoking a childlike sense of both seriousness and whimsy.

Relationship to Roald Dahl's Source Novel

A number of critics have dealt with the topic of how Anderson has been promoted as Dahl's cinematic heir by linking Anderson with Dahl through promotional materials, including the story of Anderson meeting Dahl's widow, Felicity (more commonly known as "Liccy") on a visit to Dahl's own residence, "Gipsy House," in Great Missenden, a small village in Buckinghamshire, England.[8] Anderson and co-writer Noah Baumbach were later invited by Liccy to spend two weeks at Gipsy House, where they perused Dahl's original drafts of *Fantastic Mr. Fox* (during this time they discovered Dahl's draft of the original story had the foxes stealing from a supermarket, which became the ending of the film), Dahl's remaining curio-like belongings, writing hut, and desk (Dahl wrote four hours a day sitting in an armchair with a green-felt-upholstered board across his lap), as well as carefully studying, photographing, and recreating Dahl's living spaces in parts of the film (such as the Fox home, and Badger's office).[9] The promotional materials included in the DVD, such as an essay by Anderson reprinted from *The New York Times* entitled "Welcome to the Dahl House" and photographs from that visit, draw special attention to these links between Anderson's film and Dahl himself, which act to bestow upon the film a certain critical legitimacy. It is even clear from the DVD's presentation of Dahl's original draft that Anderson based some of his vision, particularly of the tunnels and digging, on Dahl's original drawings. However, this direct critical and creative heritage has been challenged by scholars such as Adrienne Kertzer (2011) who questions Anderson's fidelity to the source material by pointing out that Anderson changed the nature of the "Felicity" character from Dahl's original story, and Tom Dorey (2012) in his article "Fantastic Mr. Filmmaker: Paratexts and the Positioning of Wes Anderson as Roald Dahl's Cinematic Heir," which examines how the marketing of the film deliberately plays up the connection between author and filmmaker.

Dahl's original story is rather short for a novel, and although it contains eighteen chapters, it is only eighty-one pages long in the Quentin Blake-illustrated version

(Blake was Dahl's illustrator for approximately the last fifteen years of his life). Some of Dahl's chapter titles (such as "The Shooting" and "The Terrible Tractors") are used directly in Anderson's film. In addition, certain passages are taken directly from Dahl's original narrative, such as the nursery rhyme used at the film's opening, and Badger's description of Bunce: "He was so short his chin would have been under water in the shallow end of any swimming-pool in the world."[10] The most significant additions to the story are the fleshing out of Mrs. Fox and the family dynamics with Ash and his visiting cousin, the "unaccompanied minor" Kristofferson – in the book Fox has four children but they remain unnamed, without distinctive personalities or physical descriptions. The character of Rat is much more developed and given much more prominence (in an unforgettable performance by Willem Dafoe: "Y'all are trespassing now … illegally") in the film (Dahl's Rat is dismissed easily by Fox baring his teeth, and Badger offers up a final summation of his character: "All rats have bad manners. I've never met a polite rat yet"[11]).

Another interesting connection between the book and the film is the discussion of the morality of Fox's acts of theft, and the somewhat belabored analysis of Fox's motivations. In chapter 14 of the book, entitled "Badger Has Doubts," Badger questions Fox by naming the crime he is committing as "stealing," whereupon Fox accuses Badger of being far too respectable:

> "There's nothing wrong with being respectable," Badger said.
> "Look," said Mr. Fox, "Boggis and Bunce and Bean are out to kill us. You realize that, I hope?"
> "I do, Foxy, I do indeed,'" said the gentle Badger.
> "But we're not going to stoop to their level. We don't want to kill *them*."
> "I should hope not, indeed," said Badger.
> "We wouldn't dream of it," said Mr. Fox. "We shall simply take a little food here and there to keep us and our families alive. Right?"
> "I suppose we'll have to," said Badger.
> "If they want to be horrible, let them," said Mr. Fox. "We down here are decent peace-loving people."
> Badger laid his head on one side and smiled at Mr. Fox. "Foxy," he said, "I love you."
> "Thank you," said Mr Fox. "And now let's get on with the digging."[12]

This passage encapsulates much of the character of Mr. Fox and dynamic of the relationship between Mr. Fox and Badger, which is given fuller expression in Anderson's film. In the book, Badger expresses himself as the hesitant, proper, law-abiding citizen, unwilling to involve himself in a moral quandary, while Fox's charm and charisma wins him (and everyone else) over. The dialogue is reminiscent of the dynamic between Dignan (as the charismatic leader) and Anthony (as the reluctant partner-in-crime) in *Bottle Rocket*. Although Dahl's original story lingers on this discussion of motive, Anderson's film takes the discussion much further by suggesting Fox's motivation is a form of midlife crisis, which reflects how the story is filtered through Anderson's lens (the addition of egotistic human psychology to complicate the hero: Mr. Fox is as selfish and self-centered as the typical Anderson male lead, but with an unusually heroic streak as well).

A significant change from Dahl's original story is found in the character of Mrs. Fox, and these alterations have incited critical discussion. In Dahl's story, Mrs. Fox is drawn rather flatly as a demure housewife who is unfailingly supportive to her husband (the two often call one another "darling"), an excellent cook, and a warm and loving homemaker who deeply cares for her children. In addition, in Dahl's writing, Mrs. Fox exhibits certain characteristics of weakness, i.e., she cries and becomes panicky when the family is threatened. During the violence of the conflict with the farmers, Mrs. Fox's physical weakness caused by the deprivation of food and water prevents her from helping further with the digging, and she seems to be more of a background figure; in this way, Dahl's story keeps in line with the more typically conservative view of gender roles. An early passage from Dahl's text after the initial digging demonstrates this conservative dynamic between Mr. and Mrs. Fox:

> They all sat down, panting for breath. And Mrs. Fox said to her children, "I should like you to know that if it wasn't for your father we should all be dead by now. Your father is a fantastic fox."
> Mr. Fox looked at his wife and she smiled. He loved her more than ever when she said things like that.[13]

By contrast, Anderson's Felicity Fox is a no-nonsense woman who confronts her husband, makes him change jobs, and during one conflict even slaps him across the face, scratching his cheek and leaving a scar that remains for the rest of the film. She threatens him fiercely: "If what I think is happening *is* happening, it better not be." At the same time, Anderson is faithful to Dahl's portrait of Felicity Fox in certain key ways, such as the 1950s "I Love Lucy" homemaker image described above: Felicity is the one who makes her husband's breakfast and brings him coffee while he reads the newspaper at the breakfast table, the one who wears an apron and runs the vacuum cleaner in the background, and the one who is sent away to safety with the other animals. Yet, Anderson challenges this view by having Mrs. Fox defend her family against Rat skillfully, and fearlessly later in the film, wielding a chain like a set of nunchucks. Other continuities with the book are Mrs. Fox's tearful, panicky line, "They'll kill the children!" in response to the first attack. Anderson turns this into a more humorous dialogue when Fox replies, "Over my dead body," and Mrs. Fox snaps back, "That's what I meant, you'd also be dead in that scenario." The film complicates the character of Mrs. Fox while retaining her loyalty to her husband; when Fox, at one of the lowest points of their plight, tries to rally the troops by asking, "Who will join me?" Mrs. Fox is the only one (at first) to respond with her support. In addition, Mrs. Fox is given a complicated past (it is implied that she had once been quite promiscuous), but here Fox defends her with "She lived. We all did." During the climactic battle scene, Mrs. Fox is shown wearing her sixties-style headband, which demonstrates an awakening that connects back to her younger, "wilder" self. In the book and film, Mrs. Fox prepares the great feast for all the animals, but while at the end of Dahl's story Mrs. Fox claims she is too shy even to make a speech, only to say once more that her husband is "fantastic," at the end of the film, Mrs. Fox makes the more playfully postmodern statement that her husband is "quote unquote, fantastic." This linguistic discrepancy represents the more nuanced viewpoint that Anderson brings to the story, elevating it from its rigid, of-its-time traditionalism by casting it in the humorous light of a more psychologically ambiguous, postmodernist paradigm.

The Complication of Gender Roles

While the analysis above of the comparison between the film's portrayal of Felicity Fox and the book's more traditional rendering of the Mrs. Fox character demonstrates that in many ways Anderson remained true to the spirit of the book, Anderson also complicates the gender dynamics in his filmic family. In the book, Mrs. Fox's maternal and wifely nature is well-determined (she is the happy wife and mother of a litter of four), while in the film, Mrs. Fox is the mother of one, a slightly "problem child" (at the end of the film, when Mr. Fox – standing literally on a soap box – makes a toast, all the characters toast with apple juice boxes while Ash alone toasts with grape juice) who must also wrestle with her husband's wild nature. Mrs. Fox's paintings (by real-life artist Turlo Griffin) throughout the film are of beautifully-executed landscapes with one unusual detail – they all portray lightning bolts or tornadoes suddenly cropping up to threaten the pastoral calm – a reference to the unpredictable "wildness" of nature and also of the "wild animal" nature within herself and her loved ones, especially her husband. Fox is a hyper-masculine character ("How can a fox ever be happy without a chicken in its teeth?" Fox says to Kylie,[14] an opossum who is added to the story by Anderson in a male-male "buddy" relationship with Fox) doomed to live life without his tail (Fox's tail is shot off in both the book and the film – only in the film does Anderson add the detail of having Farmer Bean wear the tail as a necktie). Fox is also perturbed by his son turning out to be (accompanied by hand gestures) "different," a fact that is challenging to Ash as well, as he cannot compete well in his father's best sport, "Whack-Bat" (he is replaced in the game by a substitute). In the film, Anderson adds the dynamic of Ash trying to redeem his father's masculinity by retrieving his father's tail, thus gaining the longed-for paternal recognition he craves.[15]

The viewer only learns that the first name of Mrs. Fox is Felicity[16] when her signature is shown on the large landscape mural she is painting. The name "Felicity" means "happiness," and this name, as well as "Foxy" for Mr. Fox, has a Dickensian aspect to it. Foxy is naturally a predator, a trickster, and a seducer, and yet Mr. Fox cannot have "happiness" – or "felicity" – unless he changes his essentially wild nature. This is highlighted during the tormented scene at the waterfall:

> Mr. Fox: Foxes traditionally love to court danger, hunt prey, and outsmart predators. And, that's what I'm usually good at. I think by the end of the day, I think that...
> Mrs. Fox: I know ... We're wild animals...

Haunting music by Alexandre Desplat marks this unforgettable scene in which Wolf shares Fox's raised-fist salute in solidarity to their shared wildness in the film's denouement. Anderson considers this the most important scene in the film.

The fact that this scene uses music by Georges Delerue ("Une petite île") from Truffaut's film *Les Deux anglaises et le continent* points to the connection between Mr. and Mrs. Fox and the tormented love story at the center of Truffaut's film, wherein lead actor Jean-Pierre Léaud is in love with two sisters. Foxy is likewise a seductor, and when Felicity tells Foxy that she loves him, but she should never have married him, this leads Foxy to realize he seriously has to make things right, and he decides to sacrifice himself – the ultimate for a trickster – basically giving up "the game." To keep "Felicity," Foxy has to change his ways. This same piece of music is also used in the earlier scene in the mineral deposit where Felicity says, "We all die – unless you change." Both of these scenes demonstrate that Fox must change or give up his essential wild nature in order to have "felicity."

At the end of the film, Anderson provides a much more nuanced scenario. The film ends with Fox and his gang escaping and they meet the wild Wolf. Fox salutes him – and his old self – away. The Wolf represents Fox's wild side, and he can never be too "wild" because of the responsibilities and difficulties of his domestic life, his family, his job, etc. When he comes to realize this, his eyes briefly fill with tears. The Wolf also represents the complete freedom and independence from the human world that animals, and in particular Fox, can/wishes to attain. This freedom is simultaneously something that scares Fox ("I have a phobia of wolves") because as a civilized Canidae, he is afraid of the primal animal he recognizes at his core: his unruly appetites, his selfishness, the danger he poses to his loved ones because of his natural instincts for lying and scheming. Achieving mastery of himself over these instincts is his ultimate goal, what he fights for throughout the whole movie, the struggle into which he pulls everyone around him. This scene shows that Fox has indeed overcome his own fear of freedom/responsibility symbolized here by a nuanced moment of contact with the

Wolf. When they salute one another, Wolf puts a paw into the air in a gesture of solidarity in recognition of their shared wildness. Then the film ends with the exuberant dance-party to the song "Let Her Dance" by Bobby Fuller, with a lyric about someone embarking on a brand new love affair. In essence, it is as though the "old" Foxy is looking in on the dance and realizing that Felicity is dancing with a "new" Mr. Fox – "Well, there she goes with a brand new love affair. Dancing with him [the new Fox]."

Made for Children/Adults?

Dahl began writing *Fantastic Mr. Fox* in 1969 (the same year Anderson was born) and completed it for publication the following year. According to Michael Specter's interview, *Fantastic Mr. Fox* is the first book Anderson remembers having read. "This was not only the first Roald Dahl book I read," Anderson recalls in the interview, "I think it was the first book I ever possessed."[17] Anderson's mother put nameplates in her sons' books, and the three brothers would fight over the Dahl books by tearing out one another's names and replacing them with their own. Another aspect of the book that captured the young Anderson's imagination was the importance of digging an elaborate network of underground tunnels (the appearance in the movie also suggests the careful tunneling in an ant farm), because when Anderson and his brothers were small, they were "obsessed with being underground."[18] Not only did Anderson and his brother Mel carve out a secret access to their attic through the roof (see Introduction), but they often joined a neighbors' family digging out tunnels and a large underground fort, which Anderson likened to an anthill; they only halted the digging in their own yard when they ran into underground pipes. Anderson elaborates on the importance of the book to him, even into adulthood, in an interview with Terry Gross:

> Well, it was the first Roald Dahl book that I ever read as a child, and I became a huge fan of Dahl, and he was a big part of my childhood. For some reason, this book was the one I always kept with me. Wherever I lived, when I went to college, I always had this book on my shelves. It's not a very – it's a slim book, and it really kind of – I think it's for young children, but something about it always stuck with me. And I think the character of Mr. Fox is a very Dahl kind of figure, and he's the one who rescues everybody, but he's also the cause of all of their problems, and his personality gets them into these problems in the first place. And I think something about that grabbed me.[19]

The fact that Anderson identifies Dahl as a significant influence on his childhood, as well as pointing out that he kept the book on his shelves during college, indicates the tremendous respect Anderson maintains for Dahl's work, in both childhood and as an adult. This adult/child audience hybridity of audience for the book comes into play in Anderson's film, which contains elements which are certainly not common to a children's film, and thus blurs the line between adult and child entertainment. Dahl himself did that with his own work in film, writing for both adults, with the screenplay for the James Bond film *You Only Live Twice* (1967), and for children with the fantastical film *Chitty Chitty Bang Bang* (1968). In addition, some of Dahl's short stories for adults were adapted and dramatized for television in the United States as part of the series *Alfred Hitchcock Presents* (1955–1965) and in the UK as *Tales of the Unexpected* (1979–1988). Adaptations of Dahl's children's books for film have proved challenging over the years; *Charlie and the Chocolate Factory* has been adapted twice, once in 1971 as *Willy Wonka and The Chocolate Factory*, starring Gene Wilder (Dahl worked on the original screenplay but ultimately disowned the film, the script of which was partially rewritten by David Seltzer; Dahl was disappointed by the shift in emphasis from Charlie to Willy Wonka) and later with the original name restored as *Charlie and the Chocolate Factory* (2005) starring Johnny Depp in the version directed by Tim Burton. Anderson's *Fantastic Mr. Fox* had a predecessor in Henry Selick's *James and the Giant Peach* (1996), produced by Tim Burton, which also used stop-motion animation for the sequences with the over-sized insects (and live-action for the beginning and end of the film). Henry Selick had been the animator for Anderson's *The Life Aquatic with Steve Zissou* in 2004, and Anderson hoped to work with him again, but Selick was committed to directing the stop-motion film *Coraline* (2009), and recommended Mark Gustafson to lead the teams of animators for *Fantastic Mr. Fox*.

Erica Wagner (2014) observes that Dahl's clothed animals are an updated version of Beatrix Potter's anthropomorphic animals who behave as real animals with true animal instincts, especially because despite their "civilized" adoption of human ways, they are also still "wild" and take reckless risks like the titular mammal in Potter's *The Tale of Peter Rabbit* (1902). There is also a noted similarity with Kenneth Grahame's *Wind in the Willows* (1908), another anthropomorphic animal story (depicting a toad, a rat, a mole, and a badger) set in a pastoral version of England. While these earlier works were created for children and served a didactic purpose (for example, when Peter Rabbit misbehaves and disobeys his mother, he is sent to bed early while his three sisters enjoy bread, milk, and blackberries for supper), Dahl's writing, and Anderson's film, have a more unnerving ambiguity in their narratives. Boggis, Bunce, and Bean are the evil farmers and clearly the villains of the piece, but Mr. Fox is hardly an ideal role model: the character Dahl created acts heroically by saving all the animals, but only after being himself the cause of all their problems. Anderson complicates this further by giving him the type of midlife crisis typical of an Anderson "anti-hero" father figure. The story features a lot of scheming and violence; there are explosions, guns, a knife-wielding rat, and a rabid dog (Spitz, an oblique reference to the dog that clashes with Buck in Jack London's *The Call of the Wild* [1903]). The farmers smoke and drink, as do the adult animals, who tend to drink with dinner (the rapturous enjoyment of strong cider is an element that is unmistakable in the source novel, in which Fox and Badger each compose odes to the alcoholic drink). Mr. and Mrs. Fox are shown exchanging kisses, but no sexuality is expressed (apart from Mrs. Fox's repeated pregnancies), and the language is limited to the word "cuss" being used as a substitute for stronger words (as in "What the cuss?"). This coyness with bad language also comes from the source novel, in which Dahl depicts the farmer Bunce's swearing as "cursing the fox with dirty words that cannot be printed"[20] With the repeated use of "cuss," Anderson's idea was to try to use the concept of profanity as a replacement for the profanity itself. This idea turns out to be very versatile; for example, in one scene in the village, the word "CUSS" appears as spray-painted graffiti on the wall. Anderson's film thus modulates, both in content and in subtle humor, between adult and child audiences.

Anderson deliberately selected music from children's films or music associated with powerfully nostalgic memories of children's entertainment, such as the use of "The Ballad of Davy Crockett" at the beginning of the film, and three different Burl Ives songs from the 1959 album *Burl Ives Sings Little White Duck and Other Children's Favorites* (Ives was memorably the voice of the Snowman narrator in Rankin-Bass stop-motion holiday special "Rudolph the Red-Nosed Reindeer" [1964]). There is also the song "Love" that was originally used in a beautifully romantic scene in the Disney animated version of *Robin Hood* (1973), in which the titular character was an animated fox. Alexandre Desplat also composed *Peter and the Wolf*-style (1936) themes for each animal, and the Rat's movements, especially with the knife, echo Bob Fosse-style choreography, particularly the hoodlums' dancing coordinated with flick-knives in *West Side Story* (Robert Wise and Jerome Robbins, 1961; adapted from Stephen Sondheim and Leonard Bernstein's stage musical, 1957). To round out the musical selection, the soundtrack also features the Beach Boys (including an especially arresting cover version of Oscar Hammerstein II and Jerome Kern's "Ol' Man River") and the Rolling Stones' "Street Fighting Man," in time with the arrival of "the terrible tractors."[21]

Anderson says in an interview with Michael Specter, when asked about the target audience of his film:

> There are lots of movies for kids that I like and have always liked. *The Bad News Bears* [1976] is one that I've always loved. I've always talked to people about how much I like that movie. That's a movie for kids, but it doesn't make any compromises based on the fact that it's for children. The movie ends with the Bears losing the game, drinking beers with the coach, and there's quite a lot of profanity, and one of the kids smokes cigarettes. And, you know, I don't really like the movement in children's movies toward – I'm not fond of this thing where it gets so clean and safe… [*Fantastic Mr. Fox* has] not been made deliberately safe, and instead we tried to keep it free and a bit wilder like Dahl.[22]

In making *Fantastic Mr. Fox*, Anderson deliberately chose not to design a specifically "child-friendly" film; in fact, he did not try to pose the question about whether the film would be targeting children or adults. Children who view the film are thus confronted with adult realities, especially the concept that the world is not, in fact, "safe." In doing so, Anderson remains faithful to Roald Dahl's uniquely macabre, and even disturbing, source material.

Other Influences

Anderson chose to make *Fantastic Mr. Fox* using one of filmmaking's oldest animation styles – stop-motion. Specifically, he was interested in capturing the old-fashioned, handmade quality and movement of the animal's fur in the original *King Kong* (1933):

The thing I've always loved with stop-motion, more than anything else, is puppets that have fur ... I love the way King Kong, the old King Kong, looked, with his fur – the animators call it "boiling." And for some reason, the whole magical aspect of stop-motion was one of those things where you can see the trick – I mean, you know the Cocteau movies? The visual effects in *Beauty and the Beast* [*La Belle et la bête*, 1946] for instance, are things where you can really see that a person is behind this wall sticking their arm through it, holding a torch, and the film is running backwards, and so that is how this light is coming on, or the mirror is actually water. You know, those kinds of effects, where you can see what it is, have always been the most fascinating and mesmerizing and moving to me.[23]

As Eric Anderson (who voiced "Kristofferson" in the film), explained to Michael Specter, the effect of stop-motion is like the difference between "a hand-drawn drawing versus something that is computer designed. There's a little personality somewhere in it that just, maybe it's a little warmer than something that is made by computer."[24]

Other obvious influences include the association of actor George Clooney, whose Danny Ocean is a man who concocts elaborate plans for larceny, in the *Oceans* franchise (2001, 2004, 2007) directed by Steven Soderbergh. The tunneling and elaborate motorcycle jump over the fence recall Steve McQueen in *The Great Escape* (1963). When Kylie describes the altercation between Mr. and Mrs. Fox, "You say one thing, she says another and it all changes back again," this is a direct quote from *Rebel Without a Cause* (1955). On the *Fantastic Mr. Fox* DVD director's commentary, Anderson points to an unnamed "Afterschool Special" that suggested the relationship between a larger younger cousin who fights on behalf of a smaller, older one (when Kristofferson removes his shoe to kick a larger bully in the face). Anderson also references a touching farewell scene between a father (played by Mel Gibson) and son from M. Night Shyamalan's *Signs* (2002), which Anderson imitates in Fox's farewell to Ash, holding Ash's head in his hands, before he plans to turn himself in to the farmers, heading up to "Street Level" with a white flag in his paw. In the little English village street, Anderson also makes a subtle reference to Truffaut's film *Baisers volés* (*Stolen Kisses*, 1968) with his "Dutronc Detective" sign, which matches a sign filmed near the Louvre by Truffaut.

Fantastic Mr. Fox connects to Truffaut most overtly in one of the key scenes: Fox's pivotal toast scene near the end of the film. In this scene, Anderson chose the same piece of music, Delerue's "Le Grand Choral," used in Truffaut's film *La Nuit americaine* – which he had already put to significant use in a commercial he did for American Express (see chapter 11). This scene underscores Fox's nature as "director" of the action, as he goes around defining his friends' jobs and talents and begins assigning them "positions" for the upcoming battle. The reference to Truffaut as director here again points to the auteur connection with Anderson (Fox is a stand-in for Anderson, dressed identically to the director, and also for Truffaut, signaled by the music from *La Nuit americaine*, in which Truffaut himself played a Truffaut-like director):

Mr. Fox: (*addressing the others from atop a pile of bricks*) In a way, I'm almost glad that flood interrupted us because I don't like the toast I was giving. I'm gonna start over.

(*Mr. Fox switches on his radio. "Le Grand Choral" plays. He gestures as if holding a wine glass*)

Mr. Fox: When I look down this table, with the exquisite feast set before us, I see: two terrific lawyers, a skilled pediatrician, a wonderful chef, a savvy real estate agent, an excellent tailor, a crack accountant, a gifted musician, a pretty good minnow fisherman, and possibly the best landscape painter working on the scene today. Maybe a few of you might even read my column from time to time. Who knows? I tend to doubt it. (*brief pause*)

Mr. Fox: I also see a room full of wild animals.

(*He approaches their groups as he speaks*)

Mr. Fox: Wild animals, with true natures and pure talents. Wild animals with scientific-sounding Latin names that mean something about our DNA. Wild animals each with his own strengths and weaknesses due to his or her species.

(*re-ascends the brick pile*)

Mr. Fox: Anyway, I think it may very well be all the beautiful differences among us that might just give us the tiniest glimmer of a chance of saving my nephew, and letting me make it up to you for getting us into this, this crazy … whatever it is. I don't know. It's just a thought. Thank you for listening. Cheers, everyone.

(*mimics draining the imaginary glass and smashing it to the floor*)

Kylie: Let's eat!

(*All eyes turn to Kylie*)

Kylie: What? I was just playin' along with the bit he was doing…

Here, Anderson references Truffaut as a director who motivates the group much the same way Anderson himself does in his director role. Anderson deliberately juxtaposes the strong charisma of Truffaut with the character of Fox, and at the same time, through Fox's choice of clothing, references himself as the director. Other influences mentioned by Anderson on the director's commentary include the final sequence from the 1972 film *Jeremiah Johnson*, starring Robert Redford and directed by Sidney Pollack, which helped inspire the Wolf scene, and Anderson's explanation that the final shot, in which the camera pulls back to reveal an overhead view of the seemingly unlimited abundance of the produce in the store owned by "Boggis, Bunce and Bean International Supermarkets," is a reference to similar overhead shots of the untold riches from Kane's mansion and the unmarked treasures stored in a U.S. government warehouse in the final scenes of *Citizen Kane* and *Raiders of the Lost Ark*. Moreover, the final dance sequence in the supermarket, where each character has his or her individual dance style (i.e., Fox as Fred Astaire, Ash with his Michael Jackson moves, Mrs. Fox as French dancer Zizi Jeanmaire, and Kylie's robo break-dance) echoes once again the joyous dance onstage during Bill Melendez's 1965 *A Charlie Brown Christmas*.

Discussions of Anderson's *Fantastic Mr. Fox* also center on the undefined geographical place and chronological time period of the film. Critics have questioned whether the film is British or American – whether it is Dahl's voice that takes precedence, or whether Anderson appropriated Dahl's material for an American audience. For example, scholars have questioned why the villainous "bad" guys, the humans, were cast with UK voices only (Michael Gambon as Franklin Bean, Helen McCrory as Mrs. Bunce, Hugo Guinness as Nathan Bunce, Scottish actor Brian Cox as the T.V. reporter, Jarvis Cocker as Petey), while for the "good" guys, the animals, American voices were used: George Clooney as Mr. Fox, Meryl Streep as Mrs. Fox, Jason Schwartzman as Ash, Eric Chase Anderson as Kristofferson, Wally Wolodarsky as Kylie, and Bill Murray as Badger.[25] However, critics such as Browning (2011), and Wagner (2014) suggest that this is done for humorous intent, and relates to the traditional Hollywood casting of evil characters with British accents ("in the classic tradition of silverscreen baddies"[26] according to Wagner). Both Browning and Wagner also focus on how, while the landscapes are English, there is an unusual blend of influences that lend a deliberate chronological ambiguity to the film: the cobbler's shop on a main street, the 70's-style American station wagon equipped with British right-hand drive, the helicopter modeled after the one in the American series *Magnum P.I.* (1980–1988), the conspicuous presence of the English pub "The Nag's Head," the bakery, and red mailboxes (Anderson has said the street scenery was modeled after the town of Bath) mixed with the American-style roving T.V. reporter and newspaper deliveries thrown onto front stoops. Finally, this film is tied closely to Anderson's previous film, *The Darjeeling Limited*, with the ubiquitous presence of trains: Alexandre Desplat composed unique musical themes to highlight the appearance of trains in the film and they are frequently shown running through the countryside and also in Ash's bedroom. The scene on Kristofferson's first night, after Ash makes Kristofferson cry, and then, with uncharacteristic sympathy, climbs out of bed and runs his train set for both of the boys to quietly watch together is matched in power with the train that runs through the background at the end of the long, still scene after the group has their encounter with the Wolf. Both of these scenes emphasize the train, as it did in *The Darjeeling Limited*, as a symbol of the continuity of life. Thus, Anderson uses a pastiche of influences to create his fictional worlds in order to communicate truth more vividly.

Notes

1   Roald Dahl, *Fantastic Mr. Fox* (New York: Penguin, 1970), 5.
2   Anderson claims that the skies in the film were inspired by Mark Rothko paintings. Wes Anderson, on the *Fantastic Mr. Fox* DVD director's commentary.
3   "There was a crunch. And then there was silence. And behind it, Aunt Sponge and Aunt Spiker lay ironed out upon the grass as flat and lifeless as a couple of paper dolls cut out of a picture book." Roald Dahl, *James and the Giant Peach* (New York: Penguin, 1961), 49. This type of casual gore is similar to Wes Anderson's almost cartoonish description of the dead family dog Buckley in *The Royal*

Tenenbaums:screenplay: "Buckley's leash remains tied to the railing and extends taut beneath the wheels of Eli's car." Wes Anderson and Owen Wilson, *The Royal Tenenbaums* (New York: Faber and Faber, 2001), 137.
4　Roald Dahl, *Charlie and the Chocolate Factory* (New York: Penguin, 1964), 94.
5　Roald Dahl, *Fantastic Mr. Fox* (New York: Penguin, 1970), 21.
6　Ibid., 21–22.
7　Anderson, quoted by Matt Zoller Seitz in *The Wes Anderson Collection* (New York: Abrams, 2013a), 255.
8　Dahl was clearly inspired by the natural scenery in and around Great Missenden. The grounds of his home included a walled garden, a kitchen garden, a formal garden, and an orchard, and during Anderson's visit, while walking around the property, he came across "a gigantic beech tree at the end of a fox run, which I immediately recognized from 'Fantastic Mr. Fox.'" Wes Anderson, "Welcome To the Dahl House," *The New York Times Sunday Magazine*, August 18, 2002, 45.
9　Badger's flint mine is also inspired by an actual flint mine located near Gipsy House.
10　Dahl, 1970, 3.
11　Ibid., 72.
12　Ibid., 59–60.
13　Ibid., 19.
14　"Kylie" is named for an actual person who became a hanger-on in Anderson's life when he would not move out of Anderson's New York apartment after Anderson had it renovated.
15　This complication of gender roles is extended to the younger generation, as Ash accuses his lab partner, Agnes, of being "disloyal" because she develops a crush on his cousin Kristofferson. None of this is in Dahl's source material; Anderson adds it to further emphasize Ash's troubled performance of masculinity in the film.
16　This is where it is revealed that Anderson named Fox's wife after Dahl's widow, adding an even stronger association with Dahl's real-life married relationship, rather than limiting it to the more traditional marriage dynamic portrayed in Dahl's narrative.
17　Anderson, in an interview with Michael Specter in *The Making of Fantastic Mr. Fox* (New York: Rizzoli, 2009), 23.
18　Ibid., 23.
19　Gross, Terry. "Fresh Air: Wes Anderson Covers New Ground with 'Mr. Fox.'" *TPR.org*. November 23, 2009. http://tpr.org/post/wes-anderson-covers-new-ground-mr-fox#stream/0 (accessed June 5, 2014).
20　Dahl, 1970, 29.
21　Alexandre Desplat's distinctive whistling melody in the fight scene with Rat recalls Sergio Leone's spaghetti westerns.
22　Anderson, in an interview with Michael Specter in *The Making of Fantastic Mr. Fox* (New York: Rizzoli, 2009), 23.
23　Anderson, in interview with Specter, 2009, 31.
24　Ibid., 87.

25 American voices, especially Anderson regulars, were also used for other animal roles such as Coach Skip (Owen Wilson), Linda Otter (Karen Duffy), Weasel (Wes Anderson), Field Mouse (Adrien Brody), and Rabbit (Mario Batali).
26 Erica Wagner, "Vulpine Nature," *Fantastic Mr. Fox* DVD Liner Notes Booklet. Criterion Collection Blu-Ray DVD Release, 2014, 14.

CHAPTER NINE

Reconstitution of the "Family" and Construction of Normalized Gender in Moonrise Kingdom

Moonrise Kingdom is a hybrid romance/comedy/fantasy about two twelve-year-olds, the social outcast Sam Shakusky (Jared Gilman) and the alienated Suzy Bishop (Kara Hayward), whose "amour fou" turns into an epic pre-adolescent love story. This narrative is set in a meticulously crafted Anderson cosmos, and takes as its motif children's stories – the tall tales, Sunday-school stories, boy's adventure narratives, fables, and fairy tales that once again point to the power of literary narratives in Anderson's work. He carefully evokes the experience of a childhood memory wrapped in the narrative guise of a children's story that is both exaggerated and authentic (as memory often is).[1] Using a unique mise-en-scène of carefully constructed tableaux that evoke Norman Rockwell[2] images, a thoughtfully curated soundtrack, and artful embellishments of magical realism seemingly drawn from Suzy's cherished storybooks, Anderson captures the cataclysmically heightened sense at the end of childhood and the transformative, almost magical potency of first love. This film, made from Anderson's Oscar-nominated screenplay written with Roman Coppola, clearly deals with the topic of nostalgia, bringing together many strands of cultural and personal memory, with the year of 1965 (a time heralding the end of America's cultural innocence), the fictional "Khaki Scouts of North America" organization, and the Norman Rockwell/Gilbert and Sullivan aesthetic of New Penzance Island. This film also contains a documentary element, as the gnome-like character played by Bob Balaban sets the (mythical) location within history and culture – this is "Chickchaw country." Anderson has claimed that he wanted the visuals to have a storybook feeling, a flat, two-dimensional quality, like a fable, and like a play. This film does contain an actual play, the Benjamin Britten opera *Noye's Fludde* (i.e., "Noah's Flood," 1958) written to be performed by children, as part of the story. At the same time, Anderson deliberately sets the film in 1965 at a time heralding great social change after a long period of stasis (a pre-Woodstock sensibility emerging from the social conformity of the American 1950s) and these rumblings are not far into the future, dimly hinted at by the two pre-adolescent children's longing for change.

The passionate love felt by two twelve-year-olds literally and figuratively "takes them by a storm" (this is underscored by the simultaneously-occurring squall that rages across the island, causing an actual flood). This ardent devotion upends everyone, not only the two principals, but their parents, and, eventually, their entire communities. As Anderson has explained in an interview about the film:

> A twelve-year-old with a crush – that is really the whole world for that person. In the same way, I remember that when I was that age, that when I would read a book, the book would be my whole world, and I would sort of lose a sense of quite *what is reality* and *what is the book*, and it was the same thing with a romantic feeling at that age: you sort of lose touch with [reality] and it's like entering into a fantasy right then, and I wanted to kind of do something that related to that.[3] (italics added)

Thus, once again, the narrative of *Moonrise Kingdom* has strong roots in literature. Suzy is a voracious reader, and even brings with her a small library within her suitcase, contents packed lovingly and treated with great care. She reads aloud to Sam as they continue their journey. She also "teaches" him about the contents of her books, and they share their imaginative worlds, blending Sam's love of painting with Suzy's love for literature and music (she introduces Sam to the French singer Françoise Hardy through her favorite record, which Suzy explains is a gift from her aunt in France). Books are so important to Suzy that she steals them from the library (Sam asks her why, and if she steals them because she is poor) – Suzy admits this is bad, but she does it so she can make herself feel better and have a secret. She reads aloud a series of pitch-perfect juvenile/young adult novels that never existed but could have (*Shelly and the Secret Universe, The Girl from Jupiter, The Francine Odysseys, The Disappearance of the 6th Grade*).[4] Also, towards the end of the film the book Suzy reads aloud is called *The Return of Auntie Lorraine*, a book about a return, after reading all those books about escaping. Introducing her precious library to Sam, Suzy says:

> These are my books. I like stories with magic powers in them. Either in kingdoms on Earth or on foreign planets. Usually I prefer a girl hero, but not always.

It is notable that this film ends with the dedication "for Juman"[5] – this film marks the deepest exploration yet of the female gender in a career characterized by masculinity, brothers, boys and men. Juman Malouf also designed the book cover and illustrations for *The Francine Odysseys*, one of the books carried by Suzy in the film. In every way, this film is a love letter, a grand tempest of "l'amour fou," complete with a record by the French "yeh-yeh" singer Françoise Hardy, appropriately titled "Le Temps de l'Amour" ("The Time for Love"). To represent the overwhelming emotional forces at work in the narrative, the main character, Sam, is even struck by lightning ("coup de foudre" in French, which translates as "love at first sight"), and later, in a touch of magical realism, some lighting sparks fly from his mouth as he kisses his twelve-year-old love. The film also includes some violence, as the lovers are pursued by the bully "Redford" (Lucas Hedges) and the troop of scouts, who are on a "non-violent rescue mission," yet are armed with a bow and arrow, a knife, an axe, and a brutal medieval-looking wooden club with nails pounded into the end. The idea of twelve-year-olds being left to their own devices on an island which devolves into violence has its most potent source in the William Golding literary classic, *Lord of the Flies* (1954). Hitchcock's films are also evoked, as noted by Richard Brody (2012), including most obviously *Vertigo* (1958), with the dramatic dangling of the characters at the ending, and Suzy's use of binoculars referencing James Stewart's character in *Rear Window* (1954). Brody describes another Hitchcock reference to *Vertigo*:

> Near the end of "Moonrise Kingdom," the two children, together with the chief of police, are left dangling rather precariously from a blasted steeple. Happily, all three come through just fine (though their rescue isn't shown). The same thing happens in "Vertigo" – not at the end, but after the movie's very first scene, which concludes with the detective (played by James Stewart) hanging onto the rickety ledge of a roof for dear life.[6]

Brody notes, however, that Anderson challenges Hitchcock by showing that although James Stewart's character was permanently damaged by his experience of vertigo, in the final scene of *Moonrise Kingdom*, Sam leaves the house via a ladder and has no lasting ill effects or fear of heights; this shows that despite the trauma experienced by the characters, Anderson gives his film a gentler ending compared to Hitchcock's harsher universe, like waking up from a dream at "Summer's End" (the name of the Bishop's house).

Characterization and Vulnerability in Moonrise Kingdom

The film opens with the camera lingering on a needlepoint version of the Bishop family home, adding to the "homespun" feel of the film. While the phonograph record of the Benjamin Britten/Henry Purcell overture plays, the camera pans throughout the Bishop family home displaying it like a dollhouse with wall dividers, revealing stylized rooms reminiscent of the boat cross-section in *The Life Aquatic with Steve Zissou*. Mr. and Mrs. Bishop, played by Bill Murray and Francis McDormand, are first shown seated facing each other in adjacent rooms of the house, with a literal wall between them. As the music from the phonograph continues, shifts in the positions of the characters (such as Mrs. Bishop washing her hair in the sink, or seated under a hair dryer, or walking through a room with a cigarette), and the types of games played by Suzy's three younger brothers (playing jacks, flying model airplanes, competing at ping pong, etc.), indicate that although the record plays continuously, the idea is a montage from different family moments over a period of time (and the weather, which begins as dreary rain, turns to bright sunshine by the end). At a climactic moment in the music, Mr. Bishop sets down his wine glass and closes the leaf on a large wooden dining table, suggesting the construction and connection of the family. Suzy is shown in isolation from the other family members; she appears in various rooms of the house looking through her binoculars, or walking outside to pick up the mail and idling at the bus stop to privately read a letter. Just as the Benjamin Britten recording is designed to help a young person understand how the different sections of the orchestra work together by introducing them in separate groups, the viewer is supposed to "construct" the symphony of the complete family from these short vignettes of domestic life. At one point when Suzy stares through binoculars out an upstairs window, the camera zooms out to show that Suzy is inside the house embroidered in the needlepoint that was shown at the opening of the film.

This film deals with the subject of an outsider, a societal reject, in the most tender, gentle way, by setting this story of rejection in the safe environment of an enclosed world, an island, to which the only threat seems to be the Social Services worker (never given a name) played with icy efficiency and contempt by Tilda Swinton. The sweet-natured island policeman Captain Sharp (Bruce Willis) cannot even comprehend the foster family's rejection of the child Sam Shakusky, when the foster father says: "Unfortunately, we can't invite him back at this time... It's just not fair to the others, you see... He's emotionally disturbed." Sharp replies, "I'm confused by that statement: You can't invite him back?" In a very poignant way, Anderson puts on screen the ultimate rejection, one that every child fears – a child, orphaned by his parents' early deaths, being rejected by his foster family who refuses to take him back at the end of the summer (the foster father relays this news from a telephone in the kitchen while his wife is seen in the background icing a chocolate cake). Right away, before Sam Shakusky has even appeared onscreen (except in a photograph), it is made clear that he belongs nowhere and is wanted by no one. According to his foster father, William Billingsley (Larry Pine), Sam is a problem child who does not fit in with the family. According to Scoutmaster Ward (Edward Norton), Sam is the least popular member of the troop "by a significant margin." The other scouts in the troop gossip about Sam, one saying he heard Sam ran away because his family died, another saying he heard Sam never had any family in the first place, and a third saying he heard Sam is crazy. The destructive nature of this gossip is clear when the boys feel they have to arm themselves against their fellow scout with weapons. This is made all the more poignant when, eleven minutes into the film, Sam's character is finally revealed to the viewer to be a rather naïve, good-natured boy with excellent survival skills and a penchant for the visual arts. As the film goes on, and Sam gets into further innocent scrapes, the dire threat posed by Social Services is that Sam will be committed to an institution and receive electroshock therapy. This is rejection at every level – the fearsome Tilda Swinton suggesting Sam will be abandoned to the State, and doomed to a loveless existence.

Another kind of vulnerability is revealed through Edward Norton's character, Scoutmaster Ward, who drinks and smokes alone in his tent after hours, while making very discouraging audiotapes recording his daily activities, usually failures (during one such session, he is completely silent with a look of utter despair as the recorder's reels turn, recording nothing). When Sam first disappears, Ward organizes a search party, and when the Scoutmaster asks if there are any questions, the young scouts do not ask about the search, but instead pepper him with questions about his credentials, asking if he has a "real" job in addition to scouting. When Ward says he is an eighth-grade math teacher, a scout named Lazy-Eye (Charlie Kilgore) asks him "Do you need a Ph.D. for that?" This scrutiny makes the Scoutmaster defensive, and he counters their questions with the assertion that his "real" job is actually Scoutmaster of Troop 55, underscoring that he is only a math teacher on the side, convincing them that the scouting is of supreme importance to him. This significance that he attributes to scouting with such single-minded devotion is clear from the opening tracking shot of the campground, where the scouts are observed at their various duties, including a latrine inspection, a lanyard-tying inspection, as well as a boy who receives an infraction for a messy uniform, despite the fact that he is burning ants with lighter fluid. This whole sequence is handled with a captivating seriousness that conjures for the viewer the dogged devotion typical to the scouting world.

This vulnerability extends to Suzy's character when she reveals that she once found the booklet "Coping with the Very Troubled Child: Facts, Opinions, and Misconceptions" by Dr. Romulus Trilling on the top of the refrigerator at her home.[7] When Sam laughs, Suzy is hurt, and she retreats alone inside the tent. In the sudden silence outside the tent, Sam looks stricken, one hand holding his stomach. He unzips the tent and lingers by the tent door hesitantly. It is clear from Suzy's tear-stained face that she has been crying. He apologizes and tells her, "I'm on your side," expressing not only his devotion to her, but also the idea that the two of them are on a "side" that is different from the norm. Sam recovers Suzy's affection for him by speaking about her favorite topic, when he asks her which of her beloved books she thinks is the best. In the next scene, Suzy is shown reading to Sam from *The Francine Odysseys*, which demonstrates how Suzy and Sam bond through sharing their imaginative worlds:

> Meanwhile, on the plains of Tabitha, Francine rested. There would be another time for war.

At the end of the scene, Suzy takes Sam's pipe out of his mouth tenderly while he sleeps and taps the ashes into the campfire, and through this action the two seem bonded like an old married couple looking out for each other's needs.

Suzy's vulnerability is also revealed in her packing for wilderness survival, when Sam takes an inventory. For her stay in the woods, Suzy takes with her a yellow suitcase, a basket with her kitten in it, a portable battery-operated record player, her favorite record, binoculars, lefty scissors, a toothbrush, and storybooks – this is an unrealistic set of equipment to run away with. Binoculars give Suzy her "special power": she is always looking into the distance, wishing to "distance" herself from where she is, to escape the confines of her repressive home life. Suzy has been judged a problem child because of her emotional outbursts and her "outsider" precocity and literary pursuits. Anderson shows great sympathy for his over-achieving, hyper-intelligent, well-read protagonists, first with the Tenenbaum children, and again with Suzy Bishop. Although she has faced rejection, it is also clear that Suzy does not help her own cause. She is prone to losing her temper and "acting out" her anger through violent incidents. Her moodiness is no doubt aggravated by her pre-adolescent immaturity and lack of self-control, but Suzy's instances of violence are numerous. First, in the scene when Sam first meets Suzy in the church pageant dressing room, they talk about the cut on her hand, which Suzy attributes to smashing a mirror when she lost her temper (at herself). Then, there is her friend Molly's assertion that Suzy "goes beserk" on people. Later, she even stabs the Khaki Scout bully, Redford, in the side with her pair of lefty scissors. Finally, when Mrs. Bishop attempts to have an honest talk with Suzy in the bathtub, Suzy tells her mother "I hate you," to intentionally hurt her. Suzy's violence and immaturity are mirrored by the adults, including her own parents, who fight on the dock, when Mr. Bishop takes off his shoes and hurls them at Scoutmaster Ward.

In *Moonrise Kingdom*, Anderson explores the topic of loneliness and commitment from several points of view. The adults who are married to each other address one another as "Councilor," instead of by name; they lie in bed discussing their court cases instead of enjoying physical intimacy. Suzy watches her mother through her binoculars and discovers Mrs. Bishop's affair with Captain Sharp. Scoutmaster Ward is obviously lonely, and another romantic subplot in the film is suggested when at the end of the film he has on his desk a framed picture of the switchboard operator Becky (Marianna Bassham). The story of Noah's flood is significantly about pairing off, and the film contains a flashback of Sam and Suzy's love story one year before when Sam's Khaki Scout troop attended the local church production of "Noye's Fludde" in which Suzy was appearing. Interestingly, right before Sam meets Suzy, he heads out the church door against the tide of pairs of young children in animal costumes waiting in a long line before going in to perform the opera – Sam heads in the opposite direction of these pairs, indicating that his love with Suzy will not be a typical love. Before leaving the church, Sam looks disengaged while watching the performance and is actually twiddling his thumbs, his tongue sticking out of his mouth in a slightly bored way (perhaps a sly reference to the famous scene in *Citizen Kane* where the camera pans upward to the two stage workers watching from their position near the rafters, and one of them silently expresses his opinion of the opera by plugging his nose). When Suzy and Sam finally meet, the camera focuses very closely on Suzy's eyes, seen in this instance without their binoculars.

The Music of Benjamin Britten and Hank Williams, and Filmic Influences

One of the key recordings used in the film is Benjamin Britten's "Young Person's Guide to the Orchestra" (1947) conducted by Leonard Bernstein for an album released in 1960. The opening narrative of this recording makes up the first words of the film:

> UNIDENTIFIED BOY: In order to show you how a big symphony orchestra is put together, Benjamin Britten has written a big piece of music which is made up of smaller pieces that show you all the separate parts of the orchestra. These

smaller pieces are called variations, which means different ways of playing the same tune. First of all, he lets us hear the tune or the theme, which is a beautiful melody by the much older British composer, Henry Purcell. Here is Purcell's theme played by the whole orchestra together… Now Mr. Britten lets you hear the four different families of the orchestra playing the same Purcell theme in different ways. First we hear the woodwind family: the flutes, the oboes, the clarinets and the bassoons… Here comes the brass family: the trumpets, the horns, the trombones and tuba.

Britten's "Young Person's Guide to the Orchestra" was chosen as a framing device for *Moonrise Kingdom*; it is played at both the beginning and end of the film. This piece makes an eloquent framing device because, significantly, Britten wanted to provide young people with a guide to the orchestra without talking down to them. (All of the Britten pieces in the film are either musical plays or "simple symphonies" intended to instruct young musicians in expression.)[8] This piece represents, with its guide to different "families" of instruments, an explication of how "families" must work together to harmonize their disparate elements. At the same time, these instruments/families are playing "variations," which according to Britten are "different ways of playing the same tune." The love story between a boy and a girl who have a secret relationship and run away together is one variation on the timeless tale of love, but at the same time it follows the age-old pattern – just as the family members must conform to their patterns and roles to make the family function properly. The irony is that the adults' lives in *Moonrise Kingdom* are falling apart, but nevertheless they are trying to guide the young people while doing a very poor job as role models. Ironically, the adults who have tried to guide Sam and Suzy are now trying to find them – the adults are "lost" themselves. Other Britten selections in the film include *Friday Afternoons* ("Cuckoo"; "Old Abram Brown"), *Simple Symphony* ("Playful Pizzicato"), and *A Midsummer Night's Dream* ("On the ground, sleep sound").

In *Moonrise Kingdom*, Benjamin Britten's music is used to reflect a majestic, orderly, and traditional view of the universe. These classical pieces are contrasted with the use of seven songs from the legendary American country singer Hank Williams (music supervisor Randall Poster talked about using some other country music such as Lefty Frizzell or Ferlin Husky, but both Anderson and Poster were captivated by the emotional intensity of the Williams songs).[9] Hank Williams was the leading country singer of the 1940s and early 1950s and is considered a quintessential figure of the country music genre in the twentieth century – in that sense, he is as "classical" as Henry Purcell. The use of Hank Williams music in the film, and especially its association with Bruce Willis's character (Hank Williams songs are often playing on the radio in scenes in which he appears), demonstrates how these popular songs become a blueprint through which people deal with the pain in their own lives. While "The Young Person's Guide to the Orchestra" provides a guide for young people to learn from, Hank Williams provides a context for the adults to make sense of their brokenness and failure. Songs like "Long Gone Lonesome Blues" and "Rambling Man" take as their subjects loneliness, drunkenness, restlessness, wandering, sleepless nights. Hank Williams also had an alter ego persona "Luke the Drifter," under which he published songs and mini-sermons aimed at reaching out to the lonely, the poor, and the broken-down lives of alcoholics, such as "Men With Broken Hearts" and "I've Been Down That Road Before." Williams died of heart problems compounded by drinking and drugs when he was twenty-nine years old.

Anderson himself discussed the influence of three particular films from the 1960s/1970s that had an influence on *Moonrise Kingdom*, particularly *Melody* and *Black Jack*:

> Those two films [*Melody* and *Black Jack*] were maybe my biggest inspirations. *Melody* (1971) was one of Alan Parker's first scripts. It was directed by Waris Hussein. *Melody* is contemporary, whereas *Black Jack* (1979), directed by Ken Loach, is set in the 18th century in Yorkshire. Another inspiration was *L'Enfance Nue* (1968), which was Maurice Pialat's first feature film. It had the same kind of character as Truffaut's *The 400 Blows*, but it was made 10 years later. It's a great movie and one that very much inspired me.[10]

The hole in the side of Sam's tent covered by the map is a reference to Andy Dufresne's famous escape in *The Shawshank Redemption* (1994). When Suzy's little brother sees that his record player is missing again, he goes into her room. The lights are off, and he sees something moving as he moves the door back and forth. He turns the light on and sees the papier-maché Suzy and screams; this is a reference to *Ferris Bueller's Day Off*. The *Indian Corn* magazine article about Commander Pierce (Harvey Keitel) shown towards the beginning of the film contains the quote "Are we men, or are we mice?" next to his photo, which references the film *Bad Lieutenant* (1992), also starring Keitel, in which he similarly asks his sons, "What are you, men or mice?" Anderson had Jared Gilman watch the 1963-set *Escape From Alcatraz* to get a sense of the period and the on-the-run feel of the film. Godard is also evoked: the scissors, beach, and Suzy's dress definitely suggest *Pierrot Le Fou* (1965). The dance on the beach is a fun and awkward scene that resembles something from a Godard film, the way Godard will have his characters randomly dance in the middle of his films.

Anderson uses several dated or anachronistic film techniques in *Moonrise Kingdom*. The use of the split screen during the phone calls is an older technique, allowing Anderson to display how both Norton's and Willis's characters react to the foster father's refusal to take Sam back. Sam wildly throwing off his cap and clothes before jumping into the water at the inlet is made even more humorous by the way the camera zooms in somewhat abruptly like a 1970s movie – even the picture quality resembles the 1970s. The most obvious deliberate "retro" technique is the dramatic jump of Norton's character away from the exploding tent of firecrackers – the flash of the explosion deliberately evokes cheap television stunt shots.

Spirituality/The Sacred, Order and Rightness in Moonrise Kingdom

Of all of Anderson's films, *Moonrise Kingdom* is the only one with a spiritual, supernatural, or even religious dimension to the narrative. The film begins with the local historian and narrator (who is dressed like a gnome or an elf) foretelling, as if prophetically, a giant storm. Other religious overtones are gradually revealed, for example, Penzance (Pennsans) means "holy headland" in the Cornish language, and Suzy's family name is "Bishop." The seating line-up at the camp breakfast table resembles Leonardo da Vinci's depiction of "The Last Supper" with one apostle missing. After Suzy and Sam meet, Suzy is seen onstage in the performance, where she sings a very dramatic "Kyrie eleison" ("Lord, have mercy"). Interestingly, in the pageant she is playing the role of the raven, the first bird sent out by Noah, who did not return, not the dove who actually brings back the olive leaf to prove the flood is over in the Biblical account. The nature of Suzy and Sam's love is sacred to them, and they even have a wedding ceremony to legitimize their relationship, like the young lovers Romeo and Juliet. On the map of New Penzance, a pair of islands right next to each other can be seen labeled as "Fidelity Island" and "Honesty Rock." The *Noye's Fludde* performance at St. Jack's Church is ultimately cancelled as people gather there because of the flood, but then the church becomes a metaphorical ark, protecting all those within it. The "flood" cleanses and washes over everyone like a baptism, resulting in forgiveness and peace.

In one artful shot in the film, Sam, with Suzy by his side, looks through Suzy's binoculars at St. Jack's Church where they will take refuge when suddenly the camera draws back to display the two of them set into a stained-glass window display of Noah's Ark, with Sam and Suzy pictured as Noah and his wife, as if the purity of their devotion has been inscribed into church history. This idea of devotion is reflected by other characters in the film as well, for example through the hope, service, and conscience reflected by Scoutmaster Ward, who writes his journal entries with the fervent quality of religious devotional meditations. He is also seen praying: "Please let us find [Sam] tomorrow. Don't let him fall off a cliff." Scoutmaster Ward is a sincere believer; he is completely devoid of cynicism. Anderson contrasts a world in disorder with a well-pitched campsite at Camp Ivanhoe, where everything is in its rightful place. Ward even uses his scout Swiss army knife to open the tent with the special hook tool because it was zipped from the inside. Norton's character is given a heroic "savior" quality when he breaks protocol to rescue Commander Pierce from an explosion by carrying him out on his back and leaping over a ravine. Sam, in his coonskin cap, resembles a miniature Davy Crockett, embodying the high ideals of a traditional American hero. It is ironic that each of the principal adults has a "law keeping" career – lawyer, scout master, policeman, social services worker – which is offset and made comic because of their mistakes.

Late in the film, when Sam is surrounded by the scouts in Lightning Field, he proclaims: "On this spot, I will fight no more, forever!" This is a reference to the Surrender Speech by Chief Joseph of the Nez Perce tribe, who, in 1877, attempted to lead his people on an 1100-mile journey to Canada to escape the U.S. Army. The tribe made it within forty miles of the border before they were surrounded, and Chief Joseph made his speech. When Sam first runs into the field, he is being chased by the boy scouts who want to capture him, but after he is struck by lightning, he is found by Suzy and his friends. The magical exchange of enemies for friends makes this appear like a miracle, as does Sam's quick recovery from the lightning strike. Magic is contrasted with science in one of Suzy's books, reflecting the dialectic between scientific reason and faith:

> I don't believe in magic. I used to but once I started taking introduction to life science with Mr. Massey, I realized the logical explanation for practically every mystery in the world was even more interesting than a supernatural one. Auntie Lorraine wouldn't agree. Of course that's no surprise. She's a professional witch hunter.

In Anderson's world, adults can quickly descend to childishness, while children can display maturity beyond their years. Anderson's focus is on the cusp of this maturity, the porous boundary between childhood and adulthood. Anderson explores this by providing two central scenes in the film. In one scene, Suzy, the heroine, is talking to her mother. In the next, Sam, the hero, is talking to Captain Sharp (a father figure). Suzy calls out her mother on her affair, reprimanding her mother as if she, Suzy, is the older one. Ironically, this conversation occurs in the scene where Suzy is in the bathtub, appearing "naked" and being bathed by her mother (mother and daughter are connected by these bathing scenes; this refers back to the beginning of the film when Mrs. Bishop was bathing and washing her hair). Meanwhile, Sam also quotes life's truths to Officer Sharp, and when Sharp offers Sam some alcohol, he pours his remaining milk into the ash tray. The age-swap scenes occur midway through the film. The scenes sit beside each other, and offer a sort of overt treatment of the theory that the kids are living the ideal adult love, as a centerpiece to the film.

The meaning of the film's dramatic climax, in which lightning strikes the church steeple, can be read in two ways. After the lightning strikes, Captain Sharp, Sam, and Suzy are shown in silhouette dangling from the ruined roof in an extremely non-realistic shot that resembles the primitive art of a woodcut. Jeffrey Overstreet draws this conclusion as a moral to the film:

> Abandoning family and adult guidance isn't the answer... Suzy's idealization of orphanhood earns a stinging rebuke. For all of their insights, the children need the community that assembles in the "ark" of that storm-battered church. They need loving fathers and mothers, so they aren't swept away. What will the grownups hold on to, to keep from falling? An answer is suggested in the film's climactic image.[11]

Overstreet reads the image of the characters clinging to the church tower as a visual metaphor for them clinging to religious faith, clinging to God. Meanwhile, Richard Brody, while acknowledging the miraculous and prophetic goings-on in the film and the larger Biblical metaphor, sees the lightning as destroying the belltower, so that it means an overthrow of religious moralism, nature's cosmic retribution against the moral authorities for trying to hold the ideal couple apart.[12]

The Representation of Gender Norms in Moonrise Kingdom

The character of Suzy Bishop stands out as one of the most fully-drawn female characters in Wes Anderson's oeuvre.[13] *Moonrise Kingdom* merits examination through the lens of gender studies, specifically, the feminist critical analysis of Laura Mulvey (1989), and particularly Mulvey's ideas on how women are viewed in film. In her book *Feminism in Film*, E. Anne Kaplan (2000) examines the three different ways Mulvey classifies the male gaze in film. First, Kaplan describes "the look of the camera in the situation being filmed," and that this look "is inherently voyeuristic and usually 'male' in the sense that a man is generally doing the filming"[14] (in this case, Anderson). Clearly the hero and heroine of *Moonrise Kingdom* are introduced very differently. As has already been discussed, Sam is not directly introduced until eleven minutes into the film, and the viewer's first glimpse of him is from the back as he canoes along a river. The focus of the camera is on Sam's actions and not his face. In contrast to this, from the beginning, Suzy is shown in close-up shots of her face, often on display in the center of the frame, highlighting her severe blue eyeshadow and nearly unblinking stare. Her character is on the cusp of pre-pubescence in her mini dress, knee socks, and "Sunday-school shoes." Some of these cinematography choices can be seen as promoting the use of the male gaze, and yet Anderson subverts this gaze by giving Suzy agency – she is returning the gaze right back through her constant use of binoculars. This perspective of female voyeurism gives Suzy empowerment. What Suzy views through the binoculars (for example, her mother's affair) becomes the subject of Anderson's camera as well, and the camera views the subject from a female perspective. The second gaze Mulvey outlines is the gaze of the man within the narrative, and how the male characters within the film make women the objects of their gaze.[15] This is a very strong element of Sam and Suzy's first meeting in the dressing room at the church pageant, when Sam steps out from behind a clothing rack to ask "What kind of bird are you?" Suzy is again framed in the center of the shot, wearing heavy black raven makeup around her eyes. When one girl, not knowing to whom Sam is referring, begins to answer for all of them, Sam interrupts her explanation, repeating his question and this time pointing his finger very distinctly at Suzy. After they have a short conversation, the girl beside Suzy reminds Sam that it is "not polite to stare," once again strongly reiterating that Sam's gaze is on Suzy. In this case again, however, Suzy's use of binoculars, and her constant staring at others without their knowledge, adds a sense of equality to the use of the gaze between men and women in the film. The third type of gaze mentioned by Kaplan in summarizing Mulvey's work is the gaze of the male audience, which can imitate the first two gazes.[16] Interestingly, the age of the characters restricts desire and objectification, because the audience is aware of the taboo of objectifying young Suzy (the scene in which Suzy sits for a portrait for Sam in her underwear is particularly unnatural, because Suzy is lying in a pose commonly viewed as seductive – yet her age cancels out the potentially erotic association of the pose). The age of the main characters prevents the audience's objectification of Suzy, and instead creates a feeling of innocence and purity toward Suzy.

One of the main features of Mulvey's theory is the examination of gender roles and the distinction between the active male and the passive female.[17] Sam's masculinity is already advertised by his scouting attire and his Davy Crockett coonskin cap, with the associated masculine characteristics of being strong, resourceful, outdoorsy, and rugged. For Suzy, New Penzance Island is her home, and she is a very capable girl (her fortitude is demonstrated when she knifes Redford with the scissors), but despite this, Suzy does not compete with Sam or challenge his leadership. Instead, she leaves the planning and mechanics of their adventure to Sam, while at the same time, complementing Sam by providing the storybooks, music, a pet kitten, and a feminine aesthetic to beautify their adventures and turn Sam's camp into a couple's home. Sam displays all of the masculine fundamentals of boldness, practical competence, and protective care for Suzy (providing the supplies, the shelter of the tent, and cooking for her). Suzy responds by being vulnerable, softly feminine, and receptive only to Sam, while remaining cold, hostile, and walled off in her relationships with all the other people in her life. The film supports Mulvey's theoretical conception of the passive female and active male roles in the heterosexual division of labor.[18]

There is a predominantly large representation of male characters in *Moonrise Kingdom*: an all-male group of young Khaki Scouts, Scoutmaster Ward, Captain Sharp, Commander Pierce, Mr. Bishop, the Narrator, and Suzy's three brothers. Meanwhile, apart from Suzy, the only female characters are Mrs. Bishop, Becky the telephone operator, Social Services and Mrs. Billingsley, and two of these characters have either a non-speaking role or just a few lines in the film. Frances McDormand plays a mother who encapsulates a sense of doom, of loss of control, and although she wants to maintain her buttoned-up appearance, when she tosses aside her laundry basket and climbs on her bicycle to meet her lover in secret, it is clear she is hiding deeper issues. Similar to Suzy's binoculars giving her an enhanced sense of sight, McDormand's character uses a megaphone[19] to enhance her voice, and her speech. When Mrs. Bishop tries to reach out to her daughter in the intimate bathtub conversation, Suzy rejects her coldly. This can only be expected, however, as Mrs. Bishop has hardly been a role model of warmth and care for her daughter. The character of Social Services is an institutional view of women and also shares the same coldness typical of Suzy's mother. The character is not even given a proper name, showing the institutional nature of her personhood. Becky the switchboard operator is also painted as somewhat drab and lackluster, and finally, Mrs. Billingsley is silent. These four characters represent a contrasting view of how women are viewed and how Suzy is viewed in the film. Suzy, with Sam, is a character with a fully realized emotional life, but the other female roles of Mrs. Bishop, Social Services, Becky, and Mrs. Billingsley represent a dulled-down, less feminine view of women. Through this contrast, the viewer can see how compatible Suzy and Sam are with each other.

At the end of *Moonrise Kingdom*, the three young Bishop brothers lie on the floor as usual listening to the record player in the final scene, while Suzy sits in her spot on the window seat reading *The Return of Auntie Lorraine*. The camera pans over to Suzy's kitten, now grown into a cat, lying plump and well-fed on the floor. Then the camera pans over further to show Sam sitting on a stool, painting a picture at a small easel.

The painting done by Sam which shows the name the two young runaways chose for their edenic beach cove hideaway, "Moonrise Kingdom," dissolves into a real-life shot of Mile 3.25 Tidal Inlet, erased by the storm and existing only in memory.

He wears a miniature version of Captain Sharp's short-sleeved uniform with a black necktie and a baseball cap, showing how he has now become a physical extension of his beloved guardian. The record intones: "So you see, the composer Benjamin Britten has taken the whole orchestra apart. Now he puts it back together again in a fugue." The overarching symbolism of Britten dissecting the families of instruments is reflected by the narrative of the film in which the Bishop family, Sam, Captain Sharp, Scoutmaster Ward and his Khaki Scouts, Becky, and even the Narrator, have been "taken apart" and "put back together" but in new alliances and calibrations that determine that none of them will ever be the same again.

Notes

1   Anderson has claimed that the film's narrative is written to mirror the style of the books Suzy Bishop is carrying with her, that the two are acting in a story that they themselves would enjoy reading. "Somewhere along the way, I started thinking more and more that the movie should really be one of her books, kind of, and that that really ought to be our form – that the movie is the sort of story that the two characters in it would want to read." Wes Anderson, quoted in "Wes Anderson on *Moonrise Kingdom*," Film 4 Interview, *Youtube.com*. May 29, 2015. https://www.youtube.com/watch?v=5E6i53flbdg&t=139s (accessed June 28, 2016).
2   In an NPR interview with Terry Gross, Wes Anderson refers to his "Norman Rockwell version of America" in this film. Indeed, Edward Norton was cast specifically due to the fact that, according to Anderson, "He looks like he has been painted by Norman Rockwell." Terry Gross, "Wes Anderson: Creating a Singular Kingdom," *NPR.org*. May 29, 2012. http://www.npr.org/2012/05/29/153913922/wes-anderson-creating-a-singular-kingdom (accessed October 4, 2014).

3   Wes Anderson, quoted in "Wes Anderson on *Moonrise Kingdom*," Film 4 Interview, *Youtube.com*. May 29, 2015. https://www.youtube.com/watch?v=5E6i53flbdg&t=139s (accessed June 28, 2016).
4   Six books were created in all, and Anderson wrote passages for each book, while six artists were commissioned to create the jacket covers for the books. In April 2012, Anderson decided to animate all six books and use them in a promotional video in which Bob Balaban (as both the Narrator and the librarian from the township of New Penzance) introduces the segment for each of these imaginary books, and Kara Hayward (as Suzy) reads a passage from each of them. This 2012 short is entitled *Moonrise Kingdom: Animated Book Short*, directed by Christian De Vita (Anderson is uncredited).
5   Anderson has been in a long-term relationship for many years with artist and writer Juman Malouf, who published her debut novel *The Trilogy of Two* in 2015, which she also illustrated with intricately detailed pencil drawings inspired by the black-and-white etchings in novels from Victorian-era England. Malouf, who is of Lebanese descent, grew up moving back and forth between London and Saudi Arabia, and graduated from Brown University with a degree in art history, as well as studying costume and set design while working on an MFA at New York University's Tisch School of the Arts. Malouf has been a frequent collaborator on Anderson's work; for example, she voiced the role of Agnes in *Fantastic Mr. Fox*, and most recently has served as the set and costume designer for *Moonrise Kingdom* and *The Grand Budapest Hotel*.
6   Richard Brody, "Loving *Moonrise Kingdom* for the Right Reasons," *NewYorker.com*. June 14, 2012. http://www.newyorker.com/culture/richard-brody/loving-moonrise-kingdom-for-the-right-reasons (accessed February 27, 2015).
7   Anderson based this on his own personal experience (see chapter 1, footnote 58). Terry Gross, "Wes Anderson: Creating a Singular Kingdom," *NPR.org*. May 29, 2012. http://www.npr.org/2012/05/29/153913922/wes-anderson-creating-a-singular-kingdom (accessed October 4, 2014).
8   Similarly, Camille Saint-Saëns' *Le Carnaval des animaux*, selections of which were used in *Moonrise Kingdom*, was also written for the musical education of children, and an orchestral analysis of Alexandre Desplat's musical suite "The Heroic-Weather Conditions of the Universe, Part 7: After the Storm," is narrated by Jared Gilman during the film's credits.
9   Randall Poster, "How Wes Anderson Soundtracks His Movies," *NPR.org*. May 24, 2012. http://www.npr.org/templates/transcript/transcript.php?storyId=153585829 (accessed July 25, 2015).
10 Wes Anderson, quoted by Walter Donohue, "Love on the Run," *Filmmaker Magazine*. October 17, 2012. http://filmmakermagazine.com/53944-love-on-the-run/#.Vg7O5BGqpBc
11 Jeffrey Overstreet, "*Moonrise Kingdom* and the Divine Symphony," *Patheos.com*. July 5, 2012. http://www.patheos.com/blogs/goodletters/2012/07/moonrise-kingdom-and-the-divine-symphony/ (accessed November 17, 2014.)
12 Brody, 2012.

13 Regarding the prevalence of strongly-written male characters in his films, Anderson elucidated his writing process in 2008: "There were about 11 guys in the room, and we were wondering why we couldn't write a good female main character." Wes Anderson, in Olivier Zahm and Olympia Le-Tan, "Interview with Wes Anderson," *Purple.fr*. September 2008. http://www.purple.fr/magazine/ss-2008-issue-9/wes-anderson/ (accessed June 17, 2016).
14 E. Ann Kaplan, *Feminism and Film* (Oxford: Oxford University Press, 2000), 120–121.
15 Ibid., 121.
16 Ibid.
17 Laura Mulvey, *Visual and Other Pleasures* (Indianapolis, IN: Indiana University Press, 1989), 19.
18 Ibid., 20.
19 The idea of the mother in the family using a megaphone to communicate with other members of the family comes from co-writer Roman Coppola's own childhood experience.

CHAPTER TEN

Literary Influence and Memory: Stefan Zweig and The Grand Budapest Hotel

Wes Anderson was inspired to make *The Grand Budapest Hotel* by a certain kind of early twentieth-century travel literature encapsulated in the style of Austrian novelist Stefan Zweig (1881–1942), author of numerous works, including *Letter from an Unknown Woman* (1922) and *Beware of Pity* (1939), both of which Anderson claims to have yielded ideas that were later incorporated into his screenplay, and the memoir *The World of Yesterday* (1942). The dandyistic nature of this literature matches the high farcical style of Anderson's film. The literature of Stefan Zweig is characterized by comic interludes, an arch tone, and a sense of wealth and entitlement afforded to rich travelers of the era. Anderson played off Zweig's literary ambience with the creation of his central character hotel concierge Gustave H (Ralph Fiennes). Gustave's nature as an articulate, elitist, foppish, and polysexual dandy perfectly matches the arch tone of Zweig's protagonists in his novels from the 1920s and 1930s. Anderson's film revolves around Ralph Fiennes' bravura comic performance as Gustave: vain, imperious, and mercurial yet loyal and generous – yet again, as in Anderson's earlier works, a uniquely contradictory personality in a leading role. The character's negative traits risk alienating the audience; however, the viewer sees Gustave as viewed through the eyes of the young lobby boy, Zero Moustafa (Tony Revolori). At first glance, Gustave is manipulative, shallow, self-serving, self-important, and completely self-involved. And yet, the character of Gustave is reminiscent of Gene Hackman's career-highlight performance as the simultaneously sympathetic and infuriating Royal Tenenbaum. Ralph Fiennes' astonishing portrayal wins the audience's begrudging trust and then, throughout the course of the film, wins their allegiance, which culminates at the film's denouement into an almost inexpressibly deep admiration (and with Zero's elegy, a tender love.) The viewer gradually finds himself hoodwinked into caring for Gustave, much as the lobby boy Zero did when he entered into Gustave's impulsive contract hurriedly hammered out in the train berth bunk bed scene.

Gustave's strong personality is captivating, a dynamic force that dominates the film.[1] First, the viewer is shown that Gustave's personality has a magnetic draw to women – as displayed by the numerous elderly female hotel patrons including Mme. C. V. Desgoffe und Taxis (Madame D, played by Tilda Swinton), who are his sometime-paramours, and by his easy flirtation with the young Agatha (Saoirse Ronan). Gustave's character inspires the kind of exasperated affection commonly displayed to people with such strong personalities – there is no changing them and one simply must adapt to their idiosyncrasies. Gustave's strong personality traits include his regular recitation of poetry, his speeches – more like mini-sermons – that he uses to guide his staff, and his attachment to his cologne, "L'Air de Panache." Revolori's young lobby boy quickly learns how to work in sync with his boss's controlling style and unpredictable nature, trying never to take personally Gustave's critiques and constant suggestions for self-improvement. Instead, the lobby boy named "Zero"[2] ("nothing") is inspired to become Gustave's useful right-hand man, and the two men's growing friendship becomes the cornerstone of the film. Zero begins to thrive under his patron's influence, discovering hidden talents in himself and learning as he goes. (Zero's diverse talents include concealing a painting, helping with a jailbreak, and finally, in the film's most madcap scene, commandeering a sled from a religious statue as a means of quick escape from a mountaintop monastery.)

The Grand Budapest Hotel is a confection – it contains a confection (Mendl's pastries), it exhibits a confection (the hotel's beautiful exterior), and, finally, it is as ephemeral as a confection – light, airy, soon to disappear. This layer of farcical slapstick humor and screwball comedy, however, masks the darker themes not only of totalitarianism, Eastern-bloc politics, and war, but of decay, loneliness, and personal loss (reported deaths late in the film). To lessen the intensity, the film does not seek to portray a precise location (Zubrowka is a fictional country that nevertheless evokes qualities of Hungary, Poland, or Czechoslovakia) nor does it replicate precise periods of history, but only sets out to obliquely evoke three periods of history in the twentieth century which are highly stylized in the film: the first is the "world of yesterday" which Zweig captures in his literature (pre-WWI), second, a period of indeterminate war and fascism (with the Nazi-like SS insignia changed to ZZ), and third, the period of Communism in Eastern or Central Europe. In addition, Zero Moustafa is a refugee, but his country of origin is only vaguely described (Anderson has stated that this relates to his own girlfriend Juman Malouf's Lebanese family origins).[3] The story also points clearly to the theme of writing, of authorship. In one of the most moving scenes of romance in the film, Zero gives a book as a present to his beloved Agatha while the multi-colored lights of a merry-go-round spin incandescently around her.

Finally, the film is intensely personal. The way it enfolds its complex structure as a series of stories within stories, and flashbacks within flashbacks, is a profound commentary on the function of human memory and nostalgia. The film is an invitation to a dinner, an offer to pull up a chair and dine in the hotel's nearly-empty hall with Jude Law and F. Murray Abraham.

If you're not merely being polite (and you must tell me if that's the case), but if it genuinely does interest you: may I invite you to dine with me tonight, and it will be my pleasure and, indeed, my privilege to tell you – "my" story. Such as it is.[4]

The sad, mysterious lonely man (F. Murray Abraham) in the hotel draws us in just as he draws Jude Law, and the movie slows down deliciously as Law and Abraham discuss, in the most elegant of terms, a dinner invitation, the opportunity to sit and talk and to hear a story. This part of the film engages the viewer with a powerful magnetism – an invitation to the inner circle, a world of stories and secret histories. In this way, the film recalls *My Dinner with Andre* (1981), in which Andre Gregory and Wallace Shawn share a lengthy dinner in a New York restaurant and the film lingers over each course as the characters – mainly Andre himself with Wallace Shawn playing the lesser role as an almost comical sidekick/dupe – talk about their lives. Similarly, in *The Grand Budapest Hotel*, this dinner scene creates an intimacy and an almost conspiratorial ambience that draws the viewer in as a complicit participant in the narrative.

Stefan Zweig, "The Author," and Literary Influences

The film opens with a teenage girl entering a cemetery to pay her respects at the gravesite bust of "The Author" with the book *The Grand Budapest Hotel* tucked under her arm. This is then followed by a monologue (a flashback from twenty years before) read from notecards by the character who matches exactly the features of the statue of "The Author." The opening lines of the film are as follows:

It is an extremely common mistake: people think the writer's imagination is always at work, that he is constantly inventing an endless supply of incidents and episodes, that he simply dreams up his stories out of thin air. In point of fact, the opposite is true. Once the public knows you are a writer, they bring the characters and events to *you* – and as long as you maintain your ability to look and carefully listen, these stories will continue to seek you out.[5]

In this opening quotation, the filmmaker gives his own literary analysis as the author of this screenplay, and indeed as an author of all of his screenplays. Anderson takes an authorial role in the creation of his art, and, as has been observed, guides this creative process with an unusually precise control: his vision of his films is often fully realized in storyboard form before the film is shot. He is not simply the "author" of the words the actors will speak in their roles, but the author of the film's entire ambience which has been precisely calculated down to the last detail with a sense of almost gleeful obsession.

The film segues into the opening account of the writer's stay at the Grand Budapest Hotel in the late 1960s, which is written in the elevated style of Stefan Zweig's prose:

Author (V.O.): A number of years ago, while suffering from a mild case of "Scribe's Fever" (a form of neurasthenia common among the intelligentsia of that time) I had decided to spend the month of August in the spa town of Nebelsbad below the Alpine Sudetenwaltz – and had taken up rooms in the Grand Budapest ... a picturesque, elaborate, and once widely-celebrated establishment.[6]

The film also takes its time to focus on the introduction of the elderly character whose boyhood will form the bulk of the story: The screenplay reads: "At the far end of a colonnade, beyond Reception, a dark-skinned, white-haired seventy-year-old man in a threepiece-suit sits alone smoking a pipe. He is Mr. Moustafa." The author's voice continues by way of introduction:

> Author (V.O.): A small, elderly man, smartly dressed, with an exceptionally lively, intelligent face – and an immediately perceptible air of sadness. He was, like the rest of us, alone – but also, I must say, he was the first that struck one as being, deeply and truly, lonely. (A symptom of my own medical condition, as well.)[7]

This introduction to the character of Mr. Moustafa is interrupted by an event in the film, but it continues in a further scene after this description from the screenplay:

> Author (V.O.): However, this premature intermission in the story of the curious old man had left me, as the expression goes, *gespannt wie ein Flitzebogen*, that is, on the edge of my seat – where I remained throughout the next morning until, in what I have found to be its mysterious and utterly reliable fashion: fate, once again, intervened on my behalf.[8]

What follows leads to the introduction of the most memorable character in the story, Monsieur Gustave H, seen striding imperiously across the length of an ornate hotel suite. The consummate concierge, Gustave issues orders with impeccable style and efficiency, often speaking in a lightning-fast manner characteristic of old-style high society film repartee. An example of instructions he gives to Zero is as follows:

> Run to the cathedral of Santa Maria Christiana in Brucknerplatz. Buy one of the plain, half-length candles and take back four Klubecks in change. Light it in the sacristy, say a brief rosary, then go to Mendl's and get me a Courtesan *au chocolat*. If there's any money left, give it to the crippled shoeshine boy.[9]

From this example, it is clear that Gustave speaks in the elevated fashion of a dandy or a bon vivant, capturing impeccably the anachronistic tone of Zweig's writing as it sounds to twenty-first-century ears. Even the allusion to a "crippled shoeshine boy" is an expression from a different era. This stylized language draws the reader back to the past through aural memory and connections to both early twentieth-century literature and the tone and rhythm of early Hollywood screenplays.

The plot of *The Grand Budapest Hotel* is both simple and remarkably complex. The story involves the theft and recovery of a priceless Renaissance painting and the battle for an enormous family fortune, all against the backdrop of suddenly and dramatically changing geopolitical events. It involves both a murder and a jailbreak, plus several scenes of very graphic violence. However, the intimate effect of violence on people's lives is dwarfed by what is to come: the violence of the greater catastrophe of war, which will erase certain people and past-times forever from the world stage. Rather than basing the screenplay on a single narrative from Zweig's stories, Anderson attempted to capture the spirit of Zweig's work in general, both in his novels and novellas, and in his memoir *The World of Yesterday*. In addition, the film has one of the largest ensemble casts Anderson has worked with in recent years: Saoirse Ronan, Bill Murray, F. Murray Abraham, Edward Norton, Mathieu Amalric, Adrien Brody, Willem Dafoe, Lea Seydoux, Jeff Goldblum, Jason Schwartzman, Jude Law, Tilda Swinton, Harvey Keitel, Tom Wilkinson, and Owen Wilson – a gathering of great European actors mixed with Wes Anderson's regular troupe – which makes this film feel like another Anderson masterpiece taking its place in the canon with *The Royal Tenenbaums*. The European influence of Zweig on Anderson's work enhances the director's vision even more broadly, making *The Grand Budapest Hotel* one of Anderson's most expansive and daring films.

Visual Style in The Grand Budapest Hotel

The central image in *The Grand Budapest* Hotel is, of course, the hotel itself, the outside of which is viewed as a drawing as well as a mechanized model with the funicular riding up the mountainside like a dollhouse. The interior of the hotel is given extremely detailed treatment, reminiscent of the introduction to the Bishops' house in *Moonrise Kingdom*: Anderson was determined to cut inside the house, but then not limit himself to one set, so he used different sets for different points of view. In *The Grand Budapest Hotel*, the hotel itself is dissected into its parts: the thermal baths, the pool area, the manager's quarters, the elevator, and individual guest rooms. The lobby itself is a dizzying wonder of symmetry due to its geometric shapes of detail, ornamental design, and carpeting.[10] All the signifiers are heightened and almost farcical in their obviousness and obsessive detail – the exalted language of the characters, the high art ("Boy With Apple" by the fictional Dutch Renaissance master Johannes van Hoytl the Younger), the exacting standards of the hotel (Zero running through the hotel with a chair or a newspaper), the signage ("Do Not Run," "Deposit Towels Here," the "Lobby Boy" hat), the exaggerated patterns of the convict's tattoos (which appear to be drawn on with magic marker), the parodic Wild West-style shoot-out across the hotel lobby balconies, and the iconic perfection of Mendl's pastries with their pink cardboard pastry boxes (the prison guard is unwilling to cut into the Mendl's pastries to search for a concealed weapon because the pastry is too beautiful). Anderson worked with a local baker in Görlitz to design the fictional "Courtesan *au chocolat*," a parody of a two-layered éclair-style pastry called the *religieuse*, modeled on the papal mitre or ceremonial headdress. The "Courtesan" comprises three layers (suggestive of a female shape) rather than two, and the name "courtesan," or escort, is also a parody of the name "religieuse," or nun.

Anderson also acknowledges a certain 1930s Hollywood vision of "Europe" in his work. In an interview with Matt Zoller Seitz, Anderson points to the influence of Ernst Lubitsch (*The Shop Around the Corner*, 1940, and *To Be or Not To Be*, 1942), Michael Powell and Emeric Pressburger, referencing their work in the character of Lermontov, played by Anton Walbrook in *The Red Shoes* (1948), whose costume is channeled here by Adrien Brody in *The Grand Budapest Hotel*, and also Powell and Pressburger's *The Life and Death of Colonel Blimp*, in which the flashback story is framed by the "present day" narrative in thermal baths.[11] The thermal bath scene in Anderson's film even contains a shot of a portly, naked man reminiscent of the main character in *The Life and Death of Colonel Blimp*. In addition, in the screenplay's opening description of the hotel's surroundings, Anderson references the edelweiss flower as an Alpine signifier from the Second World War period portrayed in *The Sound of Music* (1965). *The Grand Budapest Hotel* also shares similarities with *Grand Hotel*, a 1932 American film about the goings-on in a luxury hotel in post-World War I Berlin, directed by Edmund Goulding, with a screenplay by William A. Drake and Béla Balázs based on the 1930 play of the same title by Drake, who had adapted it from the 1929 novel *Menschen im Hotel* by Vicki Baum. Similarities include certain plot elements and costumes, the hotels' circular check-in desks, the presence of a black dachshund carried under a character's arm, and the uncanny resemblance between the characters Baron Felix von Geigern in *Grand Hotel* (played by John Barrymore) and Ralph Fiennes' M. Gustave. In the film *Grand Hotel*, the Baron Felix seems to charm and placate the pretty Russian ballerina Grusinskaya (played by Greta Garbo, who utters her most famous line "I want to be alone") in the same way that M. Gustave appears to comfort and coddle the aging countess Madame D (albeit for different reasons), in the *The Grand Budapest Hotel*. Ludwig's (Harvey Keitel) tattoos are a direct copy of those of Pere Jules in the 1934 film *L'Atalante*.[12] Anderson also mentioned as influences William Wyler's 1935 romantic comedy *The Good Fairy* written by Preston Sturges, Rouben Mamoulian's 1932 musical comedy *Love Me Tonight*, Frank Borzage's 1940s MGM drama *The Mortal Storm* starring Margaret Sullavan, James Stewart, and Frank Morgan, and Ingmar Bergman's *The Silence* (1963), which, like *The Grand Budapest Hotel*, is centered in a fictional Europe, set in its own invented European country with trains and hotel scenes. In addition, one of the most superbly styled Hollywood movies, Max Ophüls's *Letter from an Unknown Woman*, from 1948, is based on a book by Zweig.

The Grand Budapest Hotel was shot in three different aspect ratios – 1.37, 1.85 and 2.35:1 – to inform the viewer where he or she is in the timeline, which alternates between three time periods: 1985, 1968 and the 1930s. The 1930s part of the film was shot in Academy 1.37, which is generally how the movies at the time were shot. The 1960s part of the movie was shot with anamorphic widescreen lenses, which is a 2.35:1 aspect ratio, and this section reflects how in the 1960s many movies were shot anamorphically, with film studios reacting to the perceived threat of television. For the 1980s, Anderson used 1.85, which is more the standard format with which people shoot today. These three different aspect ratios help put the viewer into the visual mode of the different time periods; Anderson felt that by shooting in the actual format of the time, he could pose shots differently within those formats and enhance the feeling of the era. The multiple-chronology structure of *The Grand Budapest Hotel* shares similarities with *The Life and Times of Colonel Blimp*, which is also set in multiple times: 1902, World War I, the inter-war years, and finally, World War II, with even a mention of 1980 thrown in (*The Grand Budapest Hotel* also mentions a fourth time period as it opens in the present day with the young teenager in the graveyard, and is also set in multiple times, mainly 1932 and 1968 in two very different versions of the hotel: one inter-war luxury; the other Cold War Eastern Bloc). Other similarities with *The Life and Times of Colonel Blimp* include the way Ralph Fiennes as Gustave strides confidently throughout the hotel, which is similar to all of the soldiers striding about in the nursing home in Berlin in *Blimp*. *The Grand Budapest Hotel* is more heightened and cartoonish than any Powell and Pressburger film, but the dialogue is similarly full of longish literary lines delivered with a sense of panache and rapid-fire speed. Also in *Blimp*, much of the violence takes place off-screen, such as the Blimp duel, and Barbara's death, or is implied, such as the events of the two World Wars; similarly in *The Grand Budapest Hotel*, the major (and quite brutal) individual bits of death-dealing all happen off-screen or in voice-over, although some violence, such as the brutal amputation of Deputy Kovacs' four fingers, is gleefully displayed by Anderson. Finally, the films are somewhat thematically similar. *The Life and Times of Colonel Blimp* shows that Blimp, with his Victorian public school values, was becoming dated and irrelevant, not properly prepared to meet the challenges of the twentieth century. Gustave's character is similarly increasingly out of step with the times, for he was raised in a more elegant era. There are physical similarities between the sets as well, that reference this defunct style metaphorically: in *The Life and Times of Colonel Blimp*, there are the increasing number of stuffed wild game trophy heads mounted on the wall over time, while on the Author's wall in *The Grand Budapest Hotel*, there is a painting of mastodons. Both the taxidermy of the animals and the appearance of the mastodons metaphorically suggest the endangerment and eventual extinction of the aging characters' way of life, and the passing of an era.

Anderson includes sly references to popular culture as well, with these lines mimicking Tommy Lee Jones as Deputy Samuel Gerard tracking Dr. Richard Kimble (Harrison Ford) in *The Fugitive* (1993):

Henckels: I want roadblocks at every junction for fifty kilometers. I want *rail*blocks at every train station for a hundred kilometers. I want fifty men and ten bloodhounds ready in five minutes. We're going to strip-search every *pretzelhaus, waffelhut, biergarten* – and *especially* every grand hotel – from Äugenzburg to Zilchbrück. These men are dangerous, professional criminals. (At least, three of them are, anyway.)[13]

The similarity between the lines of Henckels and Gerard ("What I want out of each and every one of you is a hard-target search of every gas station, residence, warehouse, farmhouse, henhouse, outhouse, and doghouse in that area")[14] is another example of

This formal group portrait of the Grand Budapest Hotel staff draws inspiration from posed group portraits of people in hotel lobbies from the 1930s and photochromic images Anderson researched at the Library of Congress. Anderson briefly considered making the whole film resemble antique hand-tinted photography, and although he ultimately decided against it, these early photographs influenced the way certain scenes were framed.

how Anderson juxtaposes an incongruously recent pop-cultural reference to give a new level of humor to a film set in a long-ago era.

Literary Influences, Poetry, and Music in the Film

With its source in the writings of Stefan Zweig, *The Grand Budapest Hotel* is clearly a highly literary film. At the beginning of the screenplay, the Author's office is described in loving detail: "A cluttered office with French windows and ornate mouldings. There are books in shelves and stacks, first editions, dictionaries, dime-store paperbacks, translations in numerous languages. There is a typewriter on the desk and an extensive collection of literary prizes on a bureau."[15] Anderson's detailed description of the illustrious 75-year-old Author's work space is wreathed in elegance and courtly sophistication that characterize the entire tone of *The Grand Budapest Hotel*. Another literary source, closer to home for Anderson, is Kay Thompson's *Eloise* book series from the 1950s (especially the original book entitled *Eloise: A Book for Precocious Grown-Ups* [1955]), in which a little girl lives a fantasy life in the Plaza Hotel in New York City. This book, which also seems connected to Anderson's vision in *The Royal Tenenbaums* (especially when Royal lives in the Lindbergh Palace Hotel) conjures a literary/intellectual yet child-like fantasy of a charmingly opulent life in a fantastical hotel.

The sophisticated trappings of Gustave's lifestyle at the hotel are reflected in his language. One of Gustave's most fascinating habits is his inclination for sudden, extemporaneous recitations of poetry.[16] For example, when Madame D is troubled with nervous anxiety at the beginning of the film, Gustave declaims these verses to comfort her:

> M. Gustave: While questing once in noble wood of gray medieval pine, I came upon a tomb, rain-slicked, rubbed cool, ethereal; its inscription long vanished, yet still within its melancholy fissures – [17]

Later, after having escaped from Checkpoint 19, Gustave and Zero are reunited. It is clear that Gustave has had a strong influence on Zero, because when Gustave asks him about Agatha, Zero reveals his own penchant for recitation:

> M. Gustave: How's our darling Agatha?
> Zero: [*Zero starts to answer, then hesitates. He recites*] "'Twas first light when I saw her face upon the heath; and hence did I return, day by day, entranc'd: tho' vinegar did brine my heart – "
> M. Gustave: *Very* good! I'm going to stop you there because the alarm has sounded, but remember where we left off, because I *insist* you finish later![18]

As the film goes on, it becomes more and more clear that these recitations are always interrupted, unfinished, and fragmentary. This sudden cutting-off or interruption of the literary recitation represents the fact that the poet does not have time to luxuriate in his verse. Instead, because of the terrible times of war and violence in which the characters are caught up beyond their control, the poetry must be enjoyed in brief, hurried snippets, which, as the film shows, is a comically ineffective way to enjoy literature. These frantic and interrupted recitations demonstrate that during times of crisis, aesthetic concerns are the first to fall by the wayside.

One of the most memorable recitations of poetry is after the wild sled ride down the mountain, when Gustave, facing death, clings to the side of a cliff and recites a poem, while Jopling repeatedly stomps on his fingers.

> M. Gustave: 'If this do be me end: farewell! cried the wounded piper-boy, whilst the muskets cracked and the yeomen roared, "Hurrah!" and the ramparts fell. "Methinks me breathes me last me fears," said he – [19]

The overly flowery line "Methinks me breathes me last me fears" (all of these verses were written by Anderson) is a marvelous parody of poetic sensibility. Finally, toward the end of the film, Gustave speaks with eloquence about the fall of the hotel to the Fascist occupiers as he and Zero wistfully gaze on it from a distance:

> M. Gustave: The beginning of the end of the end of the beginning – has begun. A sad finale played, off-key, on a broken-down saloon piano in the outskirts of a forgotten ghost town. I'd rather not bear witness to such blasphemy.
> Zero: Me, neither.
> M. Gustave: (*elegiac*) The Grand Budapest has become a troops' barracks. I shall never cross its threshold again in my lifetime.
> Zero: Me, neither.
> M. Gustave: (*on a roll*) Never again shall –

Zero: (*alarmed*) Actually I think we might be going in there right now after all![20]

Once again, the recitation is interrupted as more pressing events present themselves. Shortly later, Zero and Gustave will go to the rescue of Agatha and reclaim the painting that Dmitri is trying to steal.

In addition to literary influences, both real and fictional, the music in *The Grand Budapest Hotel* is a combination of both existing pieces, folk songs, and yodels, as well as an original score. The majority of the soundtrack is original music composed by Alexandre Desplat, along with Russian folk songs together with pieces composed by Öse Schuppel, Siegfried Behrend, and Vitaly Gnutov, and performed by the Osipov State Russian Folk Orchestra. Wes Anderson and Randall Poster chose the distinctive sound of the balalaika to establish the musical voice of the film. Desplat's use of the balalaika begins with "Mr. Moustafa" but it returns as a repeating motif in the film. Other instruments and musical elements in this soundtrack include alphorns, whistles, organ, Gregorian chant, bells and cimbalom. The thirty-two tracks, with orchestral elements, keyboard instruments and balalaikas, feature eclectic variations and central European melodic themes. Balalaikas are used in "Overture: M. Gustave H" and church organs in "Last Will and Testament." The a cappella opening song, the Appenzell yodel "s'Rothe-Zäuerli" by Ruedi and Werner Roth, is from the Swiss folk group Öse Schuppel's album *Appenzeller Zäuerli*.

Masculinity/Bisexuality/Gender Fluidity in The Grand Budapest Hotel

Although Anderson's films generally reflect Anderson's continuous exploration of heterosexual masculinity, beginning with *Bottle Rocket* clearly being focused on the topic of male bonding, *The Grand Budapest Hotel* adds an interesting dimension to Anderson's work insofar as this is the first film he has made in which the main character displays any type of gender fluidity. While the character is shown in sexual relationships with women, there is some doubt cast upon his gender identity by other interactions in the film, which neatly references Judith Butler's seminal 1990 work *Gender Trouble*, in which Butler calls gender a performance, by which she means that one's sense of gender is an ongoing activity occurring in a relational matrix. In *The Grand Budapest Hotel*, Gustave is presented as casually bisexual, but he is also labeled with homosexual slurs by other characters. For example, Dmitri, angry about Gustave's relationship with his mother that has led her to will a priceless heirloom artwork to him, uses modern slang to call Gustave a "fruit." He goes on to have this exchange with Gustave:

> Dmitri: If I learn you ever once laid a finger on my mother's body, living or dead, I swear to God, I'll cut your throat! (*Screaming.*) You hear me?
> M. Gustave: (*clever though dizzy*) I thought I was supposed to be a f-----g faggot.
> Dmitri: (*hesitates*) You are, but you're bisexual.[21]

Dmitri is genuinely nonplussed by Gustave's gender identity – it is not easy to bully such a man, and Dmitri does not know what to make of him. Historically, Gender

Studies and Queer Studies are concerned with the interactions between people that constitute power, gender, and sexual relations. There are processes of interaction between identity markers such as gender and sexuality; "Queer theory" is largely an academic discourse that examines the constructedness of gendered and sexual identities and categorizations, with particular focus on the logocentric interdependency of gay and straight, and the centrality of queerness to "normalcy" (see Warner 1993; Messner 1997). The resulting research ranges across a wide spectrum, from a more personal, journalistic literature on self-help to controversial social critiques (Connell 1987; Kimmel 1992). Queer also became an identity category unto itself: individuals who wanted to be fluid or inclusive in their own stated desires or who wanted to challenge hegemonic assumptions of sexuality have described themselves as "queer" (Doty 1993; Jagose 1996). As Halperin (1995) states, queer is "by definition whatever is at odds with the normal, the legitimate, the dominant."[22] The queer theorist studies the webs of power and discourse: identities, sexual or not, become tools of social order and control, constantly recreated and performed by the individual. Thus, queer theory also destabilizes genders (masculine/feminine) and biological sex (male/female), questioning the assumed connectivity between sex and gender, or the legitimacy of presumed scientific classification (Drescher, 2007; Jagose, 1996).

This idea of flawed scientific classification of gender is reflected by the following exchange between Gustave and fellow prisoner Pinky, who is unaware of Gustave's gender fluidity:

> Pinky: Me and the boys talked it over. We think you're a real straight fella.
> M. Gustave: Well, I've never been accused of that before, but I appreciate the sentiment.[23]

Pinky's description of Gustave as "straight" is used humorously to underscore just how difficult it is to label Gustave, or to pin down his gender identity. These hardened prisoners ironically consider Gustave just as manly as one of their own. Anderson does not use his polysexual character for any sort of direct political statement, but in the end, it is important to remember that during the prohibitive environment of Eastern Europe during World War II, the elements of society most often attacked along with the Jews (represented by Zweig) were non-white immigrants (represented by Moustafa) and homosexuals (represented by Gustave). These were the vulnerable groups most often condemned to death in concentration camps.

While never making an overt political statement, Anderson's view toward his characters' gender issues is made clear in *The Life Aquatic with Steve Zissou*, which was the first of Anderson's films to feature a gay character, Eleanor's former husband Alistair Hennessy:

> Hennessey: We've never made great husbands, have we? Of course, I have a good excuse. I'm part-gay.
> (*Zissou shrugs. He smiles and says warmly:*)
> Zissou: Supposedly, everyone is.[24]

The character of Hennessy has a complicated gender identity in that he was once married to a woman and now claims to be gay. Anderson's films thus raise the topic of gender fluidity as early as 2004.

Despite the presence of homosexuality, more or less overt, in the two films *The Life Aquatic with Steve Zissou* and *The Grand Budapest Hotel*, the traditional view of heterosexuality and classic masculinity are still the most prevalent forces in Anderson's work. In the original screenplay, as written by Anderson, in a detail that did not make it into the final version of the film, the six-year-old boy seen in the Author's study at the film's opening plays peacefully with toy soldiers at the end. Toy soldiers are a quintessential masculine signifier as they reference male communities such as military groups.

> *The study. The author (at seventy-five) sits in an armchair writing in an identical small notebook. The six-year-old boy plays with an army of metal soldiers on the floor beside him.*[25]

This small detail did not appear in the filmed version, where instead, the boy is sitting beside his grandfather on a sofa and eating a pastry. However, it is important to remember how this small scene also reflects a moment from Anderson's earliest feature, that of Anthony straightening a toy soldier in *Bottle Rocket*. This connection ties *The Grand Budapest Hotel* to Anderson's earliest film, and expresses the strong thread of masculinity that runs throughout Anderson's work.

The Denouement: Gustave's Death/Zweig's Exile and Suicide

At the end of *The Grand Budapest Hotel*, Anderson places the tribute line before the credits "Inspired by the Writings of Stefan Zweig." Zweig was a contemporary of Sigmund Freud and Arthur Schnitzler and once one of the world's most famous and most translated authors, whose best-known works take place in elegant, long-vanished settings, like ocean liners, spas in the Alps, or a cavalry regiment stationed near a remote border of the Habsburg Empire. While this literature is characterized by its upbeat, slightly comic tone, sophisticated language, and epicurean detachment, this masks the darker reality of wistful nostalgia for a world that was already passing from view, even as Zweig was writing. Certain passages are taken almost verbatim for *The Grand Budapest Hotel*, especially the passage that opens the film, adapted from the first paragraph in the Introduction to Stefan Zweig's *Beware of Pity*:

> "To him that hath, more shall be given." Every writer knows the truth of this biblical maxim, and can confirm the fact that "To him who hath told much, more shall be told." There is nothing more erroneous than the idea, which is only too common, that a writer's imagination is always at work, and he is constantly inventing an inexhaustible supply of incidents and stories. In reality he does not have to invent his stories; he need only let characters and events find their own way to him, and if he retains to a high degree the ability to look and listen, they will keep seeking him out as someone who will pass

them on. To him who as often tried to interpret the tales of others, many will tell their tales.²⁶

Towards the end of his life, Zweig was unable to escape the ominous maelstrom of early twentieth-century history. Caught up in the rise of inter-war fascism leading to World War II, as a Jewish man in Vienna, he was condemned to end his years in exile, as detailed in George Prochnik's *The Impossible Exile: Stefan Zweig at the End of the World*, (2014). Zweig traveled to England and then the United States with his second wife, Lotte Altmann, and, like many wealthy Jews of the period, eventually fled to South America to seek refuge. Once safely ensconced in South America, however, Zweig and his wife were unable to find solace: the ugliness of war and the systematic anti-Jewish violence proved too great a mental foe against the bon vivant lifestyle that Zweig had successfully cultivated in his life and literature. On February 22, 1942, only two days after finishing his magnum opus *The World of Yesterday*, his autobiographical memoir of his pre-war life, Zweig and his wife committed suicide together in a death pact in their home in Petrópolis, Brazil. The beginning of *The World of Yesterday* expresses the darkness of that time for those who experienced it:

> The times provide the pictures, I merely speak the words to go with them, and it will not be so much my own story I tell as that of an entire generation – our unique generation, carrying a heavier burden of fate than almost any other in the course of history.²⁷

The ending of *The Grand Budapest Hotel* similarly reflects the shadow of dark events, as M. Gustave and Zero are once again confronted by militia. "Why are we stopping at a barley field again?"²⁸ Zero asks, as the train pulls up to the same frontier settlement and totalitarian-style soldiers board the train. While the first time the hotelier and lobby boy faced the soldiers, all was well due to Gustave's smooth-talking flair for words, politesse, and good connections with the army lieutenant (played by Edward Norton) who turns out to be an old family friend, this time they are not so lucky. The violence and the brutality of the war prove inescapable, and this time Gustave's charm is ineffectual against the ignorance, ugliness, and destructive malevolence of the war machine. This scene merits full quotation to demonstrate the contrast between Gustave's politesse and the stark brutality he faces in the soldiers:

> M. Gustave: I find these black uniforms very drab. I suppose they're meant to frighten people, but –
> *Three soldiers appear in the compartment doorway. They are stocky, thick-necked, and armed with carbine rifles. M. Gustave says with his usual air of fancy-meeting-you-here:*
> M. Gustave: Well, hello there, chaps. We were just talking about you.
> Soldier #1: (*blankly*) Documents, please.
> M. Gustave: With pleasure – as always.
> *M. Gustave and Agatha withdraw their passports and present them to the soldier.*

> *The soldier flips through them.*
>
> M. Gustave: You're the first of the enemy forces to whom we've been formally introduced. How do you do?
>
> *The soldier ignores this comment. He returns the passports to M. Gustave and Agatha and looks to Zero. Zero nervously hands him his little scrap of paper. The soldier frowns and studies it. M. Gustave smiles. He says lightly:*
>
> M. Gustave: Plus ça change, am I right? (*To the soldier.*) That's a Migratory Visa with Stage Three Worker Status, darling. Read this.
>
> *M. Gustave hands the soldier Henckels' special document. The soldier shows it to his associates. They confer rapidly at a whisper. There is some debate. Before M. Gustave can work his magic – the soldier rips the special document to shreds.*[29]

The contrast between the peaceful exuberance of Agatha declaiming a celebratory toast to Gustave and Zero's relationship ("Whence came these two, radiant, celestial brothers, united, for an instant, as they crossed the stratosphere of our starry window? One from the East, and one from the West"[30]) is marred by the sudden violent imposition of the soldiers, and the bloodied Gustave is whisked away to be executed in the field outside the train car. It is important that this violence happens off-screen. "In the end, they shot him,"[31] is reported by Zero. Mr. Moustafa reflects Zweig's own viewpoint of the war when he states in a voice-over: "There *are* still faint glimmers of civilization left in this barbaric slaughterhouse that was once known as humanity... He was one of them. What more is there to say?"[32] The hopelessness of frail human goodness to withstand the onslaught of war is reflected by Zweig's own tragic suicide and loss of hope in the face of the Second World War.

And yet, as Wes Anderson indicates in the final frames of the film, all is not lost. Although the Author is dead, he is remembered and honored with the words on a bronze plaque below the bust in the graveyard: "In Memory of Our National Treasure." The final sequence shows the wrap-up of Mr. Moustafa and the Author's dinner at the Grand Budapest, then the Author taking notes in a small notebook while seated on a couch next to his grandson in the 1985 documentary, and finally the conclusion of the teenage girl's visit to honor the Author's memory at the cemetery. There, in a meaningful act of pilgrimage, she sits on a bench to read the book she so adores, while earlier she had hung a key on the tombstone in tribute to "The Society of The Crossed Keys," in a display of the enduring honor attributed to that world of the past. In this way, the Author's world continues to be honored in the memories of the younger generations; similarly, Wes Anderson pays tribute to Zweig's influence in this film. To demonstrate this, in the final moments of the film, Anderson cuts to the graveyard scene:

> *The park. The girl in the trench coat and beret sits on a bench near the statue of the author. She is just finishing the final chapter of:*
> THE GRAND BUDAPEST HOTEL.[33]

By leaving the image in the viewer's mind of the girl finishing the novel *The Grand Budapest Hotel*, Anderson is making a statement about literary reception and history.

This image illustrates the enduring effect of classical narrative literature and its power to resist and overcome the darkness of war, violence, and death.

Zero eulogizes Gustave with this quote, just as he and the Author reach the elevator at the end of their evening together:

> Mr. Moustafa: To be frank, I think his world had vanished long before he ever entered it – but, I will say: he certainly sustained the illusion with a marvelous grace!
> (*Pause.*)
> Are you going up?[34]

This characteristic of "marvelous grace" could equally be applied to Stefan Zweig as well, especially to the Proustian *World of Yesterday*, and similarly, the same could be said of Wes Anderson. All three operate outside of their ages; all three wish to preserve a vanishing world of enjoyment and old-school intellectual sophistication in a world where the pace of modernization seems to be leaving them out of step with the times. Anderson invites the viewer to slow down, linger over a fine meal, and remember.

Notes

1. Of the creation of the character of M. Gustave H, Hugo Guinness, co-author of the story of *The Grand Budapest Hotel*, says the following: "I remember in Paris, 2007, Wes and I spent some time in restaurants and cafes and on walks in public parks discussing a mutual friend of ours. We talked about the things he said, his life, his mannerisms. He was an unusual character – full of anecdotes, charm and *bons mots*. He made us laugh. Wes would write occasional casual notes about him. I then returned to New York and heard nothing from Wes about this character for five or six years. He was forgotten. In 2012, out of the blue, Wes revived him. We worked together over a period of several weeks and then multiple telephone calls. The character became M. Gustave H, the bisexual concierge of a hotel in middle Europe." Hugo Guinness, in the Introduction to *The Grand Budapest Hotel* (New York: Opus, 2014), vii.
2. In an interview with Matt Zoller Seitz, Anderson states that the inspiration for Zero's name came from actor Zero Mostel. Wes Anderson, interviewed by Matt Zoller Seitz, in *The Wes Anderson Collection: The Grand Budapest Hotel* (New York: Abrams, 2015a), 46. Mostel is most famous for his 1964 Broadway portrayal of struggling Jewish patriarch Tevye who faces exile from his homeland in *Fiddler on the Roof*. This is significant because of Zero's admission of his background as an exile and refugee from his vaguely-identified homeland, where he says he witnessed the execution of his own family members.
3. Anderson elaborates on the background of the character of Zero, stating that he wanted to find an actor who was from the Middle East to give him an indistinctly foreign look, so that his background could not be easily placed: "The character is kind of half-Arab, half-Jew, maybe? He's from another made-up

country." Anderson, interviewed in Seitz, 2015a, 35. (To find the actor to play Zero, Anderson and his team looked as far as Lebanon, Israel, and North Africa. Ultimately, however, the actor cast in the role, Tony Revolori, was from Anaheim, California.)
4 Wes Anderson (screenplay) and Hugo Guinness (story), *The Grand Budapest Hotel* (New York: Opus, 2014), 12.
5 Anderson and Guinness, 2014, 3–4.
6 Ibid., 4–5.
7 Ibid., 8.
8 Ibid., 9–10.
9 Ibid., 23.
10 For the walls of the Author's study, Anderson deliberately chose a wallpaper pattern reminiscent of Stanley Kubrick's geometrically-patterned carpeting choice for the Overlook Hotel in Kubrick's famous hotel-themed movie, *The Shining* (1980).
11 Seitz also notes that the character name of Deputy Vilmos Kovacs (played by Jeff Goldblum) is an amalgamation of the names of Vilmos Zsigmond, and László Kovács, two Hungarian-born American cinematographers well-known in Hollywood in the mid-twentieth century. Seitz, 2015a, 52, footnote 5.
12 The "MAV" tattooed on Ludwig's left arm is the abbreviation of the French saying "morts aux vaches," which translates roughly to "death to the pigs/police."
13 Anderson and Guinness, 2014, 106.
14 Tommy Lee Jones' line from *The Fugitive* is as follows: "Listen up, ladies and gentlemen! Our fugitive has been on the run for 90 minutes. Average foot speed over uneven ground, barring injury, is 4 miles an hour which gives us a radius of 6 miles! What I want out of each and every one of you is a hard-target search of every gas station, residence, warehouse, farmhouse, henhouse, outhouse, and doghouse in that area. Checkpoints go up at 15 miles! Our fugitive's name is Dr. Richard Kimble. Go get him."
15 Anderson and Guinness, 2014, 3.
16 Anderson claims these regular recitations of poetry were inspired by the same habit in the mutual friend upon which he and Hugo Guinness based their story, as well as the constant referrals to people as "darling." Wes Anderson, interviewed by Seitz, 2015a, 61.
17 Anderson and Guinness, 2014, 19, 22.
18 Ibid., 98–99.
19 Ibid., 125–126.
20 Ibid., 130.
21 Ibid., 55.
22 David Halperin, *Saint Foucault: Towards a Gay Hagiography* (Oxford, UK: Oxford University Press, 1995), 62.
23 Anderson and Guinness, 2014, 72.
24 Wes Anderson and Noah Baumbach, *The Life Aquatic with Steve Zissou* [Final Draft] (Burbank, CA: Touchstone Pictures, n.d.), 1.

25 Anderson and Guinness, 2014, 150.
26 Stefan Zweig, *Beware of Pity*, quoted in Seitz, 2015a, 216.
27 Stefan Zweig, *The World of Yesterday*, quoted in ibid., 220.
28 Anderson and Guinness, 2014, 145.
29 Ibid., 145–146.
30 Ibid., 144.
31 Ibid., 147.
32 Ibid., 146–147.
33 Ibid., 150.
34 Ibid., 149.

CHAPTER ELEVEN

Wes Anderson's Short Films and Commercial Work

The discussion of Wes Anderson's oeuvre would not be complete without an examination of his unique canon of short films and work in commercial advertising. In many ways, Anderson's short films and commercial work demonstrate thematic continuities with his feature-length work that merit more detailed attention. Specifically, his original 13-minute short "Bottle Rocket," and his later commercial work for Prada and other companies expresses his clearest homage to directors of the past such as Truffaut and the French New Wave, and Federico Fellini. An overview of Anderson's commercial work demonstrates his commitment to bringing to life these references to great directors from the past and playfully engaging their cinematic styles.

"Bottle Rocket" (short, 1994)

The screenplay that Anderson and Owen Wilson crafted in their early twenties for their first short film, "Bottle Rocket," is a vivid depiction of the early originality and boldness of Anderson's "voice" as it developed in later films. From the opening scene, in which the childhood friends Dignan and Anthony carry on an intense discussion about an episode of "Starsky and Hutch"[1] while cutting through neighbors' backyards on their way to a robbery, the film signifies that the viewer will be navigating some odd terrain.[2] The character of Dignan is full of contradictions, a slacker-dude with strong career motivations, a liar with a passionate commitment to encouraging others and helping them reach their potential, a loser with absurdly self-aggrandizing notions. He speaks with an erudite diction, (when discussing the phone call from "Starsky and Hutch," both Dignan and Anthony say "This is he") and yet he confuses the words "hypocritical" and "hypothetical" ("I'm just being hypocritical now" – this malapropism occurs in both the short film and the feature-length version). It is an amusing detail that when Dignan plans to rob the house, he is carrying a white tennis bag (an object that only someone who is already wealthy would own). Anthony's character is also shown to be one of contrasts: he is the more cautious one, and the one who would naturally be more law-abiding, because he still retains a childish innocence and naïveté (for example, in the scene of the robbery, Anthony lingers over toy soldiers). He is also the one who tells his friend who is growing illegal marijuana that he should grow cinnamon instead, so that he can make his own cinnamon toast – here substituting an illegal pot grower's trade for an innocent childlike desire. In a later robbery scene, Anthony wears a shirt that has the name "Roberto" embroidered above the pocket, like a child wearing a costume.

As discussed in the third chapter on Anderson's 1996 feature-length film *Bottle Rocket*, the "Bottle Rocket" short shows three friends named Dignan (Owen Wilson), Anthony (Luke Wilson) and Bob (Robert Musgrave) preparing for a heist. The short contains scenes where Anthony and Dignan rob a house (which they enter simply by opening the front door), eat at a diner, ogle an older waitress, play pinball while arguing about how much the coin collection they stole is worth, and have the discussion that reveals that the house they robbed was actually Anthony's own family home. Anthony becomes angry when he finds out that Dignan stole the earrings he bought for his mother's birthday. Anthony defends himself by insisting that their burglarizing is "professional" and that they must simply do their job. This version begins after Anthony's breakout from the mental health facility in the 1996 version, and ends after the boys recap the bookstore robbery to Bob.

Some scenes appear in the short film that were not included in the feature-length version. For example, as the two walk past a parked car, Dignan persuades Anthony to rob a wallet that he spots on the car seat. Anthony reluctantly steals the wallet, and there is an extremely forlorn sequence of Anthony running away, which echoes the extended running of Truffaut's character Antoine Doinel (a misunderstood youth who is running away from an institution for juvenile delinquents) at the end of *Les Quatre cents coups*. After running through a dingy back alley that is rendered even more depressing by the cold, stark contrasts of black and white in the film, Anthony dutifully delivers the wallet to Dignan, who triumphantly reveals its contents to be a grand total of eight dollars. Dignan painstakingly divides the cash into two equal portions with an air of victory and magnanimity, while it is clear from Anthony's distressed face that he does not believe it was worth the risk to rob the car for eight dollars.

The next scene takes place in a bar or a coffee house, where their friend Bob reveals to them that he is growing marijuana worth US$6000 in his backyard. He claims that "Hector," his dog, is protecting his crop. Bob tells them not to tell anybody, and the two accuse Bob of being "paranoid." This is followed by Anthony's innocent question about whether Bob could grow cinnamon instead of pot. The following scene focuses on a rotund man in an "I'm a Pepper" shirt (a nuanced costume detail which would also appear in *The Life Aquatic with Steve Zissou*) with a camouflage cap that reads "Little River Gun Co.," and 70s-style glasses with huge frames. He is a gun salesman (Temple Nash, Jr.), a professional firearms dealer/security guard who appears as himself in the film. He speaks of a "ballpoint pen tracheotomy," and discusses the various common household objects that could be used as weapons: a knife, a coke bottle, a pencil. When Dignan tells him he wants to buy a gun just to "intimidate people," the gun enthusiast tells him: "You don't intimidate people with guns, you shoot people with guns." The film cuts to a shot of Bob's worried face; this is perhaps the boys' first realization that what they are planning involves any risk at all. The gun salesman punctuates his sobering speech with a hearty laugh, one of the only hearty laughs in all of Wes Anderson's oeuvre. This is followed by the iconic scene at the shooting range, when all three boys try shooting guns at hand-drawn targets (these targets are extremely childish-looking, again suggesting how young and naïve the three boys are). The use of the Peanuts' song "Skating" by Vince Guaraldi underscores this reference to childhood and childishness – the use of a Peanuts' song during the gun-shooting scene is unsettling and strangely joyful.

The "Bottle Rocket" 1994 short film is quite illuminating as an example of one of the first films from a now established director, and it clearly demonstrates Anderson's potential and the early-stage emergence of his unique voice. There are several elements of this film that hint at the rich developments in the future of Anderson's career. First, this film highlights one of Anderson's key themes in his subsequent films, the topic of male bonding, and the Wilson brothers, despite their lack of acting experience, already have a striking rapport that clearly conveys the closeness of these young men. Second, Anderson uses a unique style to introduce the bookstore into the story, and it is interesting to note how the bits and pieces of visual information are conveyed by "stolen" shots in the aisles and around the corners, highlighting Anderson's natural attention to detail as he focuses on a pay phone or a Post-It note stuck to the front of the "Employees Only" door. Third, use of the medium of black-and-white film in "Bottle Rocket", and its use of jazz, is a clear homage to French New Wave, with particular similarities to *Les Quatre cents coups*, with its Anthony/Antoine Doinel parallel (the feature-length version even begins with Anthony escaping from a mental hospital which pays homage to Antoine's escape from the juvenile delinquency institution at the end of Truffaut's film). Finally, the tone of the film, with its contrasting of "lawless" subject matter with the "innocence" of youth, is very prescient in foreshadowing Anderson's oft-revisited dichotomous themes that will come to the forefront again and again in Anderson's future work. The "Bottle Rocket" 1994 short film overall is something slight, but it works for a 13-minute short with a fairly abrupt ending. The subtlety and simplicity of the film, combined with the very genuine performances of its first-time actors, convey the burgeoning talents of the filmmaker and his cast.

Anderson's American Express Advertisement (2006)

In 2006, the American Express credit card company recruited Anderson to direct his own ad as part of their serial "My Life, My Card" campaign. Anderson's inclusion in this pantheon was a daring choice at the time considering he had made only four feature films at that point, yet his name and occupation, "Wes Anderson: Director," appeared onscreen, treated as if he had already approached the status of a "brand." The director appeared in the American Express ad as "himself," the nattily dressed (with a green scarf as an ascot), and decorously pompous (an early M. Gustave?) character, "acting out" his role as director in a sly self-parody. The spot, written and directed by Anderson, is a long tracking shot modeled on *La Nuit américaine* (*Day for Night*, 1973), a film about filmmaking directed by François Truffaut (the theme music used in the ad, the "Grand Chorale" by Georges Delerue, was also taken from this film). Thus, like Truffaut in *La Nuit américaine*, Anderson directs and stars in a film in which he explains how to make a movie while answering various questions from his cast and crew. The 2-minute television ad begins with a scene from this "fake" action movie, in which a character played by Jason Schwartzman is in conversation with Anderson film regular Waris Ahluwalia. Their discussion about a ballpoint pen is followed immediately by the fatal car accident of François (Roman Coppola). After shouting out his friend's name in a grief-stricken voice, Schwartzman dons his panama hat at a rakish angle. Wes Anderson cuts the filming, makes comments on the smoke and the snow (the snow machine is too loud), and gives notes on the lines by Schwartzman and Ahluwalia. He is handed a sandwich on a plate, and joins his banana-eating producer on a tour of the set. He passes a geisha and checks her makeup, asks for a .357 pistol with a bayonet (the pistol's mock-up is offered to him eight seconds later), listens to a draft dialogue, authorizes a $15,000 helicopter shot (using his card), and meets Lucy, the daughter of the man who loaned the team a sports car. Finally he climbs up into a floating crane with his director of photography, Bob Yeoman, to declare the ad's pitch line, that "my life is about telling stories" (he is nearly hit in the face by a flock of birds – a sly reference to Alfred Hitchcock's notorious avian horror film, and to the text *Hitchcock/Truffaut*; he asks if the birds are his, and says he needs them) and "my card is American Express."

This film is a series of humorously fanciful Andersonian moments, one after another. For example, Anderson is told that the production cannot afford a $15,000 helicopter shot, similar to an event that actually happened during the filming of *Rushmore*. In this case, instead of Bill Murray writing Wes Anderson a check to cover the expense of the chopper rental, Anderson takes out his wallet, demonstrating the power of an American Express card. In addition, the little girl who waits to meet Anderson, Lucy, is wearing pink gloves just like those of Margot Tenenbaum, while the man who introduces her is holding a tennis racquet under his arm in a reference to her brother, Richie. However, the music, the style of the ad, the pacing, the long tracking shot, and the role played by Anderson himself are all a direct homage to Truffaut. One clear example is that in *La Nuit américaine*, Truffaut plays a director named Ferrand who explains how to make a movie while responding to various questions from different crew members; at one point, Truffaut, as Ferrand, is shown a collection of pistols in a black display shelf lined with red velvet, which conspicuously resembles the prop gun case displayed to Anderson in the short. Moreover, Schwartzman's cry of "François!" at the beginning of the film is a brief elegy to Truffaut, who died in 1985. Thus, Anderson once again points to Truffaut in his work, but this time he essentially "performs" Truffaut, presenting himself as an auteur in the Truffautian tradition, albeit with tongue in cheek.

Anderson's Other Commercial Work

Anderson has designed advertisements for IKEA, SoftBank (Japan), Stella Artois, Hyundai, Sony Xperia, and AT&T. In 2002, Swedish furniture company IKEA kicked off their "Unböring" marketing campaign with an Anderson-directed commercial featuring a family drama unfolding in a very stylish living room. His IKEA advertisements all follow the same formula: a family feels so comfortable in the IKEA "set" furnishings in the store that they begin to argue just like they would at home, only to be interrupted by a salesman who asks if they would like to purchase the furniture; when Anderson pulls his camera back, it is revealed that the family was having an argument on an IKEA sales floor. In September 2007, Anderson oversaw a series of six commercials for AT&T: "College Kid," "Reporter," "Mom," "Architect," "Actor" and "Businessman." Each of the six commercials introduces the viewer to a different AT&T customer. As each of these people comes before the camera and talks about the different, far-reaching locales where he or she needs cell-phone service, the visuals behind the customer change dramatically to reflect the different destinations. For "Actor," Anderson mounted the camera on a revolving platform; the camera stayed focused on the main actor while four distinct sets revolved behind him. This series of commercials for AT&T unmistakably captures Anderson's visual style with its unique design and filming of the sets.

In 2008, Anderson shot a 30-second commercial in a seaside town in Normandy for the Japanese telecommunications company SoftBank, a lively pastiche of the films of Jacques Tati, particularly *Les Vacances de Monsieur Hulot* (*Mr. Hulot's Holiday*, 1953), featuring Brad Pitt clad entirely in bright yellow (including Mr. Hulot's signature hat) playing a bumbling but good-natured tourist. The ad is full of slapstick hijinks connected in a series of whip-pans and dolly shots, as the unnamed character purchases a peach from a local fruit stand, which, when he picks it up to take a bite, is shown to be half-eaten already; this is quickly followed by the character's helpful offer to push a stalled automobile (but his knapsack becomes entangled with the metal handle on the trunk and he loses it when the car drives off). He is then passed and nearly knocked over by a large group of bicyclists (suggestive of the peloton in the Tour de France), and then he spots a group of adolescent boys dressed in hiking garb (foreshadowing the scouts in *Moonrise Kingdom*), one carrying baguettes, who move away to reveal a bucolic scene of picnickers in a meadow, who are being painted by an artist in the open field. One of the women is topless, and the tourist snaps a photo of her bare back on his cell phone. The film ends with a close-up of this photo displayed on the cell phone. The entire commercial is set to the music of Serge Gainsbourg's 1965 Eurovision prize-winning song, "Poupée de cire, poupée de son," a well-known but controversial French bubble-gum pop song (called "yé-yé" music in France) performed by France Gall. In the song, Gainsbourg's lyrics use self-referentiality, word play, and double entendres to imply that Gall is a "singing doll" controlled by Gainsbourg.[3] Anderson would later use "yé-yé" music again for Suzy Bishop's favorite record in *Moonrise Kingdom*.

Another example of Anderson's commercial work is his collaboration with the Innocean global marketing/advertising agency for Hyundai. In 2012, Anderson directed two commercials for Hyundai which reveal his signature techniques in different ways. In the first commercial, "Talk to My Car," Anderson uses a whimsical mixture of miniatures and advanced car technology representing three different time periods of "magical" cars in the American cultural imagination. The result resembles famous smart cars from *Chitty Chitty Bang Bang* (1968) and *The Spy Who Loved Me* (1977), as well as *Knight Rider*'s KITT. At the end of the commercial, a young boy in the back seat turns around expectantly to watch the deployment of the car's rear incendiary devices, and the scene changes again to modern times, with a sleek Hyundai that can "hear" verbal commands, like the father's request for the car to locate a good Italian restaurant in the vicinity. The narrator intones, "It's always been a dream to talk to our cars – now we can!" reminding the viewer of Anderson's penchant for childlike flights of imagination, as well as his fanciful references firmly rooted in American cultural history. In the commercial "Modern Life," a mother delays returning home to the chaos of her children and husband cooking a pasta dinner – one child is eating frozen peas out of the bag, one is drumming, one is sitting in a kitchen cabinet, one is wearing a white lab coat, one has on a scuba mask, one is grating cheese, one is wearing a wizard costume, all while the husband receives instructions on cooking dinner over the phone – preferring to sit in the serenity of her "beautifully quiet" Hyundai Azera (this film is a long tracking shot that uses Anderson's characteristic color palette, centered point of view, and humorous dialogue, at the end of which the camera passes through a wall where the wife is revealed to be sitting in the car in their home's driveway). Both Hundai commercials aired during the 84th Academy Awards. Also in 2012, Anderson released a stop-motion animation commercial for Sony Xperia. Jake Ryan, who played Lionel, one of the young siblings in the Bishop family in *Moonrise Kingdom*, composed the text for the commercial during an interview in which he describes how he imagines the Xperia phone works, and the animation accompanies his explanation. The youthful narration and imaginative inventiveness of the Sony commercial and the childlike playfulness of the Hyundai ads display Anderson's enjoyment of creating these worlds, again highlighting the childlike voice behind the director's sense of humor.

Hotel Chevalier (2007)

The 13-minute film *Hotel Chevalier* was developed independently and originally envisioned as a stand-alone short film, but later incorporated as a companion piece/prequel to *The Darjeeling Limited*. It was filmed on location at the Hotel Raphaël in Paris in 2005, with Natalie Portman and Jason Schwartzman. Anderson realized while working on the film that he liked the unnamed male character played by Schwartzman in the short and that was the type of character that he wanted Schwartzman to play in *The Darjeeling Limited*, which he was writing at the time. (Anderson toyed with the idea of releasing the two films as a sequence in cinemas, and has occasionally shown the two works together; for example, *Hotel Chevalier* was screened as part of the program at the world première of *The Darjeeling Limited* at the 64th Annual Venice Film Festival on September 2, 2007.) *The Darjeeling Limited* can be viewed as a stand-alone film, and the events in *Hotel Chevalier* are touched on only remotely in *The*

Darjeeling Limited: for example, the viewer is aware from the beginning of the film that the youngest Whitman brother, played by Schwartzman, is coming from a broken romantic relationship, since he calls to check his ex-girlfriend's answering machine at various stops throughout the film, he finds the perfume she put in his luggage, and toward the end of the film, recounts some of the lines between the boy and the girl in a short story he has written. Portman also has a short cameo in *The Darjeeling Limited*, tying the two films together into a more harmonious resolution, while *Hotel Chevalier* is comparatively open-ended. There is also a line which appears in the credits: "Part I of *The Darjeeling Limited*," and another line which credits Eric Anderson with the "Suitcase Wildlife Drawings" on the Louis Vuitton luggage monogrammed with the initials J. L. W. that become a central focus of *The Darjeeling Limited*. Finally, Schwartzman's character is barefoot just as he is in *The Darjeeling Limited*, and he also wears the yellow "Hotel Chevalier" robe in the full-length feature.[4] The theme of the film is the unresolved relationship between the two main characters, a male and a female, who remain unnamed throughout the vignette. It is clear from the film that the two share a meaningful history; they broke up and they are now facing an ambiguous future. According to the timeline, the events in *Hotel Chevalier* take place two weeks before the beginning of *The Darjeeling Limited*.

The film begins with a brief shot of the concierge answering a telephone at the hotel's front desk in an ornate European-style hotel lobby. The scene cuts to Jason Schwartzman's character, lying on a bed in a vivid yellow "Hotel Chevalier" robe, reading a newspaper while ordering a meal from room service. Billy Wilder's 1953 war film *Stalag 17* is playing silently on the hotel room's television screen.[5] The first shot shown from *Stalag 17* is two corpses covered by a blanket – two American prisoners of war shot for trying to escape from the German prison camp in the film – a sly reference to the "death" of the relationship between the man and the woman in the film, and how they cannot fully escape the "prison" of their failed relationship, which ended more than a month before. After ordering room service from the concierge in broken French, the man receives a call from the woman who tells him she is on her way from the airport and asks for his room number. He then hurriedly tidies the room – pausing to play the opening bars of the song "Where Do You Go To (My Lovely)?" on his iPod – and runs a bath. He then is shown waiting for the woman's arrival, lying on the bed in a funereal dark suit, another visual cue suggesting the death of their relationship. When the woman arrives, she asks the man quizzically, "What is this music?" indicating that the song is not part of their shared past. The song "Where Do You Go To (My Lovely)" a 1969 European hit song by Peter Sarstedt that the man has chosen to play for her is not just background music, but is featured prominently. Like the Yves Montand song in *Rushmore*, setting up the song and playing it are key elements of the narrative. Although written in English and sung by an Englishman, it sounds like Serge Gainsbourg or Jacques Brel, both of whom were popular when the song was written. Anderson's use of the Sarstedt tune is an interesting way for the director to demonstrate his own self-image: this mix of an English-language song done in a French style parallels Anderson himself. Another significant feature to the song is its recounting of external references to describe the woman as talking like

"Marlene Dietrich," whose "clothes are all made by Balmain," and who keeps all her "Rolling Stones records" in her apartment on "the Boulevard of St. Michel," which also suggests Anderson's tendency to display external objects in order to communicate inner character. (Later, in *the Darjeeling Limited*, this same song is used to try to seduce Rita.) The woman observes the man's belongings displayed around the hotel room, including some porcelain figurines (one appears to be an Indian swami and the other Winston Churchill), mounted insect specimens, a miniature music box (interestingly, both Portman's character and Anjelica Huston's character play the music box when they see it – a similarity that bonds Jack's girlfriend and his mother in *Hotel Chevalier* and *The Darjeeling Limited*), and an amateur painting of pears (the girl touches it to see if the paint is still wet). As she passes the bed, she places a small package into his suitcase with a quick, secretive gesture (later, in *The Darjeeling Limited*, this turns out to be the bottle of perfume Voltaire No. 5, Le Petit Mort[6]). She then goes into the bathroom and brushes her teeth with the man's toothbrush, and he tells her he had drawn a bath for her. Emerging from the bathroom, she questions him about how long he has been living in the hotel, and he confesses that it has been more than a month. When the two lie down on the bed the first time, they are both separated by the large monogrammed suitcase between them. They are interrupted briefly by the arrival of room service, wheeled in on a fancy table-clothed cart with elaborate presentation under rounded metal warming covers even though the meal is simply grilled cheese, onion soup, and chocolate milk.

Once alone again, the two kiss and the man begins to undress the woman, first removing her boots in an erotically-charged way. They pause to have an uncomfortable exchange about not having slept with other people. Their dialogue reveals little of their enigmatic past; he is weighed down with self-absorbed dissipation, while she has bruises on her body that she declines to explain. Lying on top of him, she tells the man that she does not want to lose his friendship, and that she loves him and never meant to hurt him. He responds truthfully "I promise I will never be your friend – ever," but holds her when she embraces him. "Where Do You Go To (My Lovely)?" starts to play again, and the man, with shy pride, offers to show the woman his view of Paris. In a slow-motion shot, the woman is shown perched against an armoire; the man approaches and covers her naked body with the yellow bathrobe, and the two move together towards the window. After they step out on the balcony, the man draws a toothpick from his pocket and hands it to her with an upwards nod; she receives it with a smile. After looking out for another few seconds she clasps his neck lightly and they step back inside, while the camera pans over a typical Haussmann façade in the Paris twilight. The orderly windows and symmetry of the shot also reveal that inside the dwellings, the people in the opposite building – and all over the city – are going about their daily lives, unaffected by the passion and misery of the on-again, off-again relationship.

Cousin Ben Troop Screening with Jason Schwartzman (2012)

This 2-minute short film co-written with Roman Coppola was made as a "Funny or Die" exclusive for promotional purposes leading up to the release of *Moonrise Kingdom*.

Anderson shot this as he completed principal photography on *Moonrise Kingdom*, and it retains continuity of aesthetic and tone as a result. Cousin Ben (Schwartzman) organizes a movie night at the youth camp where "Moonrise Kingdom" is being shown, while the children paying admission to watch his tented screening all appeared in the original film. This creates a metaphysical conundrum considering they are characters watching a film in which they themselves appear.

Castello Cavalcanti (2013)

This 8-minute short made for Prada opens with a serene nighttime scene in a small Italian town, where the sign "Molto Miglia" is hung over a stone arch which serves as an entrance to the town square. The camera pans right to the sign "Caffe" and some of the evening regulars who are enjoying an evening at outdoor tables on the terrace in front of the restaurant: three older women are smoking and gossiping while one knits, two men are standing with a young boy as he plays with a toy car on top of a bale of hay (one of the men, casually conversing, holds a dead pheasant by the feet, which he uses to make a gesture in the conversation), four older men are playing an animated game of cards, and finally, the open door of the restaurant itself displays a world-weary middle-aged but still strikingly sensual waitress standing far back in the room against the counter, while another man dressed in chef's whites comes from the kitchen to announce that the racers are soon to appear. A harried Jason Schwartzman, competing in the Molto Miglia (as opposed to Mille Miglia) race,[7] appears after all of the other competitors have passed by in extremely bright-colored, almost candy-like race cars.[8] He is in last place, and appears at a slight delay after all the excitement of the frontrunners has passed, complete with an extremely zealous photographer/paparazzo transported into town by motorcycle. Schwartzman's voice alone is heard from the vehicle as he enters the town, cursing audibly. After more cursing, the yelling of the word "No!" and a blackout, there is a titlecard with the Italian flag and the words "Italy: September, 1955."

After this break in the film, the next scene is the memorable image of Schwartzman leaping out of a burning vehicle that has crashed into a statue of Christ in the town square of Castello Cavalcanti. The front end of his car is smashed in, a red race car just as shimmering and delicious-looking as the others that passed earlier. ("It wasn't my fault – the steering wheel's screwed on backwards!") A simple plot with many holes deliberately left unexplained by Anderson, the narrative could be as simple as a Formula One racer unexpectedly finding himself in his "Old Country" hometown (his last name is Cavalcanti) among his ancestors, one of whom is his colorfully named "great great grand-uncle" Michelangelo. When the bus arrives to take the racer away, he instead decides to stay among them, for the evening, or perhaps for longer, as he has made a connection with the woman at the café counter. However, another interpretation is that this is a meditation on death for the racer, who might not have survived the crash. He muses: "In a way I'm glad I crashed. It's a warning for me. I coulda got killed, you know, like that coop of chickens over there. Tarred … feathered … spitroasted.") As the racer walks away from the wreck, there is a man holding a dead chicken with white feathers foregrounded in the frame. In addition, when the car crashes into the Christ-figure statue, the square around it is suddenly covered with white chicken feathers resembling "puffballs," like those that arrive every spring and blow through the air signifying rebirth and memory. Finally, as the men from the bar douse the car with water, a priest suddenly arrives on the scene, a latecomer, holding a festive racing flag and watching the chaotic scene in slight puzzlement.

The film is set in the 1950s, which emphasizes the purity and simplicity of the village people in their conservative, set roles: a restaurant worker, several grandmotherly figures, a family with a young son, a priest, and nuns. This comes across as a contrast to the young Jed Cavalcanti's brash American manner ("I think my ancestors mighta came from here!") and expletive-filled speech. He redeems himself after cursing out his brother-in-law, Gus, over the telephone for outfitting the car badly, by saying "Stop crying, I understand. I understand," but he can't resist adding, "Plus there's a slow leak in the rear left tire, but I suppose that doesn't matter anymore since the car's totaled." The classic car race and the old-world style of the ancestral village, plus a few seconds from the original Italian broadcast of Formula One 1979 French Grand Prix, with the epic battle for second place between Gilles Villeneuve and René Arnoux voiced by the legendary commentator Mario Poltronieri broadcast on the radio, all contribute to an effortless sense of nostalgia.

Castello Cavalcanti was filmed in Fellini's studio Cinecittà in Rome, Italy, and shares a prop with Fellini's *La Dolce Vita* (1960), the Christ statue standing in the center of the square, along with the motorcycle-riding paparazzo, which are both memorably featured in the film.[9] The car race itself is an homage to the Mille Miglia car race in Fellini's *Amarcord* (1973). The film is a classic Felliniesque take similar to *Amarcord* – which is even referenced directly through the "puffballs" and the scenes of the Mille Miglia racecars passing a "Caffe" sign as they race through a small town at night. The film shares similarities with Fellini's *Amarcord* in that it is heavily and almost surreally nostalgic, and that it lacks a plot in the usual sense. Fellini's film depicts one year in the 1930s Italian coastal town of Rimini in a series of short vignettes that depict small-town life through local events and customs as well as an array of colorful, larger-than-life local characters. In *Amarcord*, Fellini creatively depicts the natural human tendency toward idealization of the past; his views on nostalgia are clearly illustrated by the way he mixes reality and fantasy in this film.[10] Characters look like caricatures, actors playing them often deliberately overact, and women, especially those who fuel the young protagonist's sexual fantasies, are often endowed with certain body parts of gargantuan proportions. Every now and then, scenes that depict 1930s reality gradually slide into fantasies of the movie's characters and Rimini becomes almost indistinguishable from the magical place in the characters' visions. Because of that, almost everything in *Amarcord* looks different, and in most cases better, than it would have looked in real life. Fellini preferred spectacle over reality, and his films are like magic tricks with the elements revealed. The question is, if one can see how a magic trick is performed, does it ruin the trick?

Prada: Candy (2013)

Prada: Candy is the second of two short films/commercials Wes Anderson and Roman Coppola made for Prada, and this one is in the form of a three-part series which runs for a total of three minutes and thirty seconds (or a little over one minute per section). Much like the first short *Castello Cavalcanti* was a tribute to Fellini, the film *Prada: Candy* is an overt homage to Truffaut with its dazzling cinematography and sharp aesthetic, while Julius and Gene's character names clearly reference Truffaut's Jules and Jim. The film illustrates the relationship between two best friends (Peter Gadiot and Rodolphe Pauly) and a woman (Léa Seydoux) as they both try to vie for her love in different ways, each of which concluding with a statement to buy Prada's new fragrance "Candy." This is the first film Anderson directed entirely in French (a fitting tribute to Truffaut), set to a soundtrack by French yé-yé singer France Gall and Jacques Dutronc; Seydoux would later appear in *The Grand Budapest Hotel*.

Come Together (2016)

This four-minute short is set aboard the "H & M Lines Winter Express" (named for the H & M clothing retailer being advertised). The title *Come Together* cannot help but bring to mind the eponymous song by the Beatles, and the sight of Adrien Brody on a train is a shorthand connection to *The Darjeeling Limited*. Brody is Conductor Ralph of Coach 14, an obsessively organized and buttoned-up conductor with his neat tie clip and his pocket watch, and jolly red-and-green trimmed vest and cap. Snowflakes fall as he looks out the train window. He tears off a calendar page revealing it is December 25, makes some calculations, checks the timetable, and turns around toward the camera with a sigh – it turns out there will be an 11½-hour delay, and it is up to him to save Christmas. The song "The Little Drummer Boy" recorded by The Harry Simeone Chorale in 1958 (and closely associated with eponymous 1968 Christmas stop-motion animated television special produced by Rankin/Bass Productions) plays, lending an instant nostalgic air to the advertisement.

The camera travels back over the outside wall of the train, offering a glimpse of all the passengers one at a time through their cabin windows, a sequence reminiscent of the cutaway shots in *The Life Aquatic*, and the imaginary train sequence in *The Darjeeling Limited*. Each passenger is displayed with gift-wrapped packages and a photo of his or her loved ones (in one case, the photo is of a dog). Brody (representing Anderson as conductor/director of the train) is presented as a slightly off-kilter Santa figure whose mad speed and efficiency, coupled with the bumbling efforts of his second-in-command, Fritz (Garth Jennings) as assistant porter and Santa's helper (the conductor pops a Santa's cap on Fritz's head), resemble an old-style comedy slapstick routine. In a visual highlight of the short, the passage of time is represented by the beautifully symmetrical pale-green Art Deco interior hallway of the train, darkening while going through a tunnel and bathed in light on the other side. With the title notation "19 Minutes Later," the passengers, having been invited to the cafeteria at the rear of the coach for a Christmas brunch, gingerly emerge from their individual compartments; the last one to come out is a young blond boy, the "Unaccompanied Minor," who peers cautiously down the hallway for a long moment before emerging.

Noticeable signifiers of Anderson's work include the setting on a compartmentalized conveyance, the cool gray-green color palette, the anachronistic vintage 1920s-style font used for the titles, the presence of a child, the reading of a book (Agatha Christie's *4:50 From Paddington* [1957]), the juxtaposition of the conductor's obsessively timed efficiency with his unlikely Christmas spirit (incongruously calling Stationmaster Fred for scissors, construction paper, aluminum foil, and an extension cord, while the male voice on the other end of the line clearly resembles the distorted "wah wah wah" voice given to all adults in the "Peanuts" specials), Fritz's awkward tossing of confetti when the young boy approaches, the "Chocolate-Flavoured Hot Beverage" and "Whipped Topping" labels on their respective containers, the tastefully designed H & M paper cups, the boy's whipped-cream mustache and lips as he drinks, and the loveliness of the final train setting with its glass-ceiling panels that flood the car with wintery light. This highly structured Anderson aesthetic is given a transcendent quality by the reappearance of John Lennon's influence during the finale with the 1971 song "Happy Christmas/War is Over" (distinctly played on a vinyl LP with its scratches and pops). The juxtaposition of the bittersweet nostalgia of "Happy Christmas/War is Over" with the title *Come Together* strongly sends a meta-nostalgic message of peace, while the visual representation of people of different ages and backgrounds[11] coming together for Christmas – estranged "orphans" and an unaccompanied minor thrown together and entertained by the master celebration-planner – is again representative of the director himself, and his oft-repeated theme of setting the lonely into "families."

Anderson and the Short Film/Advertisement: Critical Response

Many critics, such as Nicole Richter (2014), feel that the short film and the commercial advertisement are the perfect vehicle for Anderson's "heightened reality" style, because of Anderson's ability to present a complete world in microcosm, which the short form lends itself to. In particular, Anderson's talent for creative set design and unexpected storylines has made him a desirable director for television advertising, which allows him to exercise some of his greatest talents: set pieces, art direction, whimsy, and irony. Anderson creates his commercial work and his short films with the same meticulous attention to character, story, and, especially, art direction that makes his feature work so identifiable. Anderson's short films and his commercials, especially the "Bottle Rocket" short, the American Express commercial, and *Prada: Candy*, continue Anderson's tradition of referencing Truffaut and the French New Wave in his work, while *Castello Cavalcanti* is an obvious homage to Fellini and the Softbank commercial to Jacques Tati. Richter notes that *Hotel Chevalier* connects to the French New Wave omnibus film *Paris vu par...* (*Six in Paris*, 1965) and the newer anthology of short films, *Paris, je t'aime* (2006), specifically Natalie Portman's role in the segment *Faubourg Saint-Denis*.[12] Anderson's short films, like his feature-length work, demonstrate the director's penchant for borrowing signifiers from the past to create something playful and innovative in his art.

Notes

1. Owen Wilson would go on to star with Ben Stiller in *Starsky and Hutch*, the film version of the television series, in 2004.
2. The pop culture discussion at the start is echoed by similar pop cultural debates in films released during this same period, such as Kevin Smith's *Clerks* (1994), as well as subsequent Kevin Smith films, and Quentin Tarantino's *Pulp Fiction* (1994).
3. The double entendres in the lyrics include the title, which can be translated "wax doll, rag doll" (a floppy doll stuffed with bran or chaff) or as "wax doll, sound doll" – implying that the singer is a "singing doll," parroting songs created by adults, with lyrical themes purposefully introduced by those controlling adults which the young performer only partially understands. Thus, Gall herself is the "Poupée de cire, poupée de son" of the song's title.
4. The word "chevalier" ("knight") is used in somewhat comical juxtaposition with Schwartzman's hapless character, who is far from the embodiment of a chivalrous knight.
5. *Stalag 17* director Billy Wilder is yet another filmmaker like many others referenced by Anderson who, as a Jewish man in the Austro-Hungarian Empire, had to flee Europe under Hitler, eventually living in exile in America.
6. "Voltaire" is named after France's greatest philosopher/satirist. "Le Petit Mort" is French for "orgasm."
7. The "Mille Miglia" was a classic endurance race which took place in Italy from 1927 to 1957, crossing half of the country from Brescia to Rome and back. The race also appears in Fellini's nostalgic view of Italy in *Amarcord* (1973).
8. This scene strongly suggests a connection with the animated series "Wacky Races" which ran from 1968–1970 and continued in reruns in the Saturday morning cartoon lineup, which definitely would have been seen by any child growing up in the US in the 1970s, with the memorable racing outfits and vehicles belonging to characters such as Dick Dastardly, whose penchant for the interjection: "Drat, drat, and double drat!" calls to mind the impassioned cursing of Jed Cavalcanti after the totaling of his racecar in the film.
9. The homage extends beyond Fellini alone, as the title character is named after Brazilian-born director Alberto Cavalcanti.
10. Distortion between the actual past and its subjective interpretation can be found even in the title of the film – "Amarcord" is not a real word, but instead a neologism made from the contraction of the phrase "I remember" in the Romagnol dialect, emphasizing further the disconnection between reality and memory.
11. Diverse racial backgrounds are represented in *Come Together*, including an Asian businessman, a young Indian woman, and a black woman who clearly resembles Whoopi Goldberg.
12. Nicole Richter, "The Short Films of Wes Anderson," in Peter C. Kunze, ed., *The Films of Wes Anderson: Critical Essays on an Indiewood Icon* (New York, Palgrave Macmillan, 2014), 20–22.

CONCLUSION

Memory and Narrative in the Works of Wes Anderson

"In the end, the thing that strikes me the most forcefully when I think back on [*Rushmore*] was that I went home."[1]

Wes Anderson, Film 4 Interview, February 25, 2014

"I discovered Truffaut in the little video rental section at the back of a record store in Houston when was I sixteen or something like that, this movie [*Les Quatre cents coups*], which was probably panned and scanned and not really in a correct form, and I loved that movie immediately. ... I think what it is, this is such a personal story and it's the director's story, you know, it's this man's, it's like a first novel and it's his."[2]

Wes Anderson, to Paul Holdengräber in an interview at the New York Public Library in 2014

In an interview with Michael Specter published in 2009, when asked how he arrived at his particular approach to making films, Anderson responded: "I guess I try to think up a story that I can sort of tell in a way that nobody else would tell it."[3] Historically, the uniqueness of Anderson's approach has not always been well-received by audiences. In fact, his highly personal vision met with strong opposition in the cases of *Bottle Rocket*, and especially his most vilified film, *The Life Aquatic with Steve Zissou*, a complicated story that is at once an adventure film, a satire, and a dysfunctional family film carried out at sea with a murderous shark. After the early puzzlement of viewers in reaction to *Bottle Rocket*, which, as noted, nearly derailed Anderson's career, Anderson's popularity has grown over the years not because he has adapted his work to more clearly suit the sensibilities of the audience, but because his films have, over time, trained the viewer to gain fluency in Anderson's unique filmic language.

Anderson is reticent in interviews, expressing to Matt Zoller Seitz, for example, that he does not wish to "add" anything to his films by way of explication – he is the opposite of an extroverted, grandstanding director, appearing instead to duck away from questions, and respond with minimal detail, often seeming to casually deflect the question through making a gentle inside joke or simply blurting out a casual response, sometimes even what could only be construed as a non sequitur. (To many of Seitz's insightful questions, Anderson's reply is frequently, "Hmm.") In response to Seitz's questions about whether he prefers to leave his films unresolved, or open for interpretation, Anderson used a paraphrase of Harold Pinter's words in explanation:

> Well, I read about Harold Pinter that when people would ask him about the meaning of his plays, his response was, "Here is what they did. Here is what they said. This is what happened." That's your answer. And with this film [*The Life Aquatic with Steve Zissou*], but in particular with *The Darjeeling Limited*, we had so much information. For that one, the three of us – Jason, Roman, and I – spent so much time together, traveling and talking about these brothers, and playing the roles of these brothers and putting ourselves in their situations, and we created this really expansive tapestry of their lives, their biographies. But we put very, very little of it in the movie. All we ever did was pull things out. We felt the process of taking things out was making it stronger – stronger in the way we wanted it to be, anyway. That definitely appeals to me, that kind of Hemingway theory of omission.[4]

Wes Anderson's films express the tip of the iceberg; he provides visual details as a way of accessing the connections and links within his films, and the representations of his characters.

The very titles of Wes Anderson's films each evoke a sense of nostalgia in different ways. After *Bottle Rocket*, which conveys the ebullient pranksterism of youth, and the simpler pastimes of the pre-Internet era – even this film, made when Anderson himself was still a youth, looks back to the simpler pleasures of youth in the past – each title grows in sophistication and nuance. The titles of subsequent films are majestically nostalgic and conjure up old-world charm in a slightly comic, anachronistic way. *Rushmore* cannot help but bring to mind the eponymous monument, and the film feels like it could have been set in the Dakotas, or anywhere in the US – it is rootless, with its very American class war. *The Royal Tenenbaums* has a portentous and pretentious ring to it (while deliberately evoking Orson Welles's *The Magnificent Ambersons*); *The Life Aquatic with Steve Zissou* is mockably elitist-sounding, with its inverted noun-adjective imitating the style of French grammar, fittingly recalling the filmic connections with the work of French explorer Jacques Cousteau. *The Darjeeling Limited* seems to look back to an earlier, more sophisticated era with its dream-like train journey; *Fantastic Mr. Fox* is, of course, Roald Dahl's actual book title; *Moonrise Kingdom*, perhaps the hardest to recall of all of Wes Anderson's film titles, is the fictional name of a beautiful inlet reimagined by children. Finally, *The Grand Budapest Hotel*, which highlights the aging beauty and decay of the establishment over the passage of time, is Anderson's most distinctly nostalgic film to date, with its ties to the Greta Garbo film *Grand Hotel*, as well as other grand historical traditions (i.e., when M. Gustave is interviewing Moustafa, and the boy replies, "Well, who wouldn't [want to work] at the Grand Budapest, sir? It's an institution"[5]).

The ancient Greek and Latin roots of the word "nostalgia" are "to return" or "return home," an essential meaning which is particularly poignant when seen in the context of Anderson's life, due to his parents' early divorce when he was in fourth grade. Anderson, from the earliest dialogue where his two "lost boys" characters discuss an episode from the television show in the film short "Bottle Rocket," written when he was just twenty-three years old, always seems to be trying to "return" to a time of innocence, of freedom, of no serious obligation. His characters look for happiness, playfulness, freedom from the constraints of mainstream adult responsibility. Even his more jaded characters, such as Steve Zissou, yearn for a time of freedom, of being full of life, alive; they search for something – anything – to bring them back to life. "Bottle Rocket" also reveals the early presence of two selections of music from the Vince Guaraldi Trio, with its reference to Charlie Brown and the "Peanuts" gang. Similar to Charles M. Schulz's world as portrayed by Charlie Brown in the "Peanuts" comic strip, Anderson always surrounds himself with a gang of friends; in another similarity Anderson shares with Schulz, he names many of his fictional characters after his friends. Also similar to Charlie Brown's world, in many respects Wes Anderson never seemed to be a child at all, always dealing with weighty subjects and childhood grief or depression, he seems to have been a very "mannered" child, similar in many ways to Max Fischer. Anderson notes the oddity of Charlie Brown's depressive nature being foregrounded in a children's comic (Charlie Brown's smile always seems slightly awry); one of Charlie Brown's most endearing qualities is that he keeps on trying. Charles M. Schulz's personality was reflected in his central protagonist (Schulz had a dad who was a barber, he had a black-and-white dog, he flew his kite into trees, he liked to ice-skate, he had poor self-esteem due to the teasing he endured during his youth, and moreover, he even had friends play that pull-the-football-away trick on him – just like Charlie Brown). Although Schulz made it to the pinnacle of his career, even he never lost that angst and remained rather melancholic. The Zissou crew on the *Belafonte* is like the Peanuts gang all grown up and dedicated to chasing the Red Baron, watching for the Great Pumpkin, fighting the commercialization of Christmas, and scrupulously avoiding the Kite-Eating Tree – grown men in matching blue polyester outfits and silly red knit hats who sail around the world making up adventures for themselves. Their dedication to truly childlike pursuits suggests a Peter Pan-worthy aversion to growing up.

Another noticeable child-like feature of Anderson's films is that there are very few direct references to sex. In the short "Bottle Rocket," a waitress in a diner is ogled by the young men in the beginning, who refer to her as "hot," although this is puzzling since the woman in question is older than what is considered the normal "attractive" age for a woman. Anthony's interlude with Inez in 1996's feature-length version is kept very distant and fantasy-like (a white sheet passes over them in slow motion to discreetly hide their lovemaking). In *Rushmore*, Max tries to forcibly kiss Miss Cross, but the romance at the end is very old-school and traditional, represented through their sharing a dance at a cotillion. Margot and Richie in *The Royal Tenenbaums* briefly kiss, but when they lie down together, they are as chaste as they were as child runaways in the African Wing. The most explicit sex scene (although the characters remain fully clothed) in Anderson's feature-film work is in *The Darjeeling Limited*, while an unexpected glimpse of oral sex flashes by in *The Grand Budapest Hotel*, so quickly that the viewer barely has time to register what was onscreen. (In terms of nudity, Margot has a very brief erotic scene with a topless female in Paris, and all three of her early plays' titles refer to sexuality [such as "Nakedness Tonight"], but she hides the fact that she smokes, which is a metaphor for her own sexuality. In *The Life Aquatic with Steve Zissou*, script girl Anne-Marie frequently works topless; while in *Moonrise Kingdom*, Suzy's mother is seen briefly topless while washing her hair; a topless older woman is seen in *The Grand Budapest Hotel*.) The direct discussion of sexual arousal in *Moonrise Kingdom* is handled as discreetly as it would be in real life between two pre-adolescent children, and when the twelve-year-olds Suzy and Sam sleep together (again in a tent, like in *The Royal Tenenbaums*), they are as chaste as Margot and Richie.

The most erotic scene Anderson has filmed is in the short *Hotel Chevalier* in which Jason Schwartzman removes Natalie Portman's clothes, although despite the nudity, the two only kiss and no lovemaking is shown. Anderson spoke about sex and nudity in his films to Olivier Zahm and Olympia Le-Tan: "The short [*Hotel Chevalier*] is all about sex and [*The Grand Budapest Hotel*] has some elements about it that are much more overtly sexual. ... But it's funny. In *Rushmore* there was a scene written in which the teacher was naked, and I decided not to do it. In *The Royal Tenenbaums* there was nudity, but I cut it."[6] (Indeed the nudity of an artists' model named Cinnamon, who is introduced by Eli Cash, can still be seen on the deleted scenes on *The Royal Tenenbaums* DVD, and the scene is intact in the original script.) This quote makes it clear that while Anderson can be quite bold occasionally in his sex scenes, in general he tends to make his films very sexually discreet. One striking exception is the adolescent discussion of sexuality ("Frenching," and "hand jobs") and excessive use of swearing in *Rushmore* – although this is true to the "all talk and no action" bravado of adolescent boys. This is underscored by the scene after Max's "Heaven and Hell" play when Dirk and a couple of his classmates are looking at some vintage *Playboy* centerfolds taped up on the wall as part of the army barracks motif – the frank nudity of the centerfold models is juxtaposed with the open curiosity and innocence of the children.

Anderson's unusual use of violence has also been noted. In addition to the work of Hitchcock and Kubrick, one of Anderson's most inspirational films was Roman Polanski's 1968 film *Rosemary's Baby*, which had very real performances in a story that was deliberately heightened, in Anderson's opinion, almost like a comedy. In a 2005 interview with Kevin Conroy Scott, Anderson also cites Martin Scorsese as an influence for his first film *Bottle Rocket*, explaining that he and Owen Wilson had set out to make a gritty crime drama about coming of age, their own version of Scorsese's *Mean Streets* (1973). Anderson explains: "*Bottle Rocket* came from how our lives were. If you take the guns and the crime element out then it was more or less our lifestyle at the time."[7] Located in swimming pools, country clubs, and suburban houses, *Bottle Rocket* makes it clear that Anderson's experiences of growing up were far gentler than those of Scorsese, who witnessed the life-and-death dramas of gangsters play out on the streets of Little Italy. *Bottle Rocket* was rated R in the US, but it could have been rated PG except for seven uses of explicit language – for a film about armed robbery, the film is remarkably gentle and innocent. Interestingly, all of Anderson's films are rated R except for *Moonrise Kingdom* (PG-13) and *Fantastic Mr. Fox* (PG).

In many of his films, Anderson reaches back to periods of history that allude to radical change. For example, the twelve-year-old protagonists of the 1965-set *Moonrise Kingdom* will live in a very different America when they are sixteen years old in 1969 (the year of Anderson's own birth). Anderson was born into a historical period of tumultuous change – the late sixties in America – and he is unafraid of dealing with the topic of radical historical change (as in totalitarian takeover in *The Grand Budapest Hotel*). At the same time, he longs to reach back, like Stefan Zweig and Roald Dahl, and like Booth Tarkington in *The Magnificent Ambersons*, to simpler times of peace and the innocence of childhood. Cate Blanchett has said of Anderson, "He is from another time,"[8] and this seems to be the case with his heroes, the authors and auteurs of literature and film: they are men out of time. This is especially apparent in the case of Stefan Zweig, who titled his memoir *The World of Yesterday*, and who yearned for a vanished way of life before 1914; for Zweig, the end of that world would ultimately result in his suicide. The intensity of Zweig's nostalgia for that golden age is one of the great themes of *The Grand Budapest Hotel*, which is itself about a man out of time, and nostalgia for an era long vanished.

Anderson creates a heightened childhood fantasy world in his films, and they are evocative of the intensity of childhood dreams and visions. For example, in an interview at Cannes in 2012, Anderson spoke of the entire story of *Moonlight Kingdom* resembling one of the books Suzy is carrying around with her in her suitcase ("The whole movie could be in her suitcase, too")[9] and while making *The Royal Tenenbaums*, Owen Wilson commented that the whole film reminded him of "one of Max [Fischer's] plays."[10] Anderson has also commented that the story of *Rushmore* itself could be one of Fischer's plays (and indeed, the theater curtains that part to reveal the action do divide the film into "acts"). According to Anderson, *Moonrise Kingdom* was inspired in part by Susan Cooper's *The Dark is Rising* series (1965–1977), a children's book series about a land in which the inhabitants wield magical powers. When Anderson first read this series, he was so caught up in Cooper's created universe that he felt on some level that the magical powers described in Cooper's world would someday be proven to exist in reality. "I really wanted to believe these powers existed, and I desperately thought, at some point, some evidence was going to come through and we're going to be able to say 'This is real.'"[11] He likens the power of being caught up in the fantasy world while reading a story to the experience of falling in love for the first time, where reality seems heightened or even fantastic, where "you feel like you are under water or something; you feel like you're in a dream."[12] The genius of Anderson is that he has somehow retained, and is able to reproduce, the emotional wonder of a child, as if viewing something for the first time – stunned, thrilled, overwhelmed – and this results in his vivid perception of reality in his films that creates a sense of hyper-nostalgia in the viewer. Anderson's films demonstrate a genuine respect for the imaginary worlds that spring from a child's imagination and that sincerity helps all the other potentially arch and ironic elements hold together.

Anderson's nostalgia is encapsulated by the signature elements and props in his films, such as old-fashioned communication devices, which include hand-written letters on formal letterhead, a bullhorn (in *Moonrise Kingdom*), a hand-cranked siren, walkie-talkies, and switchboard telephones shown on a split screen. Students from Rushmore view educational materials on reel-to-reel film projectors; Blume's office in *Rushmore* is outfitted with pneumatic tubes for communication. Anderson's films are set apart by their lack of modern technology; he is clearly more comfortable in an analog world. *Fantastic Mr. Fox* contains many anachronistic items, from the Dictaphone and the typewriter in the law office to a seventies-style bicycle with a banana seat. "I wanted to make a children's movie like some of the ones I grew up with," Anderson says, "and that went with the idea of how you didn't have to wear helmets when you rode bicycles. I never wore a helmet riding a bicycle ... there's just a certain nostalgia for when [children] didn't. For when we didn't."[13] In addition, in his films, there are always elaborate plans or journeys, which always require plans, maps, directions, and paraphernalia. Many of these apparently childlike and old-fashioned maps and drawings were expertly executed by Eric Chase Anderson (his handpainted safari animal designs on the Louis Vuitton luggage designed by Marc Jacobs also created an unforgettable "retro" look for those items). In addition, Jason Davids Scott (2014) mentions the names Anderson gives to his characters, such as Bob Mapplethorpe (*Bottle Rocket*), Blume and Guggenheim (*Rushmore*); and Redford, Izod, Roosevelt, and Nickelby (*Moonrise Kingdom*); all of these are evocative of different periods in literature, visual art, and popular culture. Stefano Baschiera postulates about *The Royal Tenenbaums* that "clothing, technology, and artifacts all belong to a past that does not match the diegetic time of the film, contributing ... to a nostalgic dislocation of the characters from contemporary time."[14] Kim Wilkins (2014) also notes the curious interaction between the present time and various pasts that creates a fragmented sense of nostalgia:

> The merging of diffuse historical and contemporary contexts promotes identification and nostalgia that is unable to be located in a wholly contemporary or retrospective chronological context. The films occupy a chronological space imagined only by Anderson.[15]

Anderson has been accused of making the same story again and again, because of his use of similar visual tropes, and his casting of the same actors repeatedly. However, it is hardly correct to claim that a movie about an oceanographic explorer is the same movie as one about a rich family gone to ruin, and one about a play-producing student at a prep school is the same as one about a fox who burgles farmers. In addition, as Orson Welles had The Mercury Players, Wes Anderson has put together one of the great acting troupes in modern cinema. *The Grand Budapest Hotel* contains three tiers of Anderson's "players": first, veterans like Owen Wilson, as well as Jason Schwartzman and Bill Murray, are present. In addition, there are those actors who have done one or two Anderson films, including Edward Norton, Adrien Brody, Jeff Goldblum, Tilda Swinton, Harvey Keitel and Willem Dafoe, and finally there are the newcomers, including Ralph Fiennes, Jude Law and Saoirse Ronan. Each new member is adopted into the family, or the theatrical troupe, and when they repeatedly work together, according to Anderson, it is comparable to a reunion. His approach is like repertory theatre; he cultivates his friendships and the film is well-served by them: the resulting closeness comes through in the film when it is seen on the screen. For *Moonrise Kingdom*, Anderson rented a Newport mansion and by the end of the shoot, Bill Murray, Edward Norton, and Jason Schwartzman (who were all assigned to a very comfortable hotel) had moved into it with him; for *The Grand Budapest Hotel*, the entire cast took over a small hotel in Görlitz, Germany and commuted to the department-store set via a three-minute ride in golf carts. Clearly the family-like, summer camp atmosphere Anderson creates goes a long way toward convincing his big-name actors to take huge pay cuts (otherwise his modestly budgeted films could never afford such casts).[16] As Anderson says about the reunion-like atmosphere: "This is the main thing I do – I have no life outside of movies – so I'd better be with my friends."[17] He who came from a broken home has rebuilt a sense of "home" and "nostalgia" through his art. Anderson (and Wilson, in the first three screenplays) include true incidents, stories, and running jokes from their past, such as Chas's electric tie rack (which in real life was owned by childhood friend Stephen Dignan) or naming the family "Tenenbaums" after Brian Tenenbaum's family. The hand filmed in *The Royal Tenenbaums* with the BB pellet embedded near the knuckle belongs to Andrew Wilson; as a child, Owen once shot Andrew in the back of the hand with a BB gun when they were on the same team. Anderson prefers to include incidents from real life or anecdotes that his friends have told him, such as Owen Wilson using a cotton ball to shine his shoes at New Mexico Military Institute (which he also does as Ned Plimpton in *The Life Aquatic with Steve Zissou*):

> We include those because if certain people are on the set, they bring a positive feeling to it. The *memory of something you've lived* creates a kind of electricity during the shoot, and that reality is part of what gets photographed.[18] (italics added)

Both linguistically and visually, *the Royal Tenenbaums* reaches back to the past. The nostalgic description of the décor in the Tenenbaum household is painted in loving detail in the film's screenplay:

> A gallery of the children's art, done mostly in crayon, but with beautiful frames and careful lighting. The subject matter includes: spaceships, wild animals, sail-boats, motorcycles, and war scenes with tanks and paratroopers. A stuffed and mounted boar's head with its teeth bared hangs in the stairwell. A label on it says "Wild Javelina, Andes Mountains." Under the stairs there is a telephone

room the size of a closet. Old messages are tacked to the walls, and the children's heights are marked on the door frame.¹⁹

This is also reflected by the frequently-visited interior of a cupboard filled with well-used family board games – *Risk, Clue, Sorry, Go to the Head of the Class, The Ungame,* and *Operation* – in which there is a green Monopoly house tied to the end of the lightbulb's string; all of these details would instantly arouse the childhood memories of a viewer from Anderson's generation. According to Scott (2014):

> Just as his characters might be "stuck" in a displaced era that evokes the late 1970s and early 1980s, so too does Anderson seem to be recreating that era cinematically, deliberately placing elements of those eras within the visual frame to convey information about narrative and character, while simultaneously delivering to his audience members a nostalgic experience that is as disquieting and complex as it is effective and evocative.²⁰

In his insightful work on the impact of children's culture on Anderson's oeuvre, Peter C. Kunze (2014) notes Anderson's deconstruction of the child/adult binary in his films, indicating Kunze's larger argument that Anderson refuses to draw a sharp line between childhood and adulthood. Kunze states that "[Anderson] dissolves any implied social separation between childhood and adulthood, refusing to see either as advantageous, to demonstrate that such delineations are inherently superficial and impractical."²¹ Both the children and the adults in Anderson's narratives lead lives that are emotionally complex, and neither is privileged over the other. Kunze notes, for example that Anderson's reference to *From the Mixed-Up Files of Mrs. Basil E. Frankweiler* in *The Royal Tenenbaums* (as Anderson himself asserts on the DVD commentary) is due to the book's lingering resonance in his consciousness, thus suggesting that Anderson has acute memories and easy access to his boyhood experiences and perceptions. Likewise, Anderson's childhood affection for Roald Dahl remained with him as he took his own copy of *Fantastic Mr. Fox* with him to college. Kristin Thompson and David Bordwell (2014) have noted the influence of children's authors on Anderson, as Anderson's work connects with the literary tradition in which writers such as J. M. Barrie and G. K. Chesterton employ childhood fantasy as a medium to evoke a richer, livelier realm beyond ordinary, mundane reality. Thompson and Bordwell insightfully connect Anderson's art to the looking-glass world of Lewis Carroll – viewing Anderson's work in this light goes a long way toward reconciling his use of deadpan absurdity, so characteristic of Alice's earnest efforts to navigate and master an absurd world. Thompson and Bordwell cite both the way the lawyers in *Moonrise Kingdom* speak to each other as if they are always in court, and the ridiculously high but somehow functional tree house, as similarities to Lewis Carroll's looking-glass world.²²

Although rarely appearing in his own films (sitting behind Dignan and Anthony on the bus at the beginning in *Bottle Rocket*, asking the math question at the beginning of *Rushmore*, his hands lending out the eponymous novel at the beginning of *The Royal Tenenbaums*; the voice of the real-estate salesman Weasel in *Fantastic Mr. Fox* and the sports commentator describing Richie's meltdown during a tennis match in *The Royal Tenenbaums*), Anderson does cast himself in distinct ways in the main roles of his films, which become his alter egos: his Max Fischer is his boyhood stand-in, as is his Sam Shakusky, and he visually aligns himself with The Author in *The Grand Budapest Hotel* and as Fox in *Fantastic Mr. Fox* by dressing these characters in similar clothes to himself. Thus he communicates his authorial presence in the films, and puts himself in an auteurial role of authority and dominion as the one commanding the action (just as Mr. Fox does). In addition, in each of Anderson's films, whether for the 75-Year Plan in *Bottle Rocket*, the check for 187 dollars in *The Royal Tenenbaums* or the letters exchanged by Sam and Suzy in *Moonrise Kingdom*, the handwriting in every character's notes is always in the same hand. This handwriting is Anderson's own, a childish combination of lowercase and capital letters within words, and it is another thread tying together his oeuvre. Like Hitchcock's cameo appearances in his own films, Wes Anderson's childlike handwriting makes its own unique appearance.

Anderson's work embodies nostalgia, in that many of the scenes he has created seem to be taken straight from his own boyhood memories. The boyishness of Anderson's characters include small moments, such as Sam Shakusky pushing the button to turn on the water fountain in his boredom as he wanders around a church building before meeting Suzy for the first time, Max Fisher sticking his wad of gum on the basement wall of the hotel as he makes his triumphant escape after unleashing the bees on Mr. Blume, and even the grown-up Anthony straightening the toy soldier back into formation in *Bottle Rocket*. For Anderson and his characters, the past and the present occupy the same space. About nostalgia, James Agee writes:

> And so in this quiet introit, and in all the time we have stayed in this house, and in all we have sought, and in each detail of it, there is so keen, sad, and precious a nostalgia as I can scarcely otherwise know; a knowledge of brief truancy into the sources of my life, whereto I have no rightful access, having paid no price beyond love and sorrow.[23]

Anderson acknowledges a sentiment vis-à-vis the inevitability of nostalgia that echoes F. Scott Fitzgerald, whose writing Anderson often claims as a source for his films, in *The Great Gatsby*. Fitzgerald famously concludes his 1925 treatment of the brokenness of the American dreamer: "So we beat on, boats against the current, borne back ceaselessly into the past."[24] This recalls the very final scene of *Moonrise Kingdom* where Sam and Suzy part, and the camera reveals Sam's painting of Mile 3.25 Tidal Inlet. Then the film dissolves to a shot of the real place, with Sam and Suzy's yellow tent still there, and the waves still lapping at the beach, even though the storm erased it from the map. The whole scene is one of the most beautiful sequences in Anderson's oeuvre, and its message that childhood is something that disappears from everywhere except one's memory is both bittersweet and touching. Anderson's films are made in such a way that there really is not a specific year or exact date or location in which his movies take place. All of his narratives are fluid in time and they will not grow old; they share a whimsical, fable-like feeling that makes them timeless.

Notes

1. "Wes Anderson Introduces *Rushmore*," Film 4 Interview, *Youtube.com*. February 25, 2014. https://www.youtube.com/watch?v=ydGLVMCHq3U (accessed June 12, 2016).
2. Wes Anderson in an interview with Paul Holdengräber, "LIVE from the New York Public Library: Wes Anderson | Paul Holdengräber." *Nypl.org*. February 27, 2014. http://www.nypl.org/audiovideo/wes-anderson-paul-holdengraber (accessed August 14, 2014).
3. Wes Anderson, interviewed by Michael Specter for *The Making of Fantastic Mr. Fox* (New York: Rizzoli, 2009), 5. Later in the book Specter asks, "You know, creating new characters and situations in an intensely loved book is a little risky. Are you worried that people will see this movie and no matter what else they say they'll say 'But it isn't the same'?" Anderson responds: "Well, I feel like there's so many bad things that people could say about you, so why focus on one in particular?", 40.
4. Wes Anderson, quoted in Matt Zoller Seitz, *The Wes Anderson Collection* (New York: Abrams, 2013a), 188–192.
5. Wes Anderson (screenplay) and Hugo Guinness (story), *The Grand Budapest Hotel* (New York: Opus, 2014), 28. This film also cannot help drawing associations with other iconic hotel films from history, such as Stanley Kubrick's *The Shining* (1980), which has been combined with *The Grand Budapest Hotel* in a 2015 parody mashup entitled "Wes Anderson's *The Shining*" published to YouTube on May 29, 2015 emphasizing the two directors' similar shot composition, framing, and cinematography.
6. Olivier Zahm and Olympia Le-Tan, "Interview with Wes Anderson," *Purple.fr*. September 2008. http://www.purple.fr/magazine/ss-2008-issue-9/wes-anderson/ (accessed June 17, 2016).
7. Kevin Conroy Scott, "Lesser Spotted Fish and Other Stories," *Sight and Sound* 15:3 (March 2005):13.
8. Richard Brody, "Wild, Wild Wes," *NewYorker.com*. November 2, 2009. http://www.newyorker.com/magazine/2009/11/02/wild-wild-wes (accessed January 10, 2016).
9. "Moonrise Kingdom Full Press Conference – Festival de Cannes 2012," *Youtube.com*. May 16, 2012. https://www.youtube.com/watch?v=QT1ijPitGl8 (accessed June 28, 2016).
10. Wes Anderson, interviewed in Seitz, 2013a, 102.
11. "Moonrise Kingdom Full Press Conference – Festival de Cannes 2012," *Youtube.com*. May 16, 2012. https://www.youtube.com/watch?v=QT1ijPitGl8 (accessed June 28, 2016).
12. Ibid.
13. Brody, 2009.
14. Stefano Baschiera, "Nostalgically Man Dwells on This Earth: Objects and Dom-

estic Space in *The Royal Tenenbaums* and *The Darjeeling Ltd.*," *New Review of Film and Television Studies* 10:1 (March 2012): 86.

15 Kim Wilkins, "Cast of Characters: Wes Anderson and Pure Cinematic Characterization," in Peter C. Kunze, ed., *The Films of Wes Anderson: Critical Essays on an Indiewood Icon* (New York: Palgrave Macmillan, 2014), 35.

16 Mottram, James. 2014. "Wes Anderson Interview: "I Feel Happier Making Movies than I Ever Did Going to School." *The Big Issue*. February 24. http://www.bigissue.com/features/interviews/3558/wes-anderson-interview-i-feel-happier-making-movies-than-i-ever-did-going (accessed April 29, 2016).

17 "Moonrise Kingdom Full Press Conference – Festival de Cannes 2012," *Youtube.com*. May 16, 2012. https://www.youtube.com/watch?v=QT1ijPitGl8 (accessed June 28, 2016).

18 Wes Anderson, quoted by Marshall Sella, "Wes Anderson: Boyish Wonder," *New York Times Magazine*. December 2, 2001. http://www.nytimes.com/2001/12/02/magazine/02ANDERSON.html?pagewanted=4 (accessed April 5, 2015).

19 Wes Anderson and Owen Wilson, *The Royal Tenenbaums* (New York: Faber and Faber, 2001), 6.

20 Jason Davids Scott, "'American Empirical' Time and Space: The (In) Visibility of Popular Culture in the films of Wes Anderson," in Peter C. Kunze, ed., *The Films of Wes Anderson: Critical Essays on an Indiewood Icon* (New York: Palgrave Macmillan, 2014), 87.

21 Peter C. Kunze, "From the Mixed-Up Files of Mr. Wesley W. Anderson," in Peter C. Kunze, ed., *The Films of Wes Anderson: Critical Essays on an Indiewood Icon* (New York: Palgrave Macmillan, 2014), 103.

22 Kristin Thompson and David Bordwell, "Observations on Film Art: Moonrise Kingdom: Wes in Wonderland," July 20, 2014. http://www.davidbordwell.net/blog/2014/07/20/moonrise-kingdom-wes-in-wonderland/ (accessed August 12, 2014).

23 James Agee and Walker Evans, *Let Us Now Praise Famous Men* (second edition) (Boston: Houghton Mifflin, 1960), 415.

24 F. Scott Fitzgerald, *The Great Gatsby* (New York: Scribner, 2004 [1925]), 180.

FILMOGRAPHY

"Bottle Rocket" short film (1994)
Producers: L. M. Kit Carson, Cynthia Hargrave
Director: Wes Anderson
Screenplay: Wes Anderson, Owen Wilson
Cinematography: Bert Guthrie
Editors: Tom Aberg, Laura Cargile, Denise Ferrari Segell
Main Cast: Owen Wilson (Dignan), Luke Wilson (Anthony), Robert Musgrave (Bob), Temple Nash, Jr. (Temple), Elissa Sommerfield (Waitress)

Bottle Rocket (1996)
Production Companies: Columbia Pictures Corporation, Gracie Films
Producers: Barbara Boyle, James L. Brooks, Cynthia Hargrave, Polly Platt
Director: Wes Anderson
Screenplay: Wes Anderson, Owen Wilson
Cinematography: Robert Yeoman
Editor: David Moritz
Production Design: David Wasco
Music: Mark Mothersbaugh
Main Cast: Owen Wilson (Dignan), Luke Wilson (Anthony), Robert Musgrave (Bob Mapplethorpe), James Caan (Mr. Henry), Lumi Cavazos (Inez), Shea Fowler (Grace), Donny Caicedo (Rocky), Andrew Wilson (Futureman), Tak Kubota (Rowboat), Jim Ponds (Applejack), Kumar Pallana (Kumar)

Rushmore (1998)
Production Companies: American Empirical Pictures, Touchstone Pictures
Producers: Wes Anderson, Barry Mendel, Paul Schiff
Director: Wes Anderson
Screenplay: Wes Anderson, Owen Wilson
Cinematography: Robert Yeoman
Editor: David Moritz
Production Design: David Wasco
Music: Mark Mothersbaugh
Main Cast: Jason Schwartzman (Max Fischer), Bill Murray (Herman Blume), Olivia Williams (Rosemary Cross), Seymour Cassel (Bert Fisher), Sara Tanaka (Margaret Yang), Brian Cox (Dr. Nelson Guggenheim), Mason Gamble (Dirk Calloway), Luke Wilson (Dr. Peter Flynn), Andrew Wilson (Coach Beck), Kumar Pallana (Mr. Littlejeans)

The Royal Tenenbaums (2001)
Production Companies: Touchstone Pictures, American Empirical Pictures
Producers: Wes Anderson, Barry Mendel, Scott Rudin
Director: Wes Anderson
Screenplay: Wes Anderson, Owen Wilson
Cinematography: Robert Yeoman
Editor: Dylan Tichenor
Production Design: David Wasco
Music: Mark Mothersbaugh
Main Cast: Gene Hackman (Royal Tenenbaum), Anjelica Huston (Etheline), Ben Stiller (Chas), Gwyneth Paltrow (Margot), Luke Wilson (Richie), Owen Wilson (Eli Cash), Bill Murray (Raleigh St. Clair), Danny Glover (Henry Sherman), Seymour Cassel (Dusty), Kumar Pallana (Pagoda), Stephen Lea Sheppard (Dudley), Alec Baldwin (Narrator, voice only)

The Life Aquatic with Steve Zissou (2004)
Production Companies: Touchstone Pictures, American Empirical Pictures, Scott Rudin Productions, Life Aquatic Productions Inc.
Producers: Wes Anderson, Barry Mendel, Scott Rudin
Director: Wes Anderson
Screenplay: Wes Anderson, Noah Baumbach
Cinematography: Robert Yeoman
Editor: David Moritz
Production Design: Mark Friedberg
Music: Mark Mothersbaugh
Main Cast: Bill Murray (Steve Zissou), Owen Wilson (Ned Plimpton), Cate Blanchett (Jane Winslett-Richardson), Anjelica Huston (Eleanor Zissou), Jeff Goldblum (Alistair Hennessey), Michael Gambon (Oseary Drakoulias), Willem Dafoe (Klaus Daimler), Noah Taylor (Vladimir Wolodarsky), Waris Ahluwalia (Vikram Ray), Niels Koizumi (Bobby Ogata), Seu Jorge (Pelé dos Santos), Robyn Cohen (Anne-Marie Sakowitz), Pawel Wdowczak (Renzo Pietro), Bud Cort (Bill Ubell), Seymour Cassel (Esteban du Plantier)

American Express: My Life. My Card. short film (2006)
Director: Wes Anderson
Screenplay: Wes Anderson
Editor: Vincent Marchand
Set Decoration: Kris Moran
Main Cast: Waris Ahluwalia (Waris Ahluwalia), Jason Schwartzman (Jason Schwartzman), Wes Anderson (Wes Anderson), Roman Coppola (François [uncredited])

Hotel Chevalier short film (2007)
Producers: Jerome Rucki, Nicolas Saada, Alice Bamford
Director: Wes Anderson
Screenplay: Wes Anderson
Cinematography: Robert Yeoman
Editor: Vincent Marchand
Art Direction: Kris Moran
Main Cast: Jason Schwartzman (Jack), Natalie Portman (Jack's Girlfriend), Michel Castejon (Waiter)

The Darjeeling Limited (2007)
Production Companies: Fox Searchlight Pictures, Collage Cinemagraphique, American Empirical Pictures, Dune Entertainment
Producers: Wes Anderson, Roman Coppola, Lydia Dean Pilcher, Scott Rudin
Director: Wes Anderson
Screenplay: Wes Anderson, Roman Coppola, Jason Schwartzman
Cinematography: Robert Yeoman

Editor: Andrew Weisblum
Production Design: Mark Friedberg
Main Cast: Owen Wilson (Francis), Adrien Brody (Peter), Jason Schwartzman (Jack), Amara Karan (Rita), Wally Wolodarsky (Brendan), Waris Ahluwalia (The Chief Steward), Irrfan Khan (The Father), Barbet Schroeder (The Mechanic), Camilla Rutherford (Alice), Anjelica Huston (Patricia), Bill Murray (The Businessman)

Fantastic Mr. Fox (2009)
Production Companies: Twentieth Century Fox, Indian Paintbrush, Regency Enterprises, American Empirical Pictures, Twentieth Century Fox Animation
Producers: Allison Abbate, Wes Anderson, Jeremy Dawson, Scott Rudin
Director: Wes Anderson
Screenplay: Wes Anderson, Noah Baumbach (adapted from the novel by Roald Dahl)
Cinematography: Tristan Oliver
Editors: Ralph Foster, Stephen Perkins, Andrew Weisblum
Production Design: Nelson Lowry
Music: Alexandre Desplat
Main Cast: George Clooney (Mr. Fox, voice), Meryl Streep (Mrs. Fox, voice), Jason Schwartzman (Ash, voice), Bill Murray (Badger, voice), Wally Wolodarsky (Kylie, voice), Eric Chase Anderson (Kristofferson, voice), Michael Gambon (Franklin Bean, voice), Willem Dafoe (Rat, voice), Owen Wilson (Coach Skip, voice), Jarvis Cocker (Petey, voice), Wes Anderson (Weasel, voice), Robin Hurlstone (Walter Boggis, voice), Hugo Guinness (Nathan Bunce, voice), Juman Malouf (Agnes, voice)

Moonrise Kingdom (2012)
Production Companies: Indian Paintbrush, American Empirical Pictures, Scott Rudin Productions
Producers: Wes Anderson, Jeremy Dawson, Steven Rales, Scott Rudin
Director: Wes Anderson
Screenplay: Wes Anderson, Roman Coppola
Cinematography: Robert Yeoman
Editor: Andrew Weisblum
Production Design: Adam Stockhausen
Music: Alexandre Desplat
Main Cast: Bill Murray (Mr. Bishop), Frances McDormand (Mrs. Bishop), Bruce Willis (Captain Sharp), Edward Norton (Scoutmaster Ward), Jared Gilman (Sam), Kara Hayward (Suzy), Tilda Swinton (Social Services), Jason Schwartzman (Cousin Ben), Bob Balaban (The Narrator), Harvey Keitel (Commander Pierce), Larry Pine (Mr. Billingsley), Lucas Hedges (Redford), Charlie Kilgore (Lazy-Eye)

Cousin Ben Troop Screening with Jason Schwartzman short film (2012)
Production Company: Funny or Die
Director: Wes Anderson
Screenplay: Wes Anderson, Roman Coppola
Editor: Edward Bursch
Main Cast: Jason Schwartzman (Cousin Ben), Charlie Kilgore (Lazy-Eye), L. J. Foley (Izod), Gabriel Rush (Skotak)

Castello Cavalcanti short film (2013)
Production Companies: American Empirical Pictures, Hi! Production, Prada, The Directors Bureau
Producers: Roman Coppola, Jeremy Dawson, Julie Sawyer
Director: Wes Anderson
Screenplay: Wes Anderson

Cinematography: Darius Khondji
Editor: Stephen Perkins
Production Design: Stefano Maria Ortolani
Main Cast: Jason Schwartzman (Jed Cavalcanti), Giada Colagrande (Bartender), Giorgio Zancolla (Bartender), Paolo Coluccio (Cook), Francesco Zippel (Paparazzo), Fernando Lumaca (Uncle Michelangelo)

Prada: Candy short film (2013)
Production Companies: The Directors Bureau
Producers: Max Brun, Andrea Puig, Julie Sawyer
Director: Wes Anderson
Screenplay: Wes Anderson, Roman Coppola
Cinematography: Darius Khondji
Editor: Dániel Hajnal
Main Cast: Peter Gadiot (Gene), Rodolphe Pauly (Julius), Léa Seydoux (Candy)

The Grand Budapest Hotel (2014)
Production Companies: Fox Searchlight Pictures, Indian Paintbrush, Studio Babelsberg, American Empirical Pictures, TSG Entertainment
Producers: Wes Anderson, Jeremy Dawson, Steven Rales, Scott Rudin
Director: Wes Anderson
Screenplay: Wes Anderson, Hugo Guinness (story)
Cinematography: Robert Yeoman
Editor: Barney Pilling
Production Design: Adam Stockhausen
Music: Alexandre Desplat
Main Cast: Ralph Fiennes (M. Gustave), F. Murray Abraham (Mr. Moustafa), Tony Revolori (Zero), Tom Wilkinson (Author), Jude Law (Young Writer), Adrien Brody (Dmitri), Willem Dafoe (Jopling), Jeff Goldblum (Deputy Kovacs), Edward Norton (Henckels), Saoirse Ronan (Agatha), Harvey Keitel (Ludwig), Mathieu Amalric (Serge), Léa Seydoux (Clotilde), Bill Murray (M. Ivan), Jason Schwartzman (M. Jean), Tilda Swinton (Madame D)

Come Together short film (2016)
Production Companies: H&M, Riff Raff Films, The Directors Bureau
Producers: Matthew Fone, Lisa Margulis, Julie Sawyer
Director: Wes Anderson
Screenplay: Wes Anderson
Cinematography: Bruno Delbonnel
Main Cast: Adrien Brody (Conductor Ralph), Garth Jennings (Fritz)

BIBLIOGRAPHY

Agee, James, and Walker Evans. 1960. *Let Us Now Praise Famous Men*. 2nd edition. Boston: Houghton Mifflin.

Aisenberg, Joseph. 2008. "Wes's World: Riding Wes Anderson's Vision Limited." *Brightlightsfilm.com*. http://www.brightlightsfilm.com/59/59wesanderson.php (accessed June 4, 2015).

Amsden, David. 2007. "The Life Obsessive with Wes Anderson." *New York Magazine*. September 24. http://nymag.com/movies/filmfestivals/newyork/2007/38024/ (accessed September 30, 2014).

Anderson, Eric Chase. 2005. *Chuck Dugan is AWOL*. San Francisco, CA: Chronicle Books.

Anderson, Wes. 1999a [1998]. "Introduction." In Wes Anderson and Owen Wilson's *Rushmore*. New York: Faber and Faber. xiii–xvii.

_____. 1999b. "My Private Screening with Pauline Kael." *The New York Times* (Arts and Leisure section). January 31. 20–21.

_____. 2002. "Welcome to the Dahl House." *The New York Times Sunday Magazine*. August 18. 42–49.

_____. 2016. "Introduction." In *The Wes Anderson Collection: Bad Dads: Art Inspired by the Films of Wes Anderson*. Eds. Ken Harman, Matt Zoller Seitz, and Wes Anderson. New York: Abrams. 9.

Anderson, Wes, and Noah Baumbach. n.d. *The Life Aquatic with Steve Zissou* [Final Draft]. Burbank, CA: Touchstone Pictures.

Anderson, Wes, and Hugo Guinness [story]. 2014. *The Grand Budapest Hotel*. New York: Opus.

Anderson, Wes, and Michael Specter. 2009. *The Making of Fantastic Mr. Fox*. New York: Rizzoli.

Anderson, Wes, and Owen Wilson. 1999 [1998]. *Rushmore*. New York: Faber and Faber.

_____. 2001. *The Royal Tenenbaums*. New York: Faber and Faber.

Anon. 2012. "*Moonrise Kingdom* Full Press Conference—Festival de Cannes 2012." *Youtube.com*. May 16. https://www.youtube.com/watch?v=QT1ijPitGl8 (accessed June 28, 2016).

_____. 2014. "Wes Anderson Introduces *Rushmore*." Film 4 Interview. *Youtube.com*. February 25. https://www.youtube.com/watch?v=ydGLVMCHq3U (accessed June 12, 2016).

_____. 2015. "Wes Anderson on *Moonrise Kingdom*." Film 4 Interview. *Youtube.com*. May 29. https://www.youtube.com/watch?v=5E6i53flbdg&t=139s (accessed June 28, 2016).

———. 2016. "Mission: National Film Preservation Board of the Library of Congress," *www.loc.gov*. December 1. https://www.loc.gov/programs/national-film-preservation-board/about-this-program/mission/ (accessed December 15, 2016).

Arendt, Hannah. 1963. *Eichmann in Jerusalem: A Report on the Banality of Evil*. New York: Viking.

Arsel, Zeynep, and Craig J. Thompson. 2011. "Demythologizing Consumption Practices: How Consumers Protect Their Field-Dependent Identity Investments from Devaluing Marketplace Myths." *Journal of Consumer Research* 37:5 (February): 791–806.

Baschiera, Stefano. 2012. "Nostalgically Man Dwells on This Earth: Objects and Domestic Space in *The Royal Tenenbaums* and *The Darjeeling Ltd*." *New Review of Film and Television Studies* 10:1 (March): 118–31.

Best, Steven and Douglas Kellner. 1997. "Postmodernism in the Arts." In *The Postmodern Turn*. New York: Guilford Press. 124–194.

Bloom, Harold. 1973. *The Anxiety of Influence: A Theory of Poetry*. Oxford: Oxford University Press.

Bogdanovich, Peter. 2001. "Introduction." In Wes Anderson and Owen Wilson's *The Royal Tenenbaums*. New York: Faber and Faber. vii–ix.

Bordwell, David. 1985a. *Narration in the Fiction Film*. London and New York: Routledge.

———. 1985b. "Part One: The Classical Hollywood Style, 1917–1960." In David Bordwell, Janet Staiger, and Kristin Thompson's *The Classical Hollywood Cinema: Film Style and Mode of Production to 1960*. London and New York: Routledge.

———. 1997. *On the History of Film Style*. Cambridge, MA: Harvard University Press.

———. 2006. *The Way Hollywood Tells It*. Los Angeles, CA: University of California Press.

Bourdieu, Pierre. 1984. *Distinction: A Social Critique of the Judgement of Taste*. Trans. Richard Nice. London: Routledge.

Bowie, David. 2005. Liner notes for *The Life Aquatic Studio Versions Featuring Seu Jorge*. Produced by Wes Anderson and Randall Poster. Hollywood Records.

Breines, Ingeborg, R. W. Connell, and Ingrid Eide, eds. 2000. *Male Roles, Masculinity and Violence: A Culture of Peace Perspective*. Paris: UNESCO Publishing.

Brody, Richard. 2009. "Wild, Wild Wes." *NewYorker.com*. November 2. http://www.newyorker.com/magazine/2009/11/02/wild-wild-wes (accessed January 10, 2016).

———. 2010. "Voyage to India," *The Darjeeling Limited*, liner notes for the Criterion Collection DVD.

———. 2012. "Loving *Moonrise Kingdom* for the Right Reasons." *NewYorker.com*. June 14. http://www.newyorker.com/culture/richard-brody/loving-moonrise-kingdom-for-the-right-reasons (accessed February 27, 2015).

———. 2014. "*The Grand Budapest Hotel*: Wes Anderson's Artistic Manifesto." *NewYorker.com*. March 7. http://www.newyorker.com/culture/richard-brody/the-grand-budapest-hotel-wes-andersons-artistic-manifesto (accessed February 27, 2015).

Brooks, James L. 1999 [1998]. "Foreword." In Wes Anderson and Owen Wilson's *Rushmore* [screenplay]. New York: Faber and Faber. vii–xii.

Browning, Mark. 2011. *Wes Anderson: Why His Movies Matter*. Santa Barbara, CA: Praeger.

Broyard, Anatole. 1948. "Portrait of the Hipster." *Partisan Review* 15:6. 721–727.

Bruzzi, Stella. 2005. *Bringing Up Daddy: Fatherhood and Masculinity in Post-War Hollywood*. London: British Film Institute.

Buckland, Warren. 2012. "Wes Anderson: A 'Smart' Director of the New Sincerity?" *New Review of Film and Television Studies* 10.1 (March): 1–5.

Bunting, Eve. 1976. *The Skateboard Four*. Park Ridge, IL: Albert Whitman.

Butler, Judith. 1993. *Bodies That Matter: On the Discursive Limits of "Sex."* New York and London: Routledge.

———. 1997. *Excitable Speech: A Politics of the Performative.* New York and London: Routledge.

———. 2006 [1990]. *Gender Trouble: Feminism and the Subversion of Identity.* New York and London: Routledge.

Calhoun, Dave. 2014. "Wes Anderson Interview: 'I Always Used to Have Two Desserts a Day; Now I Have Only One.'" *TimeOut.com.* March 4. http://www.timeout.com/newyork/film/wes-anderson-interview-i-always-used-to-have-at-least-two-desserts-a-day-now-i-have-only-one (accessed April 29, 2016).

Callow, Simon. 1995. *Orson Welles. Volume 1: The Road to Xanadu.* New York: Penguin.

Carlson, Greg. 2005. "You Are Forgiven: Interpersonal and Familial Ethics in the Films of Wes Anderson." In *Communication Ethics, Media, & Popular Culture.* Eds. Phyllis M. Japp, Mark Meister, and Debra K. Japp. New York: Peter Lang. 249–275.

Carrigan, Tim, R. W. Connell, and John Lee. 1985. "Toward a New Sociology of Masculinity." *Theory and Society* 14:5 (September): 551–604.

Charania, Iman. 2012. "25 Years Later: Director Wes Anderson on Living, Filming *Rushmore.*" *The Review: The Official Student Newspaper of St. John's School* 63:8. 6.

Clarke, J. J. 1997. *Oriental Enlightenment: The Encounter Between Asian and Western Thought.* Routledge: London and New York.

Cochrane, Lauren. 2015. "Fantastic Mr. Wes Anderson: How Tenenbaum Chic Took Over the Catwalks." *The Guardian.* August 24. https://www.theguardian.com/fashion/2015/aug/24/fantastic-mr-wes-anderson-how-tenenbaum-chic-took-over-the-catwalks (accessed September 29, 2016).

Collin, Robbie. 2014. "Wes Anderson Interview." *The Telegraph.* February 19. http://www.telegraph.co.uk/culture/film/starsandstories/10644172/Wes-Anderson-interview.html (accessed April 27, 2016).

Collins, Jim. 1993. "Genericity in the Nineties: Eclectic Irony and the New Sincerity." In *Film Theory Goes to the Movies.* Eds. Jim Collins, Hillary Radner, and Ava Preacher Collins. New York: Routledge. 242–263.

Colloff, Pamela. 1998. "The New Kids—Owen Wilson and Wes Anderson." *Texas Monthly.* May 1998. http://www.texasmonthly.com/articles/the-new-kids-wes-anderson-and-owen-wilson/ (accessed May 30, 2015).

Connell, R. W. 1987. *Gender and Power: Society, the Person and Sexual Politics.* Cambridge: Polity Press.

———. 1995. *Masculinities.* Cambridge: Polity Press.

Connell, R. W., and James W. Messerschmidt. 2005. "Hegemonic Masculinity: Rethinking the Concept." *Gender and Society* 19:6. 829–859.

Corrigan, Timothy. 2003 [1991]. "The Commerce of Auteurism." *Film and Authorship.* Ed. Virginia Wright Wexman. New Brunswick, NJ: Rutgers University Press. 96–111.

Cousteau, Jacques-Yves. 1985 [1979]. "Introduction." *The Ocean World.* New York: Abradale Press/Abrams. 12–14.

Cousteau, Jacques-Yves, and Philippe Diolé. 1971. *Diving for Sunken Treasure (The Undersea Discoveries of Jacques–Yves Cousteau).* Trans. J. F. Bernard. London: Cassell.

Crofts, Stephen. 1998. "Authorship and Hollywood." *The Oxford Guide to Film Studies.* Ed. John Hill and Pamela Church Gibson. Oxford: Oxford University Press. 310–326.

Crouch, Ian. 2012. "Does Wes Anderson Hate Dogs?" *NewYorker.com.* June 21. http://www.newyorker.com/culture/culture-desk/does-wes-anderson-hate-dogs (accessed July 16, 2015).

Dahl, Roald. 1961. *James and the Giant Peach.* New York: Penguin.

_____. 1964. *Charlie and the Chocolate Factory*. New York: Penguin.

_____. 1970. *Fantastic Mr. Fox*. New York: Penguin.

Dean-Ruzicka, Rachel. 2013. "Themes of Privilege and Whiteness in the Films of Wes Anderson." *Quarterly Review of Film and Video* 30:1. 25–40.

Derrida, Jacques. 1990. *Limited Inc*. Trans. E. Weber. Paris: Éditions Galilée.

Desplechin, Arnaud. 2009. "An Interview with Wes Anderson." *Interview*. October 26. http://www.interviewmagazine.com/film/wes-anderson/ (accessed June 4, 2014).

Donohue, Walter. 2012. "Love on the Run." *Filmmaker Magazine*. October 17. http://filmmakermagazine.com/53944-love-on-the-run/#.Vg7O5BGqpBc (accessed July 15, 2014).

Dorey, Tom. 2012. "Fantastic Mr. Filmmaker: Paratexts and the Positioning of Wes Anderson as Roald Dahl's Cinematic Heir." *New Review of Film and Television Studies* 10:1. 169–185.

Doty, Alexander. 1993. *Making Things Perfectly Queer: Interpreting Mass Culture*. Minneapolis, MN: University of Minnesota Press.

Drake, Philip. 2013. "Reputational Capital, Creative Conflict, and Hollywood Independence: The Case of Hal Ashby." *American Independent Cinema: Indie, Indiewood, and Beyond*. Eds. Geoff King, Claire Molloy, and Yannis Tzioumakis. London: Routledge. 140–152.

Drescher, Jack. (2007). "From Bisexuality to Intersexuality: Rethinking Gender Categories. *Contemporary Psychoanalysis* 43:1. 204–228.

Duncan, Pansy. 2016. *The Emotional Life of Postmodern Film: Affect Theory's Other*. New York: Routledge.

Edwards, Tim. 2006. *Cultures of Masculinity*. New York and London: Routledge.

Elsaesser, Thomas. 2012. "Auteurism Today: Signature Products, Concept-Authors and Access for All: *Avatar*." In *The Persistence of Hollywood*. New York: Routledge. 281–304.

Felando, Cynthia. 2012. "A Certain Age: Wes Anderson, Anjelica Huston and Modern Femininity." *New Review of Film and Television Studies* 10:1. 68–82.

Fellini, Federico. 1976. *Fellini on Fellini*. Trans. Isabel Quigly. London: Eyre Methuen.

_____. 1995. *I, Fellini*. Trans. Charlotte Chandler. New York: Cooper Square.

Fitzgerald, F. Scott. 1995 [1928]. "The Captured Shadow." *The Short Stories of F. Scott Fitzgerald: A New Collection*. New York: Scribner. 412–430.

_____. 2004 [1925]. *The Great Gatsby*. New York: Scribner.

Feinberg, Scott. 2012. "Wes Anderson on His Life, Career and Biggest Success Yet, *Moonrise Kingdom*: Interview with Wes Anderson." *The Hollywood Reporter*. December 25. http://www.hollywoodreporter.com/wes-anderson-his-life-career-406295 (accessed October 3, 2014).

Fleming, Jr., Mike. 2012. "Fleming Q&A's '*Moonrise Kingdom*' Director Wes Anderson." *Deadline.com*. December 30. http://deadline.com/2012/12/fleming-qas-moonrise-kingdom-director-wes-anderson-394927/ (accessed May 25, 2015).

Foucault, Michel. 1978. *The History of Sexuality: Volume One*. New York: Vintage Books.

Gerstner, David A., and Janet Staiger, eds. 2003. *Authorship and Film*. New York and London: Routledge, 2003.

Gibbs, John. 2012. "Balancing Act: Exploring the Tone of *The Life Aquatic with Steve Zissou*." *New Review of Film and Television Studies* 10:1 (March): 132–51.

Godard, Jean-Luc. 1972. *Godard on Godard: Critical Writings by Jean-Luc Godard*. Trans. Tom Milne. New York: Da Capo Press.

Gooch, Joshua. 2007. "Making a Go of It: Paternity and Prohibition in the Films of Wes Anderson." *Cinema Journal* 47:1. 26–48.

_____. 2014. "Objects/Desire/Oedipus: Wes Anderson as Late-Capitalist Auteur." In *The Films of Wes Anderson: Critical Essays on an Indiewood Icon*. Ed. Peter C. Kunze. New York: Palgrave Macmillan. 171–180.

Govender, Dyalan. 2008. "Wes Anderson's *The Life Aquatic with Steve Zissou* and Melville's *Moby Dick*: A Comparative Study." *Literature/Film Quarterly* 36:1 (January): 61–67.

Greif, Mark, Kathleen Ross, and Dayna Tortorici, eds. 2010. *What was the Hipster? A Sociological Investigation*. Brooklyn, NY: n+1 Foundation.

Gross, Terry. 2009. "Fresh Air: Wes Anderson Covers New Ground with 'Mr. Fox.'" *TPR.org*. November 23. http://tpr.org/post/wes-anderson-covers-new-ground-mr-fox#stream/0 (accessed October 4, 2014).

———. 2012. "Fresh Air: Wes Anderson: Creating a Singular Kingdom," *NPR.org*. May 29. http://www.npr.org/2012/05/29/153913922/wes-anderson-creating-a-singular-kingdom (accessed October 4, 2014).

Guillén, Michael. 2007. "2007 MVFF30: The Darjeeling Limited—Interview with Wes Anderson, Jason Schwartzman, and Roman Coppola." *Screenanarchy.com*. October 10. http://screenanarchy.com/2007/10/2007-mvff30-the-darjeeling-limitedinterview-with-wes-anderson-jason-schwart.html#ixzz453AMLFwl (accessed November 8, 2015).

Guinness, Hugo. 2014. "Introduction." *The Grand Budapest Hotel*. New York: Hugo, vii.

Hainey, Michael. 2011. "Interview with Gene Hackman." *GQ*. June 1, http://www.gq.com/story/gene-hackman-gq-june-2011-interview (accessed November 28, 2015).

Halperin, David. 1995. *Saint Foucault: Towards a Gay Hagiography*. Oxford: Oxford University Press.

———. 2003. "The Normalization of Queer Theory." *Journal of Homosexuality* 45:2 (February): 339–343.

Harman, Ken, Matt Zoller Seitz, and Wes Anderson, eds. 2016. *The Wes Anderson Collection: Bad Dads: Art Inspired by the Films of Wes Anderson*. New York: Abrams.

Hart, Moss, and George S. Kaufman. 1998 [1936]. *You Can't Take It with You: A Comedy in Three Acts*. New York: Dramatists Play Service.

Heath, Chris. 2014. "GQ Style: Wes Anderson's Highly Influential, Slightly Tweaked Take on Reality." *GQ*. October 27. http://www.gq.com/story/gq-style-fall-2014-influencer-wes-anderson (accessed March 26, 2016).

Hill, Derek. 2008. *Charlie Kaufman and His Merry Band of Pranksters, Fabulists and Dreamers: An Excursion into the American New Wave*. Harpenden: Kamera Books.

Hirschorn, Michael. 2007. "Quirked Around: The Unbearable Lightness of Ira Glass, Wes Anderson, and Other Paragons of Indie Sensibility." *The Atlantic*. September 1. 142–147.

Holdengräber, Paul. 2014. "LIVE from the New York Public Library: Wes Anderson | Paul Holdengräber." *Nypl.org*. February 27. http://www.nypl.org/audiovideo/wes-anderson-paul-holdengraber (accessed August 14, 2014).

Holmes, Diana, and Robert Ingram. 1998. *François Truffaut*. Manchester: Manchester University Press.

Holmlund, Chris, and Justin Wyatt, eds. 2005. *Contemporary American Independent Film: From the Margins to the Mainstream*. New York: Routledge.

Hrycaj, Lara. 2014. "Life on Mars or Life on the Sea: Seu Jorge, David Bowie, and the Musical World in Wes Anderson's *The Life Aquatic with Steve Zissou*." In *The Films of Wes Anderson: Critical Essays on an Indiewood Icon*. Ed. Peter C. Kunze. New York: Palgrave Macmillan. 139–150.

Hyden, Stephen, Noel Murray, Keith Phipps, Nathan Rabin, and Scott Tobias. 2007. "10 Films that Couldn't Have Happened Without Wes Anderson." *AVClub.com*. October 9. http://www.avclub.com/article/10-films-that-couldnt-have-happened-without-wes-anderson (accessed November 20, 2014).

Ingram, Robert, with Paul Duncan, ed. 2004. *François Truffaut: Film Author, 1932–1984*. London: Taschen.
Jagose, Annamarie. 1996. *Queer Theory: An Introduction*. New York: New York University Press.
Jenkins, Henry. 1992. *Textual Poachers: Television Fans & Participatory Culture*. New York: Routledge.
Jones, Abigail. 2009. "America's Elite Prep Schools." *Forbes*. April 6. http://www.forbes.com/2009/04/06/america-elite-schools-leadership-prep.html (accessed June 28, 2015).
Jones, Kent. 2001. "Family Romance." *Film Comment* 37:6. 24–27.
Joseph, Rachel. 2012. "'Max Fischer Presents': Wes Anderson and the Theatricality of Mourning." In *The Films of Wes Anderson: Critical Essays on an Indiewood Icon*. Ed. Peter C. Kunze. New York: Palgrave Macmillan. 51–64.
Kaplan, E. Ann. 2000. *Feminism and Film*. Oxford: Oxford University Press.
Kehr, Dave. 1999 [1998]. "DVD Booklet Introductory Essay on Rushmore." *Rushmore*. Criterion Collection DVD.
Kennedy-Karpat, Colleen. 2014. "Bill Murray and Wes Anderson, or the Curmudgeon as Muse." In *The Films of Wes Anderson: Critical Essays on an Indiewood Icon*. Ed. Peter C. Kunze. New York: Palgrave Macmillan. 125–137.
Kertzer, Adrienne. 2011. "Fidelity, Felicity, and Playing Around in Wes Anderson's *Fantastic Mr. Fox*." *Children's Literature Association Quarterly* 36:1. 4–24.
Kimmel, Michael. 1992. "Reading Men: Men, Masculinity, and Publishing." *Contemporary Sociology* 21:2. 162–171.
———. 1996. *Manhood in America: A Cultural History*. New York: Free Press.
Kimmel, Michael, and Michael A. Messner, eds. 2009. *Men's Lives*. 8th edition. London: Pearson.
Kimmel, Michael, Jeff Hearn, and R. W. Connell, eds. 2005. *Handbook of Studies on Men and Masculinities*. Thousand Oaks, CA: Sage.
King, Geoff. 2005. *American Independent Cinema*. London: IB Tauris.
———. 2009. *Indiewood, USA: Where Hollywood Meets Independent Cinema*. London: IB Tauris.
———. 2010. *Lost in Translation*. Edinburgh: Edinburgh University Press.
King, Geoff, Claire Molloy, and Yannis Tzioumakis, eds. 2013. *American Independent Cinema: Indie, Indiewood, and Beyond*. London: Routledge.
Knegt, Peter. 2015. "The 50 Highest-Grossing Indies of 2014." *Indiewire.com*. January 2. http://www.indiewire.com/2015/01/the-50-highest-grossing-indies-of-2014-66644/ (accessed August 25, 2015).
Knight, C. Ryan. 2014. "Who's to Say?": The Role of Pets in Wes Anderson's Films." In *The Films of Wes Anderson: Critical Essays on an Indiewood Icon*. Ed. Peter C. Kunze. New York: Palgrave Macmillan. 65–75.
Konigsburg, E. L. 1967. *From the Mixed-up Files of Mrs. Basil E. Frankweiler*. New York: Atheneum.
Kunze, Peter C., ed. 2014a. *The Films of Wes Anderson: Critical Essays on an Indiewood Icon*. New York: Palgrave Macmillan.
———. 2014b. "From the Mixed-Up Files of Mr. Wesley W. Anderson." In *The Films of Wes Anderson: Critical Essays on an Indiewood Icon*. Ed. Peter C. Kunze. New York: Palgrave Macmillan. 91–107.
Lane, Anthony. 1998. "Renaissance Teen." *The New Yorker*. December 7. 214–216.
Lander, Christian. 2008. *Stuff White People Like: A Definitive Guide to the Unique Taste of Millions*. New York: Random House.
Lanham, Robert. 2003. *The Hipster Handbook*. New York: Anchor Books.

Lartigue, Jacques-Henri. 1986. *Jacques-Henri Lartigue*. New York: Pantheon Books.

Leland, John. 2004. *Hip: The History*. New York: HarperColllins.

Lewis, Jon. 2007. "The Perfect Money Machine(s): George Lucas, Steven Spielberg, and Auteurism in the New Hollywood." In *Looking Past the Screen: Case Studies in American Film History and Method*. Eds. Eric Smoodin and Jon Lewis. Durham, NC: Duke University Press. 61–86.

Levy, Emmanuel. 1999. *The Cinema of Outsiders: The Rise of American Independent Film*. New York: New York University Press.

Lippy, Tod, ed. 2000. "Interview with Wes Anderson." In *Projections 11: New York Filmmakers on Filmmaking*. London: Faber & Faber. 108–121.

Lorentzen, Christian. 2010. "Captain Neato." *nplusonemag.com*. April 23. https://nplusonemag.com/online-only/captain-neato/ (accessed February 7, 2016).

Lyman, Rick. 2002. "From Centimes, A Wealth of Ideas (Watching Movies With: Wes Anderson)." *NYTimes.com*. January 11. http://www.nytimes.com/2002/01/11/movies/watching-movies-with-wes-anderson-from-centimes-a-wealth-of-ideas.html?_r=0 (accessed May 14, 2015).

Lynskey, Dorian. 2014. "Film by Film: Wes Anderson on Wes Anderson." *Empireonline.com*. March 4. http://www.empireonline.com/movies/features/wes-anderson/ (accessed April 25, 2016).

MacDowell, James. 2010. "Notes on 'Quirky.'" *Movie: A Journal of Film Criticism*. http://www2.warwick.ac.uk/fac/arts/film/movie/contents/notes_on_quirky.pdf (accessed May 20, 2015).

_____. 2011. "Defining 'Quirky.'" *Alternate Takes*. March 28. http://www.alternatetakes.co.uk/?2011,3,250 (accessed May 20, 2015).

_____. 2012. "Wes Anderson, Tone, and the Quirky Sensibility." *New Review of Film and Television Studies* 10:1 (March): 6–27.

_____. 2013. "Quirky: Buzzword or Sensibility?" In *American Independent Cinema: Indie, Indiewood, and Beyond*. Eds. Geoff King, Claire Molloy, and Yannis Tzioumakis. London: Routledge. 53–64.

_____. 2014. "The Andersonian, the Quirky, and 'Innocence.'" In *The Films of Wes Anderson: Critical Essays on an Indiewood Icon*. Ed. Peter C. Kunze. New York: Palgrave Macmillan. 153–169.

Mackenzie, Susie. 2005. "Wes Anderson: Into the Deep." *The Guardian*. February 12. http://www.theguardian.com/film/2005/feb/12/features.weekend (accessed January 2, 2015).

Maltin, Leonard. 1999. "Wes Anderson." Content on Turner Classic Movies website, from an interview in *Premiere* magazine, March 1999. *TCM.com*. http://www.tcm.com/tcmdb/person/514940%7C0/Wes-Anderson/ (accessed December 5, 2015).

Mayshark, Jesse F. 2007. *Post-Pop Cinema: The Search for Meaning in New American Film*. Westport, CT: Praeger.

McGeveran, Tom. 2001. "Wes Anderson's Dream House." *Observer.com*. June 4. http://www.observer.com/2001/06/wes-andersons-dream-house/ (accessed July 17, 2016).

Messner, Michael A. 1997. *Politics of Masculinities: Men in Movements*. Walnut Creek, CA: Alta Mira Press.

Monda, Antonio. 2005. "Mondo Monda." *The Life Aquatic with Steve Zissou*. Criterion Collection DVD featurette.

Morris, Jason. 2008. "The Time Between Time: Messianism and the Promise of a 'New Sincerity.'" *Jacket Magazine*. http://jacketmagazine.com/35/morris-sincerity.shtml (accessed April 24, 2015).

Mottram, James. 2006. *The Sundance Kids: How the Mavericks Took Over Hollywood*. New York: Farrar, Straus, and Giroux.

———. 2014. "Wes Anderson Interview: 'I Feel Happier Making Movies than I Ever Did Going to School.'" *The Big Issue*. February 24. http://www.bigissue.com/features/interviews/3558/wes-anderson-interview-i-feel-happier-making-movies-than-i-ever-did-going-to-school (accessed April 29, 2016).

Mulvey, Laura. 1989. *Visual and Other Pleasures*. Indianapolis, IN: Indiana University Press.

Newman, Michael Z. 2011. *Indie: An American Film Culture*. New York: Columbia University Press.

———. 2013. "Movies for Hipsters." In *American Independent Cinema: Indie, Indiewood, and Beyond*. Eds. Geoff King, Claire Molloy, and Yannis Tzioumakis, London: Routledge. 71–82.

Olsen, Mark. 1999. "If I Can Dream: The Everlasting Boyhoods of Wes Anderson." *Film Comment* 35:1 (January/February): 12–17.

Orgeron, Devin. 2007. "La Camera–Crayola: Authorship Comes of Age in the Cinema of Wes Anderson." *Cinema Journal* 46:2 (Winter): 40–65.

———. 2010. "Wes Anderson." In *50 Contemporary Filmmakers*. Ed. Yvonne Tasker. 18–27.

Overstreet, Jeffrey. 2012. "*Moonrise Kingdom* and the Divine Symphony." *Patheos.com*. July 5. http://www.patheos.com/blogs/goodletters/2012/07/moonrise-kingdom-and-the-divine-symphony/ (accessed November 17, 2014).

Papamichael, Stella. 2005. "Interview with Wes Anderson on *The Life Aquatic with Steve Zissou*." *BBC.co.uk*. February 15. http://www.bbc.co.uk/films/2005/02/15/wes_anderson_the_life_aquatic_interview.shtml (accessed August 30, 2015).

Peberdy, Donna. 2012. "'I'm Just a Character in Your Film': Acting and Performance from Autism to Zissou." *New Review of Film and Television Studies* 10:1 (March): 46–67.

Peppard, Alan. 2012. "Dossier Dallas: Owen Wilson." *The Dallas Morning News*. September 29. http://www.dallasnews.com/entertainment/celebrity-news/headlines/20120929-dossier-dallas-owen-wilson.ece (accessed June 28, 2015).

Perren, Alisa. 2001. "Sex, Lies, and Marketing: Miramax and the Development of the Quality Indie Blockbuster." *Film Quarterly* 55:2. 30–39.

———. 2012. *Indie, Inc. Miramax and the Transformation of Hollywood in the 1990s*. Austin, TX: University of Texas Press.

———. 2013. "Last Indie Standing: The Special Case of Lions Gate in the New Millennium." In *American Independent Cinema: Indie, Indiewood, and Beyond*. Eds. Geoff King, Claire Molloy, and Yannis Tzioumakis. London: Routledge. 108–120.

Phillis, Jen Hedler. 2014. "'I Always Wanted to Be a Tenenbaum': Class Mobility as Neoliberal Fantasy in Wes Anderson's *The Royal Tenenbaums*." In *The Films of Wes Anderson: Critical Essays on an Indiewood Icon*. Ed. Peter C. Kunze. New York: Palgrave Macmillan. 171–180.

Phipps, Keith. 1999. "Interview: Wes Anderson." *The Onion A. V. Club*. February 10. http://www.avclub.com/article/wes-anderson-13580 (accessed April 22, 2016).

Piechota, Carol Lyn. 2006. "Give Me a Second Grace: Music as Absolution in *The Royal Tenenbaums*." *Senses of Cinema*. http://sensesofcinema.com/2006/on-movies-musicians-and-soundtracks/music_tenenbaums (accessed August 17, 2013).

Plevin, Julia. 2008. "Who's a Hipster?" *Huffingtonpost.com*. September 8. http://www.huffingtonpost.com/julia-plevin/whos-a-hipster_b_117383.html (accessed May 15, 2015).

Pomeroy, Alisa. 2002. "Interview with Wes Anderson for *The Royal Tenenbaums*." *BBC.co.uk*. February 27. http://www.bbc.co.uk/films/2002/02/27/wes_anderson_the_royal_tenebaums_interview.shtml (accessed October 2, 2015).

Poster, Randall. 2012. "How Wes Anderson Soundtracks His Movies." *NPR.org*. May 24. http://www.npr.org/templates/transcript/transcript.php?storyId=153585829 (accessed July 25, 2015).

Pribram, E. Diedre. 2002. *Cinema & Culture: Independent Film in the United States, 1980–2001*. New York: Peter Lang.

Prochnik, George. 2014. *The Impossible Exile: Stefan Zweig at the End of the World*. New York: Other Press.

Rich, Katey. 2010. "TIFF Review: *Submarine* is Much More Than Just the Welsh *Rushmore*." *Cinemablend.com*. September 18. http://www.cinemablend.com/new/TIFF-Review-Submarine-Much-More-Than-Just-Welsh-Rushmore-20717.html (accessed January 15, 2016).

Richter, Nicole. 2014. "The Short Films of Wes Anderson." In *The Films of Wes Anderson: Critical Essays on an Indiewood Icon*. Ed. Peter C. Kunze. New York: Palgrave Macmillan. 13–24.

Robé, Chris. 2012. "'Because I Hate Fathers, and I Never Wanted to Be One': Wes Anderson, Entitled Masculinity, and the Crisis of the Patriarch." In *Millennial Masculinity: Men in Contemporary American Cinema*. Ed. Timothy Shary. Detroit, MI: Wayne State University Press. 101–121.

Romney, Jonathan. 2002. "Family Albums." *Sight and Sound* 12:3. 12–15.

Rybin, Steven. 2014. "The Jellyfish and the Moonlight: Imagining the Family in Wes Anderson's Films." In *The Films of Wes Anderson: Critical Essays on an Indiewood Icon*. Ed. Peter C. Kunze. New York: Palgrave Macmillan. 39–49.

Said, Edward. 1978. *Orientalism*. New York: Pantheon.

Salinger, J. D. 1951. *The Catcher in the Rye*. New York: Little, Brown.

———. 1953a [1948]. "A Perfect Day for Bananafish." In *Nine Stories*. New York: Little, Brown. 3–18.

———. 1953b [1949]. "Down at the Dinghy." In *Nine Stories*. New York: Little, Brown. 74–86.

———. 1961 [*Franny*, 1955; *Zooey*, 1957]. *Franny and Zooey*. New York: Little, Brown.

———. 1991 [1955/1959]. *Raise High the Roof Beam, Carpenters/Seymour: An Introduction*. New York: Little, Brown.

Sarris, Andrew. 1981 [1962]. "Notes on the Auteur Theory in 1962." In *Theories of Authorship*. Ed. John Caughie. London: Routledge. 62–65.

Schechner, Richard. 1985. *Between Theatre and Anthropology*. Philadelphia, PA: Pennsylvania University Press.

Schiermer Andersen, Bjørn. 2014. "Late–Modern Hipsters: New Tendencies in Popular Culture." *Acta Sociologica* 57:2. 167–181.

Sconce, Jeffrey. 2002. "Irony, Nihilism, and the New American 'Smart' Film." *Screen* 43.4 (Winter): 349–369.

Scorsese, Martin. 2007 [2000]. "Wes Anderson." *Esquire*. January 29. http://www.esquire.com/news-politics/a1608/wes-anderson-0300 (accessed September 18, 2015).

Scott, A. O. 2007. "Brothers, and Their Baggage, In India." *NYTimes.com*. September 28. http://movies.nytimes.com/2007/09/28/movies/28darj.html (accessed June 4, 2015).

Scott, Jason Davids. 2014. "'American Empirical' Time and Space: The (In) Visibility of Popular Culture in the films of Wes Anderson." In *The Films of Wes Anderson: Critical Essays on an Indiewood Icon*. Ed. Peter C. Kunze. New York: Palgrave Macmillan. 77–88.

Scott, Kevin Conroy. 2005. "Lesser Spotted Fish and Other Stories." *Sight and Sound* 15:3 (March): 13–15.

———. 2005. *Screenwriters' Masterclass: Screenwriters Discuss their Greatest Films*. New York: Faber and Faber.

Sedgwick, Eve. 1990. *Epistemology of the Closet*. Berkeley, CA: University of California Press.

Seidler, Victor J. 2006. *Transforming Masculinities: Men, Cultures, Bodies, Power, Sex, and Love.* London: Routledge.

Seitz, Matt Zoller. 2009. "The Substance of Style, Part I." *Moving Image Source.* March 30. http://www.movingimagesource.us/articles/the-substance-of-style-pt-1-20090330 (accessed November 7, 2014).

———. 2010. "The Substance of Style, Part II." *Moving Image Source.* June 3. http://www.movingimagesource.us/articles/the-substance-of-style-pt-2-20090403 (accessed April 21, 2014).

———. 2013a. *The Wes Anderson Collection.* New York: Abrams.

———. 2013b. "Seitz: 24 Things I Learned While Writing My Book About Wes Anderson." *Vulture.* October 23. http://www.vulture.com/2013/10/wes-anderson-collection-24-tidbits-matt-zoller-seitz.html (accessed August 14, 2014).

———. 2015a. *The Wes Anderson Collection: The Grand Budapest Hotel.* New York: Abrams.

———. 2015b. "Behind the Scenes at '*The Grand Budapest Hotel*,'" *Telegraph.com.* February 19. http://www.telegraph.co.uk/film/the-grand-budapest-hotel/behind-scenes-wes-anderson/ (accessed March 20, 2016).

Sella, Marshall. 2001. "Wes Anderson: Boyish Wonder." *New York Times Magazine.* December 2. http://www.nytimes.com/2001/12/02/magazine/02ANDERSON.html?pagewanted=4 (accessed April 5, 2015).

Shackelford, Laura. 2014. "Systems Thinking in *The Life Aquatic with Steve Zissou*." In *The Films of Wes Anderson: Critical Essays on an Indiewood Icon.* Ed. Peter C. Kunze. New York: Palgrave Macmillan. 199–213.

Silman, Anna. 2015. "Whoopi Goldberg wants more people of color in Wes Anderson's movies: 'I would like to give you my resume.'" *Salon.com.* June 23. http://www.salon.com/2015/06/22/whoopi_goldberg_wants_more_people_of_color_in_wes_andersons_movies_i_would_like_to_give_you_my_resume/ (accessed June 25, 2015).

Slabaugh, Andy. 2005. "Wes Anderson: Genuine Auteur or Stylish Charlatan?" *Cinesthesia.* http://archive.li/4pYoh (accessed May 18, 2015).

Smith, Gavin, and Kent Jones. 2001. "At Home with The Royal Family: Wes Anderson Interviewed by Gavin Smith and Kent Jones." *Film Comment* 37:6. 28–29.

Sontag, Susan. 2001 [1966]. "Godard's *Vivre Sa Vie.*" In *Against Interpretation.* New York: Picador/Farrar, Straus, and Giroux. 196–208.

Stephenson, Barry. 2011. "'Filled with Ritual': Wes Anderson's *The Darjeeling Limited.*" *Brightlightsfilm.com.* October 31. http://brightlightsfilm.com/filled-with-ritual-wes-andersons-the-darjeeling-limited/# (accessed November 10, 2015).

Tarkington, Booth. 1998 [1918]. *The Magnificent Ambersons.* New York: Modern Library.

Thomas, Deborah J. 2012. "Framing the 'Melancomic': Character, Aesthetics and Affect in Wes Anderson's *Rushmore*." *New Review of Film and Television Studies* 10:1 (March): 97–117.

Thompson, Kristin, and David Bordwell. 2003. *Film History: An Introduction.* 2nd edition. Boston, MA: McGraw Hill.

———. 2007. "Observations on Film Art: Shot-Consciousness." January 16. http://www.davidbordwell.net/blog/2007/01/16/shot-consciousness/ (accessed October 28, 2015).

———. 2014. "Observations on Film Art: *Moonrise Kingdom*: Wes in Wonderland." July 20. http://www.davidbordwell.net/blog/2014/07/20/moonrise-kingdom-wes-in-wonderland/ (accessed August 12, 2014).

Tobias, Scott. 2007. "Interview: Wes Anderson." *The Onion A. V. Club.* October 10. http://www.avclub.com/article/wes-anderson-14161 (accessed May 14, 2015).

Turan, Kenneth. 1996. "The Gang That Couldn't Shoot, or Think, Straight." *LATimes.com*. February 21. http://articles.latimes.com/1996-02-21/entertainment/ca-38140_1_bottle-rocket (accessed October 14, 2015).

Turner, Daniel Cross. 2008. "The American Family (Film) in Retro: Nostalgia as Mode in Wes Anderson's *The Royal Tenenbaums*." In *Violating Time: History, Memory, and Nostalgia in Cinema*. Ed. Christina Lee. New York: Continuum. 159–176.

Turner, Victor W. 1988. *The Anthropology of Performance*. New York: PAJ.

Tzioumakis, Yannis. 2006. *American Independent Cinema: An Introduction*. New Brunswick, NJ: Rutgers University Press.

Verne, Jules. 1992 [1870]. *Twenty Thousand Leagues Under the Sea*. London: Wordsworth Editions.

Wachtell, Jennifer. 2008. "The Director's Director." *Good*. June 20. http://magazine.good.is/articles/the-directors-director (accessed May 12, 2014).

Wagner, Erica. 2014. "Vulpine Nature." *Fantastic Mr. Fox* DVD Liner Notes Booklet. 2014 Criterion Collection Blu-Ray DVD Release.

Wallace, Amy. 2001. "Bittersweet Dreamers." *Los Angeles Magazine*. December. 90–95, 174.

Warner, Michael. 1993. *Fear of a Queer Planet: Queer Politics and Social Theory*. Minneapolis, MN: University of Minnesota Press.

Waxman, Sharon. 2006. *Rebels on the Backlot: Six Maverick Directors and How They Conquered Hollywood*. New York: HarperCollins.

Weiner, Jonah. 2007. "Unbearable Whiteness: That Queasy Feeling You Get When Watching a Wes Anderson Movie." *Slate.com*. September 1. http://www.slate.com/articles/arts/culturebox/2007/09/unbearable_whiteness.html (accessed May 14, 2015).

Weisberg, Jacob. 2012. "The World According to Wes." *Slate.com*. May 25. http://www.slate.com/articles/podcasts/conversations_with_slate/2012/05/wes_anderson_the_complete_slate_interview_.html (accessed September 3, 2015).

Wilkins, Kim. 2014. "Cast of Characters: Wes Anderson and Pure Cinematic Characterization." In *The Films of Wes Anderson: Critical Essays on an Indiewood Icon*. Ed. Peter C. Kunze. New York: Palgrave Macmillan. 23–37.

Wilson, Karen. 2004. "A Talk with Director Wes Anderson." *Gothamist.com*. December 7. http://gothamist.com/2004/12/07/a_talk_with_director_wes_anderson.php (accessed November 24, 2015).

Zahm, Olivier, and Olympia Le-Tan. 2008. "Interview with Wes Anderson." *Purple.fr*. September 1. http://www.purple.fr/magazine/ss-2008-issue-9/wes-anderson/ (accessed June 17, 2016).

Zweig, Stefan. 2006 [1939]. *Beware of Pity*. Trans. Phyllis Blewitt and Trevor Blewitt. New York: New York Review Books Classics.

———. 2013a [1922]. *Letter from an Unknown Woman and Other Stories*. Trans. Anthea Bell. London: Pushkin.

———. 2013b [1942]. *The World of Yesterday*. Trans. Anthea Bell. Lincoln, NE: University of Nebraska Press.

INDEX

3D 2
8½ (film) 122, 130, 131

Abraham, F. Murray 48, 54, 184, 185, 187
Academy Awards 3, 4, 18, 20–21, 38, 39, 42, 50, 205
Act One (Hart) 103
Adventures of Buckaroo Banzai Across the 8th Dimension, The (film) 131
Agee, James 221
Ahluwalia, Waris 49, 123, 139, 203
Allen, Woody 2, 64, 72, 124
All the President's Men (film) 40
Alps 194
Altman, Robert 15
Altmann, Lotte 195
Amalric, Mathieu 187
Amazon river 101
American Express 9, 163, 202–3, 211
Andersen, Hans Christian 98
Anderson, Eric Chase 13, 136n28, 163, 165, 218
Anderson, Melver Leonard 13
animals 46, 154, 161
Antonioni, Michelangelo 3, 15, 52
Arnaz, Desi 153
Arsel, Zeynep 37
Ashby, Hal 8, 34, 67, 81, 88

Astaire, Fred 164
L'Atalante (film) 188
Atlantic ocean 121
auteur 1–21
Ayoade, Richard 7

Bach, J. S. 130
Bad Dads (exhibition) 53–4
Bad Lieutenant (film) 175
Bad News Bears, The (film) 162
BAFTA 21
Baker, Chet 64
Balaban, Bob 4, 54, 168
Balázs, Béla 188
Baldwin, Alec 53, 100
Ball, Lucille 153
Ballad of Davy Crockett, The 152, 162
Bancroft, Anne 86
Barrie, J. M. 220
Barrymore, Ethyl 97
Barrymore, John 97, 142, 188
Baschiera, Stefano 144, 218
Bass, Saul 92
Baum, Vicki 188
Baumbach, Noah 4, 18, 19, 122, 123, 125, 129, 130, 131, 155
Baxley, Jack 99
Beach Boys 152, 162
Beatles 88, 115, 119, 143, 210
Abbey Road (album) 143

Beauty and the Beast (*La Belle et la bête*) (film) 163
Beethoven, Ludwig van 144
Behrend, Siegfried 192
Bengal Steamship Company 145
Bennett, Richard 100
Bergman, Ingmar 9, 15, 188
Berhman, S. N. 103
Berlin International Film Festival 21
Bernstein, Leonard 162, 173
Bicycle Thieves (*Ladri de biciclette*) 143
bildungsroman 13, 85, 90
Birdman (film) 3
Black Jack (film) 175
Black Narcissus (Godden) 145
Black Stallion, The (film) 131
Blake, Quentin 155
Blanchett, Cate 5, 126, 217
Blood Meridian (McCarthy) 104
Blow, Isabella 124
Bogdanovich, Peter 12, 16, 74
Bordwell, David 34, 52, 220
Borg, Bjorn 100, 114, 115
Borzage, Frank 188
Bottle Rocket (film) 5, 6, 15–16, 17, 18, 43, 49, 50, 59–75, 111, 134, 156, 216, 217, 218, 220–21
costumes 200–201
flawed heroes 45

BRINGING NOSTALGIA TO LIFE 239

masculinity 44, 60–75, 192
nostalgia 214
reception 213
violence 46
Bottle Rocket (short film) 2, 12, 16, 44, 63, 64, 200–202, 215
Bourdieu, Pierre 37
Bowie, David 130
Boyle, Barbara 16
Braff, Zach 6–7
brand 3, 7, 9, 10, 25n33, 33, 35, 37–41, 126, 131, 202–3
Brazil 123, 130, 195
British Invasion 78, 87–9
Britten, Benjamin 14, 113, 168, 170, 171, 173–5, 180
  Noah's Flood, (*Noye's Fludde*) 14, 168, 173, 176
  Young Person's Guide to the Orchestra 173, 174
Broderick, Matthew 81
Brody, Adrien 1, 4, 137, 187, 188, 211, 219
Brody, Richard 3, 144, 170, 177
Bronzino, Agnolo 17
Brooks, James L. 16, 73
Browne, Jackson 97, 115
Browning, Mark 40, 49, 165
Bruzzi, Stella 116
Buckland, Warren 37
Budapest 47
Burnett, Frances Hodgson 153
Burroughs, Texas Ann 13
Burton, Tim 161
Bush, George W. 80–81
Butch Cassidy and the Sundance Kid (film) 131
Butler, Judith 192

Caan, James 2, 50, 61, 66
Cahiers du cinéma (journal) 2
Caicedo, Donny 67
California 21
  Los Angeles 54
  San Francisco 53
Call of the Wild, The (London) 161
Canada 176
Cannes Film Festival 20, 217
Capote, Truman 5
Capponi, Ludovico 17
Capra, Frank 97

Carlos, Wendy 130
Carroll, Lewis 200
Carson, L. M. Kit 16
Cassavetes, John 15, 19, 34
Cassel, Seymour 2, 4, 26, 81, 104
Castello Cavalcanti (short film) 209
Cavazos, Lumi 5, 66
CGI (computer-generated imagery) 2
Chaffin, Donald 151
Charlie Brown Christmas, A (TV special) 12, 64, 87–8, 114, 115, 164
Chatterjee, Soumitra 144
Chekhov, Anton 103
Cherry Orchard, The (play) 103
Chesterton, G. K. 220
Chicago 42, 85
children 5, 11, 12, 13, 43, 47, 63, 93, 125, 143, 151, 160–62, 177, 205, 208, 215, 218, 220
  Bottle Rocket 69, 73
  Dahl 153, 154, 155, 156, 157, 161
  Darjeeling Limited 140
  Moonrise Kingdom 12, 66, 169, 170, 216
  Royal Tenenbaums 66, 98–115, 134, 173, 219
  Salinger 72, 111, 125
  stories 4, 12, 14, 93, 97, 98, 153–8, 161, 168, 217
  Truffaut 10, 12, 91
Chitty Chitty Bang Bang (film) 161
Christie, Agatha 211
Christmas 68, 88, 149, 210, 211, 215
Churchill, Winston 51
Cinecittà 19, 122, 209
City of God (film) 130
Clarke, J. J. 142
Clerks (film) 39
Clooney, George 163, 165
Cocker, Jarvis 165
Cocteau, Jacques 163
Coen brothers 35, 36
Cohen, Robyn 123
Colbert, Claudette 142
Cold War 87, 189
Collins, Jim 36, 37

color 2, 53, 113, 137, 145, 147, 151, 184, 205, 208, 211
Color Forms 97
Coltrane, John 64
Columbia Pictures 12, 16, 59, 65
Communism 184
Connell, R. W. 43–4
Conroy Scott, Kevin 216
Cooper, Susan 217
Coppola, Francis Ford 8, 24n28, 30n83, 88
Coppola, Roman 19, 20, 30n83, 139, 168, 203, 207, 210, 214
Coppola, Sofia 4, 6, 58n55
Coraline (film) 161
Cornish language 176
Corrigan, Timothy 9
Cort, Bud 2, 50, 81, 126
Costello, Dolores 99
costumes 1, 25n36, 60, 188
  animals 14, 113, 173
  Bottle Rocket 200–201
  commercials 203, 205
  Darjeeling Limited 138, 145, 206
  Fantastic Mr. Fox 152–3, 157, 158, 164
  Life Aquatic with Steve Zissou 18, 36, 122, 123, 125, 126, 133, 201
  Moonrise Kingdom 178, 180
  Royal Tenenbaums 26n49, 97, 100, 104, 107, 111–12, 115
  Rushmore 14, 17, 46, 81, 83–4
Côte d'Ivoire 101, 103
Cotton, Joseph 100
Cousteau, Jacques 17, 18, 47, 85, 86, 89, 121–2, 125, 214
Cousteau, Philippe 122
Cousteau Society 122
Cox, Brian 108, 165
Cranston, Bryan 54
Criterion Collection 9, 82
Crockett, Davy 176, 179
Crouch, Ian 46
Cukor, George 97
Czechoslovakia 184

Dafoe, Willem 2, 4, 50, 123, 156, 187, 219
Dahl, Felicity 19, 155

Dahl, Roald 4, 19, 64, 92, 151–65, 217
  Charlie and the Chocolate Factory (Dahl) 153, 161
  Fantastic Mr. Fox (Dahl) 19, 151–165, 214, 220
  James and the Giant Peach (Dahl) 153
  Kiss Kiss (Dahl) 153
Darjeeling Limited (film) 1, 4, 8, 21, 35, 42, 48–54, 137–149, 165, 214
  British accents 141
  costumes 138, 145, 206
  dysfunctional family 12–13, 45
  male bonding 43
  nostalgia 214
  sex 216
Dassin, Joe 144
da Vinci, Leonardo 128, 176
deadpan 1, 35, 52, 220
Dead Poets Society (film) 83, 84
Dean-Ruzicka, Rachel 40
Debussy, Claude 144
De Luca, Mike 74
Delerue, Georges 159, 163
Demme, Jonathan 92
Demy, Jacques 98
Depp, Johnny 161
Desplat, Alexandre 4, 21, 159, 162, 165, 192
Desplechin, Arnaud 12
Deux anglaises et le continent (Roché) 98, 99
Dignan, Stephen 47, 74n3, 219
dioramas 1, 27n53, 97
Disney 128, 162
Dorey, Tom 9, 155
Drake, Nick 116
Drake, William A. 188
Drakoulias, Oseary 131
Dufresne, Andy 175
Dylan, Bob 73

Eames, Charles and Ray 92
Eastern Europe 54, 193
Ellington, Duke 64
Elsaesser, Thomas 8
Enescu, George 116
England *see* United Kingdom
Escape From Alcatraz (film) 175
Esquire (magazine) 74
Evel Knievel 125

Faces (band) 89
Fantastic Mr. Fox (film) 2, 4, 5, 7, 21, 47–54, 93, 151–65, 217, 220–21
  children 12, 93
  costumes 152–3, 157, 158, 164
  dysfunctional family 13, 43
  father 45, 161
  flawed heroes 45, 161
  gender roles 158–60
  masculinity 44
  music 152, 159, 160, 162
  nostalgia 214, 218
  violence 46, 161
Fargo (film) 74
fashion 7, 9, 17, 24n25, 25n36
Fellini, Federico 3, 8, 9, 15, 19, 41, 42, 93, 122, 130–31, 200, 209, 210, 211
Ferris Bueller's Day Off (film) 81, 83, 84–5, 175
Feu follet, Le (film) 114
Fiennes, Ralph 4, 21, 49, 183, 188, 189, 219
Film 4 213
Film Comment (journal) 82
filming techniques 1, 19, 41, 42, 51, 53, 62–3, 65–9, 90–93, 98, 138, 175, 205
Fitzgerald, F. Scott 15, 63, 103–4, 116, 117, 221
Fleming, Jr., Mike 74
Florida 146
Ford, Harrison, 189
Forster, E. M. 142
Fosse, Bob 162
Fox Searchlight 38, 39
France 10–11, 14, 90, 129, 169, 204
  Paris, 11, 14, 19, 20, 38, 54, 64, 197n1, 205, 207, 216
French (language) 47–8
French Connection (film) 40, 50, 97, 138
French New Wave 2, 3, 9, 12, 78, 89, 99, 200, 202, 211
Freud, Sigmund 194
Friedberg, Mark 137
Frizzell, Lefty 174
From the Mixed-Up Files of Mrs. Basil E. Frankweiler (Konigsburg) 112, 220
Fugitive, The (film) 189
Fuller, Bobby 160

Gambon, Michael 4, 20, 131, 165
Garbo, Greta 188, 215
Garden State (film) 2, 6–7
Gender Trouble (Butler) 192
Germany 21, 123
  Berlin 38, 188, 189
  Görlitz 219
  Hamburg 47
  Karlsbad 43
Gerwig, Greta 54
Gibbs, John 37
Gibson, Mel 163
Gilman, Jared 20, 45, 47, 168, 175
Giovannelli, Leonardo 125
Glover, Danny 50, 103
Gnutov, Vitaly 192
Godard, Jean-Luc 8, 9, 12, 15, 52, 92, 131, 175
  Pierrot Le Fou (film) 175
Godden, Rumer 145
Godfather, The (film) 40
Goldberg, Whoopi 23n12, 212n11
Goldblum, Jeff 4, 46, 54, 187, 219
Golding, William 170
Gooch, Joshua 45
Goodall, Jane 126
Good Fairy, The (film) 188
Good Will Hunting (film) 39
Gorovaia, Irina 99
Goulding, Edmund 188
Govender, Dyalan 129
Graduate (film) 8, 63, 86, 94n26
Grahame, Kenneth 161
Grand Budapest Hotel, The (film) 1, 3, 4, 6, 20, 21, 38, 41, 47–8, 72, 98, 122, 183–99, 219, 221
  costumes 188
  father 45
  flawed heroes 45
  gender 192–4
  homosexuality 192–4
  masculinity 43, 44
  nostalgia 215
  sex 216
  time period 217
  toplessness 216
  violence 46, 154
Grand Hotel (film) 188, 189, 215

Great Escape, The (film)   163
Great Gatsby, The (Fitzgerald)   114, 221
Greek   215
Gregorian chant   192
Gregory, Andre   185
Greif, Mark   37, 38
Griffin, Turlo   158
Gross, Terry   160
Guaraldi, Vince   12, 63, 64, 87, 114, 202, 215
Guinness, Hugo   4, 20, 47, 165, 197n1, 198n16
Gustafson, Mark   19, 161

Hackman, Gene   2, 21, 50, 58n48, 97, 99, 117, 183
Halberstam, David   89
Halperin, David   193
Hammerstein II, Oscar   162
H & M   210–11
Hardy, Françoise   169
Harold and Maude (film)   8, 50, 81, 88
Hart, Moss   97, 103
Hartley, Hal   8, 35, 36
Hawks, Howard   73, 142
Hawthorne, Nathaniel   63
Haynes, Todd   8, 36, 52
Hayward, Kara   20, 47, 168
HD (high-definition)   2
Heat (film)   91
Hedges, Lucas   170
Hedler Phillis, Jen   49
Hemingway, Ernest   214
Herzog, Werner   131
Hill, Derek   40, 99
Himalayas   145
Hitchcock, Alfred   9, 14, 92, 161, 170, 203, 216, 221
    Alfred Hitchcock Presents (TV)   161
    Rear Window (film)   170
    Tales of the Unexpected (TV)   161
    Vertigo (film)   170
Hockney, David   65, 76n5
Hoffman, Dustin   86
Holdengräber, Paul   47, 213
Holmes, Diana   12
Holt, Tim   99
Hotel Chevalier (film)   50, 139, 146, 205–7, 211, 216
Huffington Post (website)   37
Hughes, John   81, 84

Hungary   184
Husky, Ferlin   174
Hussein, Waris   175
Huston, Anjelica   2, 4, 5, 17, 18, 50, 99, 121, 207
Huston, John   15

Iceman Cometh, The (play)   103
I Love Lucy (TV)   153, 157
India   8, 13, 19, 21, 42, 48, 49, 54, 123, 137–149
    Himalayas   137
    Jaisalmer   137
    Jodhpur   137
    New Jalpaiguri   42
    Rajasthan   145
    Rishikesh   143
    Sealdah   42
    Thar desert   137
Indiana   102
Indiana Jones (film)   14
Indian Corn (magazine)   175
Indian Ocean   121
Indiewire (website)   38
Indiewood   3, 6, 34, 35, 39, 40
Industrial Revolution   154
Ingram, Robert   12
intertextuality   97–117
Isle of Dogs (film)   54
Italian neorealism   2, 92, 143
Italy   21
    Rome   19, 20, 21, 122, 209
Ito, Akira   54
Ives, Burl   162

Jackson, Michael   164
Jacobs, Marc   138, 218
James and the Giant Peach (film)   161
James Bond   160
Japan   123, 204
Jarmusch, Jim   4, 8, 34, 35, 36
Jeanmaire, Zizi   164
Jenkins, Henry   53
Jeremiah Johnson (film)   164
Jews   195
Johansson, Scarlett   54
Jones, Kent   18
Jones, Tommy Lee   189, 198n14
Jorge, Seu   123, 124, 130, 136n29
Jules, Pere   188
Juno (film)   2, 7

Kael, Pauline   3, 14–15, 22n9, 131–2

Kaplan, E. Anne   178
Karan, Amara   138–9
Karate Kid, The (film)   110
Kaufman, George S.   97, 103
Kazan, Elia   91
Kehr, Dave   82
Keitel, Harvey   4, 54, 175, 187, 188, 219
Kentucky   132
Kern, Jerome   162
Kertzer, Adrienne   155
Kilgore, Charlie   172
Kim (Kipling)   142
King, Geoff   2, 3, 6, 34, 39, 40,
King Kong (film)   162–3
Kinks   144
Kipling, Rudyard   142
Knegt, Peter   38
Knight, C. Ryan   108
Koizumi, Niels   123
Konigsburg, E. L.   112, 113, 220
Kubota, Tak   66
Kubrick, Stanley   216
Kunze, Peter C.   40, 220
Kurosawa, Akira   9

Labute, Neil   36
Lacan, Jacques   45
Lacoste   100, 115
Lang, Fritz   20
Lars and the Real Girl (film)   7
Lartigue, Jacques-Henri   17, 89–90, 126
Latin   47–8, 215
Law, Jude   4, 45, 48, 184, 185, 187, 219
Léaud, Jean-Pierre   11, 26n45, 30n82, 159 *see also* Truffaut, François
Leland, John   35
Lennon, Cynthia   115
Lennon, John   115, 211
Lennon, Julian   115
Leonard, Robert Sean   84
Leone, Sergio   131
Le-Tan, Olympia   216
Letter from an Unknown Woman (Ophüls)   183
Levy, Emanuel   34
Lewis, Jon   8
Library of Congress   33, 190
Liebling, A. J.   103
Life and Death of Colonel Blimp (film)   8, 91, 188, 189

Life Aquatic with Steve Zissou, The (film) 1, 4–6, 17, 18, 19, 21, 35, 37, 42, 47–54, 121–34, 139, 170, 214 *see also* Cousteau, Jacques
   animation 161
   costumes 18, 36, 122, 123, 125, 126, 133, 201
   dysfunctional family 12
   father 44
   flawed heroes 45
   homosexuality 193–4
   male bonding 43
   masculinity 44
   music 130
   nostalgia 138, 214
   reception 213
   toplessness 216
   Truffaut 17, 210
   violence 46
Life is Beautiful (film) 39
Linklater, Richard 8, 36
literary references 1
Literature/Film Quarterly (journal) 129
Little Miss Sunshine (film) 7
Loach, Ken 175
Lola Montès (film) 131
Lombard, Carole 142
London, Jack 161
Lord of the Flies (Golding) 46, 170
Los Angeles Times (newspaper) 72
Louvre 163
Love Me Tonight (film) 188
Lubitsch, Ernst 1, 8, 188
Lucas, George 8, 14
Lyman, Rick 10–11
Lynch, David 34

Macchio, Ralph 110
MacDowell, James 3, 7, 35, 36, 37
Magnificent Ambersons, The (Tarkington) 97, 99, 102, 103, 217
Magnum P.I. (TV) 165
Maharishi Mahesh Yogi 143
Malick, Terrence 8, 15
Malle, Louis 8, 114, 137, 143
   Calcutta (film) 143
   Phantom India (film) 143
Malouf, Juman 169, 184
Mamoulian, Rouben 188

Mapplethorpe, Robert 74n3, 218
Marie Antoinette (film) 19
Marshall, Garry 16
Marx brothers 104
*M*A*S*H* (TV) 70
Mastroianni, Marcello 122, 131
Matrix (film) 33
Mayshark, Jesse 3, 5
McCarthy, Cormac 104
McCartney, Paul 115, 143
McCole, Stephen 81
McCrory, Helen 165
McDormand, Frances 5, 54, 170, 179
McGeveran, Tom 18
McQueen, Steve 163
Mehta, Ved 142
Melendez, Bill 164
Melody (film) 175
Melville, Herman 64, 129
memory 1, 168–80, 183–97, 213–21
Menschen im Hotel (Baum) 188
Merchant-Ivory 137, 144
   Bombay Talkie (film) 144
   Guru, The (film) 144
   Householder, The (film) 144
   Shakespeare Wallah (film) 144
Mercury Theatre 4, 218–19
Metropolitan Museum of Art 112
Michelangelo 112
Midnight Cowboy (film) 97
Miramax 34, 39
mise-en-scène 2, 8, 24, 53, 119, 168
Mitchell, Joseph 103
Moby Dick (Melville) 129–30
Molloy, Claire 2, 3, 34
Monda, Antonio 124
Montand, Yves 89, 93, 206
Moonrise Kingdom (film) 1, 4, 12,14, 20, 21, 35, 41, 47–54, 65, 71, 79, 113, 168–180, 216–18
   absurdity 220
   costumes 178, 180
   dysfunctional family 13, 43
   father 45
   flawed heroes 45
   gender roles 178–9
   location 187, 219
   masculinity 44
   nostalgia 214, 218, 221

   violence 46, 154
Morgan, Frank 188
Morita, Pat 110
Morrison, Van 97, 119
Mortal Storm, The (film) 188
Mothersbaugh, Mark 4, 88, 96n31, 115, 119, 130, 165
   see also music
Mottram, James 40
Mulvey, Laura 178–9
Murray, Bill 4, 18, 20, 50, 125
   Darjeeling Limited 137, 138, 147
   Grand Budapest Hotel 45, 187, 219
   Isle of Dogs 54
   Life Aquatic 122, 123, 131, 134, 139
   Moonrise Kingdom 43, 170
   Royal Tenenbaums 103, 203
   Rushmore 79, 84, 94n5, 96n34
Musgrave, Bob 47, 59, 201
music 1, 4, 5, 78, 87–9, 115, 119, 143, 152, 159, 160, 162, 168–80, 202, 210, 215
My Dinner with Andre (film) 185
Mysterious Island, The (Verne) 129

Naipaul, V. S. 142
Napoleon Dynamite (film) 2, 6, 91
National Film Preservation Act 33
National Film Registry 33
Natsuki, Mari 54
Newman, Michael Z. 3, 6, 7, 34, 35, 36, 37
New York 5, 17–21, 38, 42, 50, 54, 83, 97, 99, 100, 103, 104, 112, 116, 117, 134, 139, 143, 147, 190
New York (magazine) 9, 37
New Yorker (magazine) 3, 5, 14, 46, 103, 142
New York Public Library 47, 213
New York Times (newspaper) 10, 19, 155
Nez Perce tribe 176
Nichols, Mike 63, 92, 94n26
Nico 115
Nile river 101

No Country for Old Men (McCarthy) 104
Noda, Yojiro 54
Nomura, Kunichi 54
Norton, Edward 4, 43, 53, 54, 171, 175, 176, 180n2, 187, 195, 219
n+1 (website) 35–6,

O'Hara, John 103
O'Neill, Eugene 103
Onion A.V. Club (website) 6
Ono, Yoko 54
On the Waterfront (film) 91–92
Ophüls, Max 131
Orgeron, Devin 9
Oriental Enlightenment (Clarke) 142
Orientalism (concept) 142
Orientalism (Said) 142
Osipov State Russian Folk Orchestra 192
Overstreet, Jeffrey, 2 177

Pallana, Dipak 47, 49
Pallana, Kumar 21, 47, 49, 66, 84, 85, 117, 139
Palm Beach Story, The (film) 142
Paltrow, Gwyneth 1, 5, 17, 101, 112, 115
Paraguay 67
Paramount Studios 39
parents 5, 13, 43, 44–5, 66, 72, 87, 100, 109, 153, 169, 171, 173
    divorce, 12, 13, 14, 17, 27n51, 33, 50, 84, 86, 100, 101, 105, 115, 117, 140, 215
Parker, Alan 175
Parker, Dorothy 5
Passage to India, A (Forster) 142
Peanuts (comic strip) 5, 12, 66, 87
    TV specials 12, 64, 87–8, 114, 115, 164, 211, 215
Peck, Scott 64
Perkins, Marlon 126
Perren, Alisa 33, 39
Peter and the Wolf (composition) 162
Photographs of Chachaji, The (Mehta) 142
Pialat, Maurice 175
Piechota, Carol Lyn 114

Pine, Larry 171
Pink Panther, The (film) 14
Pinter, Harold 214
Platt, Polly 16, 74
Playboy (magazine) 216
Poland, 184
Polanski, Roman 216
Pollack, Sidney 164
Ponds, Jim 68
Portman, Natalie 5, 139, 150n2, 205, 206, 207, 211, 216
Poseidon Adventure, The (film) 117
Poster, Randall 4, 174, 192
Potter, Beatrix 161
Powell, Michael 8, 91, 98, 145, 188, 189
Prada 210
Pressburger, Emeric 8, 91, 98, 145, 188, 189
Prochnik, George 195
Proust, Marcel 126
Pulp Fiction (film) 39
Purcell, Henry 170, 174

quirk 2, 3, 6, 7, 33, 35, 36, 39,

Raiders of the Lost Ark (film) 52, 164
Rankin-Bass 162
Raphael 128
Ravel, Maurice 116
Ray, Satyajit 3, 8, 137, 141–2, 143, 144, 145
    Charulata (The Lonely Wife) 143, 144, 145
    Jalsaghar (The Music Room) (film) 144
    Pather Panchali (Song of the Little Road) (film) 142, 143
    Sonar Kella (The Golden Fortress) (film) 145
    Teen Kanya (Three Daughters) (film) 143
    Unvanquished (Aparajito) (film) 142
    World of Apu (Apur Sansar) (film) 142, 144
Rebel Without a Cause (film) 163
Redford, Robert 164
Red Shoes (film) 98, 188

Remembrance of Things Past (Proust) 126
Renoir, Jean 8, 18, 19, 137, 141, 142, 143, 145
    Boudu Saved from Drowning (film) 141
    Golden Coach, The (film) 141
    Grand Illusion (film) 141
    River, The (film) 8, 19, 143, 145
    Rules of the Game, The (*La Règle du jeu*) (film) 18, 141
    Southerner, The (film) 141
Renoir, Pierre-Auguste 141
Revolori, Tony 49, 183, 184
Rhode Island 20, 21
Robbins, Jerome 162
Robé, Chris 116
Robin Hood (film) 162
Roché, Henri Pierre 98, 99
Rocket Science (film) 6
Rogers, Roy 10
Rolling Stones 68, 73, 87, 97, 106, 130, 144, 162
Rollins, Sonny 12, 64
Roma (film) 92
Ronan, Soairse 5, 184, 187, 219
Rosemary's Baby (film) 216
Ross, Katharine 131
Ross, Lillian 103
Roth, Joe 74
Roth, Ruedi and Werner 192
Royal Family of Broadway (film) 97
Royal Tenenbaums, The (film) 1, 3, 4, 5, 7, 8–9, 13, 18, 21, 41, 43, 47–54, 97–117, 152, 190, 217, 219, 220–21
    animals 108–10
    children 66, 98–115, 134, 173, 216, 219
    costumes 26n49, 97, 100, 104, 107, 111–12, 115
    dysfunctional family 12
    flawed heroes 45
    kissing 216
    masculinity 44
    music 5, 114–16
    Salinger 8, 97
    sexuality 216
    Truffaut 10
    violence 46, 154
Rubens, Peter Paul 128

Rudolph the Red-Nosed Reindeer (TV) 162
Rushdie, Salman 142
Rushmore (film) 3, 4, 6, 12, 13, 18, 21, 37, 41, 43, 46, 47–54, 74, 78–93, 134, 213, 218, 220
  acquatic themes 85–9
  British accents 141
  costumes 14, 17, 46, 81, 83–4
  father 44, 87
  flawed heroes 45
  kissing 216
  masculinity 44
  music 78, 87–9, 114
  nostalgia 214, 218
  nudity 216
  plays 79, 86, 89, 92, 217
  Salinger 8
  screenplay 16, 17, 111
  sexuality 216
  Truffaut 10
  violence 46
Rushmore Academy (website) 3, 53
Ruther, Camilla 138

Sagan, Carl 126
Said, Edward 142
Saint, Eva Marie 91
Salinger, J. D. 5, 8, 17, 63, 71, 82, 103, 111–12, 114, 117, 125, 146, 147
  Carpenters/ Seymour: An Introduction (Salinger) 111
  Catcher in the Rye, The (Salinger) 8, 72, 83, 84, 111
  Franny and Zooey (Salinger) 97, 111, 112
  Nine Stories (Salinger) 111
  Raise High the Roof Beam (Salinger) 111
Satie, Erik 116
Saturday Night Live (TV) 53
Sayles, John 34
Schiermer Andersen, Bjørn 38
Schnitzler, Arthur 194
Schreiber, Liev 54
Schroeder, Barbet 139
Schulz, Charles M. 5, 12, 87, 115, 215 *see also* Peanuts
Schuppel, Öse 192

Schwartzman, Jason 1, 4, 19, 26n45, 165, 203, 214
  Darjeeling Limited 31n96, 49, 139, 143
  Grand Budapest Hotel 1, 219
  Hotel Chevalier 205–9, 216
  Rushmore 17, 78–93
Sconce, Jeffrey 36, 37
Scorsese, Martin 8, 15, 19, 74, 216–17
Scott, Jason Davids 218, 220
Seattle 83
Second World War *see* World War II
Secret Garden, The (Burnett) 153
Selick, Henry 5, 161
Sellers, Peter 67
Seltzer, David 161
Serpico (film) 40, 89
Seven Samurai, The (film) 131
sex, lies, and videotape (film) 34, 39
Seydoux, Lea 187
Shakespeare in Love (film) 39
Shane (film) 10
Shankar, Ravi 143–4
Shaw, Artie 61, 64
Shaw, George Bernard 20
Shawn, Wallace 185
Shawshank Redemption, The (film) 175
Shire, Talia 17
Shop Around the Corner, The (film) 8, 188
Shyamalan, M. Night 163
Signs (film) 163
Sigur Rós (band) 130
Silence, The (film) 188
Silence of the Lambs (film) 92
Simon, Paul 5, 97
Skateboard Four, The (film) 13, 76n10
Sling Blade (film) 39
Smith, Elliot 114, 116
Smith, Gavin 18
Soderbergh, Steven 163
Solondz, Todd 36
Something Wild (film) 92
Sondheim, Stephen 162
Sony Studios 75
Sound of Music, The (film) 188
South America 195
Specter, Michael 160, 162, 163, 213

Spielberg, Steven 8, 14
Spoke Art Gallery 53
Sports Illustrated (magazine) 107
Squid and the Whale, The (film) 6
Stamps Farish III, William 80
Stardust Memories (film) 124
Starsky and Hutch (film) 212n1
Starsky and Hutch (TV) 61, 200
Star Wars (film) 14
Statue of Liberty 117
Stephenson, Barry 142
Stevens, Fisher 54
Stevenson, Robert Louis 85
Stewart, James 170, 188
Stiller, Ben 17, 101
Sting, The (film) 40
St. Mark's preparatory school 80
St. John's preparatory school 14, 46, 78, 80–81
Stockholm 38
Stone, Oliver 89
Streep, Meryl 5, 165
Sturges, Preston 142, 188
Submarine (film) 7
Suicide (band) 130
Sullavan, Margaret 188
Sundance Film Festival 2, 12, 16, 34, 39, 40, 73
Swinton, Tilda 4, 5, 54, 171, 184, 187, 219

Tadpole (film) 7
Tagore, Rabindranath 143
Takayama, Akira 54
Tale of Peter Rabbit, The (Potter) 161
Tanaka, Sara 80
Tarantino, Quentin 36
Tarkington, Booth 97, 99, 102, 103, 217
Tati, Jacques 204, 211
Taylor, Noah 123
Terms of Endearment (film) 16
Texas 10–11, 21
  Austin 12, 15, 21, 54
  Dallas 12, 16, 21, 47, 54, 63
  Houston 10–11, 12, 14, 21, 54, 75, 78, 143, 213
  University of Texas 11, 12, 15, 17, 121
Thomas, Deborah J. 37
Thompson, Craig 37

Thompson, Kay 190
Thompson, Kristin 34, 220
Thurber, James 103
Time-Life Books 128
Tintin 20
Titian 128
Transcendental Meditation 143
Truffaut, François 1, 3, 9, 15, 20, 47, 78, 164, 213 *see also* Léaud, Jean-Pierre
  400 Blows, The (Les Quatre cents coups) 10–11, 17, 61–2, 71, 91, 93, 175, 201–2, 223
  children 10, 12, 91
  Day for Night (La Nuit americaine) (film) 47, 163
  filming techniques 63–4, 90
  Jules and Jim (Jules et Jim) (film) 10, 91, 131, 210
  Lachenay, Robert 12
  Mischief Makers, The (Les Mistons) (film) 11
  Small Change (L'Argent de poche) (film) 10, 11, 20, 91
  Stolen Kisses (Baisers volés) (film) 163
  Two English Girls (Deux anglaises et le continent) (film) 98, 159
  Wild Child, The (L'Enfant sauvage) (film) 11
Tsioumakis, Yannis 2
Turan, Kenneth 73
Turturro, Amedeo 99
Twain, Mark 17, 64, 82–3, 95n17
Twentieth Century (film) 142
Twenty Thousand Leagues Under the Sea (Verne) 86, 127

Umbrellas of Cherbourg, The (film) 98
United Kingdom 21, 80, 154, 155, 161, 195
  Bath 165
  London 19, 38, 54

Yorkshire 175
Universal Studios 39
University of Alaska 124
U.S. Army 176
Ustinov, Peter 131
Utne Reader (journal) 64

Vance, Courtney B. 54
Van Sant, Gus 8
Verne, Jules 64, 86, 127–8, 129
violence 3, 46, 50, 153, 154, 157, 161, 170, 173, 187, 189, 191, 195–7, 216
Vivaldi, Antonio 116

Wachtell, Jennifer 101
Wagner, Erica 161
Walbrook 188
Wall Street Journal (newspaper) 90
Warhol, Andy 34
Wasco, David 68
Watergate 89
Waters, John 8, 34
Waxman, Sharon 40
Weir, Peter 83, 84
Welles, Orson 1, 3, 4, 9–10, 74, 103
  Citizen Kane (film) 164, 173
  Magnificent Ambersons, The (film) 97, 99, 101, 102, 214
  Mercury players 4, 218–19
Wellingtons 152
West Side Story (film) 162
White, E. B. 103
Wilder, Gene 161
Wilkins, Kim 218
Wilkinson, Tom 48, 187
Williams, Hank 174–5
Willams, Olivia 79
Williams, Robin 84
Willis, Bruce 50, 171, 174, 175
Willy Wonka and The Chocolate Factory (film) 161
Wilson, Andrew 16, 47, 68, 84, 219

Wilson, Luke 4, 21, 47, 59, 63, 65, 75, 81, 84, 101, 201
Wilson, Owen 1, 4, 11, 12, 16, 17, 18, 21, 47, 50, 60–75, 138, 217, 219
  Armageddon (film) 21
  Grand Budapest Hotel 187, 219
  Life Aquatic 121–34, 219
  Royal Tenenbaums 97, 98, 219
  Rushmore 12, 78–93
  screenwriting 17
  University of Texas 12
Wilson brothers 12, 16, 47
Wind in the Willows (Grahame) 161
Wise, Robert 162
Wölfflin, Heinrich 52
Wolodarsky, Wally 4, 123, 127, 132, 138, 165
Wood, Frank 54
World Book Encyclopedia 128
World War I 188, 189
World War II 116, 121, 154, 188, 189, 193, 196
Wyler, William 188

Yeoman, Bob *see* Yeoman, Robert
Yeoman, Robert 4, 51, 203
You Can't Take It with You (play) 97
You Can't Take It with You (film) 97
You Only Live Twice (film) 160
YouTube 53

Zahm, Olivier 216
Zoller Seitz, Matt 2, 53, 87, 91, 93, 188, 214
Zombies (band) 130
Zweig, Stefan 4, 20, 64, 183–97, 217
  Beware of Pity (Zweig) 183, 194
  World of Yesterday (Zweig) 183, 195, 197